CONTEMPORARY AFRICAN ISSUES

Macmillan International College Editions will bring to university, college, school and professional students, authoritative paperback books covering the history and cultures of the developing world, and the special aspects of its scientific, medical, technical, social and economic development. The International College programme contains many distinguished series in a wide range of disciplines, some titles being regionally biassed, others being more international. Library editions will usually be published simultaneously with the paperback editions. For full details of this list, please contact the publishers.

Contemporary African Issues series

General Editor: Chris Allen, Centre of African Studies, University of Edinburgh

G M Carter & P O'Meara: *Southern Africa: the Continuing Crisis*
O Oyediran (ed.): *Nigerian Government and Politics under Military Rule 1966–79*
D E Albright (ed.): *Africa and International Communism*
R Rathbone: *Nationalism in Africa*
C Allen (ed.): *Decolonisation in Africa*
C Stoneman (ed.): *Zimbabwe's Inheritance*
G Chaliand: *The Struggle for Africa: Conflict of the Great Powers*

Other Related Titles:

O Oyediran (ed.): *The Nigerian 1979 Elections*
M Joye & K Igweike: *An Introduction to the Nigerian 1979 Constitution*

An Introduction to Nigerian Government and Politics

BILLY J. DUDLEY

Macmillan
Nigeria

First published 1982 by
THE MACMILLAN PRESS LTD
London and Basingstoke
Companies and representatives throughout the world

Typeset in 11/12pt Baskerville by
STYLESET LIMITED
Salisbury · Wiltshire

ISBN 0–333–28438–0
ISBN 0–333–28439–9 Pbk

Printed in Hong Kong

Contents

Preface

I am honoured and saddened to write a brief preface to
Professor Dudley's book. He was a scholar of international
esteem whose work was rooted in the study of the politics
and government of Nigeria. It was his life's task to which he
brought great learning and independent judgement. He was
nobody's servant but his own, although in that respect he was
a hard taskmaster. He did not spare himself.

He devoted nearly two years of his research and writing
time to this book but he left us before he could complete the
task. An intended chapter on political behaviour and the
Conclusion were thus never written.

Reading the chapters ably brought together and edited by
Professor Yahaya, and reflecting on Dr Dudley's earlier
writings, I could think of no one that could presently match
his skill in interpretation. To read his analysis of the political
life of Nigeria is to be aware of the play of a powerful mind,
always courteous in argument, although properly critical of
what was seen to be false.

Others, however, will follow Dr Dudley, for he was also a
teacher. He drew around him at the University of Ibadan, and
during the brief time he spent in the Faculty of Economic
and Social Studies at Manchester, a number of younger
scholars who are now writing about Nigerian politics. The
memory of him will not die, and it is certainly how he would
have liked to be remembered. He took as his life's work the
study not only of Federal politics in Nigeria, but of politics

in Africa, and of man as a political creature adrift in his own troubled times. They were themes that Dr Dudley used to convey his sense of compassion for the fate of his country and the predicament of our age. I should add too that he was as skilful in the resolution of constitutional problems in the committee room as he was learned in the classroom. He served his country well. This last book will stand as a memorial to a notable African scholar.

It is a pleasant duty also to pay tribute to those who were particularly helpful to Professor Dudley in the last months of his life: to his friends and colleagues in Northern Ireland, especially Professor A. J. A. Morris and Professor Robert Gavin, a friend for many years who gave so much practical assistance and friendship; and to Doris Assi David and Audrey Kelly, of the Nigerian Universities Office, London, for their help in typing the manuscript.

Prof. Dennis Austin,
University of Manchester

List of Abbreviations

ACB	African Continental Bank
ACP	African Caribbean and Pacific
AG	Action Group
BYM	Bornu Youth Movement
CCD	'culture of critical discourse'
CDC	Constitution Drafting Committee
CPIB	Corrupt Practices Investigation Bureau
DPA	Distributable Pool Account
ECOWAS	Economic Organisation of West African States
EEC	European Economic Community
ESIALA	Eastern States Interim Assets and Liabilities Agency
FEC	Federal Executive Council
FEDECO	Federal Electoral Commission
FESTAC	(Second World Black and African Festival of Arts and Culture)
FJSC	Federal Judicial Service Commission
FNLA	National Front for the Liberation of Angola
FPSC	Federal Public Service Commission
GDP	Gross Domestic Product
GL	Grade Levels
GNPP	Great Nigeria Peoples' Party
ICSA	Interim Common Services Agency
JMA	Jam'iyyar Mutanen Arewa
KPP	Kano Peoples' Party

MDF	Midwest Democratic Front
MPLA	Popular Movement for the Liberation of Angola
NA	Native Authority
NCNC	National Council of Nigeria and the Cameroons
NEPA	Northern Elements Progressive Association
NIPC	National Investment and Properties Company
NNA	Nigerian National Alliance
NNDP	Nigerian National Democratic Party
NPC	National Population Council
NPN	National Party of Nigeria
NPP	Nigerian Peoples' Party
NSC	National Security Council
NTA	Nigerian Television Authority
OAU	Organisation of African Unity
OCAM	Organisation Commune Africaine et Malgache
OFN	Operation Feed the Nation (Green Revolution)
OPEC	Organisation of Petroleum Exporting Countries
PF	Patriotic Front
PR	Proportional Representation
PRP	Peoples' Redemption Party
PSC	Police Service Commission
SMC	Supreme Military Council
UDI	Unilateral Declaration of Independence
UMBC	United Middle Belt Congress
UNIP	United Nigeria Independence Party
UNITA	Union for the Total Independence of Angola
UPE	Universal Primary Education
UPGA	United Progressive Grand Alliance
UPN	United Party of Nigeria
UPP	United Peoples' Party

1

Introduction

An Introduction to Nigerian Government and Politics is Professor Billy Dudley's permanent legacy to students of Nigerian politics. But it is not the only legacy. His other major works, *Parties and Politics in Northern Nigeria* and *Instability and Political Order: Politics and Crisis in Nigeria*, have both been acclaimed as standard works on Nigerian politics. These publications are not just fine works of scholarship, they also provide an insight into Professor Dudley's thoughts and ideas on Nigerian political development. These published works also reveal the man as a committed scholar who was preoccupied with the articulation and dissemination of ideas for the attainment of a clearly defined objective for his country which in this case was a viable political framework for Nigeria. Consequently, his work of scholarship exhibits some clearly identifiable traits. The works are analytical, rigorously logical, perceptively critical, validly sceptical, and in some instances deeply reflective. All these traits, combined, constitute what one can designate as Dudley's approach to political analysis. These works also reveal the development pattern in Dudley's ideas on nation-building in Nigeria. It will therefore be necessary to expatiate on these two points, his approach to political studies and his ideas on nation-building, as an introduction to his works.

First, his approach to political studies. Dudley's works are not merely descriptive accounts of political events. They are high-quality analytical studies developed within a conceptual framework. Even in his first book, *Parties and Politics in Northern Nigeria*, which is conceptually less rigorous than the subsequent books, Dudley demonstrated his capacity for logical analysis, and his considerable knowledge of the subject-matter and other relevant studies in the field. The study was related to the theoretical formulations on the politics of 'new states' as articulated by American political scientists. He, in fact, explicitly stated that one of the objectives of the book

> albeit implicitly, is to question some of the assumptions of much of the academic writing on the politics of 'new states' such as Almond and Coleman's *The Politics of Developing Countries* (Princeton, 1960); Lucien Pye's *Politics, Personality, and Nation Building* (Yale, 1962) and the series on *Studies in Political Development* sponsored by the Committee on Comparative Politics of the Social Science Research Council.

In this study, Dudley went on to question 'Apter's hypothesis that a hierarchical authority stemming from a single king can innovate much more easily than any type of authority'. It was Dudley's view that a system which places premium on loyalty and which tolerates maladministration but not impartiality cannot be said to be adaptable to innovation. For him, only a modern bureaucracy which operates on 'legal—rational' basis can be deemed to be impartial and adaptive. Implicit in this conclusion is his strong belief in the sanctity of 'regulatory' and 'constitutive' rules in every political organisation. This is perhaps why he regarded any organisation which did not exhibit the attributes of a modern bureaucracy and which does not operate in a 'legal—rational' form, as an aberration. Accordingly, he made the point that in Northern Nigeria, the Native Authority (NA) system in which power was concentrated in the emir, and

> which places him in a position to control all appointments in the state, the relations of clientage and vassalage . . . which places a premium on loyalty to other considerations, . . . all of these militate against and are dysfunctional of a bureaucratic system.

He went on to show that the Northern Peoples' Congress

(NPC), the dominant party in Northern Nigeria, was the political expression of the NA system, and the party maintained its dominance by the manipulation of instruments of control, and by converting the Northern political arena into a 'closed system' by successfully forging an alliance between the legislature, the executive arm of government, the judiciary, and indeed other institutions of government. Each organ of government regarded the preservation of the dominance of the NPC as consistent with its interests. Despite the existence of opposition parties, political competition was not free and opposition groups were intimidated, oppressed, and considerable legal restraints were imposed on their mobilisation effort. Given the pattern of alignment of the period and the distribution of seats among the regions, the NPC as the dominant party of the North was also in control at the Federal level. It is, however, the disruptive consequences of the political process of the time that Dudley was concerned about. His recipes for averting political instability are structural transformation by way of the creation of more states, for free and fair political competition on the basis of prescribed rules of the game, and for political leadership to uphold the norms of political behaviour.

It is his second major book, *Instability and Political Order: Politics and Crisis in Nigeria*, that one finds an analysis of Nigerian politics from the perspective of a conceptual framework. By adapting the theoretical formulations of games theory, Dudley proceeded to account for the instability of the Nigerian political system. For him, instability is an inevitable condition of the development process and should not be seen as abnormal. It should rather be seen 'as a necessary and inescapable condition in the creation of political order and is thus intimately bound up with the process of modernisation and political development'. Political instability may, therefore, have some positive features. It may lead to the realisation of a viable political order. Thus, stability to preserve a decadent political order or a corrupt and repressive regime cannot be advocated. Stability is only preferred because it is a necessary condition for the attainment of the objectives of a state.

His account of the instability of the Nigerian political system was based on his analogy of the political process with a game situation. He asserted his long-held view that stability can only be maintained if the behaviour of leadership and actors is consistent with the rules of the game or if the boundary-determining rules are respected. Correct behaviour according to the rules of the game is a *sine qua non* of political stability. By implication, this argument can be reversed to explain that stability is conceivable only in political systems that uphold the norms of political behaviour and respect established rules and regulations of political behaviour. It is ultimately a moral argument. From the perspective of the survival of the Nigerian political system, Dudley demonstrated that a three-person game by its very nature is inherently unstable and this thesis enabled him to consistently maintain the necessity for structural transformation in the Nigerian political system. The collapse of the first civilian regime and the civil war were the consequences of the breakdown of political order as a result of the severe strains and stresses in the system.

In this his third book, *An Introduction to Nigerian Government and Politics*, Dudley has attempted to show how values structure political behaviour. After revealing the 'handicaps' of the student of African politics, he expressed his scepticism of the whole conceptualisation enterprise. In particular, he was concerned about the 'conceptual bias' of the 'functionalists', 'developmentalists', and 'modernisers' and he was also critical of these approaches because 'they also mislead by seeking to parade what is patently ideological as a "theoretical", "conceptual" construct'. It was his view that the

> bias arises from the fact that the competitive, market model is not the only model there is — there are other non-competitive, 'non-market' models for the African polities to copy and there is no logical reason why the one should be preferred to the other.

Yet in much of the conceptual literature

> the countries of the 'West' are held up as 'models' of developed states, the underlying assumption being that as 'models', they are what all states aspire to become: the

architechtony of historical and political change is for all
states to become, in the words of C. B. MacPherson, 'open
market societies', the competitive capitalist society.

Dudley therefore rejected the established conceptual 'theories'
developed by American social scientists and opted to formulate
a new theoretical construct for the explaining and understanding of the politics of African states. For him, values
which are 'socially conditioned' influence political behaviour,
and he consequently proceeded to analyse the government
and politics of Nigeria from the perspective of the values of
the people.

Dudley's ideas on the development of Nigeria can be delineated from his works. As a committed scholar his works,
though objective, cannot be said to be neutral. Indeed, no
developed mind can be neutral about events around him and
so a man of Dudley's intellect cannot be expected to be neutral.
His commitment as a scholar has also portrayed him as a
critical and autonomous personality who consistently highlighted the inadequacies of every political regime in the
country. As stated by Lalage Bown, these 'criticisms were
never made in a negative spirit, or for catchpenny sensational-
ism . . . but for Billy Dudley, a patriotic scholar ought to put
his knowledge and ideas at the disposal of his fellow citizens'.
It is precisely for this reason that Dudley's works all relate to
the major political issues of the time.

His early works were primarily concerned with the establishment of a firm political framework for the survival of
Nigeria as one, indissoluble political unit. Underlying his
works during this early period, which coincided with the first
civilian regime, is a strong desire for the attainment of a viable
political order in the country. It was his belief that a firm
foundation for the political survival of the country is a
necessary precondition for the attainment of a viable political
order in the country. It was in an effort to realise this manifest goal that he was preoccupied with issues capable of
creating strains and stresses in the political system. Issues like
regionalism, ethnicity, abuse and misuse of power, political
oppression, coercion and violence featured prominently in his
political discourse. The struggle for this viable political order

was not carried out at the intellectual level only. The struggle was extended to the realms of popular literature. Here his role as the editor of the *Nigerian Opinion* is pertinent. The *Nigerian Opinion* was a weekly commentary on political issues in Nigeria published by a group of scholars in the University of Ibadan. It contributed a great deal to the political awareness and enlightenment of the Nigerian people, and had a very strong influence on intellectual opinion with respect to the political issues in the country. The influence of the *Nigerian Opinion* was perhaps strongest during the era of intense crisis in Nigeria. The *Nigerian Opinion* ceased to be published in the early 1970s and was succeeded by the *New Nationalist* which also ceased publication when Gowon's regime was displaced.

Occasionally, Dudley had the opportunity of translating his ideas into practice. One such opportunity he cherished most was his participation in the Ad Hoc Constitutional Conference of August/September 1966 as an adviser to the Midwest delegation. If it is recalled, only the Midwest delegation advocated the preservation of the federation as a united and indissoluble country when the three other regions were seeking for the break-up of the federation or for a confederal arrangement. The Midwest line was later accepted by all the regions except the East with the result that the future of Nigeria as a united and indissoluble country was resolved in the theatre of war. So the survival of Nigeria as one country owes much to the Midwest delegation, with which Dudley was associated. As a member of the Constitutional Drafting Committee he also participated in framing the present Constitution of Nigeria. His specific contributions are those provisions which relate to Citizenship, Fundamental Rights, Elections, and Political Parties, because he was a member of the Sub-Committee on Citizenship, Citizenship Rights, Fundamental Rights, Political Parties, and Electoral Laws. As a man who was strongly committed to the democratic principle in the liberal tradition, he would argue that a proportional representation electoral system would enable parties to win seats in proportion to their electoral support. Furthermore, proportional representation on a single slate would 'encourage parties when composing the list of candidates to make a more "balanced" choice if only to escape the accusation of ethnic bias'. In principle, it should be possible by such an approach for an Ibibio person to find himself sitting in the Oyo state assembly and an Urhobo likewise sitting in the Sokoto state assembly. Thus, for Dudley, proportional representation would eliminate the ethnic factor in politics and would bring about the realisation of the 'idealistic underpinning of the Constitution'. The 1979 elections revealed to him, despite

> all the care taken in the new Constitution – and in the Electoral Decree – to play down the element of ethnicity in Nigerian political life and prominence given to the need for national integration . . . electoral behaviour was still a far cry from the ideals of the framers of the Constitution.

His ideas on the unity of the country also include the need for adherence to 'constitutive' and regulatory rules. But this did not preclude him from ignoring the human factor in political relations. It simply means that adherence to rules is consistent with constitutionalism. He regarded 'constitutional propriety' as a mark of good leadership. In his later works, and especially in this book a discernible shift in his orientation is perceptible. When the survival of the country ceased to be a political issue, he started showing concern for the condition of the common people in the country. Dudley regarded the common people, especially those resident in the rural sector, as the producers of wealth for the country, but it is these producers that are exploited to satisfy the consumption of the privileged elite. This is a qualitative shift. The chapter on the Economy, for instance, devotes a section on the Individual and the State, the problem of distribution, social justice or equity. He was critical of the distributive aspect of economic management under the military and he drew attention to how the military and their civilian aides collaborated in the exploitation of office for personal aggrandisement. He concluded that military rule 'fostered the growth and spread of what might best be described as "commercial capitalism", enabling the military hierarchy and their civilian aides – the top bureaucrats, a few university men and the indigenous mercantilists — to emerge as the new dominant property-owning "class" in the society. Whereas under the civilian regime, the key sectors of the economy — finance, banking, and insurance, construction and manufacturing, prospecting and mining — had remained economic enclaves within the larger economic system and were controlled and dominated by foreign business interests, the spread of commerical capitalism has enabled the new property-owning class to make an incursion into these sectors, in some cases displacing the foreign interests, in others, collaborating with such interests in extracting the surplus which control makes possible. But in this enterprise, the main losers have been the rural farmers whose interests have been almost totally neglected by the "new rich" in the pursuit of their collective interest, the utilisation of state power to accumulate wealth'.

This shift in Dudley's orientation is by implication a recognition of a new political reality of the Nigerian nation. The political future of the country as one indivisible nation is resolved with the end of the civil war and a successful policy of rehabilitation, reconstruction and reconciliation executed by the military government. It is, therefore, not conceivable for the present generation of Nigerians who were so much part of the struggle for the survival of the federation to resuscitate the unity of the country as a political issue. The major political issue today is, therefore, not the unity of the country. It is in fact the problem of distribution of wealth between the elite and the producers. If this problem is not resolved the country is likely to be confronted with a major social and political upheaval. Even the political parties recognise this reality. On a Left–Right ideological positioning, Dudley placed the National Party of Nigeria (NPN) on the Right and the Peoples' Redemption Party (PRP) on the Left, while the Nigerian Peoples' Party (NPP) is in the Centre, the Great Nigeria Peoples' Party (GNPP) Right of Centre, and the United Party of Nigeria (UPN) Left of Centre. A reference to the manifestos or programmes of the parties would reveal the major issue identified by each party. The parties of the Left and Right would be taken to demonstrate this point. It is apparent that with the NPN and the PRP, the class phenomenon is an important feature of politics. In the case of the

NPN, Dudley revealed that the

> distinctive feature of the NPN's electoral manifesto was the party's promise of 'more of the same': more funds to small-scale farmers; more large-scale mechanised farms; more meat, dairy, and live-stock farming; more tree crop farming; more housing for the urban areas and improved quality of rural housing; more educational institutions — but with private schools being allowed to co-exist side by side with state schools; more health facilities; more. . . . However, the business orientation of the party is brought out clearly . . . in the following statement:

>> As Nigerians are energetic people they should be encouraged by themselves, or where suitable, in cooperation with foreign expertise and finance, to take a leading role in the manufacturing sector of the economy. To further this objective, it will be the fundamental policy of the party if voted into power to encourage, protect, and induce foreign capital into Nigeria so that it may contribute to the sound development of the national economy, the improvement of the balance of payments, and the introduction of advanced technology into the economy.

> For a party with predominantly business interest representation — and one which had to rely on the London public relations firm of Michael Rice and Company to handle its publicity — perhaps that was not a surprising ideological and electoral position to take.

In the case of the PRP, on the other hand, the party sees the major political issue not in terms of conserving and maintaining the existing structure of society as is the case with the NPN. In the General Programme of the party, the PRP unequivocally identified the major issue as a class struggle which should lead to the creation of a new social order. It is the view of the party that:

> Two great forces face each other, and are locked in a grim struggle for survival and ascendancy. On the one side, the

forces of privilege are resolved to protect their interests at all costs under the existing social order. These are the conservatives, because their political stand is to protect, retain and sustain the existing social order. On the other side, the forces of the people are determined to replace the existing social order that harbours so much hardship and frustration for them with a new social order in which there will be equality, liberty, freedom from want, and social justice. These are the progressives, because their political stand is to replace a system of oppression and exploitation with a new society that guarantees a freer and fuller life for all.

During military rule, the alliance which was forged between the military and the technocrats, and the enormous wealth which they and their clients accumulated, led to the emergence of a privileged class. Members of this privileged class cut across all the ethnic groups and it is, therefore, the case that politics in Nigeria during the second republic is beginning to be defined in class terms rather than on ethnicity. It is the emergence of this new phenomenon in the political equation of Nigeria that has given rise to a new pattern of political alignment in the country and that has made it possible for the Constitutional requirement to be fulfilled. It is, however, not correct to conclude that the ethnic dimension has been eliminated in the Nigerian political process. Indeed, some will argue that a high proportion of the voting decision in the 1979 elections was strongly influenced by the ethnic factor. It was Dudley's view that 'ideological disputes have never been a prominent feature of Nigerian politics and . . . the rhetoric of the class struggle and class conflict is not something which has won wide recognition'. Nevertheless, he recognised that the people are concerned about food, jobs, education, and health care. Consequently Dudley, in this book, began to articulate ideas around issues of equitable distribution of wealth, and the provision of social and welfare amenities for the underprivileged.

In order to understand the existing reality, it is pertinent to analyse the dynamics of the demilitarisation process. One consequence of military rule was the politicisation of the public service. The effect of this politicisation led to the emergence of a class of technocrats who owed their power and influence to the control of the bureaucratic machine and access to the sources of patronage and economic opportunities. These technocrats provided the ideas, the expertise, and the skills for the solution of national problems. These ideas were usually articulated and debated in national seminars and conferences which were a feature of military rule. It became a tradition during the military era to organise these seminars and conferences as forums for the articulation and dissemination of ideas appropriate for nation-building. It is, therefore, not out of place for this class of technocrats to take an interest in the return to civil rule. According to Dudley, 'the top bureaucracy who, used to having their way, could hardly be expected to cherish the prospect of being brought under the control of politicians' and so by the end of 1971

> the handing over of power to an elected civil authority, had been ruled out, and the idea of a one party state was seriously considered. . . . Basically, the notion involved proclaiming Nigeria a single party state, with the party centred around General Gowon who would become President.

In 1973, Mr Ayida, the Permanent Secretary of the Ministry of Finance then, articulated this idea in his 'Presidential Address' to the Nigerian Economic Society by advocating for a 'National Movement outside which no serious opposition will be allowed'. This proposal

> has very serious implications and should not be lightly embarked upon without a full appreciation of the repercussions. There cannot be such a national movement without a revolutionary vanguard made up of highly dedicated men and women with a clearly defined national purpose and a sense of mission. It is difficult to see how such a group can be formed without the military hierarchy politicising itself.

But the National Movement which was subsequently formed in 1978 with the sanction of the military, was a wholly civilian affair. It was the National Movement which was converted into the NPN. In this sense, therefore, the NPN is the political expression of the alliance between the top Military command, the technocrats, the civilian aides of the military, and their clients.

According to Dudley, Mr Asika said that 'the military could not be expected to be indifferent to the nature of its successor'. But this desire to be succeeded by approved groups is not peculiar to the Nigerian military. Richard Joseph had revealed that according to Claude Welch, the 'relative fit' theory is one of the several factors which facilitate military disengagement. This means that the military will be more disposed to be succeeded by a political group that will uphold the policy of the military and that will be more inclined to protect the corporate interest of the military. Thus, ideological continuity and the security of the departing military are decisive issues in the decision to disengage. Perhaps the NPN more than any other party fulfils this requirement. The policy of the party at the federal level gives credence to this supposition. The Green Revolution, for instance, is the OFN (Operation Feed the Nation) in a new garb, Nigeria's policy on the liberation of southern Africa is not changed, a new housing policy has, however, been launched but defence expenditure is to remain high according to the party's manifesto. Thus, there is continuity in policy between the Obasanjo regime and the second civilian regime. However, a valid assessment of the Constitutional propriety of the regime, federal/state relations and the issue of social justice, will at this stage be premature and an objective assessment can only be made at the end of the first term of the Presidential experiment.

A. D. YAHAYA
July 1981

2

The Conceptual Framework: Values and Politics

The student of the African political scene suffers from two main handicaps in trying to understand that which he studies. The first is the ever-changing nature of the scene itself. Regimes, governments and political institutions in general change with such rapidity that no sooner has one succeeded in describing a given situation, event or institution than that description becomes outdated: a military coup has occurred, a head of state or a leading politician has been assassinated, or a ruling coalition has fragmented and what was thought to be the case, immediately ceases to be so.[1]

The second difficulty which confronts the student of African politics is the conceptual. There are two aspects to this: the one relates to the terms which we use in talking about African politics, terms, for instance, like 'elite', 'class', 'the bourgeoisie', and 'peasants'; the other relates to the way in which one conceptualises, makes sense of, the complexity of observational data, something we refer to when words like 'theory' or 'model' are used. The terminological problem arises from the fact that certain words which feature in political discourse have, within the contexts in which these words originated, come to acquire fairly standardised and acceptable connotations, connotations which bear little similarity to the political reality of African societies when such words are used in descriptions of these societies.

A good example is the word 'nation-state'. Does that word refer to the same, or a comparable, reality when applied to France and to Nigeria? In Europe the term has come to be associated with a territorial sovereign unit embracing a people who, in the main, share a common culture, speak the same language and are united by the same historical experience.[2] It was on this basis — of making the state coterminous with the people — that the statesmen of Germany engineered the unity of Germany in the nineteenth century[3] thereby establishing a principle which was to be applied in the reconstruction of Europe after the First World War. But in Nigeria, as in most African states, the notion of the nation-state must refer to a collection of over 200 peoples, each speaking a different language, with different cultures and separate histories, united only through living within a given territorial unit whose boundaries were demarcated by an external and foreign power. Apart from the determination of such states to remain free and sovereign political units, we can hardly be talking about the same social reality when we use terms like the 'French nation' and the 'Nigerian nation'.

Terminological precision is no doubt something which should be desired in itself, but in so far as English remains the medium of communication, the difficulty remains that there are certain words in that language, notorious for their imprecision and ambiguity, yet which have gained widespread currency, the use of which one cannot escape from — an example being the word 'democracy'. To suggest that one should not use the word 'democracy' with reference to, say, the African countries, because democracy when used about these states means something totally different from what is normally understood when the same word is used about the European states, would be to ask for the impracticable. One cannot expect of any natural language the same precision as can be achieved with a formal language.

The second aspect of the conceptual difficulty confronting the student of African politics, is the enterprise of conceptualising within an overarching framework of 'theory' a mass of complex, sometimes loosely related, observational data. The early studies of African politics — mostly written in the middle fifties and early sixties — were largely descriptive and institutional with either an historical or a constitutional orientation. Classic examples of these, to restrict the field of reference to West Africa, and Nigeria in particular, are

James Coleman's study of *Nationalism in Nigeria* (Berkeley: University of California Press, 1960), Ruth Schachter's *Political Parties in French Speaking West Africa* (Oxford: Clarendon Press, 1964), Kalu Ezera's *Constitutional Development in Nigeria*, O. Odumosu's *The Nigerian Constitution* (London: Sweet & Maxwell, 1963), D. Austin's *Politics in Ghana* (London: Oxford University Press, 1964), A. Zolberg's *One Party Rule in the Ivory Coast* (Princeton: Princeton University Press, 1969), K. Post's *The Nigerian Federal Elections of 1959* (London: Oxford University Press, 1963) and even before the foregoing, T. Hodgkin's *Nationalism in Colonial Africa* (London: Muller, 1956), and K. Robinson's edited *Five Elections in Africa* (Oxford: Clarendon Press, 1960).[4]

But these studies were not just descriptive and historical, institutional or constitutional; they followed what seemed to be a pattern or rather, a sequence. With the end of the Second World War and as the demand for independence accelerated, scholarly concern was devoted to the phenomenon of nationalism which was seen as the driving force behind the demands for independence. That concern soon gave way, however, following the attainment of independence, to a new interest in political parties, and, specifically, the single-party state, then as the single-party state was eclipsed by a succession of military coups in one African state after the other, interest swung over to concern with the military and military takeovers. With the change in interests also went attempts to explain, to make some sense of, the experience of change itself. The conceptual enterprise had begun. The initial impetus derived from the discovery by political scientists of the works by social anthropologists and sociologists and that which was supposed to explain all, to provide the key to understanding, came to be known as 'structural—functional analysis' or 'structural—functional theory'.[5] The key publication, from the viewpoint of African political studies, could perhaps be said to be the collection of essays edited by Gabriel Almond and James S. Coleman under the title *The Politics of the Developing Areas* (Princeton: Princeton University Press, 1960).

The relevance of 'structural—functional theory' to the study of African politics was designed by those who saw a 'unique' character in the less developed polities and put them in a totally different category, the 'non-Western political process'.[6] In reality, however, to talk of a 'non-Western political process' reflected the growing pessimism of students of African politics at the inability of the 'Westminster model' to take roots in those societies to which it was transplanted. Others who were less pessimistic began to think in terms of alternative conceptualisation. Thus, for instance, rather than talk of 'non-Western political process', it was suggested that changes within African states should be seen in terms of a 'development process' and with that emerged the notion of 'political development'. A similar suggestion was that change should be seen in terms of these societies seeking to modernise themselves, and hence one should rather talk of the 'process of modernisation'. These days, however, it is often argued that to understand African politics, it would be necessary to understand the relationship between African states and European states. This approach to the study of African politics is found to be more rewarding through the political economy perspective. The result of this conceptual framework is the dependency theory which will now be examined.

On looking at a great amount of the conceptual literature, a feature which immediately strikes the reader is the way in which the countries of the 'West' are held up as 'models' of developed states, the underlying assumption being that as 'models', these are what all other states aspire to become: the architechtony of historical and political change is for all states to become, in the words of C. B. MacPherson, 'open-market societies',[7] the competitive capitalist society.[8] But in this, the 'functionalists', 'developmentalists' and 'modernisers' not only exhibit a form of conceptual bias, they also mislead by seeking to parade that which is patently ideological as a 'theoretical', 'conceptual' construct. The bias arises from the fact that the competitive, market model is not the only model there is — there are other non-competitive, 'non-market' models for the African polities to copy and there is no logical reason why the one should be preferred to the other. If anything, the non-competitive model could be regarded as being more apposite to the historical experience of the African states. The charge of misrepresentation derives from the fact that the conceptual constructs of the 'modern-isers' and the developmentalists not only misdescribe the political processes of the Western states, but, in that mis-description, prevent students of the African polities from confronting the reality of African politics, which is that the 'problematics' of the African polities can only be made comprehensible if put within the perspective of a world political order in which the African states feature as nothing more than peripheral enclaves of the Western capitalist system. The misdescription can be very briefly stated. The Western states are class-stratified societies in which the pattern of dominance is that of class dominance: the property-owning class who control the means of production and distribution dominate the non-property-owning class, which is the working class. In these societies, any talk of equality of access must necessarily be empty, for the property-owning classes not only control the reins of political power, they manipulate the judicial and other processes of social control to create the illusion of access. The working class may believe their material conditions of living have improved – and this may indeed be so – but nevertheless they remain an exploited class since they do not and cannot receive the full reward of their labour. The logic of a capitalist system entails that the 'social surplus' the product of labour, be expropriated by the property-owning classes. If equality of access is illusory so also is political participation. The reality of working-class exploita-tion not only keeps the workers apathetic; what participation there is, is allowed only to the extent that such participation does not threaten the hold of the capitalist class.

Given the above more realistic description of the 'Western' political system, it is not difficult to see that the 'rhetoric' of 'developmentalism' and 'modernisation' (and 'functionalism') is nothing more than a collection of class-inspired ideologies designed to keep the African states as peripheral enclaves to be exploited by the Western capitalist states to which they were formerly tied as colonies. (It is not without some interest to note that these constructs were in fact created by academic committees set up by the Social Science Research Council of the United States, the members of which were themselves part and parcel of the power structures of the state system.) To begin to understand the nature of politics and political change in the African states, it would be necessary to understand what relationship these states have with the metropolitan, European states. That relationship is an asymmetric relation of dependence between the 'core' or 'centre' states (the European metropolitan powers) and the 'periphery' (African) states. Though the dependency relation was created initially and historically through a colonial tutelage, nevertheless that relation has been maintained in the post-independence era from common class interests which exist between the 'centre' and the 'periphery' states. A simple description of the structure of the 'centre' and the 'periphery' state will easily show this.

In the 'centre' state, one can distinguish between the 'centre of the centre', the group or class who hold political power and control of the economic system, and the 'periphery of the centre', those outside the sphere of political power, in the main, the dominated class. Paralleling that structure, one can also distinguish in the 'periphery' state between the 'centre of the periphery' and the 'periphery of the periphery'.[9] The foregoing can be put schematically as follows:

CENTRE STATE (X)	PERIPHERY STATE (Y)
Centre of centre (X_1)	Centre of periphery (Y_1)
Periphery of centre (X_2)	Periphery of periphery (Y_2)

The argument, as presented by protagonists of this viewpoint, is that Y_1 — the national bourgeoisie as Fanon styled them — were largely created by X_1, the former 'inheriting' the positions held — in the pre-independence period — by representatives of X_1 — the colonial administrators. But having emerged as the ruling group, the national bourgeoisie becomes preoccupied by the wish to maintain itself as the ruling group, a process in which it is aided by X_1 but only in so far as X's economic interests — largely foreign investments in extractive enterprises — in Y are not in any way endangered. But since X's interests in Y can be protected only at the expense of Y_2 — the masses of Y — a common bond is thus developed between X_1 and Y_1 which is aimed at the exploitation of Y_2. Though the interests of X_1 and X_2 are basically opposed, relative to Y_2, they are non-antagonistic, the improvement in the material conditions of living of X_2 being predicated on the effective exploitation of Y_2. We thus have a pattern of shared and at the same time conflicting interests within which Y_1 acts as the agent of X_1 in the systematic exploitation of Y_2. Unless one therefore appreciates the strategic role of X_1 in shaping the behaviour of Y_1 — and hence determining the dialectical relationship between Y_1 and Y_2, which constitutes the politics of Y, one cannot adequately explain that politics. An explanation of the politics of Y therefore requires a conceptual schema which incorporates the relationship between X and Y.

This form of conceptualisation, now commonly known as the 'political economy approach', obviously owes much to Marx and Marxist political thinking and, as such, is equally susceptible to the type of criticism commonly levied against Marxism. For instance, when it is said that there are interests which are 'shared', 'held in common' between X_1 and Y_1, or that those between Y_1 and Y_2 are in opposition, it is not exactly clear in what sense the word 'interest' is being used.[10] Be that as it may, what is perhaps more damaging is the conspiratorial premise on which much of the schema rests, for unless one accepts such a premise, then it becomes difficult to see what sense it makes to talk of X_1 and Y_1 joining together to exploit Y_2. Unfortunately, there is no known way of disproving that premise, for even if Y_1 were to be overthrown, for example through a military coup, that could still not be taken as a disproof. It could be contended that Y_1 was overthrown only because they no longer served the 'interest' of X_1 which would 'prove' the conspiracy thesis. Equally Y_1 remaining in power could be taken to show there was a 'common interest', thereby 'proving' the existence of a 'conspiracy'. The political economy approach served a useful function in calling attention to the ideological bias of 'developmentalism' and similar conceptualisations, but its weakness lies in seeking to show more than can legitimately be claimed for it.

What the 'political economists', the 'developmentalists', the 'modernisers' and the 'functionalisists' have tried to do is to explain and understand the nature of the political realm in the African states and societies as part of all the states and societies now generally referred to as 'developing countries' or 'developing nations'. In what follows, an attempt is made to provide such an understanding, using as a starting point the notion of political values, or simpler still, values and belief.

WEBERIAN THEMES

This section has been titled 'Weberian themes' with some deliberation, though what is subsumed under it is now more fashionably referred to as 'political culture'. But the former expression has been chosen because its formulation is less ambiguous than the formulations associated with the notion of 'political culture'.[11] Weber showed that a correspondence can be drawn between particular values and given structural relationships, for example, authority relations.[12] Thus, he argued, where values are of an 'instrumental' nature, there is a strong likelihood for a given pattern of dominance, which he termed 'rational—legal', a pattern which is characteristic of bureaucratic institutions, to be associated with such values.

The Weberian schema can be extended into an explanatory model in which values are taken as the 'independent variable' and behaviour patterns and institutional structures are the 'dependent variables'. (We could, if we so choose, make either 'behavioural patterns' or 'institutional structures' an 'intervening variable': which we choose could be a matter of individual or methodological preference, but for the present purposes, both variables will be taken as 'dependent variables' with no attempt being made to specify which is 'intervening' and which is not.) In broad terms, then, what the 'model' specifies is simply that behaviour patterns and institutional structures are to be, or can be, explained in terms of individual and collective values.

Values structure behaviour, for called upon to explain or justify a particular action, the individual — or group — appeals to certain reasons, the expression of given ends sought. Consider, for example, the utilitarian answer to the question of political obligation. One obeys the state because the state contributes to the greatest happiness of the greatest number.

The pursuit of the individual's happiness is an end in itself. We may want to pick logical faults with that answer but that does not make it any the less intelligible.[13] And certainly were the state *not* to contribute to the welfare of its citizens, they would sooner or later rebel.[14] For the community, where behaviour comes patterned and ordered, we could talk of such patterned behaviour as a 'practice' or an 'institution', and 'institutions' which become formalised in terms of procedural rules we could refer to as 'political structures'. Schematically, we could formulate the foregoing as follows:

$$VALUES \longrightarrow BEHAVIOUR \longrightarrow INSTITUTIONS.$$

But values are not uniformly distributed. Even where we have a fairly homogeneous population, homogeneity being defined in terms of attributes like language and a shared common history, there will be found within such a population marginal and sub-marginal groups holding different values and beliefs. Beliefs could be defined as those propositions which are generally accepted because they are thought to be true though they need not be so. In other words, beliefs need not be true or false. One could not say, without being inconsistent: 'I believe X but I know it is false', though one could say 'I believed (used to believe) X but now I know it is false'. Once a belief is shown to be false, that belief is either given up or changed but one cannot, knowing that a belief is false, continue to uphold it.

Even where two individuals share the same values or uphold similar beliefs, it is not inconceivable they might behave differently. In talking about values and beliefs, one therefore has to take in the way a given society is structured and to examine the behaviour patterns of the different strata. Values, like beliefs, are not immutable, unchanging. Values change over time or as circumstances alter sufficiently to compel a change just as beliefs are given up or changed once they have been shown not to be true, or the material conditions which gave rise to the belief are seen no longer to hold. In effect then, the schema outlined above should read more properly as follows:[15]

VALUES/BELIEFS → BEHAVIOUR PATTERNS →
INSTITUTIONS → VALUES → BEHAVIOUR
PATTERNS . . . . —

A simple example can be used to illustrate the foregoing. Consider the notion of 'power'. For most Nigerians, 'power' (Yoruba = *agbara*) is not a relation, as it would generally be construed to be,[16] but a 'property', (or put differently, a predicate), and as such something to be valued not only for its own sake, but because its possession is what makes everything else possible. The closest approximation to this conception of power is perhaps the Hobbesian and it does not need too much imagination to see, as Hobbes himself has shown, how politics in a community in which 'power' is so construed could look like that described in Hobbes's 'state of nature' and in this respect, one could compare this 'state of nature' with politics in the First Republic (1960—66) in Nigeria. In the day-to-day proceedings of the Constitutional Drafting Committee (1975/76), this conception of power came out very clearly and it certainly underlines the office of the Presidency around which the Second Republic was founded. Admittedly, there were 'checks and balances' created to circumscribe the exercise of Presidential power. But it is not yet certain how effective these 'checks and balances' will turn out to be. And more importantly, they could be interpreted as attempts at value modification arising from past behaviour or experience.

Participation in the affairs of any political unit is undertaken in the light of the values held by the participant. Thus any coherent discussion of the political affairs of a community must seek to take account of the values held by its members. These values will be part of the general 'mental furniture' which each individual acquires as a member of a given community or group: a 'Robinson Crusoe', alone on an island, would have no reason to believe in the value of free speech on that island. But to say this is not to suggest that the individual's total mental furniture is something which he owes to the community, is, in other words, socially conditioned.

There are 'bits' of our mental furniture, like our understanding of mathematics, physics, or formal logic, which may not be due to being members of a community. But those parts of the 'mental furniture' which have to do with interpersonal relations — and thus are involved in the existence of law, politics, ethics, religion, economics, and so on are socially conditioned.

To say that the individual acquires his set of values from being a member of a given community should not be taken to suggest that there could be no incompatibility between the individual's values and those of the community. First, the individual is not a member of just one community but of several communities, some of which may in fact overlap, one with the other. By virtue of the language which he speaks, he could be a member of one community, while by residing in a given locality, he could be a member of another. Again, owing to his lineage antecedents, he could be a member of still another group and because he practises a given form of religion, a member of yet another. In societies with a system of age sets or age grades, because of his age, he could belong to a community or a specific age range just as, because of his occupation, he could find himself being a member of a particular trade union. The values which he acquires from membership of these different 'communities' need not all be consistent. Secondly, values are not immutable; they can change as the circumstances which gave rise to them change, but we would expect values held by the community as a whole, what we might want to call 'community values',[17] to be less mutable than the individual's.

In fact, though the individual's values may be 'socially conditioned', they do not necessarily vary from one community to the other and where differences do occur these could be due more to status differentials than to the simple fact of inclusion in a particular community. Thus, for instance, in an attempt at finding out people's conception of equity, a survey on 'social change, public policy and national unity in Nigeria' conducted in 1973/74 showed that, when asked whether they thought most people in Nigeria got their 'fair share' in life, of a total sample of 8414 individuals, 55.8 per cent agreed most people got 'much less' than their fair share,

27.4 per cent thought a 'little less', 14.2 per cent were not sure one way or the other, while only 2.6 per cent conceded most people got 'more than' their fair share (See Table 2.1). A disaggregation of this distribution by states gave the following result. With some exceptions (Bendel, Imo, Benue and Borno on the one hand, and Niger, Kaduna, Oyo and Plateau on the other) it is easy to see that there is not much divergence in people's conception of fairness. In those states which showed a significant variation from the 'norm', the variation could in fact be explained in terms of relative deprivation (Bendel, Imo and Benue) or in terms of the general level of education — and hence the social awareness (Plateau, Niger and Kaduna). However, were the percentages for the 'much less' and the 'little less' cells to be added to give a tripartite categorisation of 'less than', 'more than' and 'fair share/no opinion', then the level of agreement turns out to be quite remarkable. Given a convergence such as this, it would appear

TABLE 2.1   *Question: Do most people get their fair share in life?*[18] *(percentages)*

State	Much less	Little less	Fair share/ no opinion	More than fair share
Lagos	58.5	14.4	15.8	11.3
Oyo	31.1	45.0	17.4	6.6
Ogun	63.1	17.5	18.2	1.2
Ondo	54.8	37.3	6.0	2.0
Kwara	45.3	47.1	7.5	0.2
Bendel	72.0	8.1	17.5	2.4
Imo	71.2	10.6	18.2	0.0
Anambra	69.3	17.9	12.7	0.0
Rivers	52.8	28.9	12.8	5.6
Cross River	62.5	26.7	10.1	0.7
Plateau	20.1	65.0	14.6	0.3
Benue	80.4	11.3	5.4	2.9
Borno	86.9	11.5	1.3	0.3
Bauchi	75.8	23.9	0.2	0.1
Kano	43.4	31.1	24.3	1.2
Kaduna	48.1	18.6	25.8	7.5
Niger	30.5	51.0	18.4	0.0

that there is more to be gained in terms of convenience and clarity if one talks in largely aggregative terms and to disaggregate — on the basis of education, occupation and space (state) — only when such a disaggregation serves to improve the quality of the data, that is, when it can be qualitatively justified.

THE VALUE SYSTEM

As was pointed out in the previous section, the 'notion of the state' was hardly a concept which was to be found among any of the Nigerian peoples. Admittedly, there were social anthropologists who talked of societies with a 'state organisation', in contrast to what they called 'stateless societies', but the word 'state' used in such contexts has to be interpreted 'extensionally'. The so-called 'state societies', which were associated with the Habes of Northern Nigeria, the Yoruba-speaking peoples of the west and the Binis of the south-west, had ruling dynasties — with well-established rules of succession — and chiefs, Emirs or Obas (the ruling 'monarch') who wielded seemingly sovereign power over his 'subjects'. But rather than call the 'unit' of rule a 'state', or even a kingdom (P. C. Lloyd and a few others, for instance, talk of 'Yoruba kingdoms'), it would perhaps be more appropriate to describe these units as 'principalities', for, with the possible exception of the Binis (for whose system the word 'kingdom' is quite appropriate), the scope and range of rule hardly extended over the totality of the language group, the Oba or Emir being no more than the 'principal' of those over whom he was said to rule.

It should not be difficult to see that in the 'principality' there could be no such value as that of 'patriotism', meaning by this the sort of sentiment conveyed by the expression 'love of country', and this applies with just as much, if not more, force to the so-called 'stateless societies'. Professor James O'Connell, who was Professor of Politics at Ahmadu Bello University, Zaria, between 1968 and 1975, has recounted an experience which is illuminating in this respect. Just before the civil war, O'Connell visited what had by that time become 'Biafra' in the hope of 'persuading Ibo academics who had fled from the University of Ibadan to return' in the expectation that such a move could reduce the tension that then existed between the rest of the federation and 'Biafra'. In Enugu, he ran into a former Ibadan colleague, a Professor of Medicine, who decried what he saw as the 'unseriousness' of his people. The Professor of Medicine had attended a meeting of his village which he thought would be discussing the serious crisis then confronting 'Biafra', only to find that the only issue that interested the village elders, and the only thing they were prepared to talk about, was how to raise funds for a new village hall. On remonstrating with the elders about what he took to be their frivolousness, he was calmly told 'Young man sit down! Biafra may come and go, but Nimmo (the name of the village) will be here forever'. The dismay of the Professor was to find that, for most people, 'Biafra' was too much of an abstraction to be comprehensible; for the average Ibo man what was real was the village, the clan group, which constitutes the focus of 'loyalty' for the individual. In operational terms, we could regard the focus of loyalty of the individual as defining the boundaries of what is the 'community' for the individual.

The significance of this conception of 'community' is shown in a number of different ways such as, in many urban centres, the pattern of residence. Thus in the northern 'principalities', different communities cluster in different spatial settings so that to state where one lives is to specify what community one belongs to. This phenomenon is to be found in the southern part of the country as well. An obvious outcome of this is that communities become 'closed communities' and urbanisation, the process of persons moving from rural into urban settings, far from helping to broaden community boundaries, only serves to reinforce community barriers, a phenomenon which some, like Abner Cohen, have described as 'retribalisation',[19] the effect of which is to confer on the community the status of a moral category.[20]

Because the community is conceived of in moral terms, and hence 'dictates' of the community are injunctions which must necessarily be followed unquestioningly, society itself becomes extremely authoritarian. To conceive of alternative forms of social arrangement, or of different ways of bringing about a given outcome, becomes, in a manner of speaking, something 'heretical', since the existent, sanctioned as it were by 'tradition', takes on the character of the immutable, and being immutable, of the sanctified. Admittedly to say that society is authoritarian is to make a modern comment, the judgement in fact of the 'external' observer, for to the internal participant such a judgement would not just be inconceivable, it would be meaningless. But then critical evaluation would itself be impossible if only 'internal' judgements were permissible. For anyone concerned with the modernisation of society, it seems fairly obvious that unless the negative aspects of societal authoritarianism can be eliminated, social modernisation could prove to be impracticable and as Wiredu has pointed out, 'political authoritarianism (with which goes the intolerance of opposition, the denial of individual rights and freedoms, the suppression of competing perspectives and the coercion of minorities) is only an unsurprising reflection of this grass roots authoritarianism'.[21]

But that is not all. While relations within the community are seen as stable and predictable, extra-community relationships are regarded as unpredictable and, all too often, risky. This perception of extra-community relations as risky and uncertain results in the environment generally being taken to be hostile, which in turn leaves the individual with an all-pervading sense of personal insecurity. The reaction to this sense of insecurity takes a variety of forms. On the part of the businessman, for example, insecurity is reflected in the reluctance of members of the 'entrepreneurial class' to form joint enterprises with the result that most indigenous concerns tend to be of the 'one man' type of business enterprise, relatively poorly capitalised and with the thrust of activity being channelled mainly into those sectors where the risk is low and the rate of return high. In addition, the businessman's employees have also to be close relations and dependants as these are mainly those whom he can trust because they, like him, are bound by the same 'moral' ties. For those in the public service, the 'men at the top' have to ensure that immediate subordinates come from the same community — the well-known phenomenon of nepotism — while those at the bottom seek to attach themselves to a 'godfather' who, more often than not, is a kinsman of some kind. Because the 'environment' is seen as something hostile, hardly anyone believes that success can be a reward for merit and achievement and thus success, upward mobility in the bureaucratic hierarchy, has to be explained in some other terms — for example, the existence (or non-existence in the case of failure) of a 'godfather'.

Insecurity is guarded against not just by safeguarding the present but also by insuring against the future, which in practice means the use of one's office to enrich one's self, the widespread practice of corruption and abuse of office, a practice which has been commented upon by almost all observers of the Nigerian political scene.[22] But while it is seemingly impossible to escape from the issue of corruption in practically any discussion about Nigerian society and politics, there is some moral ambivalence about it amongst Nigerians as the survey on social change and public policy showed. Thus, asked whether the rich get richer because they are corrupt, the response gave the following result (see Table 2.2). If the 'don't know/no opinion' category is eliminated by distributing the numbers under that category proportionately between the 'agree' and 'disagree' groups, then the percentage of the former rises to 56.13 per cent and the latter to 43.87 per cent, which could indicate that the population are almost evenly divided over whether the rich get to become rich by being corrupt, a surprising finding give the pervasiveness of talk about corruption. It could of course be the case that the question itself is ambiguous, for there is no necessary inconsistency in believing that public officers and holders of public office are corrupt and yet maintaining that the rich are not corrupt. The two sets could be mutually exclusive but as it is highly unlikely that there would be many who would subscribe to that viewpoint, the possibility of a moral ambivalence becomes all the more probable. Given that the elite — the rich and the powerful — are a first-generation elite, then to judge that the elite are rich because corrupt could amount to judging adversely members of one's own community, and as that would be an unacceptable contravention of community codes an ambivalent value position would seem a perfectly rational position to take, particularly as often it turns out to be the case that those who decry corruption do so not so much becaues they accept that corruption is morally reprehensible as because they are not in a similar position to exploit the opportunities that the holding of specific offices confers. If this appears to be 'double-think' it is appropriate, for double-think bedevils all approaches to corruption in Nigeria. How can a citizen be said not to accept corruption as morally reprehensible and yet equally be said to be reluctant to accuse members of his own community of corruption because to do so would be to judge them adversely? For an explanation of this seeming contradiction it is necessary to understand that the values which have been totally internalised by an individual will be those of his community. And in so far as a successful individual is seen to contribute to the welfare of his community, he is not seen as corrupt. That he has not kept faith with the wider society — and by this betrayal may in fact be damaging the long-term interests of the community — is not readily appreciated. Loyalty to the community is seen as the paramount virtue. But many Nigerians know that the socially acceptable viewpoint is that corruption is morally reprehensible; it is a convenient stick with which to attack an outsider and as a topic of conversation it never loses its fascination. And it is possible, too, that the constant reiteration of alleged instances of corruption makes it more likely that, when the opportunity occurs, the individual will become corrupt; he has heard of so many others behaving in this way and has rarely seen them destroyed by the revelations. When the skeleton in the cupboard becomes a party attraction, it has perhaps lost its power to shock.

The thesis about ambivalence gets reinforced when we examine the value placed on material success, a concept with a wide-ranging connotation. Though in the folklore of the community, success, in whatever endeavour, to be really appreciated, has to be seen to be something painstakingly and slowly earned — the rhetoric of the self-made person is hardly ever to be scorned — increasingly, with the modernisation of the society, success has come to be taken as its own justification. The successful person is simply that individual capable of fully exercising the Machiavellian quality of *virtu*, the ability ceaselessly and ruthlessly to exploit every opportunity as it arises. But this notion of success has to be qualified in some respects, at least in so far as the 'principalities' of the North, where the population is predominantly Moslem, are concerned. For the peoples of these areas, while it is no doubt true that a

TABLE 2.2   *The rich are richer because they are corrupt*
(percentages (N = 8627)

State	Agree	Not sure/ no opinion	Disagree
Lagos	31.3	30.6	38.1
Oyo	48.8	15.8	35.4
Ogun	59.5	19.2	21.3
Ondo	52.2	17.9	29.9
Kwara	33.1	27.3	39.5
Bendel	45.6	17.2	37.2
Imo	55.5	12.6	31.9
Anambra	46.0	9.3	44.7
Rivers	35.0	34.4	30.6
Cross River	33.4	11.1	55.4
Plateau	70.0	12.4	17.6
Benue	60.4	13.3	26.3
Borno	60.9	33.3	5.8
Bauchi	15.3	37.4	47.4
Kano	48.1	22.6	29.3
Kaduna	64.4	29.6	6.0
Niger	50.3	26.4	23.3
National	46.2	21.5	32.3

certain degree of individualism and ruthlessness are necessary prerequisites for success, in themselves they are not sufficient to guarantee that state. For the sufficient condition, providence, whether Divine or otherwise, is required, for the people of this area believe that without the intervention of providence, an individual could struggle all he wants, have every opportunity put his way, and yet in the end turn out to be a failure. But in saying this, it is important to note that to talk of providence is not to imply any notion of fatalism or predestination. Logically, one cannot both be a fatalist and hold any expectations about the future, but – as the survey on social change and social policy showed – most Nigerians do hold favourable expectations about the future of their children, for asked whether they believed their children

TABLE 2.3   *Expectation that children would be better off (percentages) (N = 8627)*

State	Better off	Same/not sure	Worse off
Lagos	72.4	26.6	1.0
Oyo	94.3	5.4	0.3
Ogun	83.0	16.7	0.3
Ondo	97.2	2.8	0.0
Kwara	96.3	3.5	0.2
Bendel	96.1	3.6	0.3
Imo	83.4	6.1	10.5
Anambra	83.7	6.3	9.9
Rivers	87.2	10.7	2.1
Cross River	78.7	6.8	14.6
Plateau	96.0	2.2	1.8
Benue	73.9	20.9	5.2
Borno	70.7	16.7	12.6
Bauchi	81.8	16.5	1.7
Kano	73.4	18.1	8.4
Kaduna	64.2	24.3	11.6
Niger	95.1	4.8	0.1

would be better off than they were, 83 per cent (of 8627 respondents) agreed their children would be better off, 11.7 per cent thought their children were likely not to be better off while only 5.3 per cent said the children would be worse off. The distribution of the response by states is shown in Table 2.3. While it is true that, in very general terms, the peoples of the North are less sanguine about the future than their counterparts in the South, it is also true that, roughly, they all hold similar expectations about the future and the place of their offspring in that future.

But however success is explained, throughout Nigeria it still needs to be 'legitimated', made acceptable to the community. Legitimation involves the demonstration of the fact of success in a whole variety of ways: for the businessman or rentier landlord this could mean residence within the community confines, which would be interpreted as living with the 'people' and being 'part' of the 'people'; maintaining a whole retinue of 'hangers-on', part of whose function would be to maintain and propagate the rhetoric of the self-made man — and generally, serving as a broker, the link person, between the less fortunate members of the community and those in power, the bureaucrats and politicians. For the latter, who perforce have to live in the more exclusive residential areas of the main urban centres, there is the obligation (which derives from traditional expectations about the behaviour of the relatively successful towards other members of the community) to provide jobs for members of their community. But as this is often not possible — certainly the demands on the bureaucrat and the politician far exceed their capacity to deliver — the politician and the bureaucrat can become the 'them', the 'outsider' whose interests stand counterposed to those of the community.

Be that as it may, the legitimacy accorded the rentier/ businessman does pose something of a dilemma for the community, for as Adrian Peace has pointed out, 'whilst in their search for prestige and legitimation they [the rentier/business-man] contribute to a shared identity and cultural unity [of the community], in pursuing their economic and social interests they undermine the possibilities for collective action' by the less successful of the community as the latter are gradually and increasingly led to accept that their welfare depends crucially on their maintaining their clientage relations with the broker-patrons of the community. Thus, to quote Peace again:

> in attempting to legitimate their own positions of privilege within the community, they (the successful) also legitimate the economic system of relationships and declare that system to be right and proper, but in doing so they divorce the internal economic order from the wider system of power relationships which determine its fundamental form.[23]

But the foregoing merely points to a basic ambiguity in the notion of the community as a source of value for while as a 'moral order', the community is seen as a fountain of imperatival injunctions for its members, as an 'economic order' it represents a pattern of unequal and exploitative relationships which are not only incompatible with the moral basis of the community but are in fact subversive of that order. While on the one hand inter-communal comparisons of welfare would seem to indicate that most communities are reasonably satisfied, as Table 2.4 shows, within the several communities the degree of inequality is becoming more pronounced. From the data shown in the table, only Bendel, Imo, Anambra, Cross River, Rivers, and Plateau give percentages lower than the national average, or put differently, believe their communities to be more relatively deprived. It might be of some interest also to note that other than Imo and Anambra (Ibo-speaking areas where feelings of deprivation can be attributed to the aftermath of the civil war), these states would fall into the category of states usually referred to as 'minority areas'. However, asked whether they

TABLE 2.4 *Your ethnic group economically better off than others (in percentages) (N = 8627)*

State	Better off	Average/no opinion	Worse off
Lagos	37.5	54.3	8.2
Oyo	54.4	43.1	2.5
Ogun	38.6	58.1	3.3
Ondo	40.6	55.9	3.5
Kwara	18.5	75.3	6.2
Bendel	16.0	48.4	35.6
Imo	27.9	32.1	40.0
Anambra	14.7	29.4	55.9
Rivers	9.8	78.8	11.4
Cross River	4.2	39.6	56.2
Plateau	8.5	59.3	32.2
Benue	20.4	63.5	16.1
Borno	53.7	44.6	1.7
Bauchi	16.5	81.7	1.8
Kano	22.1	71.9	6.0
Kaduna	52.3	38.6	9.1
Niger	32.7	66.9	0.4
Population column percentage	27.8	54.3	17.9

thought the rich were getting richer, a preponderant number, 76.8 per cent, gave an affirmative response while 4.8 per cent were either 'not sure' or had 'no opinion' to offer. Only 18.3 per cent, or less than one in five, disagreed. The perception of inequality gains in credibility when the answer to the question whether respondents thought their status had declined relative to what they believed it was ten years earlier, is examined. Whereas 32.3 per cent agreed that it had, only 40.9 per cent thought they had improved status-wise while 26.8 per cent were undecided. However, when that response is stratified in terms of the assets owned by the respondent, some 87 per cent of the total sample, who would fall into the category of the 'relatively poor' gave answers which were three or four percentage points lower than the average, while 13 per cent of the sample who could be classed as wealthy gave replies which were between seven and thirteen percentage points higher than the average of the total who agreed their status had improved.

Paralleling the dichotomy between the 'us' and the 'them' at the community level, is that between the community and the principality at the society level and a value which is central to the whole notion of a principality is that of leadership. The principalities were relatively complex organisations with fairly well-differentiated structures and roles so that in talking about 'leadership' it might perhaps be well to be clear in what sense that term is being used. There are at least two broad ways in which we can interpret the notion of leadership: the 'collectivist' and the 'individualistic' sense. In the former, the focus would be on a 'class' or group of persons, as when we talk for instance of bureaucratic leadership or leadership by a vanguardist party, or by people with a clearly defined economic interest – the bourgeoisie or the proletariat or whatever other surrogate one might want to name. In the latter case, the notion of leadership is something more personalised, a capacity of individuals to act out of their own personal convictions, to mobilise support from others in the pursuit and furtherance of those convictions; an ability to elicit trust and loyalty, to rise above one's own economic interests and to act in the interest of the collectivity. It is in this second, individualistic sense that the term 'leadership' will be used in the discussion that follows.

Within the traditional community, there was nothing which closely corresponded to the notion of leadership in the individualistic sense: what there was, was essentially collectivistic — the 'leaders' were simply the elders of the community and leadership was just a function of age.

It is when we turn to the level of the principality that we come across ideas bearing some relation to the notion of individualistic leadership distinguished above. Thus, in the northern Islamic principalities, in which leadership is said to be prescriptively based, one finds Abdullahi dan Fodio, the brother of the founder of the Islamic principalities, writing that it was necessary, in fact obligatory, for the leader of the community to be selected by a council of learned mallams (the intelligentsia of the principality) from among the most qualified men, suitable qualifications being a high standard of scholarship, deep concern for justice and fair play, respect for the law and, naturally, being a 'believer'. In another context, Abdullahi was to write that responsibility should be divided from the highest authority, the honourable Imam (i.e. religious leader) to the least authority, the 'servant in charge of his master's wealth' which is just another way of saying that 'the Imam [must] be a watchman over all the people, but since it is impossible for him to be responsible for all their affairs, he must have deputies'. The 'good' leader is thus the man who knows when and how to delegate, but in delegating, care should be taken for to give 'responsibility to irresponsible persons is a sin'. Leadership therefore involves not just responsibility for the welfare and good governance of the people, but also responsibility for the actions of one's deputies.

At this point it might be as well to note that this notion of leadership is in no way unique to the Islamic principalities of the North but is a characteristic feature of all those collectivities in Nigeria in which the unit of social organisation is larger than the 'moral community', which in effect means most of the collectivities in Nigeria apart from the well-known examples of Ibos, the Tivs and the Urhobos. If in fact anything can be said to be unique about the Islamic principalities, it is not so much the form of the social organisation which the Moslem Fulani conquerors inherited from the Habes, the Hausa-speaking peoples – but the way in which the Fulani conquerors elaborated the notion of leadership to a level where it came close to becoming an 'ideology' of governing. It was that elaboration which so impressed the colonial administration that it sought to universalise the idiom into a principle of general applicability.

In order to be able to govern effectively the newly colonised territory which became known as Nigeria, the colonial administration guaranteed the leaders of the various principalities virtually monopolistic advantages in their respective principalities – the policy that came to be known as 'indirect rule' – first by delimiting the boundaries of the principalities, thereby removing the uncertainty surrounding what constituted the actual domain of a principality; and secondly, through such delimitation, minimising the reliance which the leader placed on his intermediaries, his clients, to ensure the security of his domain of power. But perhaps much more significant was the fact that the colonial administration, by incorporating the various principalities into an interconnected framework of administration, helped to engender a new sense of identity amongst linked sets of principalities, which sets gradually assumed a closed character as the leaders sought to maintain monopolistic advantages within the boundaries constituted by a set of principalities. Some elaboration might help to make this point clearer, and in this respect, we could consider the case of the 'Yoruba' principalities.

Though some Yorubas now talk of being descended from a common ancestor – Oduduwa – who, they claim, was the 'founder' of the various Yoruba kingdoms (or principalities), nevertheless there is not much evidence to suggest that before the end of the nineteenth century there was any conglomerate set of peoples who were known as the 'Yoruba peoples' or 'Yoruba-speaking peoples'. But, there were, and still are, groups who identified themselves as Oyos, Ijesas, Ijebus, Egbas, Ebgados, Ekitas, Akokos, Ilajes and so on. And for much of the nineteenth century what could be called a 'history' of the Yoruba peoples was nothing other than a record of bitter internecine warfare between these different groups. An Ijesa song, for example, extolling the exploits of one of their nineteenth-century warriors, tells of the warrior taking Oyos into slavery and having them slaughtered in ritual sacrifices to the gods while over their conquered land he placed Ijesas to rule as princes. In itself, that may not amount to much since the killing of captives taken in battle would seem to be a well-documented historical fact common to the different peoples of the world. But what is significant is not the slaughter of captive Oyos; it is the claim that Oyos were to be regarded as ritual sacrificial objects, which in effect was to claim that they were in some respects less than human. Similar claims have been made about other groups, for instance, the Ijebus. However, by the late nineteenth century, with the introduction of 'modern' education following the start of the colonial penetration of Nigeria, it became possible to show that these different groups were in fact sub-groups of a parent group which became known as the 'Yoruba'. With the imposition of colonial rule and the incorporation of the various groups into the new politico-administrative framework that became Nigeria, a new sense of identity was gradually formed amongst linked groups. Competition for differential rewards within the new administrative framework further encouraged the move towards greater cohesion, a cohesion which increasingly took on the characteristics of a closed system as leaders sought to protect their respective power bases.

The foregoing brief description of incorporation among the Yoruba could equally have been of any of the other linked groups, for example, the Ibos or the Urhobos. But if incorporation helped to foster a new value dimension in the form of a collective social identity it also, in a seemingly paradoxical way, reinforced the sense of (sub-group) community identity. Among the Ibos, for example, where the collective social identity found organisational expression in the Ibo State Union, the 'communal' — that which gave to the individual his sense of the existential present (and which consequently tended to be 'taken for granted', a datum, so to speak of social existence) also became endowed with organisational concreteness in the form of a plethora of sub-group associations like the Orlu Progressive Union, the Nnewi Improvement Union and numerous others.

POLITICAL ACTION AND THE ARENAS OF POLITICS

It is not difficult to see that we could possibly distinguish some four relatively well-defined 'arenas' (or fields) of political action. There is, first, what was described above as the community; second, there is the 'principality'; third, the social aggregate, or what we could call the language or ethnic group; and fourthly, the universalistic system, or the state system that is Nigeria. The relationship between the different arenas can also be conceived of in a variety of ways; for instance, as a hierarchic order, with the community at the bottom of the hierarchy and the state system at the top. An alternative form of representing the hierarchy is to take each arena as a circle, in which case we could picture the four arenas as a set of concentric circles with the community as the innermost circle and the state system as the outermost. Then again, we could look at the arenas simply as constituents of a composite whole, with the community as the elementary unit of the composite, a conjunction of elementary units then making up the principality, a set of which conjoined would then yield the social aggregate or language group. Finally, we would have the state system which could then be said to be composed of a set of language groups. Looked at from this perspective, we could then talk of Nigeria as a multinational or polyethnic state.

We can now appreciate, begin to understand, the kinds of dilemmas that could confront political actors operating within these different arenas. Some of these dilemmas have been analysed and discussed above but underlying all of these is a central dilemma. Political structures and institutions have to draw their inspiration from the requisites of the mass society. This has to be so since it is of the nature of the other arenas that they are incapable by themselves of generating or giving political consciousness to those who are not, and *ex deficione* cannot be, members of these arenas. Given then that institutions have to be structured in terms of the features and norms of the mass society, it also follows that role profiles have to be conceived in terms of those features and norms. But this immediately leads to an incongruity as role expectations – beliefs which people have about what constitutes proper behaviour – are in the main determined or shaped by the norms and values defined by the other arenas. The result is to produce a mix of role profiles which neither meets the demands of the mass society nor satisfies the expectations of the populace for whom the mass society is still an alien arena. (This is vividly shown in Chinua Achebe's novel *A Man of the People* (London: Heinemann, 1966).)

Not surprisingly, therefore, the argument has sometimes been made that to escape from role incongruity (or value dissonance) a return has to be made to 'traditional' values – the rediscovery of 'Africanism' – and institutions must be created which are consonant with such values. Professor Ayandele, the Nigerian historian, expressed this quite succinctly when he wrote:

> Borrowed ideas, customs and institutions have their value, but only to the extent that they are adapted, or adaptable, to the indigenous milieu in which they are being adopted. To miss this point is to miss one's bearings, to cease to know oneself. History is yet to reveal genuine nations born out of a cultural womb completely alien to it. It is a law of nature that the pride of any people is found in those customs and institutions peculiarly their own. Not that these customs or institutions are fixed, immutable entities, but they cannot reasonably or easily or peacefully be effaced or wished away overnight, just as they did not come into existence overnight. The process of their being changed is necessarily gradual. The extent to which a people ignores this fact and turns its back on its culture is the extent to which it is inviting humiliation and effeteness.[24]

But then the question is not really one of 'backs being turned', it is simply that any talk of 'adaptation' in the manner suggested by Ayandele – and those who argue like him – cannot but be regarded as naive, precisely because we cannot meaningfully talk of a culture but of cultures, a plurality of cultures. Conceivably, with time, the fact of value dissonance will be transcended or resolved, perhaps with the spread of education. The alternative would be that the people will have to accommodate themselves to such dissonance as a characteristic of the political system.

3

Political Institutions of the First Republic

In contemporary political discourse, the word 'institution' is often used in a variety of ways, of which two would seem to be the most common. First, there is the sense of 'institution' which features in such expressions as 'the institution of monarchy', the 'institution of the Presidency' or the 'institution of Leadership' where the word 'institution' has much the same meaning as 'office' or 'role'. Thus, we can substitute the words 'office' or 'role' for the word 'institution' in the above expressions without any loss of meaning whatsoever. This sense of the word is the one more commonly used by sociologists and those political scientists with a sociological orientation. The second, equally common, usage is that in which the word 'institution' carries the sense of a mechanism or machinery for doing things, a machinery which has parts, each part fitting into the other to form a complex whole, a structure. Thus, we can talk, for instance, of 'legislative institutions' and mean by this no more than the mechanism – organisation – for the making of laws. Equally, we can talk of the 'institution of political parties', meaning by this simply the organisations through which the interests of individuals and groups are aggregated and articulated. In talking about the political institutions of the first republic, the word institution will be used in this second sense to refer to those organisations, or structures, through which the political affairs of the first republic were conducted and managed.

To be strictly constitutional, the term 'first republic' should be used to refer only to that period between the years 1963 and 1966: 1963 when Nigeria became constitutionally a republic, and 1966 when that republic was brought to an end by means of a military coup. More usually though, the term 'first republic' is used to refer to the period 1960 to 1966 in Nigeria, that is pushing the time back to 1960 when Nigeria became an independent and sovereign state. Much of this chapter will therefore be concerned with the period 1960 to 1966, but we can hardly expect to appreciate and understand what took place within that period without taking a look at what went before. For one thing, 'institutions', in the sense in which the word is being used here, are not things which develop overnight. They have a history, but as with all history, the problem often arises of how far back in time one wants to go; but 1946 is the time when Nigerians first came to be actively involved in the management of their own affairs, so a start will be made from there.

The year 1946 marked the introduction of the 'Richards Constitution', so named after the man who was the Governor of Nigeria at the time, Sir Arthur Richards. It also marked the beginning of regionalism, which was to create many difficulties, subsequently, for Nigerian political leaders. What is perhaps much more important is that it was the year when the administration of Northern Nigeria was brought into the general framework of the government of Nigeria. What today is known as Nigeria is the product of the amalgamation in 1914 of the territories known as the Northern and Southern provinces of Nigeria by Sir Frederick (later Lord) Lugard. But though the two territories were supposed to have been amalgamated into one political unit, for all practical purposes they were administered as separate entities, more so after 1916 when Lugard left Nigeria. In 1923, a Nigerian Legislative Council[1] was created to afford a selected[2] body of Nigerians a limited opportunity to express their views on the colonial government's legislative programme, but the former Northern provinces were kept outside the purview of the Council.

Basically, the political isolation of the Northern provinces from the rest of the country was a form of quarantine. After the subjugation of Sokoto in 1905, Lugard had come to an agreement with the Emirs who effectively ruled much of the territory of the Northern provinces. Among other things, it

was agreed that (a) the colonial government would not inter-
fere with the religion of the people, essentially Islam as two-
thirds of the population were Moslem; and (b) unlike in the
Southern provinces where the Christian mission had been
allowed a free hand to proselytise, the activities of missionaries
would be restricted only to those areas of the North where
the religion of the people is not Islam, which meant in effect
such areas as came to be known as southern Zaria, Kabba,
Adamawa, Benue and Plateau provinces. The reason for this
is easy enough to understand. The Christian missions had
brought with them 'modern, western' education which the
colonial administration believed had given the people 'dangerous' ideas which might lead them to demand the vote, the
right to equal employment opportunities with the colonial
administrators and the right to be self-governing. The political
isolation of the Northern provinces was therefore an attempt
to prevent the North from being infected with similar ideas.

But it was hardly possible to keep the North effectively
quarantined, nor quarantined for an indefinite period. In the
first place, though the colonial administration sought to control the media of information in the North,[3] they could not
control trade and commerce between the provinces and this
meant the movement of people and with the movement of
people, the exchange of ideas. Secondly, the maintenance of
certain central services such as the railways, and posts and
telecommunications, meant bringing southerners to the
North, and even though, in some of the Northern Emirates,
such southerners were kept in particular parts of the towns —
the Sabon garis (or strangers' quarters) — the control of residence could not prevent the interaction between northerners
and southerners and hence the transfer of ideas and sentiments.
Last, even in the North itself, the need to maintain some
framework of administration meant that the people themselves could not be altogether insulated from forms of western
education and the very ideas which the administration regarded
as so pernicious.

The spread of education and the creation of a new educated
class, the growth of the railway and other forms of transport,
which led to increased opportunities for trade and commerce
and the emergence of new business groups, coupled with

political changes in other parts of Britain's colonial empire, for instance in Ceylon and India, meant that the participation of these new classes in the political power of the state could not be delayed for much longer. By 1938, for instance, the then Governor, Sir Donald Cameron, had already put forward proposals for political reform but these had to be postponed because of the start of the Second World War. With the end of the war, the ideas of Sir Donald were resuscitated by his successor, Sir Arthur Richards, who put these into the form that came to be known as the 'Richards Constitution'.

Basically, the 1946 constitution provided for the establishment of regional assemblies in the three regions into which Nigeria had been divided in 1938 but in the North and the West, besides the assemblies, there was also to be a House of Chiefs. The assemblies were composed of (a) representatives of the colonial administration, who formed the majority; and (b) nominated persons chosen from the various 'native authorities' (local government units). The assemblies could discuss legislative proposals put before them by the administration but could not pass these into law. For the latter purpose, a central legislature was created. This, like the regional assemblies, was composed of designated officials and members nominated from the regions but the North had fewer 'representatives' than either the East or the West. The arguments in support of the new arrangement were that it would (a) enable each region to develop at the pace best suited to it; (b) provide a training ground for future political leaders; and (c) help to create a sense of belonging to a common nation.

Though the 1946 arrangement was supposed to last for nine years, it only survived for three. By 1949, dissatisfaction with the Richards Constitution was so widespread that changes were felt to be imperative. As a preliminary, discussions were held at the level of the provinces on what directions these changes should take. The provincial discussions led to regional conferences being held, after which a general conference of delegates from the various regions was summoned which finally produced what came to be known (again after the Governor) as the 'MacPherson Constitution'. This came into effect in 1951, and its significance lies in four things: (i) it gave to the regional assemblies the right, for the first time, to make laws for the region; (ii) it provided, for the first time, for the election, admittedly indirectly, of the members of the regional assemblies; (iii) it provided for the establishment of executive councils, composed of Ministers, in the various legislatures; and (iv) at the level of the central legislature, it provided for an equality of representation among the three regions. But what is of great importance is that the MacPherson 'settlement', by providing for indirect elections, facilitated the process of political party formation.

THE PARTY SYSTEM

Political parties in Nigeria date back to 1923 when, with the introduction of the Nigerian Legislative Council, the franchise was given to the inhabitants of two towns, Lagos and Calabar. The granting of the franchise led to the formation of the Nigerian National Democratic Party in 1923, and subsequently, in 1938, to the formation of the Nigerian Youth Movement. Both parties could, however, more properly be called, following Thomas Hodgkin, 'proto-parties'.[4] Their influence barely extended beyond the immediate environs of Ibadan and Lagos. Parties, properly so called, are formal organisations which compete through the electoral process to control the personnel and policies of government, and these in Nigeria were a product of the post-Richardson constitution. The first of these to emerge was the National Council of Nigeria and the Cameroons (NCNC), which was formed in 1944, but only came into prominence between 1946 and 1947.

The NCNC was led by Herbert Macaulay, a veteran nationalist leader, and on his death in 1947 he was succeeded by Nnamdi Azikiwe, a journalist and newspaper proprietor. The NCNC caught the imagination of the people when its leadership travelled round the country rallying opposition to the Richards constitution and certain legislative proposals then before the Legislative Council. In furtherance of its opposition, the party led a delegation to London to meet the Secretary of State for the Colonies but its efforts met with little success. Thereafter the Party went into relative abeyance until it was given a new lease of life as a result of the coming into being of the MacPherson constitution.

The NCNC has been described as a 'mass party' in that unlike 'elite parties', its membership was open to everyone and it derived its finances from the contributions of its members. In actual fact, however, all Nigerian parties have tended to rely either directly or indirectly on the government of the region which they control to provide the bulk of their finances. In the case of the NCNC, the main source of its funds was 'loans' from the African Continental Bank (ACB) a bank whose principal shareholder was Nnamdi Azikiwe (and Zik Enterprises Ltd, a company again largely owned by Nnamdi Azikiwe) but whose assets were later to be taken over by the East regional government when the ACB was almost on the point of liquidation. From 1951 until the military coup of January 1966, the NCNC controlled the government of the Eastern region and for much of the same period formed the main opposition in the Western House of Assembly. Between 1954 and 1957 and from 1959 to 1966, in coalition with the NPC (Northern Peoples' Congress) it formed the Federal government.[5]

Unlike the NPC and the Action Group (AG), the other two main parties of the first republic, the NCNC drew much of its electoral support from its association with various interest and value groups. In the East itself it relied largely on the Ibo State Union, a federation of diverse clan unions of Ibo-speaking peoples, for mobilising the electorate. In the North, its support derived from the alliance it formed with the Northern Elements Progressive Union (NEPU) and with the Bornu Youth Movement before the latter switched its support in 1958 to the AG. In the West, the NCNC derived its strength from its association with such 'cultural' unions as the Otu Edo Youth Union (lit. association of Edo, i.e. Bini-speaking peoples, youths) and the Urhobo Progressive Union. And on the labour front, the party sought support from organisations such as the Railway Workers Union and the African Tin Mineworkers Union. This eclectic approach to electoral support meant that the NCNC had to be different things to different groups, and hence its ideological orientation had perforce to be essentially pragmatic. Nevertheless, were one to characterise its position within a 'left'/'right' ideological spectrum, the NCNC would be placed to the left of the AG and the NPC.

The second major party was the AG, which was formed in 1948 and was itself an offshoot of the Yoruba cultural association, Egbe Omo Oduduwa (lit. association of the children of Oduduwa, the mythical ancestor of the Yoruba speaking peoples) started in London around 1945 by Obafemi Awolowo who was then a law student. Awolowo provided the rationale for the Egbe in his book, *Path To Nigerian Freedom* (London; Faber & Faber, 1947), which was published with a Foreword written by Dame Margery Perham. The argument was straightforward enough: it was that in a heterogeneous society such as Nigeria's, political stability could be achieved only if ethnic conglomerates were grouped together to form a single self-administering political unit. Put differently, this is to say for example that all Yoruba-speaking peoples should form one single political entity and only by such means can the cultural heritage of the different ethnic groups be protected and safeguarded and political advance assured. When therefore the AG emerged from the Egbe, it was with the purpose of espousing the notion of cultural nationalism.[6] But while such a move could assure the AG the prospect of control of the Yoruba-speaking areas, it was not likely to command support in other areas. Hence the ideological image of the AG had to be modified and the AG did this by promoting a welfarist programme encapsulated in the party's slogan of 'life more abundant' and 'freedom for all'.

Be that as it may, the AG was essentially a 'caucus party', deriving its active support from the business class of merchants, transporters and contractors and the educated elite. This was clearly brought out, for example, in the way the party obtained its finances. The 'Coker Commission Report',[7] for example, showed that to secure the resources the party needed to contest the 1959 federal elections, the party had had to found the National Investment and Properties Company (NIPC), a company controlled wholly by top AG functionaries, through which government funds from the National Bank (owned and controlled by the Western government), the Western Regional Development Corporation and the West

Regional Marketing Board, were channelled to the coffers of the party. Between 1958 and 1960, some six and a half million pounds of public funds found its way through the NIPC to the AG treasury.[8] In actual fact, the funds provided by business interests had enabled the AG to buy its way into forming the government of the Western region in 1951 and devices such as the NIPC were little more than ways of repaying the business interests which had invested in the AG in its early days.[9]

For all the AG's cultural traditionalism, its hold on the electorate of the Western region was not as strong as the NCNC's in the East or the NPC's in the North. Ibadan, the Western region's capital city, remained lost to the AG, at least until 1958,[10] as were such centres as Ilesha, Akure and Owo. And other than in the 1959 federal elections, at no time did the AG poll up to 50 per cent of the votes in the West. One explanation for this tenuous hold lies in the historical animosities between the various Yoruba kingdoms, but to go into that would be beyond the scope of this chapter.[11] However, the AG did secure some support in other areas besides the West, particularly in the Benue province of the Northern region and in the Calabar, Ogoja and Rivers provinces of the East, areas with marked separatist tendencies which the AG effectively exploited. Throughout the years of the first republic, 1960–66, the AG formed the opposition in the federal Legislature and before that was a member of the coalition federal government in the period 1951–53 (by constitutional provision) and from 1957 to 1959 when at the invitation of the NPC/NCNC ruling coalition, the AG joined the federal executive in the attempt of the ruling coalition to create the consensus needed to secure Nigeria's independence. Relative to the NCNC and the NPC, the AG could ideologically be described as a 'centre' party, though the party leadership did attempt to move to the left during the period 1959–66 when the party proclaimed it was subscribing to the ideology of 'democratic socialism', a proclamation which in 1962 was to cause a split within the party, a split which initiated the series of events which was to culminate in the military coup of 1966.

The third, and the most influential, party of the first republic was the NPC, which could be said to have been formed in

1951 and somewhat like the AG, was an offshoot of a 'cultural' association, the Jam'iyyar Mutanen Arewa (JMA) (lit: the association of peoples of the North). The JMA was formed in 1948 by members of the north's intelligentsia who wanted a forum within which the political change then taking place in the country could be discussed. An earlier attempt, also by members of the intelligentsia, to found a political party with a base in the North — the Northern Elements Progressive Association (NEPA) — had led to most of the founding members losing their jobs — in the bureaucracy and in the native authorities — or being imprisoned. To escape the fate of the founders of NEPA, leaders of the JMA had to call their organisation a 'cultural association'. After the indirect elections of 1951, the newly elected members of the Northern House of Assembly — most of them native authority functionaries and a number of whom were also members of the JMA — decided to proclaim themselves members of the 'Northern Peoples' Congress' and in a sense the JMA was thus converted into the NPC. The NPC, unlike the NCNC or the AG, could thus be properly called a 'parliamentary party'. But more importantly, because most members of the NPC were also native authority functionaries, the NPC became closely wedded to the structure of the native authority system of the North and since the NA system was the only effective administrative system in the North at that period, the party and the administration became one and the same thing and the NPC could thus proudly take as its motto: 'One North; One People, Irrespective of Religion, Rank or Tribe'. The party was the only party with a restricted membership, this being open only to 'people of Northern Nigerian descent' as the party's constitution was later to specify.

The NPC's leader, Alhaji Sir Ahmadu Bello, the Sardauna of Sokoto, was Premier of the North until his death in the military coup of 1966; in this the NPC was unlike the AG — whose leader, Chief Obafemi Awolowo, left the Premiership of the West regional government to become Leader of the Opposition in the federal legislature after the 1959 elections — and the NCNC, whose leader, Dr Nnamdi Azikiwe, left the Premiership of the East regional government to become first, Leader of the Senate, the federal second chamber, in 1960, then Governor-General in 1962 and a year later, first President of the Republic of Nigeria. The fact that Alhaji Sir Ahmadu Bello remained the Premier of the North gave his deputy, Alhaji Sir Abubakar Tafawa Balewa, the opportunity to become the first and only Prime Minister of the Federation of Nigeria, a position the latter held until his death in the military coup of 1966. From 1954 to 1966 the NPC remained the dominant coalition partner in the federal government but the preference of the leader of the party to remain Premier of the North showed where the NPC's priorities lay with respect to the Nigerian political process and also where ultimate power in the federation resided: that power resided in the North.

There were, besides the three main parties, numerous other smaller parties such as the Northern Elements Progressive Union (NEPU), the United Middle Belt Congress (UMBC), the United Nigeria Independence Party (UNIP), the Bornu Youth Movement (BYM), the Kano Peoples Party (KPP) and the Midwest Democratic Front (MDF). But these were highly localised parties, based essentially on specific interests and whose main significance was that they provided avenues for one or the other of the three dominant parties, through alliances by means of which they could extend their electoral reach into regions outside their principal sphere of influence. Thus, for instance, the AG by entering into an alliance with the UMBC was able to reach into the North while the NPC succeeded in extending its electoral appeal into the Midwest through its alliance with the MDF. For the smaller parties, entering into an alliance with a major party had two advantages: first, an alliance assured the smaller party some access to funds which such parties lacked; and secondly, it enabled party stalwarts to enjoy some form of party patronage such as being appointed to the management boards of government-controlled para-statal organisations. Electorally, however, they were of not much significance since, taken together, at no election did these parties poll as much as 15 per cent of the votes.

INTEREST GROUPS

In talking about interest groups, it is conventional to make a distinction between 'interest groups', properly so called, and 'promotional' or 'value' groups. Both, of course, exist to further the interests which their members share in common but they differ in three ways, the first of which is that whereas interest groups seek to satisfy some other interest besides the main interest of the group — e.g. a trade union providing welfare services for its members besides the more obvious interest the members have in wages and conditions of work — promotional groups usually have one and only one interest. The second way in which they differ is that while interest groups tend to maintain a more or less permanent organisation, the promotional group maintains only a rudimentary organisation which in fact soon disappears once the interest is realised. Thirdly, while interest groups tend to achieve their interests through the exercise of pressure, for example, on the government or on the bureaucracy, promotional groups more usually seek to realise their aim through lobbying to change people's opinions and attitudes. Generally, in developing polities like Nigeria, the more common type of groups to be found are interest groups. There are a whole variety of interest groups such as the Nigerian Ex-Servicemen's Association; trade union associations like the Nigerian Railway Workers Union, the Union of Posts and Telegraphic Workers, the Nigerian Union of Dockworkers, etc., and employers' associations such as the Nigerian Employers Consultative Association and the various Chambers of Trade and Commerce, and of course associations like the Market Women's Association.

Before the emergence of political parties, interest groups featured quite prominently on the political scene, exerting pressure wherever possible on the colonial authorities. Thus, for example, but for the opposition of the Nigerian Cocoa Merchants Association, the colonial government would have given the expatriate-controlled firms a monopoly over the buying and marketing of Nigerian export produce in 1938. In Lagos the Market Women's Association has played a not inconsiderable role in determining the location of market sites in the city, besides influencing the rates of stallage fees. In the absence of parties, the avenues left for influencing policy formulation and articulating grievance were the interest groups and that these groups functioned in the manner they did was therefore only to be expected.

However, with the emergence of parties, interest groups have on the whole had their roles emasculated by the parties, which have tended to regard interest groups as rivals rather than as complementary organisations. In fact as the parties gained control over the machinery of government, they increasingly came to see interest groups as oppositional groups whose activities had to be curtailed or, if that proved impossible, suppressed. The result, not surprisingly, has been the elimination of these groups as centres of 'countervailing forces', balancing and moderating the influence of the parties, thereby leaving the latter with a near monopoly of political power, a power which they have exercised more often than not to the detriment of the individual and his rights.

REGIONALISM AND THE THEORY OF REGIONAL SECURITY

The MacPherson constitution marked the start of a full-scale swing towards regionalism, and between 1954 and 1959 the region became the principal *arena* of politics, the field 'where the action is'. Though the 1951 constitution had conferred on the regions the power to make their own laws, there still remained some constraints on that power. There was first the constraint that the regional appropriations act still had to be passed by the central legislature before any disbursements could be made from the regional budget. Secondly, there was an administrative constraint in that though there were now ministers supposedly in charge of ministries, the effective head of the ministry was the administrative head and not the minister and the former was not obliged to follow the directives of the latter. The difficulties which these constraints created led to demands for increased autonomy for the regions, a demand which was met with the introduction of a new constitution, the Lyttelton Constitution, in 1954.[12] The key points of this constitution can be summarised as follows:

(i)   Nigeria was to be a federation made up of a federal government and three regional governments, each with specified powers such that no one government could legislate on matters not allocated to it. Matters not allocated either to the federal or a regional government were to be contained in a 'concurrent list' over which any government could legislate, but where regional legislation — on a concurrent matter — conflicted with a federal act, then the regional legislation was to the extent of such conflict or inconsistency null and void.

(ii) The federal legislature, to be composed of an equal number of members from each of the three regions, was to be directly elected, and whichever party won a majority of the seats in the federal legislature would form the federal government.

(iii) There would be a Federal Supreme Court whose functions would be (a) to interpret the constitution — that is, have original jurisdiction in the first instance; and (b) hear appeals from the regional High Courts. Appeals from judgements of the Supreme Court would be to the Privy Council.

(iv) Regional assemblies, elections to which were to be specified by laws passed by the Assembly, were to have full legislative sovereignty over matters arrogated to them by the constitution.

(v) There were to be Regional High Courts — and such other courts as might be specified by law — whose function would be to interpret and execute all laws passed by the regional legislature.

(vi) In the North, besides the regional High Court, there was to be a Shari'a Court of Appeal, to hear appellate cases involving Muslim personal law. In the event of a conflict between decisions by the Shari'a Court of Appeal and the regional High Court, such a conflict was to be adjudicated by a Court of Resolution.

(vii) Each region was to have its own civil service which would be headed by the regional executive to which the bureaucracy would be responsible.

(viii) Each regional government would be responsible for the purchasing and marketing of all export produce produced within the region.

(ix) In each region, the titular head of the government was to be known as the Governor, and in the case of the federal government, the Governor-General.

(x)   Each region was to have the power to determine when it would become internally self-governing.

The constitutional changes which had taken place between 1946 and 1953 probably had little impact on the daily life of the average Nigerian but the 1954 constitution affected him directly. As an employee, he now found that the level of his tax varied with the region in which he resided: he paid the most in income tax if he resided in the East and the least if his residence was in the North. And as a farmer growing export crops, he found that the price he got for his produce varied with the region in which the produce was sold. Thus, for example, he got more for his cocoa if he sold it in the East — which grew little cocoa — than if the same cocoa was sold in the West. As a parent, with children of school-going age, he found that if he resided in the West, he did not have to pay fees for his children in primary schools but he had to do so if his place of abode was in the East or in the North.[13]

In many different ways the Nigerian 'citizen' now found he had to live with the fact of regionalism. The 'regionalisation' of the bureaucracy — and all the structural changes that went with it[14] — meant that the civil servant no longer had a choice of in what region he could serve or, for the prospective civil servant, a choice in where to seek employment. The regional-isation of the public service meant that the civil servant could now work — or seek employment — only in his 'region of origin'. Easterners working in the West had perforce to move to the East or face a loss of employment, and what applied to the West applied equally to the other regions. And the process did not stop with the main civil service: it was gradually extended to the corporations, the para-statals and where possible, to the private sector.

At the governmental level the head of the regional executive, previously known as 'Leader of Government Business', became the 'Premier' of the region and, to ensure that the regional ruling party remained in effective control, various instruments of social control were instituted. In the West for example, this meant the creation of a regional police service[15] parallel with, and complementary to, the Nigeria Police Force. The latter had also been regionalised with each region forming a 'regional command' headed by a Commissioner who, for the day-to-day purposes of law and order, was directly accountable, for the force under his command, to the Premier of the region.

The process of consolidation gained further momentum after the federal elections of 1954. In that election, the NPC had won all the seats from the North, while the NCNC had won all those from the East. But in the West, the AG lost the election to the NCNC, which won a majority of the seats. Because it had won the majority of the seats the NCNC insisted it should have the right to nominate which of the members from the West were to represent that region in the Federal executive. In this way the AG was denied a place in the Government of the federation. As a reaction, the AG-controlled west regional government dissolved the local councils in all those areas which in the 1954 election had returned an NCNC candidate. In many cases, 'caretaker committees' composed of AG loyalists were appointed to run the affairs of the dissolved councils. In others, the Instruments setting up the councils were revoked and the area itself either broken up to form smaller units of local administration, or amalgamated with an adjoining authority to form a larger unit.

It should not be thought that the process described above was unique to the West. In the North, in areas such as Benue, Borno, Ilorin and Plateau provinces where the NCNC or the AG had won some marginal following, the same phenomenon of persuasion—coercion was to be observed. By 1956, when the regional elections were held, so successful had been the process of party consolidation that all ruling parties experienced little difficulty in ensuring that they retained control of their respective regions. By 1956, in fact, it seemed as if there had emerged an unwritten agreement between the three main parties that none was to seek to extend its influence outside the region it dominated. Regionalism had given way to the notion of 'regional security' and this seemingly had received 'confirmation' when the East and West regions became 'internally self-governing' in 1957. In that same year the AG was also brought into the federal coalition in a new consensus which was to persist into 1959 when the North also became internally self-governing. But it was a fragile consensus which by 1959 had in fact begun to show the first signs of cracks.

The break can be attributed to two broad factors — economic and political. On the economic front regional governments found that it was becoming increasingly difficult for them to meet the annual recurrent costs of running the various welfare programmes they had initiated. In the East and the West, there had been a programme of rapid expansion of education, particularly primary education, the building of hospitals, roads, the expansion of electrification to rural areas, and ill-conceived schemes like agricultural resettlement programmes for primary-school-leavers. These and a variety of other programmes had placed an unbearable burden on government finances, which had in fact suffered a decrease as a result of successive falls in the export prices of primary products, the main source of regional government revenues. In other words, while revenues were falling, expenditure was rising. The gap thus created had in the past been met through external borrowing, but the spectacle of the different regional governments competing for limited external funds, funds which were often wastefully utilised but which nevertheless had to be guaranteed by the federal government – against revenue payments – had led the federal authority to impose some restraint on external borrowing. But where the regions were faced with severe budget deficits the federal government was experiencing rising budgetary surpluses, and access to these surpluses could only be gained through control of the machinery of government at the federal level. Here we confront the political.

Increasingly, since 1953, the minority groups had been demanding that more regions should be created in the country; the political framework as it then existed, they claimed, resulted in their legitimate claims, particularly in the distribution of economic goods, being denied by the controlling major ethnic groups. And to the clamour for independence by the political elite, the colonial government had retorted by saying independence would only be granted after a thorough examination of the demands by the minorities, a position which the political elite itself welcomed. Though the major political parties were opposed to any area being carved away from their domain of influence, nevertheless each and every one supported the idea of more 'regions' being created in the hope that such new regions would be in areas other than those they controlled. In a sense this was indicative of the fact that there was as yet no basic agreement amongst the political elite on the overall structure of the federation. In addition to the demand that more 'regions' be created, there was a demand by the North for a redistribution of seats in the federal legislature. The North, it was claimed, had a population greater than the combined population of the East and the West and it was inequitable, by any democratic criterion, for the regions to be accorded equal representation in the federal parliament. A conference to resolve these issues was therefore decided upon which was to be held in London.[16] Whatever was agreed by the conference was then to be the basis on which independence was to be granted.

THE INDEPENDENCE CONSTITUTIONAL SETTLEMENT

The London conference of 1958, like its predecessor five years before, showed that the Nigerian political elite were much more concerned with protecting their respective power bases than with resolving the structural deficiencies within the political framework. Though the NCNC and the AG leadership would have liked to see more 'regions' created, nevertheless, in the face of opposition from the NPC, both parties readily accepted the report of the Commission appointed to enquire into the grievances of minorities, the Wellinck Commission, which recommended against the creation of new regions. On its part, the British government, host to the conference, had insisted that any move towards the creation of new regions could only mean a delay in the granting of independence, and the political elite, anxious to take over the accoutrements of sovereign power, was only too willing to see that independence was not delayed. As Dr Azikiwe, leader of the NCNC, was later to put it, the Nigerian electorate owed the delegates to the conference a debt of gratitude: they, the delegates had won independence for Nigeria 'on a platter of gold'. It mattered little if less than six years later, what was thought to be gold was to be shown to be nothing other than the glitter masking some baser metal. Rather than meet the challenge of the problem posed by the minorities, who make up about 45 per cent of the population of Nigeria, the leadership opted for the somewhat empty solution proffered by the Wellinck Commission, that a chapter providing guarantees for 'fundamental human rights' be written into the constitution of an independent Nigeria, ignoring thereby the very obvious fact that questions of individual rights and those of group rights belong to different logical orders. However, almost as a concessionary recognition that something of a sop had to be offered to the minorities, the delegates agreed to have written into the constitution, provisions under which new regions could in the future be created. For the minorities, though, there was not much doubt that their demands had been sacrificed before the Nigerian altars of ethnic chauvinism and political sovereignty, and of political expediency.

With the minorities problem out of the way, the other issues were quickly resolved. The NPC's claim that representation should be based on population, given the premise of a democratic system, seemed hardly contestable and on a representational ratio of one representative to 100,000 people, this gave a federal legislature of 312 members and given a population ratio between the North and the other two regions combined of approximately 54 : 46, the North was allowed a representation of 174 members, the East 73, the West 62, and Lagos 3. But it should be noted that while the North was prepared to argue that representation should be based on the principle of 'each to count for one and no one to count for more than one', it did not apply that principle to the adult community in the North itself: women were still to be denied the vote. It is uncertain what difference it would have made to the outcome of the 1959 elections had women been allowed to vote. But on the principle that the NPC was then propounding, representational apportionment should have been based on the eligible voting population and not on the total population. The NPC would then have been forced either to enfranchise women, or accept that the North's representational quota be halved. But so overwhelming was the imagery of 'the platter of gold' that principles were freely conceded before the seemingly pragmatic consideration that independence was worth any price. But of course, the primary concern was power for its own sake and not what could be done with political power. Nkrumah's Ghana had at least shown that much since that territory became independent in 1957 and if 'little' Ghana could show that much, then how much more 'big' Nigeria?

However, to provide some safeguards for regional interests, it was agreed that there should be a federal second chamber, the Senate, which should be composed of 48 members, 12 each nominated by the government of a region and 12 nominated by the central authority to represent federal interests. The Senate would have the power to (a) initiate bills, though such bills would have to go through the House of Representatives before they could become law; (b) delay 'money bills' but only for a period not exceeding 30 days; and (c) delay other bills for up to six months, after which if the same bill were again to be passed by the House of Representatives, it was to become law. Only the House of Representatives could initiate 'money bills' and in the case of a disagreement between the two chambers, such disagreement was to be resolved at a joint committee meeting of members of both Houses presided over by the Speaker of the Senate. In the main, the Senate, like much else in the first republic, was modelled on the British second chamber, the House of Lords.

But though most of the institutions of the first republic drew their inspiration from the 'Westminster model', they lacked those conventions and practices which make that model what it is. For instance, when in 1962 the Auditor-General, whose office was supposed to be independent of executive control and whose salary was thus charged to the Consolidated Fund of the Federation, queried government overspending and waste, he was immediately dismissed by the Federal Minister of Finance for properly carrying out the duties of his office. In the same manner, the federal executive dissolved the Public Accounts Committee of the House of Representatives when in 1963 members of the committee questioned items of overspending in the audited accounts of the government. The committee was never reconstituted before the federal elections of 1964, and no meetings of the Committee were held before the overthrow of the government in 1966. Throughout the history of the federal legislature, only once, in 1960, did the government withdraw a bill on a motion by the Opposition. This bill proposed the renewal of the Anglo-Nigerian Defence Pact, and though the Opposition tabled a motion opposing the bill, it was in fact the opposition organised by university students, who marched from Ibadan, about a hundred miles away from the capital city of Lagos, and converged on the federal parliament, that led to the government withdrawing the bill. The Defence Pact was never renewed.[17] The only other instance when the government was obliged to withdraw one of its bills — in 1964 — came as a result of widespread public disapproval, initiated and orchestrated by the Nigerian Union of Journalists, of the proposed Newspapers (Amendment) Act the purpose of which was to convert the libelling of a federal Minister from civil to criminal libel. The Act would have made the author of a libellous article, and the editor of the newspaper in which the article was published, both jointly criminally liable.[18]

Throughout the first republic, at no time did a legislature anywhere in the federation sit for a total of more than 42 days in the year. The longest time for which the Northern House of Assembly sat in any one year was for a period of 29 days and the record of the Eastern and Western Houses of Assembly was not much better. Membership of a legislature was, for all practical purposes, part-time membership as most members were either school or University teachers, lawyers, doctors, businessmen and contractors or native authority functionaries. Members were therefore only too content to let the executive have its way, and though it has been said of the British House of Commons that it has become little else but a 'debating chamber', nevertheless it remains a chamber where, as Laski put it, members at least 'can ventilate grievance, extract information, criticize the administrative process and discuss large principles which test the movement of public opinion'. Of no legislature in the first republic could this have been said to be the case. In modelling the institutions of the first republic on the 'Westminster model', therefore, the political elite showed not only how little they understood of that model but also demonstrated how completely they had accepted Nkrumah's dictum to: 'Seek ye first the political kingdom and everything else shall be added unto you'.

PARTY POLITICS IN THE FIRST REPUBLIC

The 1959 elections, which ushered in the constitutional settlement for an independent Nigeria, were the first-ever direct elections covering the whole country to be held in Nigeria. It was therefore a critical election, critical not just because it would decide which party was going to rule the independent state of Nigeria, but also because there was no information base of any description whatsoever on which a prediction of the outcome of the election could be made.[19] The final results showed that the NPC won 134 seats, the NCNC 89, and the AG 73, with independent candidates winning the remaining 16 seats. But before all the results were returned, the Governor-General, Sir James Robertson, invited the Deputy leader of the NPC, who had become Prime Minister in 1957, to form a government.

Constitutionally, it was the duty of the Governor-General to invite that person who in his opinion was best placed to form a government, to become Prime Minister, and to that extent Sir James could be said to have acted properly. Nevertheless, it was open to question whether the Governor-General could exercise his constitutional right before all the results were known. In thus inviting Sir Abubakar to become Prime Minister with the obligation of forming a government before all the seats were declared, Sir James could be said to have pre-empted the outcome of the elections and to that extent to have acted without due constitutional propriety. It could of course be argued that at the time Sir James invited the incumbent Prime Minister to form the new government, it was inconceivable that the undeclared results would in any way materially alter the outcome of the election, and the issues of constitutional propriety are therefore largely irrelevant. But so to argue would be to miss the point, for what was at issue was not whether Sir James could have acted in any way other than the way he acted, but *when* it could be said that he was obliged to exercise his constitutional right. The argument here being made is that at the time Sir James acted, he had no obligation to act and therefore to that extent acted improperly. The point is important in that it could always be argued that had Sir James waited till all the returns were in, it was logically conceivable that the ruling coalition which could have emerged would have been different from that which actually did emerge. By foreclosing that possibility Sir James ensured that no other ruling coalition could emerge without creating a political crisis.

However, in the end, though the AG made separate offers to the NPC and the NCNC to form a government, neither of these offers was accepted. Instead, the NCNC agreed to join the NPC and together they became the new government of Nigeria, the AG being left to form the opposition. It is easy to see why the NCNC would have found an NPC rather than an AG coalition attractive. In an NCNC/AG coalition, both parties would have had roughly equal bargaining strengths and therefore would have posed equal threats to each other. Pay-offs to either party would thus have had to be on the basis of roughly equal shares. On the other hand, in an NPC/ NCNC coalition, though the NCNC would be the 'minor' partner, nevertheless it could expect to play a pivotal role and therefore be capable of exercising the power of *blackmail*: the NCNC could always threaten to vote with the AG and such a threat could be compelling. Thus, in an NPC/NCNC coalition, the NCNC could expect a pay-off somewhat greater than what its relative bargaining weight would have assured it. And at a time when regional governments were not only hard-pressed for development funds but also faced with sharply rising recurrent expenditure, an NPC/NCNC coalition would therefore have appeared the safer proposition to the NCNC. But here the NCNC would seem to have miscalculated.

By the end of 1960 not only had all the 16 independent members switched over to the NPC but also some members of the smaller parties allied to the AG and who had been elected on the platform of such an alliance had crossed over to the NPC with the result that, at the beginning of 1961, the NPC already had a working majority in the federal parliament and could, if it had wanted to, have done without the support of the NCNC. Thus far from being pivotal, the NCNC found itself an 'irrelevant' party.

For the Nigerian political elite, politics involves not the conciliation of competing demands arising from an examination of the various alternatives entailed by any course of political action, but the extraction of resources which can be used to satisfy elite demands and to buy political support. The political relationship is essentially a relation between patrons and clients in which the patron survives only to the extent that he satisfies the demands of his clients, and clients give their support in so far as the patron 'delivers the goods'. The ability to extract, and therefore to deliver, is of course directly related to the extent of control over the instrumentalities of government. And once the NCNC lost its pivotal role, it naturally suffered a loss in its extractive capability. An index of this loss can be easily seen by a cursory look at the 1962–68 (Six Year National) Development Programme. Under the Plan, expenditure by the federal government and its controlled agencies was expected to account for 61.0 per cent of total plan expenditure, an expenditure which did not include aid, grants and loans to the regions. But the distribution of federal spending showed the North to be the main beneficiary. Thus, one can compare items connected with coastal waterways (the main items under transport and aviation with a plan expenditure of £14.6 million), Lagos Affairs (£21.2 million), Information (£2.3 million), Communications (£30.0 million), with the major items of capital spending which went to the North: the Niger Dam, estimated at £68.1 million (it eventually cost more than £88 million) represented more than 10 per cent of total federal government spending; almost all of the £29.7 million scheduled for Defence; the major proportion of the £39.2 million to be spent on health and education, and the bulk of the £35.3 million to be spent on roads. Of the £10 million earmarked for regional agricultural expansion, the first £4 million disbursed in 1963/64 showed the following distribution: North £2.2 million, East £1.1 million and West £0.7 million. As the authors of the North's own development plan noted, 'a reallocation of revenues between the federal and the regional governments [was] imperative', adding that while such a redistribution 'obviously does not add to total resources of plan implementation, [it] will influence each of the separate plans which together form the national plan'.

The National Development Plan was the federal government's proposal for strategic action aimed at rapid social change, and whatever the NCNC's expectations may have been in joining the NPC/NCNC coalition, it seemed these expectations were not being realised, certainly not in the way the NCNC conceived of them. And if the party was to meet the expectations of its clients, expectations which the clients would have been encouraged to hold from the NCNC's membership in the coalition federal government, it was obvious the party would have to rethink its strategy. Three alternatives would appear to have offered themselves. The first would have been for the NCNC simply to dissociate itself from the coalition, but there were at least two objections to this: (i) the NCNC could not be sure that were it to break with the NPC, the AG — though this might look unlikely — would not take its place, and for the AG, some loaf would be better than none; (ii) whatever the disadvantages of belonging to the ruling coalition might be for the NCNC, the advantages of membership still outweighed the disadvantages (as they would do for the AG).

The second alternative would be for the NCNC to seek to extend its power base: for instance, given the marginality of the AG's control over the West, to seek to take over control of the West. Should the NCNC succeed in such a move it could prove to have crucial significance should the NCNC want to make political capital with the provisions relating to the creation of new states. In other words, undermine the support base of the NPC. The sporadic violence in the West, occasioned by the claims and counterclaims of the AG and the NCNC (the former saying that the Ibos were 'grabbing' all the top jobs in the federation and were deliberately and without cause having Yorubas dismissed from their posts to facilitate this and the latter making similar counterclaims) seemed a suitable opportunity for the NCNC leadership to seize upon. Dr Michael Okpara, the successor to Dr Azikiwe as Premier of the East, touring the West in 1961, proclaimed that the violence was enough evidence that law and order had broken down in the West and he demanded that the federal government should therefore declare a 'state of emergency' in the West. The idea behind this was that, given such a state of emergency, the NCNC as the opposition in the West would be able to insinuate itself into becoming the new government of the West and would then use the opportunity so offered to demand that a Midwest state be carved from the West, which, given the party's support in that area, would come under the control of the NCNC. With an NCNC government in the East, West and Midwest, the party could then move in the federal parliament a motion calling for more regions to be created, a move which the NCNC was certain would be rejected by the NPC. The effect of such a rejection would thus be to make the NPC be seen as the only party opposed to the minorities realising their aim of autonomous status and therefore unite the minorities behind the NCNC in opposition to the NPC. Moreover, there would then be a complete polarisation between the North and the 'South'. The NPC leader, Alhaji Sir Ahmadu Bello, had stated in his autobiography that should such a polarisation ever occur and the North find itself in the opposition, the North might have to reconsider its whole position in the federation.

Unfortunately for the NCNC, the Prime Minister — Deputy Leader of the NPC — refused to swallow the bait, which left the NCNC with its third alternative, to seek to alter the bargaining weights of the three main parties, that is, the representational ratio between the North, East and West, through changing the population ratio between the North and the South. The census to be held in 1962 seemed a good enough opportunity, but with each region inflating its population figures while accusing the other of gross inflation, the overall figures came under such heavy questioning that the Prime Minister had little choice but to announce the cancellation of the census data, promising at the same time that a new census would be held in 1963.

With the cancellation of the 1962 census it seemed the NCNC would have to accept the status quo. However, events in the West played into the hands of the party, affording it a chance of combining its second and third options. The occurrence in the West was a dispute between the leader of the AG, Chief Awolowo, and his deputy and successor as Premier of the West, Chief Akintola, over the new ideological stance of the party, a dispute which led to a split within the party. An attempt by the Awolowo faction to have Chief Akintola removed from office as Premier of the West and to replace him with another party leader, Chief Adegbenro, who was more acceptable to Chief Awolowo, led to disturbances in the Western House of Assembly causing the federal government to dissolve the House, suspend the Governor of the region and proclaim a state of emergency in the region. With the emergency proclaimed and an Administrator, Chief Majekodunmi, appointed to administer the affairs of the region, it became possible for the NCNC to introduce a motion in the federal legislature demanding that the Midwest be carved out of the West and constituted into a separate region, a motion which was passed by the House and subsequently approved by the legislatures of the East and the North and ratified by the Administrator of the West. The legislative procedures duly completed, a referendum was held in the Midwest at which some 83 per cent of those present and voting assented to the Midwest being made a separate region and in 1963 the Midwest emerged as Nigeria's fourth region and came immediately under the control of the NCNC, with Chief Osadebay, an NCNC party leader, as Premier of the new region.

In the West itself, the six months state of emergency over, Chief Akintola was restored as the Premier[20] but as his faction of the AG, which he named the United Peoples' Party (UPP) did not have a majority in the Assembly, Akintola had to rely on the support of the NCNC members of the Assembly, thereby forming a UPP/NCNC coalition. Thus, almost by inadvertence, the NCNC had emerged by the end of 1963 in control of the East, West (in coalition) and Midwest to confront the NPC with the bipolarisation which the NPC so much wanted to avoid. With a federal election scheduled for 1964 and the new (1963) census figures again in question, the NPC could see its chances of continued control of the federal government slipping away. To forestall this, the NPC could do nothing else but seek to break the UPP/NCNC coalition. This the party did by offering to go into an alliance with the UPP, Akintola being encouraged to (i) convert his UPP into a new party, which then became the Nigerian National Democratic Party (NNDP); (ii) announce the dissolution of the UPP/NCNC coalition; (iii) offer the NCNC members of the coalition the ultimatum of either joining the new NNDP or being removed from the government of the region.

The ultimatum to the NCNC members of the coalition was a calculated move on the part of Chief Akintola, for had they called his bluff, Akintola would have found his NNDP in a minority and would have had to ask for a dissolution. But he had banked on the fact that the NCNC members would not want to face a dissolution for two reasons: (a) not all the members could be sure of being re-elected and most would be worse off economically if not re-elected; and (b) those in the executive were not sure that, even if they were re-elected, they would retain their cabinet appointments. The bluff succeeded. Akintola got himself a new party with a majority in the Assembly, and the NCNC temporarily lost the West. The immediate outcome was that the new government of the West was able to ratify the disputed 1963 census figures (which gave Nigeria a population of 66 million with the ratio between the North and the South unchanged) as did the Midwest, under threat of having federal aid, on which the government relied, withdrawn. Since the figures were acceptable to the North and the NPC majority in the federal parliament had assured the acceptance of the census returns by the federal government, the NCNC-dominated East regional government found itself fighting a losing battle[21] and ended up acquiescing to the figures. This left the NCNC with but one chance to improve its bargaining strength — the 1964 federal elections.

THE COLLAPSE OF THE FIRST REPUBLIC

Two broad coalitions, the Nigerian National Alliance (NNA), made up of the NPC and the NNDP, and the United Progressive Grand Alliance (UPGA) composed of the NCNC and the AG, emerged to contest the 1964 federal elections. The choice of coalition labels is not without some significance. For the NNA, the use of the word 'national' was intended to emphasise that the coalition was not sectional and to play down the dominant role of the NPC, an essentially sectional party, within the alliance. UPGA, on the other hand, wanted to

convey by 'progressive' what they saw as the antithesis represented by the two competing alliances: the antithesis between
the radical and the conservative, between the modernising
and the traditional, the populist and the hegemonic elitist,
the socialist and the neocolonialist capitalist and between the
liberationist and the 'feudalist imperialist'. Put briefly, the
conflict between UPGA and the NNA was to be presented as
the antithesis between the forces of enlightenment and those
of reaction, represented, in this instance, by the 'South' and
the 'North' respectively.

In ordinary circumstances, given the heterogeneity of the
society, the use of such highly emotive terms could be expected
to incite people to violence. In the politically sensitive atmos-
phere of 1964 this became all the more pronounced, particularly when it became all too easy to cast members of the
NNDP, for instance, in the role of traitors to the cause of
'progress', traitors who had 'sold out' to a reactionary NPC
and a tradition-bound North. Violence did break out in the
West, which had become the main arena of political controversy and political competition. By October/November, so
inflamed had the electorate of the West grown, that the
President had to summon the key political figures to a meeting
in Lagos to agree on a 'code of conduct' to govern the elections
which were scheduled to be held at the end of December.[22]

But though all the political leaders subscribed to the code,
few, it would seem, observed it. The violence persisted and it
became accepted practice for party politicians to go about
campaigning with the protection of paid personal bodyguards,
usually armed with a variety of offensive weapons. Electoral
officers were terrorised into absconding from their offices
once they had received the nomination papers of governing
party candidates, leaving opposition candidates with no
opportunity of registering their nomination papers. So fla-
grantly was the electoral procedure abused that at the close of
nominations some 88 out of a total of 174 NPC candidates in
the North had their candidature unopposed and as such had
to be declared elected unopposed. In the West, about 30 per
cent of the NNDP candidates were supposed to have been
unopposed. The situation in the East was not much different.
By election day, 31 December, it was obvious the election

had become nothing but a farce and the UPGA announced it was boycotting the elections. (But the announcement was made so late and the boycott itself so ill-organised that in the North, West and the Midwest, the electorate went to the polls. Only in the East, where the NCNC could use the machinery of the government to ensure that the returning officers were not present at the polling stations to enable the election to proceed, was the boycott effective and no elections were held in the region.)

Nevertheless, even though some members of the Federal Electoral Commission had resigned from the Commission in an attempt at demonstrating they were not prepared to underwrite the elections, the Chairman of the Commission went ahead and announced the results of the elections which showed, as might have been expected, that the NPC had won all but eight of the 174 constituencies in the North; the NNDP had won the majority of the seats in the West and the NCNC a majority of the Midwest constituencies. With an NNA overwhelming majority, Tafawa Balewa then called on the President, Dr Nnamdi Azikiwe, to request that he, the Prime Minister, be reappointed to head a new government of the federation. The President refused to accede to the request of the Prime Minister, thereby creating a constitutional stalemate.[23] It was obvious the President was not acting solely on his own initiative for, even before the results of the elections were announced, he had invited the Head of the Armed Forces, Major-General Welby-Everard, to find out if the army would support him (he the President being constitutionally Commander-in-Chief of the Armed Forces) in the event of a 'showdown' between himself and the Prime Minister. For his own part the Prime Minister, knowing what moves the President was making, had informed Welby-Everard that the loyalty of the army should lie with him as Head of Government.[24] Eventually (after over a week of negotiations) the President, on the intervention of the Chief Justice of the Supreme Court and the Chief Justices of the regional High Courts, relented and agreed to invite the Prime Minister to form a new government[25] but on the understanding that:

(i) such a government was to be a 'broad-based government', that is, it was to include, wherever possible, representatives of the two competing alliances;

(ii) the 'boycotted' elections in the Eastern region were to be rescheduled for March 1965 after which NCNC members would be appointed to the government; and

(iii) there should be elections to the West Regional Assembly in October — no doubt intended to test the legitimacy of the NNDP.

The constitutional crisis was over, but it had revealed gaping cracks in the body politic which not even the 'understanding' that contributed to the resolution of the crisis could quite paper over.

Before we examine some of these cracks, certain facets of the elections, specifically the behaviour of the political elite, should be noted. First, the elections did show that for the political elite, power was an end-in-itself and not a means to the realisation of some greater 'good' for the community, and whatever the instrumentalities employed in the pursuit of power, such instrumentalities were legitimate. It follows from this that any talk about 'rules of the game' must be irrelevant, for to talk about 'rules of the game' is to presuppose some end or ends which such rules are intended to subserve but there can be no such ends since power has been taken as an end in itself. But as we cannot conceive of politics, in any significant sense, without conceiving of some notion of rules, then it follows that there can be no proper notion of politics either. The only possible kind of ethic thus becomes that of privatization, the preoccupation of the individual with his personal rather than his social situation. The constitutional crisis brought this out only too clearly.

There was first the President. The constitution showed succinctly enough that the President had little discretionary power and even that which he had, largely over such issues as the prerogative of mercy, he had to exercise on the advice of the Prime Minister. Admittedly, the constitution did empower the President to invite that person who in his opinion was best placed to form a government to do so. But while this may *look* discretionary, that discretion was open to the President only when the electoral outcome left the issue undermined. In the 1964 elections this was not the case. The NPC had a clear majority. There may be doubts as to the validity and/or legality of the elections but these were not questions over which the President could make any judgements. The President could of course have claimed that on moral grounds, taking all the facts surrounding the elections into consideration, he could not in good conscience invite Sir Abubakar Tafawa Balewa to be the new Prime Minister. In this case the President, rather than invite Sir Abubakar, should have resigned. But not only was Dr Azikiwe unprepared to make that sacrifice, he showed by his actions that he could not distinguish between his role as *de facto* leader of the NCNC and his status as the ceremonial head of the federation. In effect, Dr Azikiwe 'privatised' the office of the Presidency.

The Prime Minister, Sir Abubakar, behaved no differently. Having been told by the President that he, the President, was in good conscience unable to invite him to form a new government, Sir Abubakar, as leader of the victorious party, could have asked the Supreme Court to rule on the constitutionality of the President's action, which was about the only proper option open to the Prime Minister. But perhaps aware that such a move could cause a legal 'mare's nest', the Prime Minister chose to resort to political pressure[26] to finally end up with an 'understanding' which only served to call in question both the electoral process which brought him to power and the government which he subsequently formed. The fact that both he and the President, individually and separately bargained for the loyalty of the armed forces, only succeeded in making the armed forces ultra-conscious of the blurred boundary lines separating the 'military' from the 'civil' and the 'legal' from the 'political'. In the struggle for personal survival, both men, perhaps inadvertently, made the armed forces aware they had a political role to play and so paved the way for the military coup which followed in 1966: both men, in different ways, ended up subverting the constitution they were under an obligation to uphold.

In the same way the judiciary was critically weakened by the intervention of the Chief Justice of the Supreme Court and the Chief Justices of the regional High Courts. Their action showed that they were unprepared to differentiate their social roles as pillars of the law from their roles as ethnic leaders and party political figures. It is possible that, by intervening in the way they did, they foreclosed the chances of any of the key political leaders resorting to the law as a means of resolving the constitutional crisis. The judicial blurred with the political, and thus the judiciary could no longer be looked to as an instrument of effectuating rule adherence.

In March 1965 the 'suspended' elections in the Eastern region were held to complete the farce which had begun three months earlier. The outcome was an extended federal executive which was to bring the holders of executive office to a total of 80. In other words, just about one in four of the members of the federal legislature held executive appointments of one type or the other. There could be no clearer demonstration of the judgement of Fanon that in the African state, once independence has been won, government becomes no more than a holding company of the national bourgeoisie intent only on sharing out the national booty. People talked of change but it was not clear how this was to come about. Fanon's prescription had been to advocate a 'cleansing by fire', a violent revolution led by the dispossessed, the 'wretched of the earth', the peasants. In some respects what occurred came close to this, and the October election to the West regional assembly provided the catalyst.

UPGA leaders, having in a sense 'lost' the federal elections, had looked to the promised West regional elections as a source of change, but in this they only displayed their naivety, for in a context where the rule is that there are no rules — the federal elections had shown this only too clearly — to trust to an election as a means of change could only be sheer naivety. As might have been expected, the NNDP 'won' the 'elections' in the West. Chief Remi Fani-Kayode, Deputy leader of the NNDP and also Deputy Premier of the West, had in fact said before the elections that whether the electorate voted for the NNDP or not, the NNDP would 'win' the 'elections'. He was proved right. But though the NNDP 'won' the elections, their inheritance was an empty treasury. Disaffected over the federal election and its outcome, most of the electorate had given up paying taxes and, with the payment of salaries to government employees highly erratic, there had in fact been little incentive to collect government revenues.[27] On the point of becoming bankrupt, there was not much the government could do but to exploit the one sure source of income open to it; that is, to skim off the 'surplus' which accrued to the cocoa farmers, the producers of the region's main export crop. The first act of the new government was thus to cut the price paid to the farmer from £110 per ton of cocoa to £60, but in thus almost halving the income of the farmers – and they formed the bulk of the population – the government opened the flood-gates for violence and revolt.

The violence started in the rural areas with farm labourers setting cocoa farms on fire in protest against not being paid their wages by farmers who now found they could not meet their costs at the new prices declared by the government. It soon spread to the towns where it was taken up by the unemployed, and party-paid thugs who in the increasing state of lawlessness seized their opportunity to terrorise, to burn, and to loot. Lacking any semblance of legitimacy, the NNDP government of the West proved incapable of arresting the situation, while the police, faced with the growing anarchy and the impotence of the government, was neither willing to act nor even capable of acting to check the wave of revolt and violence. The NPC-dominated federal government, rather than accept that its western ally, the NNDP, had no support in the region and was therefore incapable of governing, preferred to turn a blind eye to the anarchy in the West. Instead of taking realistic action the federal authority preferred to play host to a Commonwealth Conference, as if by that act the government could win some respectability, if not acceptability, for itself. On the sidelines, however, waited a group of young army majors with their handful of supporters. A day after the Commonwealth conference ended, in the early hours of 15 January 1966, they decided to act, to bring to an end what many had come to see as an insufferable government. It is one of the tragic and ironic twists of fortune that though the majors led the coup that brought the first republic to an end, they failed to be the inheritors of their bloody act and, in their failure, they were to sow the seeds of a cruel and bitter civil war which all but tore apart the federal framework they had so desperately sought to preserve.

4

The Military and Politics

The new (1979) constitution of the Federal Republic of
Nigeria makes it unconstitutional, and hence illegal, for the
military to 'take over' through a coup d'etat the instrumentalities of government from the elected representatives of the
people. It is not exactly clear what legal force such a provision
has. Who, for example, is supposed to enforce the provision
once the civil authority has been overthrown? For ultimately,
the really coercive power which underpins the authority of
the civil regime is the military. It could of course be that the
'force' of such a provision is in fact exhortatory, a 'call' on
the people to rise against the military in defence of the 'constitutional order'. But there are two difficulties with that
interpretation. First, the 'people' do not just 'rise in revolt'.
They require to be organised and led and history is replete
with examples of the consequences to those who have attempted to fill that leadership role. The second difficulty is
related to the first. To demand that an unarmed electorate
rise against the army is to demand nothing short of self-
immolation on the part of the electorate and no rational
electorate would accede to such a demand; hence the demand
itself cannot but be empty and meaningless. But perhaps the
real force of the provision could be seen as both 'descriptive'
and 'moral': descriptive in that it calls attention to the pre-
valence of military coups in countries such as Nigeria; and
moral, in that in some sense of the word 'moral', it points
to the fact that a military coup is 'bad', or 'morally undesirable', something that ought not to occur no matter what.

The most plausible interpretation would be the descriptive/ moralistic since any other interpretation only leads to some form of absurdity. But then the question arises: why does the military intervene to overthrow civilian regimes?

IS THERE A 'LOGIC' OF MILITARY INTERVENTION?

The word 'logic' is here used in the most general sense, to mean that which is rational, consistent and comprehensive. Any such 'logic' would be rational in the sense that the terms used in the explanation of military intervention would be readily intelligible and/or verifiable — there would be no appeal to that which is outside immediate experience; it would be consistent in that the sentences which constituted the explanation would not be mutually self-contradictory, and would be not isolated one from the other but interconnected, the one following from the other in some ordered fashion; and it would be comprehensive in the sense that the explanatory schema would cover all instances of military interventions with no instance being excluded on the grounds that the circumstances were unique or exceptional. Put in these terms, the simple answer is that there is no logic and there can be no logic of military interventions. All there can be, and all there can be expected to be, is a 'logics', a set of explanatory schemas of military coups, some more plausible than the others, or some more coherent than the others. But this requires some amplification before which we must consider the statement that there can be no logic of military coups.

For a logic of military coups to be possible, we would require the political system to be a closed system and hence completely describable, but that is neither conceptually nor empirically feasible. It is conceptually not feasible because whatever the set of statements we make about the political system, it is logically the case that we can always add one more statement to that set and thus we could never have a complete set or a finite set and the conceptual impossibility entails that all we could ever empirically expect to achieve is a partial description of the political system. Furthermore, for a logic of coups to be possible, we would have to have complete information on the motives of those involved in the coup and this is patently not possible. Were it even to be possible, we could still be faced with the epiphenomenalistic problem that there could be an incongruence between a man's description of his motives and an observer's account of that man's motives as inferred from his behaviour, a real enough problem since it is not inconceivable that the man himself may be mistaken in his account of his motives.[1] In brief, then, a 'logic' of coups is logically impossible and we are therefore left with partial, incomplete explanatory schemas and this must of necessity be the case. But to say this is not to suggest that all partial explanatory schemas are of the same satisfactory order or of the same degree of plausibility. A brief examination of some of the explanatory schemas that have been put forward will easily reveal their differences.

It has, for instance, been suggested that coups occur in certain countries because these countries have a 'low' political culture. A country has a 'low' political culture when, among other things, its political structures have not been institutionalised or only weakly institutionalised, and dominant political norms, the 'rules of the game', have not been sufficiently internalised. Thus, states in which political structures have been institutionalised and political norms have been internalised are said to have 'high' political cultures while states with 'medium' political cultures presumably would be those in between. In effect then we could have two propositions stating this putative correlation between military coups and political cultures: a strong and a weak formulation. The strong proposition (P(i)) could be formulated in the following terms: weakly institutionalised political structures and inadequate internalisation of political norms inevitably lead to military coups. The weak proposition (P(ii)) could be stated as: military coups are more likely to occur in societies with a low political culture than in societies with a high political culture. Whichever formulation we accept, certain difficulties immediately arise.

First let us assume that there is some general agreement — and this may be questionable — on which societies fall into what category; in other words, let us assume that there is little difficulty in categorising any given society as a 'high', 'medium' or 'low' political culture. On this assumption P(i) can be seen to be false as there would be societies with low political cultures where no coups had occurred, while P(ii) would be unhelpful as we would not be any the wiser why a coup had occurred in society A and not in society B. The difficulty increases when we find that coups have occurred in societies (Greece, for example, in 1967) which cannot conceivably be categorised as societies with 'low' political cultures. If we attempt to get over this latter difficulty by simply denying that societies like Greece are societies with a 'high' political culture, we only run into the difficulty that the correlation between political culture and military intervention turns out to be nothing but circular: if military intervention takes place in society A then society A must have a 'low' political culture, and the only evidence that a society does not have a 'low' political culture is the simple fact that it has not experienced a military takeover.[2]

A different type of explanatory schema is that which derives from reference group theory. The basic underlying notion here is the observable fact that an individual's behaviour tends to be conditioned or influenced by the behaviour of those he admires, or in other words, takes as his point of reference — the reference group. Involved in this is a comparison by the individual of the actual behaviour of the reference group as against his expectations of what that behaviour ought to be. Translated into the mechanics of a coup, this means in effect that the military are most likely to intervene (a) when the role performance of the political leadership falls short of the expectation of the leadership held by the military, and (b) when the military feels it is comparatively disadvantaged relative to other groups that it can compare itself to. If we take the condition of (a) as a necessary condition for military intervention, then the conjunction of (a) and (b) provides both the necessary and the sufficient condition for the military to intervene. Some such schema was offered to explain the military intervention in Ghana in 1966.

The 'reference group' schema is, in some respects, just a sophisticated extension of the 'custodian' theory, sometimes put forward by the military itself. The 'custodian' theory, the notion that the military is the custodian of the nation's constitution and as such feels impelled to intervene when

constitutional propriety is being flouted, was employed, for
example by Col. (later Major-General) A. A. Afrifa, in his
book *The Ghana Coup* (London: Frank Cass, 1966) to
explain the overthrow of President Nkrumah in 1966, and it
was also used by Brigadier (later General) Murtala Muhammed
to explain the overthrow of General Gowon. In much more
recent times (1980) it was appealed to by Master Sergeant
Doe to account for the overthrow of President Tolbert of
Liberia. But while the dividing line between justification and
explanation may be very thin, there cannot be much doubt
that the 'custodian' theory is more of a justification than an
explanation, for the theory simply says the military intervenes
when they want to intervene, the military by self-arrogation
claiming the right to determine when the constitution is
being flouted. On the other hand, the reference group theory,
while it does bring out one of the important considerations
which prompt the military to intervene, leaves unexplained
the now familiar cycle of military coups — characteristic of
Latin American countries where neither of the conditions
indicated by the theory could be said to hold.

There are other schemas or theories but little purpose
would be served examining each and every one of such
schemas. It is sufficient, at this point, to point out that a
distinction can be made between predisposing or orientating
factors and what might be termed facilitative factors. Predisposing factors would include such variables as the structure
and composition of the armed forces, taking into account the
possibilities for mobility within the military; the commitment
to, or degree of professionalism of, armed forces personnel;
and the prevailing ideology held by, or normative orientation
of, the military. Predisposing factors would determine the
likelihood or otherwise of the military intervening but
whether the military actually intervened or not would depend
on the facilitative factors which would include such things as
the degree of permeability of military boundaries, by which
is meant the extent to which societal and extra-societal factors
could influence military behaviour; the extent to which military communication channels were independent of societal
communication media; the institutional complexity, that is
the extent to which there were countervailing forces — forces

which on the one hand complement each other and on the other balance each other — in the society; and, of course, the coercive power of the military. The importance of each of these variables and their mix would vary from one society to the other; this fact means that one cannot give a satisfactory explanation of a coup without any reference to the contextual environment of the coup. Each coup is thus, in a significant sense, a unique occurrence and has to be accounted for as such. And it is from this perspective that the Nigerian experience will now be examined.

THE NIGERIAN EXPERIENCE

Between January 1966 when the first military intervention occurred and 1 October 1979, when the military handed over power to a civil regime, Nigeria witnessed two other coups and an attempted coup.

The environmental political background to the coup — the erosion of legitimacy and the final breakdown of law and order, particularly in the West, with the anarchy of mass violence — was described in Chapter 3. The army, in 1966, was a relatively small force, composed of some 10,500 men but the middle cadre of captains and majors, in which 'southerners' predominated, provided the leadership of the coup. A meeting of top officers in Lagos provided a suitable opportunity as it meant that the coup leaders had a relatively free hand in their various locations. But of the four main areas in which the action was supposed to have taken place — Enugu, Benin, Kaduna and Lagos — only in Kaduna was the planned action successfully executed. The result of the failure in Benin, Enugu, and Lagos was that it was not those who led the coup who emerged as the new rulers: the General Officer Commanding, Major-General Ironsi, became the inheritor of the Majors' failure. The coup had led temporarily to a 'split' within the army, between the men in the south and those in the North and with the threat that the country would be faced with the spectre of a 'civil war' if the civil authorities did not hand over power to him, Ironsi succeeded in 'persuading' members of the executive to surrender political control to him. He became Head of State and Supreme Commander of the Armed Forces. With his first Decree, the Constitution (Suspension and Amendment) Decree – Decree No. 1 – Ironsi suspended the legislature and transferred the full executive power of the state to himself, power which he was free to exercise at his sole discretion and for which he could not be held accountable by anyone.[3]

Ironsi had only held power for seven months when he was overthrown in what was in effect a counter-coup. The coup which brought Ironsi to power had had all the characteristics of a sectional coup. The majority of the coup leaders were Ibo-speaking and all but one of those killed in the coup[4] were non-Ibo-speaking. Ironsi's handling of affairs after coming to power tended to confirm this initial sectionalist image of the coup. Examples of moves that appear to support this image are the attempts to replace the federal framework with a more unified and centralised political system, promotions within the army and the move towards appointing military perfects,[5] and Ironsi's choice of political advisers. There was therefore little surprise when in July 1966 there was a counter-coup, organised by Northern elements in the army – the section that had lost the most in the January coup – and Ironsi was replaced with 'Northerner', Lt. Col. Yakubu Gowon (later General). However, what no one had expected was the virulence with which the second coup was carried out, a virulence which led to the wanton killing of Ibo-speaking peoples (and a number of non-Ibo-speaking peoples from the Midwest and other parts of the Eastern region) which persisted into October 1966. The mass killings not only forced Easterners from all over the federation to migrate to the East in search of security, but were eventually to lead to a bloody and costly civil war which lasted for some 30 months, from July 1967 to 15 January 1970. Nine years later, almost to the day of the coup which had brought him to power, Gowon was himself overthrown in what can perhaps best be described as a 'palace coup' and was succeeded by Brigadier (later General) Murtala Muhammed. To most Nigerians the Gowon administration, by the time he was overthrown, had become synonymous with the most blatant form of venality in public life. In 1966/67 total federal revenue was just about £170 million. By 1974/75 that figure had risen to the astronomical figure of ₦5514.7 million but that rise was barely reflected in the quality of life of the average Nigerian. In contrast, however, the military governors, commissioners and those closely associated with the regime were not only believed to have amassed huge fortunes, they in fact flaunted their wealth in a manner which most people found extremely distasteful. A commission of enquiry set up to investigate the assets of the principals of the regime found that only two of the twelve military governors could be claimed not to have illegally enriched themselves. Before the collapse of the regime one of Gowon's civilian commissioners had been obliged to resign as a result of allegations of corruption made against him. A military governor had had an affidavit sworn against him alleging gross abuse of office and gross corruption (and there were plans to have other affidavits sworn) yet Gowon pronounced him innocent of the numerous charges made against him, and though the allegations were subsequently proved to be true, the man who swore the affidavit was arrested and detained in prison without any trial, only to be released after the coup.[6] Nor was the regime shown to be only corrupt; its management of administrative affairs was also inept. In 1973/74, the administration contracted for the supply of 20 million tons of imported cement (demands by the Ministry of Defence alone accounted for 16 million tons) which was ten times the known handling capacity of the Nigerian ports. (The total demand by all African states was estimated at 30 million tons). By late 1974 there were over 450 ships laden with cement waiting to berth, and the government was having to pay over 500,000 dollars a day in demurrage charges, and this at a time when the country was short of much-needed imported food items, a shortage which contributed to a steadily worsening domestic inflationary situation (estimated to be rising at over 34 per cent per annum). To the above catalogue of abuse of power and gross economic mismanagement should be added the frustration of dashed hopes of a return to civil rule. In 1970, immediately after the end of the civil war, Gowon had pronounced that the military would hand over power to a civil administration in 1976 and he had announced a 'nine-point programme' of transition. But four years later, on 1 October 1974, Gowon was to announce to an uncomprehending and astounded nation that it would be 'unrealistic' for the military to hand over power in 1976 as he had earlier promised. The frustration, though, came not so much from the statement that 1976 was no longer realistic as from the fact that no alternative date was proposed. Gowon had simply said that he would rule indefinitely.

Gowon could conceivably have ruled for much longer — if he had had the continued support of his own 'constituency', the armed forces. But the 'constituents' over the years had become alienated from their 'representative'. The former, who repeatedly had demanded that the latter dispense with his aides (the military governors), whose behaviour they claimed was bringing the constituency into disfavour and disrepute, had been promised time and again that the demand would be met. But Gowon somehow found one reason or the other to desist from acting, and to some members of the military hierarchy it seemed Gowon was incapable of acting, had in fact become a 'prisoner' of his own aides. As Brigadier Murtala was later to put it, Gowon had not only isolated himself from his colleagues in the various military formations, he had become insensitive to all advice from the military itself. Faced with the choice of having to prop up a regime which had seemingly lost the will to act, and which it was claimed had brought the army into disrepute with the populace, or having to remove the principal and so terminate the regime, the military hierarchy chose the latter course of action. Gowon left for Kampala to attend the OAU (Organisation of African Unity) summit meeting of Heads of States only to hear over the radio that he had been deposed. He had lost his 'constituency' and left Kampala to go into voluntary exile in Britain.

The Muhammed regime began with the avowed purpose of improving the tarnished image of the military, eliminating the stigma of corruption with which the society had been tainted during the Gowon regime, and returning the country to a form of civil rule, the pattern of which the people would themselves be free to decide on. Within two months of taking over power, the regime embarked on the second item on their programme of reform — the elimination of corruption — with the summary dismissal or retirement of certain public service employees (those employed in the civil service, para-statals, universities and the state security services, that is, the army, police and prisons) on the grounds of 'abuse of office', 'divided loyalty' or 'declining productivity'.[7]   In all, close to 10,000 people had their careers abruptly terminated. In fact, the military government had to call a halt to the exercise when it belatedly realised that (a) the 'great purge' — as the media characterised the exercise — was being used to settle 'old scores'; and (b) the destabilising effects were tending to outweigh whatever positive 'cleansing' advantages the purge might have.[8]

In furtherance of the third item, the return to civil rule, the regime began with the appointment of a series of commissions to look into various vexed questions — such as the need to create more states — thought to be vital to any successful hand-over of political power, and the setting up of a Constitution Drafting Committee which was to provide the working outline of a constitutional framework on which a Constituent Assembly (to be wholly elected) was to deliberate. With respect to the military establishment itself, a start was made with the retirement of all those above the rank of Brigadier within the army, a move supposedly dictated by the necessity to remove the 'deadwood' composed of those who had been elevated under the Gowon regime; the aim was to create more openings at the top of the hierarchy for the more able, and younger 'fighting' soldier (in contrast to the 'political' soldier favoured by Gowon). This was followed by the application of the 'purge' to the army with a promise that this was the first step towards reducing the size of the army and would be followed by controlled demobilisation with the aim of improving the army's operational efficiency and effectiveness.[9]
But before any meaningful start could be made, General Murtala (he had, since assuming office as Head of State, been promoted to the rank of General) was assassinated in an attempted coup, which, though it failed to effect a complete change in the composition of those who controlled the reins of political power, resulted in effecting the replacement of Muhammed by his second in command, Lt. General Olusegun Obasanjo. Ten years after the coup which had first brought

the military to power, Nigeria was being governed by the fourth military person to take over as Head of State and Commander-in-Chief.[10]

The Nigerian army, due to the demands of the civil war, had grown from a force of some 10,500 men at the start of 1966 to something of the order of 270,000 men at the end of the war (1970). In 1965/66 defence spending had formed only 9.4 per cent of total recurrent federal government expenditure. By 1974/75, some five years after the end of the civil war, the proportion of recurrent federal spending taken by defence was 45.9 per cent and 85 per cent of that figure went essentially into the payment of wages and salaries[11] which meant that resources were being diverted from other sectors of the economy — education, health, communications, agriculture — to pay for a service which in a sense was totally unproductive. Members of the military hierarchy admitted that much,[12] and argued the need for demobilisation not only to enable resources to be released for more productive uses (including raising the operational efficiency of the armed forces) but also to take account of the steadily mounting civilian complaint that a more than proportionate share of the nation's resources was being spent on the military to the relative neglect of everything else. Gowon was aware of the problem but, being perhaps more conscious of its complexity,[13] characteristically chose to leave it alone. The Muhammed regime, no doubt disliking the idea that they might be accused of saddling a civilian successor with an unmanageable Leviathan, chose to tackle the problem, but in making that choice they aroused feelings of insecurity among the rank and file, whose fears ultimately cost Muhammed his life.

Little need be said of the Obasanjo administration as it was essentially a 'monitoring operation', the basic outlines of policy having been laid down during the Muhammed era. The administration's one innovation was in the field of local government where it sought to lay down the framework of a uniform system of local administration throughout the federation.[14] Apart from this, the administration's achievement was simply to bring to completion the programme of military withdrawal begun under Muhammed. The Constitution Drafting Committee having completed its task by August 1976, the next step was the setting of the stage for elections to the Constituent Assembly, the electoral framework being the newly reconstituted units of local administration. The Constitituent Assembly began its deliberations early in 1977 and after a year of almost continuous debate submitted its proposals for a Constitution for the Federal Republic of Nigeria, which, after some amendments by the military authorities, was formally adopted by the Supreme Military Council. At the end of September 1978, after 12 years of military rule, the Decree imposing a state of emergency, declared in May 1967, was abrogated thereby permitting the formation of political parties. In July/August 1979 elections to the newly created offices of President and Vice-President, State Governors and Deputy Governors, and to the National Assembly and state Assemblies, were held. On 1 October 1979 General Obasanjo formally handed over power to Alhaji Shehu Shagari, the newly elected President, thereby bringing to an end 13 years of military rule. The precise nature of that rule and its impact on the political system will now be examined.

THE MILITARY AND THE POLITICAL SYSTEM: THE NATURE AND FORM OF MILITARY RULE

After the seizure of political power, the not uncommon practice is for the military to 'abolish' all political parties and para-political organisations. The rationale for this is not difficult to understand: such organisations are usually seen by the military as instruments of disunity, agents of strife and discord, of corruption and nepotism, agents which create those conditions which warrant the military intervening in the first place. The simple equation is therefore made: political parties and like organisations are synonymous with political discord. Abolish parties and you automatically abolish the basis of political strife. But there is also a further reason why parties and the like are unacceptable to the military. They could constitute a source of opposition, a base for social mobilisation, against the military and their aims and programmes. However, while there is no doubt some element of truth in equating extreme factionalism with party competition, what is often ignored is the fact that in abolishing parties and para-political associations, political strife is not eliminated — for party competition is but one factor in the generation of political discord — but a vacuum is created, a vacuum between the leaders and the led. This causes problems for the military, for in the absence of any intermediary between the political leadership and the electorate, the political leadership soon finds itself cut off from the electorate; it is not sensitised to the demands of the electorate which gradually becomes alienated and disgruntled.

To fill the gap and provide some link with the people, the military has perforce to rely on the civil service, with top civil servants now being required not only to advise and execute but also to take on decisional roles. A symbiotic relationship is thus formed between the military and the bureaucracy, and there are a number of characteristics of this relationship which need to be noted. First, because the bureaucratic personnel are, generally, better educated than their military bosses, are more experienced and skilled at handling administrative problems, and from their association with the ousted politicians, more adept at dealing with political issues, the military soon finds itself having to rely more and more on the bureaucracy for the management of the polity. In the process the bureaucrats end up not just acquiring greater influence and independence of action but also new fields of activity over which they could begin to exercise such influence as they have acquired. Secondly, wanting to safeguard and protect their newly won influence and independence, the bureaucrats discover not only that they have to identify themselves with the objectives of the military but also that they have another interest, an interest in seeking to perpetuate the system of military rule itself. Thirdly, wanting to perpetuate the system of rule, the civil service seek to insulate the military authorities from the people with the consequence that the military becomes all the more isolated and remote from the people they are supposed to govern. Normally, a way out of this dilemma is for the military to inject some civilians into the policy-making process. But this creates new difficulties: conflict is generated between such civilians and the bureaucrats as the latter see the former as competitors wanting to encroach on those areas of action which civil servants have come to regard as their special preserve. One outcome of such conflict is to slow down the decision-taking process as policy differences take longer and longer to resolve and the regime becomes characterised by a debilitating immobilism. Lastly, the symbiotic relationship between the military and the bureaucracy involves above all a greater centralisation of political power than ever before. This has the effect that not much can be achieved without the goodwill of the authorities, which opens up greater possibilities for the abuse of power and the corruption which the abuse of power brings about, a corruption which is exacerbated as the decision-making process becomes increasingly immobilised.

An examination of the Ironsi and Gowon administration will provide an empirical demonstration of the foregoing. When the civilian authorities handed over power to Ironsi on 17 January 1966, one of his first acts was to proclaim the abolition of all political parties, quasi-political bodies and various ethnic associations and unions. In all, 88 associations were said to have been proscribed. In addition, all legislators and ministers were removed from office, leaving Ironsi to become the sole legislative and executive authority, and the Constitution was suitably amended by Decree to reflect this change. Similarly in the regions, military governors assumed the legislative and executive roles of the previous regional governments. To assist him, Ironsi created two councils, a Supreme Military Council (SMC), composed of Ironsi and the four military governors,[15] and a Federal Executive Council (FEC) made up of federal permanent secretaries. (In the regions, regional executive councils were also instituted, composed of regional permanent secretaries.) The FEC was supposed to be subordinate to the SMC, but there was not much doubt that in reality the FEC carried greater weight than the SMC: the SMC met too infrequently to be able to exercise an influence commensurate with its position in the new schema of things and its members were often too preoccupied with regional matters to give adequate attention to federal issues. Besides, in the last analysis, Ironsi, as Supreme Commander, was the sole authority and he was in daily contact with the permanent secretaries.

On taking over power, Ironsi had promised that as soon as practicable there would be a return to a civil system of government but that before that return was made certain changes would have to be effected to guarantee the future stability of the federation and to minimise the incidence of political strife. In furtherance of that end, Ironsi appointed two 'commissions'; the first, a Constitutional Review Commission, headed by Nigeria's leading constitutional lawyer, Chief Rotimi Williams; and the second, an administrative review commission, with Mr F. Nwokedi (a federal permanent secretary) as 'Sole Commissioner'. He had the job of looking into the feasibility of 'integrating' the federal and regional public services into a single unified service. One would have thought that whatever changes were to emerge from the administrative review exercise would be contingent on the findings of the Constitutional Review Commission, but Ironsi and his permanent secretaries apparently believed otherwise. Before the Williams Commission could even embark seriously upon their task, Nwokedi submitted his report and on the basis of that report (and what other advice he had received from the bureaucracy) Ironsi proceeded, on 24 May 1966, to announce far-reaching political and administrative changes in the federal framework. In effect, these amounted to the following:

(i) the administrative class of the various civil services was to be unified;
(ii) the existing regions were to be abolished and in their place there would be 'groups of provinces';[16]
(iii) regional military governors were to be replaced by military governors of 'groups of provinces'; and
(iv) military prefects would be appointed who would be in charge of the various provinces.

These changes were being embodied in a Decree, Decree No. 34. In essence, the federal system of government was being abolished and in its place was being imposed a unitary format.

Politics, it has been said, is the art of the possible. But perhaps that statement should be modified to read 'the art of the practicable and acceptable' as there could be many courses of action which would be possible, of which only a limited number might be practicable and still fewer would be acceptable; 'acceptable' in this context meaning 'acceptable to the populace'. And while a course of action which was practicable and acceptable might not be the most desirable – in the sense of being both rational and efficient – provided it was thought acceptable, it would stand a good chance of succeeding. The art of the politician lies in his ability, through the various linkages which he has to maintain if he is to succeed – that is, to be re-elected – to determine, from the different possible courses of action open to the government, that which is practicable and politically acceptable. The changes proposed by Ironsi's Decree No. 34 could well have been highly desirable, but with the loyalties which had been built around the regions for over two decades by the politicians it was highly unlikely that a move aimed at abolishing these loyalties would be found acceptable, particularly when such a move had not been accompanied by any attempt at ascertaining the preferences of the populace.

The move was not found acceptable. Five days after the changes were announced, students from Ahmadu Bello University and the Institute of Administration, both in Zaria, came out in open demonstration, protesting against the changes. The populace soon seized upon the excuse provided by the demonstration to ventilate their opposition as street mobs took over from the students and a hunt for Ibo-speaking people began. The hunt rapidly spread to other towns as the story got around that Ibo men were being massacred in Zaria. Of particular significance is the fact that the law-enforcement agencies, the Nigeria and local authority police forces did little to stop the rioting mob. Even the military governor, Lt. Col. (later Major-General) Hassan Usman Katsina, refrained from calling out the troops who could very easily have called a halt to the killings.[17] Instead the killings went on for some three days, the time it took for the mobs to exhaust themselves.

The massacres brought forcefully to Ironsi the gap which had developed between his administration and the populace.

Belatedly, Ironsi began a tour of the federation, starting with the North, to solicit support for his administration from community and religous leaders and the Emirs, the traditional rulers of the various Emirates. But the damage had already been done. Two months to the day when the first rioting had broken out in Zaria, Ironsi was arrested by mutinous soldiers. He had gone to Ibadan in continuation of his support-rallying tour, and was arrested at the house of his host, the military governor of the Western region; together with his host, he was taken away and killed.

Ironsi's 'successor' Lt. Col. Yakubu Gowon, sought to remedy the 'communications gap' by bringing in civilians to shore up his administration. Former politicians, including men like Chief Awolowo and Chief Enahoro who were released from jail on Gowon's orders, were brought in to serve as commissioners. Structurally, Gowon maintained the same framework of decision-making as Ironsi but with the significant difference that the FEC was now composed of civilians and military personnel. No civil servant sat at the FEC as a member. This is not to say that the bureaucrats had been made to take second place to the new civilian commissioners. In reality, their influence suffered hardly any decline. If anything, their relative importance grew as they became in effect the powers behind the throne.

Gowon had actually been in power for more than nine months before civilian commissioners were appointed. During this period, perhaps one of the most critical in recent Nigerian history, the policy-makers were Gowon and his top bureaucrats. Over the monitoring of the Ad Hoc Constitutional Conference, the Aburi Meeting and its aftermath, the division of the country into twelve states, and the initial moves towards mobilisation for the civil war, it was the top bureaucrats who defined the federal position for Gowon.[18] The one crucial move by the federal government before the start of hostilities — the creation of states and the proclamation of the state of emergency — was taken by Gowon independently even of the military governors and the only people privy to that move were the group of top civil servants who came to be known as the 'super permanent secretaries'.[19] Thus by the time civil commissioners were injected into the administration, a rapport had been established between Gowon and the civil service. When the civilian commissioners were brought into the government, it was only for them to find an established power group within the government with which they had to contend, and Gowon was on the side of the angels, the 'universal class', as Hegel described the bureaucrats.

But what further reinforced the position of the civil servants relative to the civilian commissioners was the use to which Gowon put the SMC. Ironsi had made little use of the SMC but under Gowon that body became the final decision-making — or ratifying — organ. Using the SMC as a ratificatory body to give the seal of approval to FEC decisions (which could also be overturned by the SMC) created the impression of greater military involvement in the decision-making process, but more importantly, it enabled Gowon to have his way on most issues. All the members of the SMC (with the exception of the Administrator of the East Central State, Mr Ukpabi Asika who was a civilian and former lecturer at the University of Ibadan) were either military men or members of the police force, and given the command hierarchy of the military, were under an obligation to accept the ruling of their military superior. Gowon as head of the military government of course insisted on personally presenting all federal memoranda that went before the SMC which in the nature of things presented the other SMC members with a dilemma, for to question a federal memorandum amounted to questioning a military superior. Inevitably, therefore, Gowon invariably had his way.[20] But this also meant that in the event of a disagreement between a permanent secretary and his commissioner — a situation that normally most permanent secretaries would try to avoid — provided the permanent secretary could persuade Gowon to accept his views, he could have such views brought before the SMC in the form of a federal memorandum and be guaranteed that such views would receive the approval of the SMC.[21] Significantly, while civilian commissioners could attend a meeting of the SMC only when invited to, permanent secretaries were expected 'to be on hand' during a meeting of the SMC just in case Gowon needed to have something or the other clarified. It is hardly surprising therefore that when Muhammed became

Head of State after the overthrow of Gowon he forbade permanent secretaries to attend meetings of the SMC unless they were specifically invited. Muhammed had been Commissioner for Communications under Gowon from January 1975 until the coup that overthrew Gowon.

At the level of the states, things were of course somewhat different. The commissioners entered the political arena at almost the same time as the military governors and were thus better placed to make their presence felt, to put the bureaucracy in its 'proper place' and thus ensure that they were the effective links between the bureaucracy and the military governor. There was, however, an important difference between the federal and regional commissioners. Whereas most of the federal commissioners were former politicians with established links with the grass roots, the broad generality of regional commissioners were 'new men', new to the political arena and relatively unknown. To a greater extent than their federal counterparts, the regional commissioners held their appointments largely on sufferance and their services could be dispensed with at will. Therefore not only did they feel more compelled to identify themselves with the goals of the military, they had to be seen to so identify themselves. These differences point to one important fact about the military administration. Where at the federal level, civil commissioners could be seen as constituting, in a weak sense, some kind of 'opposition', at the regional level that place was taken by the bureaucracy.[22]

One outcome of this complex web of relationships was that it made any programme of demilitarisation that the military might envisage highly problematic. Some 10 months after the end of the civil war, Gowon announced his 'nine-point' programme for a return to civil rule by 1976. There was nothing particularly new in that promise: it was but an elaboration of statements he had made even while the civil war was still on. However, in announcing his programme on 1 October, 1970, it would seem that Gowon had not adequately taken into account certain factors. The first was petroleum. In 1969/70, revenue from oil accounted for 26.3 per cent of total federal revenue (₦166.4 million out of a total of ₦633.2 million) but by 1970/71 the percentage had risen to 43.6 per cent (₦510.2 million of ₦1,169 million) and to 54.4 per cent in 1971/72 (₦764.3 million of ₦1404.8 million). It was not just that income from petroleum was growing faster than other sources of revenue, oil had opened new visions of wealth, greater than anything the former politicians could have dreamed about. The second factor was the ambition of the 'political military' — the group of military (and police) personnel holding political offices — and their clients, the civilian commissioners. During the civil war, the need for the successful prosecution of the war had led to the subordination of everything else to the demands of the military. But at the end of the war the post-war plan of reconstruction and rehabilitation (which envisaged an invest-ment programme of some ₦2,200 million) brought with it the prospects of contracts to be awarded and the expecta-tion of profits to be made from such contracts. The oil boom of 1973/74 made the prospects still rosier. By 1974 when work started on the Third National Development Plan, the government had already started thinking in terms of an investment programme of ₦20,000 million (subsequently revised upwards to ₦30,000 million). Since military governors are not accountable for their disbursement of public funds, it seemed hardly an opportune period to start talking of handing over power to a civil authority. To this must be added the anxiety of the top bureaucracy who, used to having their way, could hardly be expected to cherish the prospect of being brought under the control of politicians.

Several possible courses of action confronted the military and their clients: they could:

(a) convert the administration into a one party state, with Gowon as President;
(b) institute a system in which power was shared between the military and an elected civilian element but with the military holding a veto power, a form of the type of government known as 'dyarchy' advocated by Dr Nnamdi Azikiwe;
(c) hand over power to a popularly elected civilian govern-ment; and
(d) maintain the status quo.[23]

By late 1971 it would seem that the third choice, the handing over of power to an elected civil authority, had been ruled out,[24] and the idea of a one-party state was being seriously considered. The idea had been suggested by some of the civil commissioners from the states (including the Administrator of the East Central State), and not unexpectedly, the top cadres of the bureaucracy.[25] Basically, the notion involved proclaiming Nigeria a single-party state, with the party centred around General Gowon who would become President. Early in 1972, some members of the bureaucracy[26] were sent to Egypt, Zaire and Guinea to study the systems in these states as possible models for a Nigerian one-party state. At the conference on national policy held in Zaria in October 1972[27] the representatives of the federal bureaucracy present talked of the need for a platform which would bring together, as Mr Asiodu[28] put it, men of distinction who would take over the management of the polity. They argued that party systems derived from representative models tended to be divisive and in any case, such systems had failed Nigeria in the post-independence civil regime. In one of his numerous statements, Mr Asika, the Administrator of the East Central State (who was being cast as the ideologue of the regime) said the military administration could not be expected to be indifferent to the nature of its successor. Mr A. A. Ayida, the permanent secretary of the Ministry of Finance (he later became secretary to the military government and Head of the Federal Public Service) was perhaps more explicit and enlightening. In his 'Presidential Address' to the Nigerian Economic Society in 1973 entitled 'The Nigerian Revolution 1966–76', Mr Ayida claimed he wanted to share some of his 'inner thoughts on the past, present and future of Nigeria' with his audience, his 'underlining political assumption' being 'predictive rather than prescriptive'. Contending that the changes which had occurred in Nigerian society since 1966 could qualify as 'the beginnings of a national revolution', Ayida noted that 'unfortunately, the Nigerian revolution is a revolution without a vanguard. The prediction' he went on to say 'is that unless we can evolve a vanguard to provide the leadership and the impetus for the revolutionary forces at work, the Nigerian revolution is bound to prove abortive.'

After examining what forms future constitutional changes could take he went on, in a passage which merits being quoted at length, to say,

> the crucial question [about the political future of Nigeria] relates to the organisations of political parties. A party can have support in more than one state and not be 'genuinely national' in outlook and vice versa. But the unanswered question is, who is to determine the criteria for assessing the national character of their [sic] performance.

His answer was: 'it is either the electorate or the powers-that-be. This is the most sensitive issue in programming the return to civil rule.'

Mr Ayida then suggested that 'there were two models' that one could work 'from the lessons of experience'. The first would be 'for the military administration to declare party politics open and leave it to the "democratic forces" to settle the issue of national leadership', but the 'lessons' of the Ad Hoc Constitutional Conference[29] would suggest that this was not a promising approach.

> The second approach is for the military to sponsor a National Movement outside which no serious opposition will be allowed. This alternative [he pointed out] has very serious implications and should not be lightly embarked upon without a full appreciation of the repercussions. There cannot be such a national movement without a revolutionary vanguard made up of a body of highly dedicated men and women with a clearly defined national purpose and a sense of mission. It is difficult to see how such a group can be formed without the military hierarchy politicising itself.

Arguing 'that military rule without the total mobilisation and involvement of the people is an aberration and is basically unstable', Ayida, however, was quick to note that 'in the light of our recent history, there is equally convincing evidence to demonstrate that a national leadership acceptable to the country as a whole will not emerge in 1976 through an autono-

mous election like a deus ex machina'. Nevertheless, while
he would not advocate a 'political role' for the armed forces
'as such', the truth is that

> Nigeria no longer has a ceremonial army. We are [he said]
> building a large modern army, of well trained, self-conscious
> and intelligent young men who will not be content to be
> relegated to the barracks for keeps. . . . The military leader-
> ship [Ayida concluded] in the new set up is of necessity
> obliged to conceive an interventionist role for itself. The
> constitutional settlement must take into account this new
> and crucial factor.[30]

Shed of all the rhetoric, Ayida's 'prediction' was the advocacy
of a National Movement led by a 'revolutionary vanguard'
headed by a 'politicised military hierarchy', a circumlocutory
way of describing a one-party state backed by a 'large modern
army of well trained, self-conscious and intelligent young men'.

But if the self-interest of the 'political military', the 'new
men' civil commissioners and the top hierarchy of the bureaucracy dictated the logic of a 'national movement' should
demilitarisation be seriously considered, that proposal was
hardly likely to command acceptance amongst those with
competing interests, and there were many of these. First,
there were the former politicians, a few of whom were
serving as federal commissioners and who, chafing at having
to play the role of hand-maiden to the 'military boys' and
fully aware of the possibilities opened up by 'petro-naira',
were hoping for a return to civil rule when they could recover
the position they saw as rightfully theirs. Having supposedly
been found wanting — and discredited — it was hardly likely
that such men would be allowed a place within a proposed
'national movement' aimed at preserving the impetus already
gained by the 'Nigerian revolution'. It could of course be
argued that the claims by this 'discredited' class of men could
be conveniently ignored by the military administration but
the wave of strikes in 1973 which came near to paralysing
the economy suggested that there already existed an explosive
potential, which given the skills at mass manipulation which

the politicians no doubt possessed, could be exploited to the detriment of the military as a whole.

The second group was the intelligentsia, composed in the main of men from the universities, and specifically, the intelligentsia from the 'North'. One of the by-products of the 'alliance' between the military and the bureaucracy was the isolation of the universities, some members of which had been associated with the former political leaders, had taken a part in politics along the periphery of the 'banned' political parties and who had become increasingly critical of military rule.[31] In the 1950s and early 1960s university employment tended to be more highly regarded than comparable jobs in the civil service. But since the military takeover that position had somewhat been reversed with bureaucrats earning more and having more perquisites of office, a situation hardly calculated to endear the military authorities to the universities. In 1973 the universities had in fact gone on strike in protest against their relatively worsened position, a strike which led to a confrontation between the military authorities and the staff of the universities. On that occasion Gowon had issued an ultimatum to the universities: return to work within three days or be faced with forced eviction (by military personnel) from university-provided housing. Though the staff capitulated to the government, capitulation turned them into an alienated group and the least likely to welcome a 'national movement' which would only serve to entrench rule by the military and their bureaucratic aides.

But over and above the generalised opposition of the univsities, the 'Northern' intelligentsia had particular grounds for concern at the idea of a 'national movement'. A number of these, through their links with the military hierarchy, had exercised considerable influence within the military administration as a whole.[32] By 1973, however, this group had become concerned at what they saw as the 'southern' influence[33] surrounding the Head of State, General Gowon. For instance, there was talk that though the media had been eloquent about the sufferings of farmers in the North due to the Sahelian drought, the General had hardly thought it fit to examine at first hand the plight of the people he was supposed to be governing. A 'national movement' dominated by the 'Southern' influence around Gowon seemed certain to be detrimental to the interests of the North. Late in 1973 Gowon decided to tour the drought-affected areas and was met by members of the 'Northern' intelligentsia who sought to persuade him of the need to curb the ever-increasing influence of the 'Southern' bureaucrats, an influence which they took to be antithetical to the real interests of the North. But as one member of that group subsequently reported, Gowon only 'talked at' them, exhibiting what they took to be total unconcern.[34] In reaction, the 'Northern' intelligentsia embarked on the process of mobilising support for the other two groups whose opposition was to bring about the collapse of the Gowon administration.

These two groups, the 'native authority' functionaries and the 'far North' elements of the military hierarchy, have close links with the intelligentsia. Two schools – Government College, Zaria (later renamed Barewa) and Government College, Keffi – have provided the main recruiting grounds for the bulk of the top brass of the army from the 'far North', the same schools that have provided the core of the North's intelligentsia. Thus, more often than not, members of both have been schoolmates or even classmates and there are close linkages, often kinship ties, between the military and the native authority functionaries – councillors, district and village heads, and the top administrative cadre.[35] Though there was no convergence of interest between the military subset and the native authority functionaries – the latter would have wanted to see a return to civil rule while some members of the former would not have objected to a continuation of military rule – both groups were nevertheless agreed on the minimum, opposition to what they saw as a 'Southern' predominance centred around Gowon, a predominance which a 'national movement' as being conceived could only enhance. In various ways, such as by meetings between Gowon and the native authority functionaries, and between Gowon and the 'far North' military hierarchy, it was made clear that not only was the system as it then existed not acceptable, but any notion of a national movement would meet with opposition.

Faced with opposition from these different groups, Gowon had little choice but to scuttle the notion of a national movement. The second alternative open to the administration, that of dyarchy, was for all practical purposes no different from the system then in operation. But if dyarchy meant going through an electoral process to recruit civilians who would form an adjunct to the military, then the military might as well go the whole way — operationalise the programme of demilitarisation. Within the military, however, it would seem there were more in favour of the continuation of a military regime than were opposed to it, though most members of the military would have preferred to see a change, particularly, a change of military governors. It was not so much a question of the military governors being corrupt — and hence bringing the image of the military into disrepute — as that there were those within the military hierarchy who, claiming they had made sacrifices to preserve the existent system, thought they ought to reap the same rewards as the military governors were believed to be reaping — and there were good grounds to suppose that belief was not unfounded.[36] But to have removed the military governors would have been to have opened a hornet's nest, and Gowon was fully aware of this. In the first place there were too many claimants seeking to be appointed and it was hardly likely that Gowon could have escaped the charge of bias or favouritism no matter what he did, which could have had destabilising effects on the military. In the second place, there was the question of what to do with the military governors once they were removed from their political assignments. They could not be sent to their former units for that would have meant having to displace the command hierarchy in such units and hence changing career expectations — owing to the promotion of most of the military governors, many were in fact senior in rank to those in command positions. They could of course have been retired but some reasons would have had to be given (all were relatively young, being in their early or mid-thirties). In any case retirement would only have lent some credence to the charges of corruption and Gowon had already said publicly that he believed in the honesty of his military governors. Thus, given the opposition to the idea of a 'national movement', the impracticability of 'dyarchy' and pressure from the administration — and the business and commercial interests who had profited immensely under military rule — not to demilitarise as it was claimed this would lead to instability, Gowon had little choice but to maintain the status quo and hence the announcement on 1 October 1974, that 1976 — the date earlier set for a return to civil rule — was no longer realistic. Nine months later Gowon was himself thrown out of office in a classic 'palace coup'. As his successor, Murtala Muhammed, was later to say:

> After the civil war, the affairs of state, hitherto a collective responsibility became characterized by lack of consultation, indecision, indiscipline and even neglect. Indeed, the public at large became disillusioned and disappointed by these developments. This trend was clearly incompatible with the philosophy and image of a corrective regime. Unknown to the general public, the feeling of disillusion was also evident among members of the Armed Forces whose administration was also neglected but who, out of sheer loyalty to the nation, and in the hope that there would be a change, continued to suffer in silence. . . . Responsible opinion, including advice by eminent Nigerians, traditional rulers, intellectuals etc., was similarly disregarded. The leadership, either by design or default, had become too insensitive to the true feelings and yearnings of the people. The nation was being plunged inexorably into chaos.[37]

If one allows for some element of exaggeration — the armed forces 'suffering' in silence, the nation being plunged into chaos — Muhammed's statement amounts to saying Gowon fell because he could not resolve the problematic posed by Kemal Ataturk: when the military seizes power, either the soldiers must leave the army and become politicians, or they must hand over power to the politicians. Gowon's successor chose the alternative of handing over power to the politicians.

THE SEARCH FOR A VIABLE POLITICAL ORDER

Muhammed was assassinated some nine months after assuming office as Nigeria's new Head of State, but his successor,

General Obasanjo, hardly changed the major policy goals stated by Muhammed. In what follows therefore no attempt will be made to differentiate the Muhammed and the Obasanjo administrations.[38] Basically, the problem confronting Nigeria, as the Muhammed administration saw it, was one of creating 'a new political order' capable of realising 'the yearnings of the people'. This could be called the 'operational premise' of the administration. But underlying that premise was an assumption, the assumption that the structural—institutional framework within which Gowon operated was somehow inadequate. That assumption was nowhere explicitly stated and because it was never explicitly stated, it was not thought there was any need to defend it. But given that it was assumed to be true — perhaps intuitively — the operational premise followed necessarily. Given then that premise, there were at least three related ways in which the administration could and did proceed; (i) improving the efficient working of the inherited system; (ii) eliminating bottlenecks to the efficient operation of the system; and (iii) changing the structure of the system through the creation of new institutions.[39]

The first move towards improving the efficiency of the administration was the alteration of the decision-making structure, which was done by interposing a new decision level between the SMC and the FEC and ensuring as much as possible that there was the minimum of overlap in the membership of all three bodies. The new intermediate body was the Council of States which was composed of all the military governors of the 12 states (before the number was increased to 19 with the creation of new states). Members of the bureaucracy were excluded from attendance at any meeting of any one of the three bodies unless their attendance was specifically commanded. The exclusion of bureaucrats, it was thought, should eliminate the deleterious effects which their presence was alleged to have had on decision-making during the Gowon administration, while by removing all military governors from the SMC and relegating them to the Council of States, it was thought a clear distinction could and should be made between federal affairs and those matters which concerned the states only. But more importantly the separation, it was argued, would have the effect of removing political — that is 'state' – considerations from having a bearing or influence on the goals of the administration *qua* military administration. The presumption, no doubt, was that members of the SMC – and a number of these were directly responsible for, and involved in, the coup that removed Gowon – were and would be, above 'politics' – motivated by the most nationalistic of ideals.[40] It is not, of course, easy to test any of these propositions but in at least one case there is good reason to believe that the political interests of at least one member of the SMC had a bearing on the number of states that were created.[41] Given human weakness, and the linkages which members of the SMC had with various groups in the larger society, it would hardly be rational to accept that the SMC could be above politics as the members would want Nigerians to believe.

The decision-making structure having been set up, various other measures were then taken to improve the working of the system, measures which included the creation of such bodies as the Public Complaints Bureau, the Corrupt Practices Investigation Bureau and the National Security Organisation. The Public Complaints Bureau was supposed to have a function similar to that of an 'Ombudsman', investigating alleged cases of administrative abuse and seeking redress against it where such cases were proven. Each state was expected to set up a state Complaints Bureau (though a number of states could set up one Complaints Bureau such as the Oyo, Ogun and Ondo States Public Complaints Bureau) which was to be responsible to, and to be under the jurisdiction of, the Federal Public Complaints Bureau. How effective these bureaus were was never very certain. There were complaints by bureau commissioners of lack of co-operation from public servants, and in some cases, complaints of commissioners exceeding the boundaries of their jurisdiction. But worst of all was the complaint by commissioners that they had neither the resources nor the administrative capacity to investigate the majority of the cases of abuse reported to them. The Bureaus, like the Rent Control Decrees,[42] are perhaps to be remembered more for the intention that went into their creation than for what they actually achieved or could achieve.

The Corrupt Practices Investigation Bureau (CPIB) was an odd creation. Since the first steps were taken towards the introduction of representative institutions in the early fifties, Nigerians have developed what may perhaps be described as a morbid fascination with the subject of corruption which tends to occur in, and to dominate, every discussion no matter what subject the discussion started with; the institution of the CPIB is best seen as a reaction to that morbid fascination.[43] Be that as it may, the CPIB turned out to be just another 'white elephant', for though the Commissioner was empowered to investigate allegations of corrupt practices reported to his Bureau (for which he did not have the staff or the skills required) and to command the production of whatever evidence might be needed, he had no power to initiate any action for prosecution. All he could do was to report to the police with a recommendation for action, a recommendation which the police were not obliged to act upon. Apart from its limited staff, the CPIB's principal handicap was perhaps the undefined relationship it was supposed to have (if any), with the Criminal Investigation Department of the police, the department directly responsible for the prevention and prosecution of cases of corrupt practices. Whatever the achievements of the CPIB may have been, it did succeed in the one respect that perhaps mattered most: in simply demonstrating that the administration was concerned about the problem of corruption even if it had no real intention of going beyond the avowal of that concern.[44]

The National Security Organisation was supposed to be the 'watchdog' of public 'security' but is perhaps better described as the 'para-political' organ of the Muhammed–Obasanjo administration, geared more to the intimidation of critics or alleged critics of the administration than to ensuring the 'security' of the nation. A good many of its members were barely literate, which in many respects summarises all that need be said about the organisation.

If the administration's measures aimed at improving the performance of the political system do not seem to add up to much, its record with respect to the elimination of impediments to efficiency must certainly look impressive, though opinion could be divided about the overall impact of the several measures taken. Holders of political appointments — military governors and commissioners — were removed from office and a commission of enquiry was appointed to investigate the assets acquired by these officers since holding public office, the aim being not to prosecute for abuse of office but to seek restitution for any assets found to have been illegally or improperly acquired. Other investigatory panels were set up to look into the question of 'abandoned properties', a main focus of controversy between the three 'eastern states';[45] the operation of the 'Indigenisation Decree';[46] the functioning of the Interim Common Services Agency (ICSA) and the Eastern States Interim Assets and Liabilities Agency (ESIALA);[47] and into revenue allocation between the federal government and the states. And as each of these panels reported, appropriate action was taken, examples being the abolition of ICSA and ESIALA and the setting up of an authority to monitor the extent of compliance with the Indigenisation Decree by the firms involved. In the field of higher education, to streamline resource use and ensure greater accountability, all universities were brought under federal control, while steps were taken to create six more universities.[48] In the same spirit, all television broadcasting was brought under federal control with the creation of a national Broadcasting Authority of Nigeria, a move which was followed by the institution of the News Agency of Nigeria (to cover the news media) and the takeover of a majority shareholding in the two principal newspapers in the federation, the *Daily Times* and the *New Nigerian*. On a still more ambitious scale, the administration extended its 'reforming' zeal to include the trade unions, and adopting an 'industry' approach, regrouped the over 250 'house' unions which comprised organised labour into some seven or eight organisations, which collectively became the Nigerian Trades Union Congress, the leadership of which the government then proceeded to appoint.

But of all the steps taken to improve performance, certainly what became known as the 'great purge' was and will remain the most controversial. This was the removal by retirement or dismissal from office of some 10,000 public servants, approximately 1.5 per cent of all those in public employment. For a regime that was, by self-proclamation a 'corrective regime', it was a curious action, as what characterised the 'purge' more than anything else was that it contravened every notion of natural justice.[49] It was a measure which was supposed to remove the 'corrupt' and to clear away the 'deadwood' in the policy-formulation process; thus it is not without some interest to note that over 80 per cent of those removed were from the lower rungs of the service, people who had had little or nothing to do with policy formulation and who at the worst could only have been guilty of some minor misdemeanour or the other. And in the higher positions it was far from certain whether those who moved into the shoes of the displaced were as efficient or competent as the people they replaced.[50] Moreover, as the military authorities admitted, there was no evidence that the incidence of corruption was in any way affected or reduced by the purge. Whatever benefits may have been expected from the purge, it involved one major cost, the loss of that sense of job security which has been found essential in most bureaucracies if the civil servant is to give of his best. To that must also be added the cost of the loss of the sense of an esprit de corps, the mutuality of co-operation, which is vital to an effective and efficient working of the bureaucracy. It would be impossible to place any quantitative measure to these costs, but what is certain is that the purge has left the civilian successor to the military with a civil service riddled with suspicion and unsure of itself, a loss of morale and confidence which will take years to rebuild. The purge was just one of those acts, characteristic of military rule, where the unintended consequences are of greater significance than the intended.

The real achievement of the administration lies in its attempts to create new institutions, a consequence of the decision to demilitarise, to hand over power to a popularly elected civilian government not later than 1 October 1979. The actions taken in this respect were: (i) the creation of new states; (ii) the introduction of a new system of local government; and (iii) the drawing up of a new constitution. The description of the processes leading to the drawing up of the constitution, and an analysis of the constitution itself, will be taken up in the next chapter. Discussion in this section will therefore be restricted to the first two items: the creation of states and the introduction of a 'uniform' system of local government.

In order to generate support for the federal government and hence be in a better position to prosecute the civil war which was then imminent, Gowon had been induced to create new states, literally by fiat, in May 1967. The underlying logic of that exercise was (a) to seek to remove the fear of continued 'domination' of the federation by the Northern region — which meant that the Northern region had to be broken into smaller units; (b) to seek to create new foci of loyalty and attachment for the non-Ibo-speaking peoples of the Eastern region — in other words, to break up the solidarity of the peoples of what, during the civil war, was to become known as 'Biafra' — which meant breaking up the Eastern region into smaller units; and (c) to seek to secure a geographical area which could not be easily threatened by any of the states and within which the security of the federal authority and its agents could be adequately protected — which meant extending the boundaries of the federal capital territory to cover such an area from which the federal government could readily contain any threat from the Western region were this ever to be made.[51] This became the Lagos state. Breaking up the Northern and Eastern regions posed the problem of into how many units each could be split, while at the same time preserving traditional linkages and community of interests, and incurring the minimum administrative costs and loss of information. The twin criteria — traditional linkages and community of interests; and minimum administrative costs and loss of information — are not necessarily compatible but the attempt at reconciling the two, given the strategic objective of the federal government, dictated a minimum of six states in the North and three in the East. Nigeria therefore ended up with 12 states in 1967.[52] Given the time constraint under which Gowon acted, it would have been surprising if the exercise had not left some problems unresolved. In fact it is a great tribute to Gowon and his civil service advisers that their division of the federation into 12 states caused fewer difficulties than might have been expected, as time was later to show. However, some problems remained — one of the states, the North-East state, covered an area which was one-third of the total land area of the federation — and Gowon therefore promised that the whole issue of states would be reviewed at a later date, but oddly enough with the end of the civil war, despite pressing demands for a review, Gowon chose to 'let sleeping dogs lie'.

Three weeks after taking office, the Muhammed administration appointed a five-man panel under the chairmanship of a Justice of the Supreme Court, Mr Justice Ayo Irikefe:

> to examine the question of the creation of more states in the federation and, should the committee find the creation of more states necessary and desirable to: (a) advise on the delimitation of such states; (b) advise on the economic viability of the proposed states; (c) advise on the location of the administrative capitals of the proposed states; and (d) examine and advise on all other factors that may appear to the committee to be relevant, so as to enable the government to take a decision which will ensure a balanced federation.

The panel was enjoined to receive and examine written representations that appeared relevant to its deliberations.

For all the years that Nigerians have been talking about the creation of states, the protagonists of the need for more states have never really seriously faced the logic of their own demands. Thus, to talk for instance, as the Muhammed administration did in its terms of reference to the Irikefe committee about the 'desirability' of creating more states, or the 'economic viability' of such states without spelling out what these terms mean, is simply to beg the question. 'Desirable' from whose point of view? If it is to be that of those making the demands, then one could end up with as many states as there are clans or villages in the federation which would be totally absurd. One may speculate on what the word 'state' would connote under such circumstances. The talk of 'economic viability' for example, is not particularly helpful when not spelled out. Viable with respect to what? Or in terms of what? In a context where federal allocations account for more than 70 per cent of a state's total revenue, surely any talk of 'economic viability' must be empty or grossly misleading. Before 1967, when the Northern region constituted more than two-thirds of the total land area of Nigeria and allegedly had more than 54 per cent of the country's total population so that the representation of the North outweighed the representation from all the other states combined, talk of an 'unbalanced' federation surely had a meaning.[53] But in the context of the 12 states, what could possibly be meant by a 'balanced federation'? Or alternatively, in what sense could one have said that the '12-state system' was 'unbalanced'?

The Irikefe Commission obviously thought these terms had a meaning though their interpretation of the terms was some-what unconvincing and simplistic. The committee decided to accept the following as criteria for recommending the 'necessity' and 'desirability' of having more states: the need to (a) bring government closer to the people; (b) ensure even development; (c) preserve the federal structure of government; (d) maintain peace and harmony within the federation; and (e) minimise minority problems.[54] Though the committee admitted that they were not sure what weight should be given to each of their selected criteria, they did not seem to have considered the internal consistency of the criteria themselves; for instance, what might contribute to 'peace and harmony' might not necessarily 'minimise the minority' problem, or that which might minimise the minority problem might be incompatible with preserving 'the federal structure'.

However, on the basis of their accepted criteria and con-sidering the various proposals submitted to the committee, the members recommended breaking the federation into 19 states. Briefly, the recommendations were as follows:

Western State — to be divided into three states — Oyo, Ogun and Ondo;

South-Eastern — to be divided into two states — Cross River and Qua Iboe;

East-Central — to be divided into two states — Udi (re-named Anambra by the federal government) and Imo;

Benue Plateau — to be divided into two states — Benue and Plateau;

North-East — to be divided into three states — Borno, Bauchi and Gongola;

North-Central — to remain as it was but renamed Kaduna state;

North-West — to be divided into two states — Rima (the federal government preferred Sokoto) and Niger;

Kano — to remain as it was but to be named Bagauda (the federal government retained the name Kano);

Midwest — to remain as it was but to be renamed Bendel;

Rivers — to remain as it was and the name Rivers retained;

Kwara — to remain unchanged (though some boundary changes suggested);

Lagos — to be merged with the proposed Ogun State.

With two exceptions, the federal government accepted the recommendations of the committee. They rejected the recommendation that Lagos state should be merged with Ogun state, and that the South-Eastern state be split into two, preferring instead to retain the state as a single unit but with the name changed to Cross River State.[55]

At this stage only one further comment need be made which relates to one of the criteria stipulated by the committee and which in a way brings out the 'vicious circle' involved in the whole argument about the creation of states. To justify their recommendation that the West and East-Central states should each be broken into two or more states, the committee stated that if more states were not created, 'the resources open to the government would be too thinly spread on the ground and would constitute in effect a relative holding back of development *within* the state'.[56] But at an earlier point in their report, the committee had noted that:

the panel considered that the principle of even development should be applied not so much to areas *within* states but, rather to the achievement of general progress between one state and another. In other words no state should be so economically backward when compared to others in the country. In this regard therefore, the concern of the panel was directed more towards determining those areas of chronic or extensive economic backwardness and advising on how to alleviate such situation.[57]

In effect then, the committee had to resort to a totally ad hoc argument, and one incompatible with their own chosen criteria, to justify breaking the West and the East-Central states into more states. Moreover, an outcome of the panel's recommendation has been that *more* resources have been put into areas which were already the most economically advanced areas in the federation.[58] In the future, then, the fact that a state is relatively more developed than others could become grounds for breaking up that state if only because not to do so would result in 'a relative holding back of development within the state'. The Irikefe committee — and the military government — have opened up, no doubt unwittingly, a 'pandora's box' the effect of which could well be to undermine that which they have sought to create and protect, a viable political order.

A month after setting up the panel to examine the necessity and desirability of creating more states, the Muhammed administration directed the states as they then existed to initiate discussion on proposals for the reform of the system of local government. The government itself set up a co-ordinating committee within the 'Cabinet Office' to collate the views from the states. Local government had in the past met with little success and its practice varied from one region to the other. The West had been the first in the 1950s to pass legislation aimed at converting the colonial system of 'native administration' — administration by traditional rulers, chiefs and elders — into a modern participatory form of grass-roots self-government through elected representatives. The West was followed by the East but by the end of the decade not only had the initial structures been changed, but party political pressure to have local authorities function as voting machines for ruling parties had led to most elected councils being suspended and in their place 'caretaker committees', composed of government nominees, substituted. Local participation had been made to give way to direct administration by the state governmental ministries. In the North, on the other hand, though some attempt had been made to introduce an elective element into the native authority system in the non-Moslem areas of the 'Middle Belt' for much of the region, the colonial framework was retained with barely any change, what change there was being simply the conversion of what used to be known as 'sole native authorities' — the Emir acting as sole administrator — into what was termed 'Emir-in-Council', that is, a system in which the Emir was to be advised by his 'council' though he was under no obligation to accept what advice was proffered.[59]

By 1975 this pattern had barely changed. In some of the 'Southern' states — Midwest, East-Central, South-East, and in the 'North' Benue Plateau — there were admittedly experiments with what the authorities chose to call 'development administration', but while the fact of 'administration' could not be denied — the direct management of local affairs by state bureaucrats — there was not much evidence of 'development'. At the grass roots, government remained as remote and removed from the daily concerns of the people as ever, while the resentment against the intrusion of ministry officials, whose main interests seemd to lie in controlling and regulating to the exclusion of everything else, grew. An expression of that resentment was the revolt of peasants — who had formed themselves into an association they called *Agbe ko'ya* (lit. farmers reject suffering, refuse to suffer any longer)[60] — in the Western state in 1969, a revolt which required the use of military force before it could be controlled. As the government was to point out in the 'Guidelines for Local Government Reform':

Local Government have, over the years, suffered from the continuous whittling down of their powers. . . . Lack of adequate funds and appropriate institutions had continued to make local government ineffective and ineffectual. . . . Excessive politicking had made even modest progress impossible. Consequently, there has been a divorce between the people and government institutions at their most basic levels. . . . The Federal Military Government has therefore decided to recognise local government as the third tier of governmental activity in the nation.

As 'third tier', the unit was to include between 150,000 and 600,000 people (later increased to 800,000)[61] with specified functions to be administered by an elected council elected on a popular vote. The basic framework was arrived at after a series of discussions between federal and state officials. Some questions arose as to the place of 'traditional rulers' within the new scheme, but a compromise formula was arrived at which allowed (a) a traditional ruler to serve as President, that is as (symbolic) head of the council; or (b) where the council was coterminous with the domain of a traditional ruler, for a traditional council, parallel with the elected body but presided over by the traditional ruler, to be instituted; or (c) where the traditional domain spanned a number of units, for a similar traditional council to be formed but with its members recruited for the area spanned. Traditional councils would have only advisory powers.

Elections to the new bodies were held in late 1976 and the new councils came into existence in early 1977. Schoolteachers, members of para-statals and people in a similar position were legally disallowed from contesting elections to the new councils, with the result that, particularly in the Northern states, most members turned out to be illiterate, unable to read or write even in the vernacular. By early 1980, only in two states were fully elected councils functioning. In the other states most if not all of the councils had been dissolved. The 'great experiment' in civic training and participatory politics was already turning out to be another unrealised dream of the military. Changing the metaphor, the foundation, it would seem, was incapable of taking the weight of the superstructure, but the nature of that superstructure will be examined in the next chapter.

THE POLITICAL ECONOMY OF MILITARY RULE

At the time that the military took over, agriculture was the mainstay of the Nigerian economy. In 1958/59, just before the country became independent, agriculture accounted for 65.9 per cent of the Gross Domestic Product (GDP), the figure falling to 53.8 per cent in 1966/67 and to 41.8 per cent in 1971/72. By 1974/75 the figure had declined still further, to 28.1 per cent. After nine years of military rule, agriculture — which had in the past contributed more than half of the gross domestic product — had fallen to the position where it accounted for only just over a quarter of the GDP. Before the wrong inference is made, it might be as well to point out that whereas industrial output accounted for just about 7.0 per cent of GDP in 1965/66, this had only risen to 10.2 per cent in 1974/75. Mining and Petroleum, on the other hand, which in 1966/67 made up just about 5 per cent of GDP had risen in 1974/75 to 14.2 per cent. Thus after nine years of military rule, Nigeria remained as dependent as ever on the export of primary products for its foreign-exchange earnings, the main difference being that whereas the proportions of agricultural exports and petroleum to total domestic exports was of the order of 61.6 per cent and 25.9 per cent respectively in 1965, the proportions had changed to 4.6 per cent and 94.0 per cent respectively in 1975.

In the main, the civilian regime had skimmed off the agricultural surplus, through the Marketing Boards, not only to pay for their 'welfare' schemes such as scholarships and programmes of free primary education — particularly in the West and East — but also to buy political support through the selective provision of pipe-borne water and electricity to those communities which had had the 'good sense' to vote 'the right way'. But that was not all. Part of the surplus had gone into the importation of consumer goods to satisfy the demands of a burgeoning educated elite of civil servants, teachers and various managerial and professional groups, and also to reward business and commercial interests — who had to be party men — through the award of contracts for building and construction undertaken by the governments. Agriculture and the rural communities were thus made to pay for the privilege of keeping the politicians in power, and to satisfy the increasing demand for imported consumer items by the urban-educated elite. But this meant that in concentrating on the extraction of the agricultural surplus the civilian regime had to relegate the control of major segments of the economy — extractive industries such as mining and prospecting, finance, in the form of banking and insurance, and major constructional activity — to expatriate interests with the result that these spheres of activity became isolated enclaves within a largely agricultural economy dominated by Nigerians.

That the strategy of maintaining Nigeria as a 'dual economy' — misleadingly described as a 'mixed economy' — was a consciously pursued policy is shown, for example, in the following statement from the First National Development Plan 1962– 68:

> Nigeria's economy is a mixed one. The Governments have taken an active part not only in providing the social but also the basic economic services, such as electricity and ports. They also intend to participate in the operation of various industries, such as a steel plant and an oil refinery. The attitude of the Government of the federation, however, is entirely pragmatic and accepts the desirability of a mixed economy. At the same time, the Governments are convinced that no amount of Government activity can effectively replace the efforts of a *broadly based and progressive* private sector.[62]

To encourage the growth of 'a broadly based' private sector, the civilian regime passed a whole host of legislation highly favourable to, and intended to foster, foreign private investment. Thus by 1964, of total identified foreign investment in Nigeria estimated at ₦258.1 million, Nigerian participation (Government and private) accounted for only ₦54.8 million or 21.2 per cent of the total. Another way of looking at the same picture is to examine the ownership of the paid-up capital invested in the 'enclave economy'. In 1963, 68.1 per cent of such capital was owned by non-Nigerian (foreign) interests with the federal and regional governments accounting for 22.0 per cent and private Nigerian interests for only 9.9 per cent. By 1965, foreign ownership had only marginally declined to 61.9 per cent, while private Nigerian ownership increased, still more marginally, by 1.2 per cent.[63] Translated into socio-political terms, the economic strategy of the civilian regime can be interpreted by saying that while the 'ruling class' of politicians and the indigenous business interests exploited the essentially rural agricultural stratum to satisfy their political power objectives, they were content to serve as agents of foreign investors whose primary interest was in the exploitation of Nigeria as a whole. Much of this was, however, to change with the military.

Agriculture, the mainstay of the economy, had been declining under civilian rule,[64] and with the advent of military rule and buoyant revenues from the export of crude oil — which made reliance on agricultural surpluses no longer necessary — agriculture suffered a near-total neglect. From being a major exporter of items like cocoa, palm produce, groundnuts, cotton and rubber, by 1975 Nigeria had become an importer of palm products and groundnuts while the export of cocoa and rubber had declined considerably. Within the two years 1975/76 and 1977/78, it has been estimated that the area under active cultivation fell from 18.8 million hectares to 11.05 million, a fall of 41.3 per cent or close to half of the total area being cultivated. Within the same period, the food import bill rose from ₦353.7 million to over ₦1000 million.[65] Though data on income distribution in Nigeria are difficult to come by, it has been estimated, for example, that by 1974 the minimum average urban wage was just about twice the rural agricultural wage. With the wage and salary awards of 1974 — the Udoji awards (made possible by petroleum revenues) which did not include the rural population — the differential could, in all probability, be expected to have doubled. Given the price index which in 1970 stood at 150.6 (1960=100) and which by 1974 — before the Udoji 'awards' — had risen to 214.7, while by 1976 it was 348.2, the conclusion can hardly be escaped that though the living standards of the rural population had been anything but comfortable under the civilian regime, the impact of military rule on the quality of life in the rural areas can only be described as catastrophic.

If the 'oil boom' was a disaster — in its effects — for the rural population, for the military political decision-makers and their civilian aides it can only be described as 'manna from heaven', opening up opportunities few could have dreamed of. The 'boom' itself can be viewed from different perspectives. As exports, its value rose from ₦262 million in 1969 to ₦5365.7 million in 1974, the year just before the overthrow of Gowon; in terms of its contribution to the net external earnings of the government, the figures were ₦106.6 million in 1969 (or 40.7 per cent of petroleum exports) and ₦5192.9 million in 1974 (or 96.8 per cent of the value of petroleum exports); and in terms of its contribution to federal government current revenue, its value rose from ₦166.4 million in 1970 (or 26.3 per cent of total current revenue) to ₦3726.7 million in 1974 (or 82.1 per cent of total revenue).[66] One result of the 'boom' is easily seen by a comparison of planned expenditure in the second and third national development plans. Whereas in the former, planned expenditure was put at ₦2000 million by the time the third national plan was being prepared the government's horizon had extended sufficiently for it to envisage a planned expenditure of some ₦30,000 million.

While it would be interesting to look at the effect of the boom, as seen from the perspectives of the national development plans, in terms of sectoral distribution of expenditure and their expected contributions to GDP, growth rates of GDP and per capita income, the expansion of employment, education, health programmes and other social services, it will perhaps be more enlightening to examine the sociopolitical consequences of the boom, the perspective usually taken to distinguish the 'new' 'political economy'. Under military rule, with no constituents to conciliate and no electorate to be accountable to — in however weak a sense one interprets the notion of accountability — the effect of the oil boom was to convert the military political decision-makers and their bureaucratic aides into a new property-owning, rentier class working in close and direct collaboration with foreign business interests with the sole aim of expropriating the surpluses derived from oil for their private and personal benefit.

The collaboration took a variety of forms, one of which was to ensure that a particular foreign interest won a valuable government construction contract for which a suitable reward was then made to the official or officials in a position to influence the award of contracts. Another method was to arrange for bulk purchases of items required by the government or a para-statal — cement, buses, aircraft, or newsprint — from overseas suppliers with highly remunerative kickbacks built into the supply price. Yet another method was participation in a joint enterprise. A good example of the last form, direct participation in a joint enterprise, is provided by the case of the Federal Ministry of Works, which was by no means unusual. The Commissioner for the Ministry was Alhaji Femi Okunnu, one of the 'new men' commissioners. The Ministry was responsible for the award of most of the construction contracts — for roads, public buildings, airports and the like — undertaken by the federal government. Siemens (Nig.) Ltd, a West German construction company, was introduced into Nigeria by Alhaji Okunnu and his Lagos state counterpart, Dr Seriki, the Lagos State Commissioner for Works and Planning. Most of the Siemens contracts were awarded initially by the Lagos State, but these were subsequently taken over by the Federal Ministry of Works. In 1974 Siemens guaranteed a loan of ₦35,000 by the United Bank of Africa to the Federal Commissioner. The Commissioner then used the guaranteed loan to purchase shares in Siemens (Nig.) Ltd. In their comments on the report of the Federal Assets Investigation Panel, which brought the above facts to light, all the Federal government had to say was that 'Alhaji Okunnu's acquisition of Siemens shares as well as Siemens Bank loan guarantee were indiscreet and showed bad judgement for a high government official in view of the connections of Siemens (Nig.) Ltd, and the Federal Ministry of Works of which Alhaji Okunnu was the political head'.[67] The choice of words is highly significant. It was not said that the Commissioner's action was illegal, or even improper, or, as the Forster-Sutton Commission was to say about the conduct of Dr Nnamdi Azikiwe, 'conduct unbecoming' (of, in this case, a Federal Commissioner), it was that the Commissioner was 'indiscreet' in his action.

A variant of the above theme is provided by the case of Mr F. A. Ijewere who, before his dismissal from the public service, was Chief of Banking Operations with the Central Bank of Nigeria. Under the 'indigenisation' programme of the government, Mr Ijewere gained ownership of the company Smeaton (Nig.) Ltd., a firm of electrical and plumbing contractors which initially had been foreign-owned. As the Assets Panel put it, 'from the evidence available to it, it was not clear whether Smeaton (Nig.) Ltd, was totally bought or that the original owners were simply displaced'. It was clear, however, that Smeaton (Nig.) Ltd was being owned and managed in the same way as Ebako and Co Ltd (another company owned and managed by Mr Ijewere and whose account with the United Bank for Africa was marked 'company owned by the Chief of Banking Operations, CBN'). Between mid-1973 and mid-1976, Smeaton (Nig.) Ltd

> handled electrical and plumbing contracts worth ₦18,418,361. Of this sum of contract, ₦2,160,783 was awarded by the Central Bank of Nigeria . . . and another contract worth ₦3,739,352 was sub-awarded to Smeaton (Nig.) Ltd, by G. Cappa [an Italian building and construction company] who have been major contractors with the Central Bank.

(Mr Ijewere also owned ₦40,000 worth of shares in G. Cappa, shares supposedly acquired through 'Loans and Dividends' in 1974).

The foregoing is of course only a partial picture. With the prospects of the oil boom before it, the military, in the second national development plan (1970—74) had stated that one of its objectives would be to have Nigeria and Nigerians gain control of 'the commanding heights of the economy', which in effect meant reducing the foreign domination of the productive sector of the economy. In furtherance of that objective, the Nigerian Enterprises Promotion Decree (the Indigenisation Decree) was promulgated in 1972,[68] a decree which became fully operative on 1 April 1974. To facilitate the provisions of the Decree, a Nigerian Enterprises Promotion Board and a publicly funded Bank for Commerce and Industry was set up by the government, which also directed that the commercial banks were to allocate at least 40 per cent of all loans and advances to Nigerian businesses. Not surprisingly, some of the major beneficiaries of the directive to the commercial banks were political office-holders — military and civilian — and members of the top ranks of the bureaucracy. Two examples will suffice. First, there is the case of Dr Adetoro, a one-time lecturer in education at the University of Lagos who subsequently became one of the 'new men' commissioners. He was able to secure loans worth ₦118,932 which enabled him to purchase some 60,201 shares in 13 different companies even though, at the time the loans were being acquired and the shares purchased, he was supposed to have a deficit with the banks amounting to some ₦121,959. The second case is that of Mr Philip Asiodu, who before his compulsory retirement from the civil service had been, at different times, a permanent secretary in the Ministry of Mines and Power; Energy and Petroleum; and Urban Affairs and Housing. Between 1974 and 1975, while having a 'total credit balance of ₦15,107 with various bank accounts', Mr Asiodu was able to raise first a loan of M345,000 in his personal capacity, then one for ₦1,105,000 'by companies of which members of his immediate family alone or with himself as partner were sole owners'. It should be pointed out that these examples are in no way unique but merely illustrative. Also, it should not be understood that it is being suggested that the behaviour of this 'class' as described is in some way or the other illegal. All that could be inferred from the description, which has already been stated above, is simply that with a high degree of centralisation of political power, and the absence of any form of public accountability, the exploitation of office-holding for personal, private ends becomes inevitable and inescapable. Since a military regime is characterised by centralisation of power and the absence of accountability, the exploitation of office in the form described becomes an essential characteristic of military rule.

Resources from bank loans and 'kickbacks' from the award of contracts went into the purchase of stocks and shares and on-going enterprises – made possible under the 'indigenisation' programme – or into commercial housing and the acquisition of 'farm estates'. The disclosures before the Assets Investigation Panel showed, for example, that at the time the military governors were thrown out of office following the July 1975 coup, the average commercial property holdings of each of the governors was some eight houses ranging in value from ₦49,000 to ₦120,000 and no fewer than seven of the high-ranking members of the military – including the last military Head of State, General Obasanjo – retired or was retired from the army to start a new career in large-scale farming. All acquired their farming estates while the military was in power.[69] The bulk of the commercial property holdings of the regime managers, interestingly enough, were in the middle-class residential areas of the main urban centres. The Rent Decree of 1976, which was aimed at controlling rents in the urban areas, actually led to an increase in rent, an increase of between a third and a half, in these areas. As most of the residents in such housing were public servants who therefore had their rents highly subsidised by state agencies — the various governments, para-statals and universities — the effect of the Rent Decree was simply to legalise the transfer of public funds — in the form of rent subsidies — from the state's coffers into the pockets of those who held the reins of political power.[70]

Summarily then, military rule and the oil boom could be said to have fostered the growth and spread of what might best be described as 'commercial capitalism',[71] enabling the military hierarchy and their civilian aides — the top bureaucrats, a few university men and the indigenous mercantilists — to emerge as the new dominant property-owning 'class' in the society. Whereas under the civilian regime, the key sectors of the economy — finance, banking and insurance, construction and manufacturing, prospecting and mining — had remained economic enclaves within the larger economic system and were controlled and dominated by foreign business interests, the spread of commercial capitalism has enabled the new property-owning class to make an incursion into these sectors, in some cases displacing the foreign interests; in others, collaborating with such interests in extracting the surplus which control makes possible. But in this enterprise, the main losers have been the rural farmers whose interests have been almost totally neglected by the 'new rich' in the pursuit of their collective interest, the utilisation of state power to accumulate wealth.

MILITARY RULE IN PERSPECTIVE

Were one to take a random sample of a year's newspapers of most of the developing countries, say a couple of years after independence, some of the recurring themes would be found to be political harassment — and imprisonment — of political opponents, strikes, riots and demonstrations and inter- and intra-communal conflicts exhibiting varying degrees of violence. There is perhaps nothing specifically unique in this. If one were to carry out the same exercise in some of the developed countries, for instance Italy, the picture that emerged would probably not be too different. Nevertheless, such events are often taken by political commentators and social scientists as evidence of the instability of the new states. One might want to say that this is just another example of bias, but such a reaction would hardly be helpful; for there is one crucial difference between the developing and the developed state with respect to what are taken as 'indices' of instability: the difference is that where the developed states are capable of absorbing such events — that is, such events leave the basic economic processes and the economic market place relatively undisturbed — in the developing states the reverse is the case; sociopolitical conflicts usually lead to a disruption of the economic market. Since in the last analysis the primary concern of most people is the economic market, it is hardly surprising therefore that there is concern with questions of political instability.

It is in this context that one should see some of the attempts to *justify* military intervention in the new states. It is not being suggested that such attempts are in any way recommendatory — inviting the military to intervene — though the dividing line between recommendation and justification can be very thin. But once the military have intervened, such intervention, which in the context of the developed states would have been decried, is seen as warrantable and to be approved. The steps involved in this justificatory exercise are straightforward enough. There are supposed to be certain characteristics which distinguish military organisations from other organisations — a hierarchical chain of command, discipline, an esprit de corps, and an interest in and concern with the most modern and sophisticated weapons. These characteristics are then said to make the military 'modernity-oriented'. From the foregoing, it is supposed to follow that once the military have intervened, they are strategically placed to start the process of modernising the society, with modernisation bringing about the desired stability.[72] Though taken as a justificatory argument, it is obvious that the 'modernisation thesis' could just as easily be construed as a recommendation for the military to intervene.

However, whether interpreted as recommendation or as justification, there are many points about the 'modernisation thesis' which are open to question. First, even if it is conceded that armies are interested in the technology of modern warfare, it does not follow from this that they are 'modernity-oriented'.[73] Secondly, the frequency with which particular armies stage coups and counter-coups cannot but cast serious doubt on any talk of an 'esprit de corps' among the armies of the developing countries. But more importantly, the historical evidence of the military in power in the African states runs completely counter to the whole notion of the 'modernising' soldier, and however logically neat the modernisation thesis may seem, one cannot escape from the hard empirical evidence. Where the theory does not fit the facts, since we cannot change the facts, it seems obvious that it is the theory which will have to be changed.

A different thesis, somewhat contrary to the 'modernisation thesis' but nevertheless aimed at the validation of military intervention and military rule, has been put forward by Ali Mazrui.[74] For Mazrui, to explain the instability of the new states of Africa, we would have to look at the character of the members of the ruling elite who took over power at the time of independence. In the main, a good many of these had had their education at the metropolitan centres where they were exposed to alien cultures, cultures which they inadequately assimilated, but nevertheless were sufficiently influenced by to make them alienated from their indigenous cultural heritage. Put differently, the inadequate assimilation of the metropolitan culture only served to turn these members of the elite into cultural schizophrenics, or as Fanon was to put it, men with black skins but wearing white masks, whose only interest is to be like the white man but who succeed only in 'aping' the white man.

Cut off from their cultural roots, the elite find themselves isolated from the masses whom they despise but pretend to lead. The cultural—intellectual divorce means in effect that the elite are incapable of mobilising. Yet to retain their power positions the elite has of necessity to rely on the support of the masses. This sets up conflicts between the elite and the masses which become exacerbated as the elite themselves compete to broaden their individual power positions. The outcome of this cross-conflict is of course the instability that has become all too familiar a phenomenon.

With the military, on the other hand, the position is different. Not having been culturally traumatised like the elite and being less educated, on the whole, than the elite, they are closer to people and therefore can share their hopes and aspirations, fears and anxieties. The military, or as Mazrui would call them, the *lumpenmilitariat*, share the same cultural idiom with the people, and particularly, the workers, the *lumpenproletariat*. If the military, on taking power, could join forces with the working class, the marriage of the lumpenmilitariat and the lumpenproletariat, of the forces of destruction and those of production, then we would have the recipe for a cultural rediscovery — it is taken that colonialism was destructive of indigenous culture — and cultural resurgence, and hence the assertion of a political identity rooted in the traditions and history of the people. And for political stability to be achieved a necessary condition (it is not clear if Mazrui is not also suggesting that it is a sufficient condition) would be the assertion of such an identity.

The 'Mazrui thesis' looks plausible enough, but like the 'modernisation thesis', the plausibility derives largely from a seemingly logical coherence — conclusions appearing to follow from stated premises — in the presentation of the thesis. But once deny the premises and the whole thesis collapses. Statements about cultural alienation and depersonalisation are put forward as 'facts' and hence tend to be accepted when in reality they are no more than mere assertions, the truth of which is yet to be demonstrated. Again, to talk of a cultural resurgence presumes that there is a homogeneous culture when in actuality what is so characteristic of African states is not so much a cultural homogeneity as one of extreme heterogeneity. Given Mazrui's perceptiveness and intellectual sensitivity, it is particularly disturbing to find that his approach to 'culture' is so crudely archaeological. Culture is spoken of as if it is a thing to be 'dug up' and exhibited, to be 'discovered' (or rediscovered?). That was precisely the notion which underlay the Nigerian military's excursion into 'cultural rediscovery', the colossal exercise in waste and futility which was called FESTAC, the Second World Black and African Festival of Arts and Culture.[75] FESTAC may have provided a titillating entertainment for the various dignitaries – and the elite segment of the Nigerian population – invited to watch the many displays of dances and 'culture' but it had little to do with the oppressive poverty of the present and the relative intellectual emptiness of the past which represents such a crucial part of the African experience. This is his culture, for culture if it means anything must represent something living and dynamic and not just a fossilised remnant of the past. Lastly, if the military can be said to be culturally closer to the 'people' than the elite, it is not because the military, unlike the elite, have not been exposed to the alienating impact of a foreign culture, it is because the military are yet to be freed from the bonds of illiteracy which still continue to handicap the mass of the African population. And it must surely be an odd argument which would seek to justify, in the extremely complex world of the present, in which Africans form such a large proportion of the 'wretched of the earth', a system of rule by the largely non-literate.

There may be no way of preventing the military, for as long as they have a superiority in the means of mass destruction, from seizing political power in the newly independent states of Africa. But by the same token, we do not have to go out of our way to try to justify such seizures.

5

Political Institutions of the Second Republic

Though it is not uncommon to find the period of military rule, the period from January 1966 to September 1979, being referred to — for instance, in the Nigerian press — as the 'second republic', that expression will be used here specifically to refer to the system of rule which was inaugurated on 1 October 1979 and which was marked by two events: first, the coming into being of *The Constitution of the Federal Republic of Nigeria 1979*; and second, the installation of a popularly elected civilian as Executive President of the Republic of Nigeria. Thus, references in this book to the political institutions of the second republic will be to the institutions provided for in *The Constitution of the Federal Republic of Nigeria 1979*.

There are no set procedures to dictate the pattern of military withdrawal from politics. On the one hand, demilitarisation could involve nothing more than a formal handing over of power to a selected body of civilians as was the case in Sierra-Leone when Dr Siaka Stevens was invited by the military to form a government after Brigadier Juxton-Smith was overthrown by his own non-commissioned officers.[1] In this case, Stevens simply 'inherited' the pre-existent constitution though he was to change that constitution once he assumed power as Prime Minister. On the other hand, the process can be more elaborate, involving the setting up of a constituent assembly, the drawing up of a new constitution, the holding of popular elections and the final handing over to a successful party. That was the procedure adopted by Ghana in 1969 when the military administration headed by General Afrifa handed over power to Dr Kofi Busia and his United Peoples' Party. In this instance, the military did not seek to set any limits on what the constituent assembly could do or to modify in any way the constitution produced by the assembly.[2] The pattern adopted by Nigeria followed closely the Ghanaian example, but departed from it in two significant respects. First, the 'preparatory stage' was more complex: it involved two stages, a constitution drafting stage to prepare a 'draft constitution', and a constituent assembly stage which produced the formal constitutional document. Secondly, unlike in Ghana, not only did the military amend certain sections of the constitution produced by the assembly, but it had written into the document decrees which the military itself had passed, thereby conferring on the decrees the status of a constitutional enactment which could not be altered except by the process of a formal constitutional amendment.[3]

The Constitution Drafting Committee (CDC), a body of 50 men,[4] was composed on the basis of two 'representatives' from each state and a number of others chosen to represent 'disciplines considered to have direct relevance to Constitution-making, namely — history, law, economics and other social sciences, especially, political science'.[5] The CDC's function was 'to produce an initial draft of a Constitutional arrangement which would provide a sound basis for the continuing existence of a united Nigeria'. The CDC was required to produce a 'draft' before the end of September 1976 — in other words, it had a year within which to produce the 'draft' which would then be submitted to a Constituent Assembly of representatives elected by the newly constituted local government councils.

In his address to the opening session of the CDC on 18 October 1975, the new Head of the federal military government, Brigadier Murtala Muhammed, had talked of the type of Constitution which he thought Nigeria needed: 'the Constitution which we need has to reflect our experience, while at the same time paying attention to the equally important fact that a good Constitution must also be capable of influencing the nature and orderly development of the politics of the people'. Put differently, what was required was a 'mix' of behavioural norms and institutional structures such as would prevent not only a 'reopening of those deep splits which caused trauma in the country' but also 'help to solve problems that may arise in the future'. Part of the 'trauma' of the country — which was to be prevented — was the tendency to regard the winning of elections as 'a life and death struggle which justified all means — fair and foul'; the fact that 'the interest of the party leaders came to supplant the interest of the public and indeed of their parties, because once in power there was hardly any question of public or party accountability'; and the fact that 'orderly succession to power was virtually impossible'.

Given these facts then, 'a good Constitution' should seek to (a) 'eliminate cut-throat political competition based on a system or rules of winner-takes-all'; (b) 'discourage institutionalised opposition to the Government in power, and instead, develop consensus politics and Government'; (c) 'establish the principle of public accountability for all holders of public office'; (d) 'eliminate over centralisation of power in a few hands, and as a matter of principle, decentralise power whereever possible'; (e) 'evolve a free and fair electoral system which will ensure adequate representation of our peoples at the centre'; and (f) 'considering our past difficulties with population counts', provide 'measures which will have the effect of depoliticizing population census in the country . . . '. It was, however, not sufficient to state what was to be avoided, discouraged or eliminated, for as Muhammed went on to say, the military administration had also given thought to what was required and it was the administration's view that this included: (i) 'genuine and truly national political parties' though to 'avoid the harmful effects of a proliferation of national parties', the CDC might want to consider the desirability of working out 'specific criteria by which their number would be limited'. (More specifically still, if indeed the CDC could 'discover some means by which Government can be formed without the involvement of political parties', then Muhammed said that the CDC should feel free so to recommend); (ii) 'an Executive Presidential system of Government', a system 'in which the President and Vice-President are elected . . . [and] are brought into office in a manner so to reflect the Federal character of the country'; (iii) 'an independent Judiciary to be guaranteed by incorporating appropriate provisions in the Constitution as well as by establishing institutions such as the Judicial Service Commission'; (iv) ' . . . corrective institutions [such] as the Corrupt Practices Tribunal and Public Complaints Bureau'; and (v) 'constitutional restriction on the number of states to be further created'.

But here a distinction should perhaps be made. While the foregoing prescriptions were 'conclusions' which the Supreme Military Council had reached, they were only being commended for the 'careful consideration' of the CDC and in that respect were different from what the military were committed to, these being 'a Federal system of Government; and a free democratic and lawful system of Government which guarantees fundamental human rights'; and 'the creation of viable political institutions which will ensure maximum participation and consensus and orderly succession to political power'. It is, however, one thing to say one is committed to something which is expressible in the present continuous, and another to say one is committed to something expressible in the future conditional. In the former case, commitment entails action which can be taken in the present, in the latter, to action which will be taken only if certain states are not realised. The latter could therefore be taken as a form of warning: 'if there is no orderly succession to political power, then . . . '. In which case, one could take the commitment to a federal system of government as a parameter set by the military from which the CDC ought not to deviate, or in any way vary.[6]

Finally, Muhammed said that since the announcement of the appointment of the members of the CDC, an ongoing debate had been generated over the place of ideology within any constitutional framework. In so far as the military were concerned, 'the evolution of a doctrinal concept is usually predicated upon the general acceptance by the people of a national political philosophy and consequently', the considered view of the military administration was that 'until our people, or a large majority of them, have acknowledged a common ideological motivation, it would be fruitless to proclaim any particular philosophy or ideology in our Constitution'. The CDC's approach should therefore be pragmatic, the aim being to produce a draft which 'must be workable and acceptable to the majority of [the] people'.

The CDC's final 'draft' followed in its broad outlines the various points 'commended' to it for 'careful consideration' by the Head of the Military Government, but this is not to say that the 'commendations' dictated the main provisions of the draft. It is enough to say that there was a broad coincidence of view between the commendations of the military and what the CDC had proposed in its draft. The Constituent Assembly, which met about a year after the CDC submitted its draft, produced a Constitution which followed very closely the proposals put forward by the CDC. In discussing the institutional structure of the second republic, it will therefore be more convenient to follow what was proposed in the Constitution, reference being made to the CDC's draft only in so far as there are differences between what the CDC proposed and the Constitution devised by the Constituent Assembly. In what follows, then, there will be (i) a description of the constitutional framework; (ii) some discussion of what sort of consensus that framework represents; (iii) a tentative assessment of the federal nature of the constitutional settlement. But before all of this, it might be useful to pinpoint in which respects there has been a departure in the second from the first republic.

DEPARTURES FROM THE FIRST REPUBLIC

The most fundamental way in which the second republic departs from the first is in the form of government. Whereas the system of government in the first republic had been based on a 'Cabinet' form of government drawn on the lines of the 'Westminster model', the executive being part of, and deriving its power from being included in, the legislature, the second republic's form is Presidential, with close parallels to the American system of government, in which there is a clear separation between the executive and the legislature, the executive deriving its power from the direct popular vote of the electorate and from the constitution. But though there are parallels and similarities between the Presidentialism of the second republic and the American form, the two do differ in at least one very important respect. In the Nigerian system, the two Houses of the National Assembly, the House of Representatives and the Senate, have equal powers and either can initiate bills to appropriate monies from the Consolidated Fund of the Republic. And since the Senate in the Nigerian system, like its counterpart in the United States, is also given the power to approve specific classes of appointments by the President, one might argue that political power is weighted more towards the Nigerian Senate than the American Senate.

Secondly, the process of government under the second republic is to be informed by specifically stated fundamental objectives and directive principles of state policy. As the 'Report' on the 'Draft Constitution' put it:

> [the] 1963 Constitution like its predecessors spoke only in terms of power and of rights, but never of duties. The latter are taken for granted. The Constitution assumes that those who wield the power of the state will be conscious of, and responsive to, its obligation and responsibilities. And so it says nothing of the duties of the government towards its subjects.[7]

But as was shown in Chapter 3, power became an end in itself, to be used mainly in the pursuit of the self-interest of the political 'ruling class', a class which claimed rights and privileges but refused to recognise any correlative duties or obligations to the rights claimed. To quote once more from the CDC 'Report':

> Governments in developing countries have tended to be preoccupied with power and its material perquisites. Given the conditions of under-development, power offers the opportunity of a lifetime to rise above the general level of poverty and squalor that pervade the society. It provides a rare opportunity to acquire wealth and prestige, to be able to distribute benefits in the form of jobs, contracts, scholarships and gifts of money and so on to one's relatives and political allies. Such is the pre-occupation with power and its material benefits that political ideals as to how society

can be organised and ruled to the best advantage of all hardly enter into the calculation.[8]

A statement of 'fundamental objectives and directive principles of state policy' is thus an attempt at stating 'how society can be organised . . . to the best advantage of all'. Fundamental objectives refer to those goals and long-term ends which a government, it is thought, ought to commit itself to, while the directive principles of state policy refer to those means by which the stated objectives are best to be achieved. Examples of 'fundamental objectives' as stated in the 1979 Constitution are the following: '. . . national integration shall be actively encouraged, whilst discrimination on the grounds of place of origin, sex, religion, status, ethnic or linguistic association or ties shall be prohibited' (s.15(2)); 'every citizen shall have equality of rights, obligations and opportunities before the law' (s.17(2)(a)); while 'directive principles' are illustrated by the following: 'the composition of the Government of the Federation or any of its agencies and the conduct of its affairs shall be carried out in such a manner as to reflect the federal character of Nigeria . . . there shall be no predominance of persons from a few states or from a few ethnic or other sectional groups in that government or any of its agencies' (s.14(3)); and '[the government shall] encourage intermarriage among persons from different places of origin or different religious, ethnic or linguistic association or ties' (s.15(3)(c)).

However, there are two points which should be noted about the statement of the objectives. The first is that they are not rights in the sense of 'fundamental rights'. To say, as the Constitution does say, that it shall be an objective of the state to provide free education for all citizens is not to say, and certainly does not entail, that the citizen thereby has a 'right' to free education. The statement 'it shall be the objective of the state to provide free education' is an elliptical statement which expanded would read something like: 'subject to the availability of resources — human and material — and there being no equally competing but more pressing demand on those resources (for example, the demand for food), then, an objective which it should be the duty of the state to pursue would be that of providing free education'. Fundamental objectives are thus strictly speaking contingent and therefore dependent on certain other factors which are yet to be specified. Because they are contingent, they are not, or cannot be made, justiciable (s.6(c)), that is, made the subject of an action before the courts of law. In this respect, 'fundamental objectives' are unlike 'fundamental rights' which are made justiciable. Admittedly 'rights' are also contingent but contingent in a different sense altogether. To say, for example, that one has the right to free speech is to say that one is free to say what one likes but only subject to the conditions (a) that one recognises a similar right in others, and (b) that the right to free speech does not include the right to slander or libel others. The contingency on which a 'right' depends is thus the contingency of equal recognition and not a dependency on the *prior* existence or provision of particular facilities or states of affairs.

The second thing that needs be noted about 'fundamental objectives' is that they can only be stated in the most general way. They therefore lack specificity, a lack of specificity which is in large part a direct consequence of the contingent nature of the 'objectives'. And it is the high level of generality of the 'objectives' that makes the statement of 'directive principles' necessary. The 'directive principles' thus add content to the objectives which would otherwise be 'empty'. But then, the question may be asked: if the objectives can only be stated in the most general way and cannot be made justiciable, unlike the large body of constitutional provisions, why include them in the Constitution and hence confer on them the look of spurious legality? The simple answer is, of course, that though not justiciable, the objectives do provide a yardstick against which the activities of government can be measured and evaluated, and, as such, they serve to provide a normative standard to guide government action and the behaviour of public officers. They serve as a charter by which action can be validated and explained. Like the Preamble to the American constitution, the objectives are a statement of the collective faith of the people not just in the present but also in the future of their society.

The third point of departure lies in the composition of the

state assemblies. In the first republic, regional Houses of Assembly were empowered by the constitution to determine the way in which the House was to be constituted. This enabled regional governments to determine not only the total membership of the Assembly, but to draw and redraw constituencies, a practice which made for gerrymandering.[9] The membership of the Northern House of Assembly, for example, was increased from 90 to 130 in 1956 and again to 177 in 1961. Similar increases took place in the Western region. In the second republic, on the other hand, state constituencies are tied to federal constituencies such that for every one constituency for elections to the Federal House of Representatives, there must be three state constituencies (s.85) and since the composition of the House is put at 450 members, a number which can only be altered by a process of constitutional amendment, it follows that the membership composition of a state assembly can be altered only through an amendment to the federal constitution.

Fourthly, political parties are for the first time given constitutional recognition, in that not only are parties defined in the Constitution (s.209) but the way in which party constitutions and rules are to be formulated (s.203), the control and regulation of party funds (s.201), the mode of election of party leaders and restrictions on the form in which party funds are to be held (s.205(3)) are all provided for in the Constitution. Even the right to change one's party affiliation is regulated. Thus s.37(b) of the Constitution provides that:

> a person elected to a legislative house as a candidate who was not sponsored by any political party shall not be entitled to join or declare himself to be a member of a political party until the general election next following his election as such candidate.[10]

This, in effect, rules out the possibility of the carpet-crossing which was so common a phenomenon during the first republic but in the context of a 'separation of powers', it is not by any means clear whether the restriction provided by s.73(b) is as significant or important as it might be in a system with a parliamentary executive as was the case in the first republic.

Fifthly, the second republic gives constitutional recognition to local government authorities as 'third-tier' agencies of government, with particular functions which are specified in the Constitution.[11] As the Constitution puts it (s.7(1)):

> The system of local government by democratically elected local government councils is under this Constitution guaranteed; and accordingly, the Government of every State shall ensure their existence under a Law which provides for the establishment, structure, composition, finance and functions of such councils.

The reference to 'finance' and 'functions' should not be misconstrued. With respect to the functions of local government councils, while state Assemblies can delegate specific powers to local councils, in other words, add to the constitutionally prescribed powers of local authorities, they cannot, without being in contravention of the Constitution, derogate from the prescribed list. Similarly, with respect to the finance of local councils, state Assemblies can only make provision for *additional* or *supplemental* funds to local governments since by s.149(4) and s.149(5) it is provided that:

> the amount standing to the credit of local government councils in the Federation Account[12] shall also be allocated to the States for the benefit of their local government councils on such terms and in such manner as may be prescribed by the National Assembly (s149(4));

and:

> each state shall maintain a special account to be called 'State Joint Local Government Account' into which shall be paid all allocations to the local government councils of the state from the Federation Account and from the Government of the State (s.149(5)).

But more important is the requirement that:

> each state shall pay to local government councils in its area

of jurisdiction *such proportion of its total revenue on such terms and in such a manner as may be prescribed by the National Assembly* (s.149(6)) (Italics mine).

It would therefore seem, on a strict construction of s.149(6), that with respect to finance, all the state Assembly could do would be to give legal recognition to the 'prescriptions' of the National Assembly.

But the question could be asked: 'What legal force is to be attached to the expression "is under this Constitution guaranteed" in s.7(1)?' Who does the 'guaranteeing'? And what does it mean to talk of 'democratically elected local government councils'? Taking first the question of 'guarantee', one could consider the extreme case, the case where a state Assembly refuses 'to ensure' the existence of local government councils. It is by no means certain if there is anything anyone can do, but presumably, there could be two possibilities. These are: (a) action by the individual citizen. Any voter resident in the state, by claiming to 'have an interest' could appeal to the courts for an order of specific performance enjoining the state government to 'ensure the existence' of local government councils.[13] But even if the courts were to recognise the voter's 'interest' and therefore rule in his favour, it is difficult to see how such a ruling could be enforced; (b) the federal government could seek a ruling by the courts that the state government in not 'ensuring the existence' of local government authorities was thereby undermining the Constitution. On the assumption that the federal authority secured a favourable ruling by the Courts, the President could then proceed to claim that the state government's action constituted a 'threat' to law, order and security and under s.265(5) attempt to proclaim a 'state of emergency' in the state, which if successful would enable the National Assembly to pass the necessary legislation to 'ensure the existence' of local authorities in the state. There are many imponderables involved in such a procedure. But this leads to the 'weak case'. Once such councils were established, there is nothing to prevent a 'recalcitrant' state government dissolving such elected councils as there might be and replacing them with 'caretaker' committees made up of the government's nominees. Faced with such a challenge, perhaps the only course of action open to the federal authority would be to withhold the state's share of the revenue allocated to local governments. But on the present evidence, such a course of action hardly seems likely.[14] In seeking to find remedies for the ills of the first republic through constitutional provisions, it would appear that the 'founding fathers' of the second republic may have succeeded in creating a legal 'Pandora's box' which if opened could easily overwhelm the ends they sought to achieve.

The sixth point of departure of the second from the first republic lies in the provision of a 'Code of Conduct', backed by a 'Code of Conduct Bureau' and a 'Code of Conduct Tribunal', to regulate the public behaviour of public officers and so check abuses in the exercise of state power on the part of public officers. As argued in the CDC 'Report':

> Our recent experience has spot-lighted the extent to which corruption and abuse of office has eaten deeply into the fabric of the public service of this country. We are all convinced that if a recurrence of that experience were to be effectively checked it is essential that provisions be made in the Constitution to ensure that persons who are entrusted with public authority do not abuse their trust and enrich themselves or defraud the nation.[15]

Generally, the 'Code' prohibits public officers[16] from putting themselves in any position in which there could arise a conflict between their personal interests and their official duties and responsibilities. Thus, for instance, the President, Vice-President, Governors and Deputy Governors, Ministers (and commissioners) 'or any public officer who holds the office of a Permanent Secretary or head of a public corporation, university, or other para-statal organisation' are forbidden from accepting: 'a loan, except from government or its agencies, a bank, building society or other financial institution recognised by law; and any benefit of whatever nature from any company, contractor, or businessman, or the nominee or agent of such a person'.[17] More or less the same class of people are prohibited from maintaining or operating a bank account in any country outside Nigeria;[18] and all public officers are required within three months of the 'Code' coming into operation or 'immediately after taking office and thereafter (a) at the end of every four years; and (b) at the end of his term of office' to submit to the Code of Conduct Bureau 'a written declaration of all [his] properties, assets and liabilities, and those [of their] spouse[s], or unmarried children under the age of 21 years.[19] In operational terms, the assets requirement could mean that in the space of four years, the Bureau would have to process some four million[20] 'declarations' of assets and liabilities, a task which would require an 'army' of public servants, who themselves would have to declare their assets. Logically, one could end up with a situation in which every citizen would be employed processing each other's declaration of assets, which would make of the whole exercise a meaningless and purposeless task. No doubt more careful judgement will prevail but it will do so at the price of the heavy cost involved in having the constitution amended.

Be that as it may, there is to be the Code of Conduct Bureau,[21] whose function, beside receiving, retaining and examining the declarations of assets made by public officers, is to receive complaints about 'non-compliance with or breach of [the] Code and . . . to refer such complaints unless the person concerned makes a written admission of such breach or non-compliance, to the Code of Conduct Tribunal'.[22] Where the Tribunal finds the report of a contravention proved, it could impose any of the following penalties:

(a) vacation of office or seat in any legislative house as the case may be; (b) disqualification from membership of a legislative house and from the holding of any public office for a period not exceeding ten years;[23] and (c) seizure and forfeiture to the State of any property acquired in abuse or corruption of office.[24]

The guilty officer could also be liable to criminal prosecution where the conduct is also a criminal offence. There is provision for appeal to the Federal Court of Appeal 'at the instance of any party to the proceedings' against any punishment imposed by the Tribunal, but should any such appeal fail, the offender may not apply to the President for the latter's exercise of his prerogative of mercy.

Finally, the second republic departs from the first in the way the Constitution allocates the 'functions' or 'powers' of government as between the federal and the state authorities. Whereas in the first republic, the respective powers of the federal and state governments were listed in separate schedules to the constitution, and the areas of joint jurisdiction enumerated in a concurrent list, in the second republic, only a 'Concurrent List' and an 'Exclusive Federal List' are shown, the presumption being that any power not included in either the Exclusive Federal List or the Concurrent List is thereby reserved to the state governments.

From the foregoing, it is obvious that a radical departure has been made with the second republic, but just how radical that departure is will become still clearer when the main institutions of government, the executive, the legislature and the judiciary are examined.[25]

THE INSTITUTIONS OF GOVERNMENT UNDER THE SECOND REPUBLIC

Given the experience of other African states with an executive presidential system of government, it is somewhat surprising that the CDC should nevertheless have recommended it as the system most suited to Nigeria, the statements of the Head of the Federal Military Government at the opening session of the CDC notwithstanding. Admittedly, the CDC's Sub-committee on the Executive did present a set of persuasive arguments in support of their recommendation of a presidential system[26] — a recommendation which the CDC in plenary session accepted and which the Constituent Assembly ratified — but persuasive as these arguments were, they were nevertheless not conclusive. Ultimately, the rationale for accepting the change to an Executive Presidential system can be seen to lie in the near complete disillusionment of Nigerians with a parliamentary executive type of government and hence the desire to experiment with something different. At the worst, the system may be just as 'bad', as intolerable, as that which was being rejected. On the other hand, it might just succeed and given an even chance of success or failure, one may as well 'experiment'. The odds in favour of experimenting improve to something better than even when one adds the fact that an executive presidential system has, at least in principle, the added advantage of discouraging a zero-sum conception of politics, the conception which underlay much of the behaviour of government officials during the first republic.

THE EXECUTIVE

The central institution and the key figure within the configural framework of the second republic is the President, who is the Head of State, the Chief Executive of the Federation and Commander-in-Chief of the Armed Forces of the federation (s.122(2)). His being Chief Executive means that the executive powers of the state are vested in the President, power which he may exercise either directly or through the Vice-President, ministers of the Federal Government or officers of the federal public service (s.5(1)(a)). This means that either directly or through his ministers, the President is empowered to give effect to all acts of the National Assembly, the federal legislature. Acts of the National Assembly, on the other hand, cannot have the force of law, unless they are assented to by the President. That assent, however, must be given within a period not exceeding 30 days from the day the Act, having been duly passed by the two houses of the National Assembly, is received by the President.

The Constitution is silent on the question whether, in giving his assent, the President has to assent to the whole, or a part, of a bill of the National Assembly, but the presumption would perhaps be that he has to do so in whole and not in part. In other words, if the President feels that only a part of a bill meets with his approval, then he will either have to repress his objections to the parts of the bill he does not approve of and therefore assent to the whole bill, or veto the whole bill. If, however, a bill is vetoed by the President, and the same bill is passed by a two-thirds majority of *each* house of the Assembly, then the bill becomes law irrespective of the President's veto (s.54(5)). In the case of a 'money bill', that is a bill which imposes a charge on the revenues of the Federation, a veto by the President will be bypassed if the same bill is passed by a two-thirds majority of the National Assembly sitting in a *joint* meeting (s.55)(4)).

Besides the power to assent to bills, the President also exercises a wide range of other powers. He and he alone is empowered to present before the National Assembly a statement of the estimated revenues and expenditure of the Federation, that is, the annual Appropriations Bill, and he can do so 'at any time in each financial year'.[27] Should, however, the National Assembly fail to pass the annual Appropriations Act before the beginning of the financial year — on the grounds, for instance, of a fundamental disagreement with the President's proposals — the President could nevertheless still authorise the expenditure of monies from the Consolidated Revenue Fund for the purposes of meeting expenditure necessary to carry out the services of the government of the federation for a period not exceeding six months, provided the amount so authorised does not exceed the sum 'withdrawn from the Consolidated Revenue Fund of the Federation under the provisions of the Appropriation Act passed by the National Assembly for the corresponding period in the immediately preceding financial year, being an amount proportionate to the total amount so authorised for the immediately preceding financial year.'[28] The President can also authorise the withdrawal of monies from the Contingencies Fund of the federation to meet exigencies not envisaged in the annual appropriations bill, but he needs the approval of the National Assembly before such withdrawals can be affected (s.77(1)). Unlike ministers of the federation who can attend a meeting of the National Assembly only when invited to do so, the President can attend any meeting of the Assembly for the purposes of delivering a message to the legislature (s.63(1 & 2)). And subject to the provisions of the Constitution, he can deprive a citizen of Nigeria of his citizenship (s.27(1 & 2)); grant an 'immigrant status' to non-Nigerian spouses of Nigerian citizens (s.29(1)) and generally, make regulations regarding the granting or otherwise of citizenship. The President can also enter into a treaty with other states on behalf of the federation but such a treaty can only be effective if enacted as a law by an act of the National Assembly (s.12(1)).

Certain classes of appointments can only be made by the President, though there are some qualifications to his powers in this respect. For example, he appoints the Auditor-General of the federation, but in doing so he has to act on the advice of the Federal Public Service Commission (FPSC) and the appointment has to be ratified by the Senate.[29] The President could, however, appoint someone to *act* as the Auditor-General without the advice of the FPSC or the approval of the Senate, but anyone so appointed could only act for a period not exceeding six months.[30] The President also appoints the ministers of the federation, subject to ratification by the Senate and the qualification (a) that at least one minister should be appointed from each state of the federation (of which the minister must be an indigene) (s.135(1 & 2)); and (b) that in making such appointments the President give due regard to the 'federal character' of the state, by which is meant that there is no predominance of any one ethnic group among the rank of ministers (s.14(3)). Ministerial appointments, however, become valid where the Senate does not make a return within 21 days of the receipt of the list of nominees sent by the President (s.135(6)). In the appointment of his advisers, the President acts solely on his own discretion, though it is left to the National Assembly to regulate the numbers and remuneration of such advisers (s.139(2)).

The Secretary to the Government of the Federation, the Head of the Civil Service of the federation, permanent secretaries or other chief executive 'in any ministry or department of Government of the federation however so designated', all ambassadors, high commissioners or other principal representatives of Nigeria abroad, and any person on the personal staff of the President, are all appointed by the President. He does not, however, have complete freedom in this respect. The appointment of ambassadors, high commissioners, etc., requires the approval of the Senate to become effective (s.157(4)), and in the appointment of the Head of the Civil Service, the President is required to make his appointment 'from among members of the civil service of the federation or of a state' (s.157(3)).[31] In addition, in making these appointments he is to bear in mind the 'federal character of Nigeria' (s.157(5)). The appointment of the Chief Justice of the Federal Supreme Court is made by the President subject to approval by the Senate but he must seek the advice of the Federal Judicial Service Commission when appointing the President of the Federal Court of Appeal — which appointment, like that of the 15 other judges of the Supreme Court, requires Senate ratification — not fewer than 15 other judges of the Court of Appeal, the Chief Judge of the Federal High Court and such other judges of the High Court as the National Assembly may determine. In contrast, the President is only required to *consult* the Police Service Commission when appointing the Inspector-General of Police (s.196(2)) to whom he may issue any directives as he may deem necessary for the proper maintenance of law and order, directives which the Inspector-General is required to obey.[32] Presumably, then, over his appointing powers, there is a difference between the requirement that the President 'consult' and the requirement that he acts 'on the advice of', the difference being that where in the former case the President need not accept the outcome of his consultation, in the latter, he is expected to follow the advice given.

To the foregoing should be added the power of the President to appoint persons to certain bodies set up under the Constitution, these being the National Population Council (NPC), the Federal Judicial Service Commission (FJSC), the Federal Electoral Commission (FEDECO), the Federal Public Service Commission (FPSC), the Police Service Commission (PSC), the National Security Council (NSC) and the National Defence Council. In appointing the Chairman and members of the NPC, the FJSC, and the FEDECO he is required to *consult* the National Council of State but does not require Senate approval for these appointments. On the other hand, for the FPSC, the PSC, the NPC and the NDC (in the case of the latter two, for the non-*ex officio* members only) he acts on his own initiative but requires Senate approval before those appointments can become effective.[33]

In making these appointments the President exercises the executive powers vested in him. But he is also the Commander-in-Chief of the Nigerian Armed Forces, a role which enables him not only to determine the operational use of the armed forces, but also at his discretion to appoint the Chief of Defence Staff, the Heads of the Army, Navy and Air Force 'and such other branches of the armed forces of the federation as may be established by an Act of the National Assembly' (s.198(1 & 2)). These are extensive powers, including as they do the power to promote and discipline, and are made subject to only two limitations, which are: (a) that the President pays due regard to the federal character of the federation in the appointments he makes; and (b) that the National Assembly can make laws regulating the exercise of the powers of the President as Commander-in-Chief of the Armed Forces. But as the latter constraint is in all likelihood to be exercised *ex post*, this in effect leaves the President with an almost unfettered control over the use of the ultimate coercive powers of the State.[34] Even the requirements which (i) forbid the President from declaring war between the federation and another country without the sanction of a resolution of both Houses of the National Assembly sitting in a joint session; and (ii) state that there has to be the prior approval of the Senate before the President can deploy the armed forces for combat duty outside Nigeria,[35] are hardly likely to prove very effective, as the American experience – in South-East Asia – clearly demonstrates.

Another wide-ranging power of the President is his power to declare a state of emergency by the simple process of causing to be published in the *Official Gazette* of the Government, a proclamation that a state of emergency exists. The conditions which warrant this being done are clearly specified: a state of emergency may be declared when (i) the federation is at war; (ii) there is imminent danger of invasion or involvement in war; (iii) there is a breakdown of public order and public safety which is considered to be serious; (iv) there is a clear danger of such a breakdown occurring; (v) a natural catastrophe or calamity affects a community or section of a community; (vi) there is a threat to the continued existence of the federation; and (vii) there is a request by a state governor supported by a two-thirds majority vote of the state Assembly stating that conditions (iii), (iv) and (v) exist within the state.

On the proclamation of a state of emergency the President is required to send a copy of the *Gazette* containing the proclamation to the President of the Senate and the Speaker of the House of Representatives, both of whom are then obliged to have the notification in the *Gazette* circulated to all the members of their respective Houses and also immediately summon a meeting of the two Houses. If within two days, when the Houses are in session, or ten days if they are not in session, the proclamation is not supported by a two-thirds majority of *all* the members[36] of each House the emergency immediately expires. The emergency also expires once it is revoked, but if it is not, then the state of emergency can only be extended beyond the initial maximum of six months if there is a resolution to that effect by the National Assembly, provided that no such extension exceeds a period of six months at any one time. The main effect of a state of emergency being declared is to suspend the provisions regarding fundamental rights contained in Chapter four of the Constitution.

In 1962, the federal government proclaimed a state of emergency over the Western region as it was then constituted, during which period the federal government not only dissolved the Regional Assembly but also 'suspended' the governor of the region. The emergency afforded the federal government the chance it needed to excise the 'Midwest' from the West. Obviously states of emergency can be exploited by the Executive to assert federal will over any 'recalcitrant' state. To prevent such possible abuses from occurring under the second republic, the Constitution stipulates quite clearly that not only can the federal government not dissolve a state assembly during a state of emergency, but the National Assembly can legislate for the state — over those matters within the state's sphere of jurisdiction — only when it is physically impossible for the members of the state Assembly to meet (s.11(4 & 5)).

Finally, there are the President's powers with regard to the prerogative of mercy: the power to grant any person concerned with or convicted of any offence created by law a pardon, either conditionally or unconditionally; grant a respite from the execution of a punishment imposed, either for a fixed, or an indefinite period; substitute a less severe punishment for that imposed; and remit, either in whole or in part, any punishment imposed for an offence. In exercising his prerogative of mercy, the President is required to consult the Council of State (s.161(2)).

A candidate for the office of the Presidency must be a Nigerian citizen by birth; he has to be at least 35 years old and must not have any characteristics which would have disqualified him from contesting to be a member of the Senate.[37] The President holds office for a term of four years after which he must vacate the office. No one can therefore hold office for a period exceeding two terms (s.128(1)(b)). However, when there is a war in which the territory of Nigeria is physically involved and the President 'considers that it is not practicable to hold elections', the National Assembly may by resolution extend the period of four years from time to time, provided that no such extension exceeds a period of six months at any one time (s.127(3)).[38] To be considered to have been duly elected,[39] a candidate for the office of President, even where he is the only candidate nominated,[40] will still be required to poll a majority of Yes over the No votes and not less than 25 per cent of the votes cast at the election *in each of at least two-thirds* of the states.[41] In other words, it is not possible to have a candidate for the office of the President 'returned unopposed'. The electorate would still have to decide whether they wanted him or not, and should he poll less than 50 per cent plus one of the total votes, he would be considered to have been rejected by the electorate. The situation is somewhat different when there are (a) two and only two competing candidates; and (b) more than two candidates. In the former case, the successful candidate must poll a simple plurality of the total votes cast and he must poll not less than 25 per cent of the votes cast in each of at least two-thirds of the states. In the latter case — a contest with more than two candidates — the successful candidate would still have to satisfy the same conditions as if there were only two candidates. But should no one candidate satisfy the double plurality requirement, then there would have to be a further contest in which the contesting candidates would be (i) the candidate with the highest proportion of the total votes cast; and (ii) the candidate with the majority of votes in the highest number of states. Should more than one candidate meet the condition stated in (ii), then the second candidate would be the candidate with the highest total (of the majority of votes cast in the highest number of states). In which case, the outcome would be determined as in a case where there are two and only two contestants in the first instance. But in the event that the outcome is undetermined, that is, in the improbable case of a 'tie', then the outcome would be determined by constituting the two Houses of the National Assembly and all the state Assemblies into an 'electoral college' and the candidate who had a majority of the votes cast by the college would become the elected candidate. The electoral college is expected to meet within seven days of an 'undetermined' electoral outcome (s.126(4)). The military, before it left office, amended, by decree, the provisions relating to the 'electoral college'. Under that amendment, in the case of an 'undetermined' outcome, there would be a re-run of the whole process with new nominations being called for by the Federal Electoral Commission. (The 1979 elections for the Presidency resulted in a disputed outcome in which the central issue was the interpretation to be given to the expression 'in each of at least two-thirds of the states'. Basically, the courts were asked to resolve what could be construed to be two-thirds of 19 states, the number of states in existence at the time of the elections. The resolution of that dispute will be discussed below when the nature of the 'federal settlement' under the second republic is being examined.)

That the executive arm of government has very wide-ranging powers, powers which could quite easily be abused, should by now be obvious from the description given. But that description has been made in more or less formal terms. What use is made of the powers of the executive, the effectiveness of the checks which the 'separation of powers', associated with a Presidential form of government, is supposed to provide — these and related questions can only be realistically examined by looking at the actual processes of government; at the personality and 'style' of the President, the relationship between the executive and the legislature and the party composition of the legislature, and of course, the diligence of the judiciary. A number of these questions will be discussed when the nature of Nigerian federalism is being examined. But at this stage, it will perhaps be more helpful to complete the description of the formal institutional structure of the governmental system by looking first at the legislature, and secondly, at the judiciary. In the next chapter the question of parties and the electoral system will then be discussed. First, the legislature.

THE LEGISLATURE

The President administers the law, but it is left to the legislature to make the law, and the legislature in this context means the National Assembly, which is composed of the Senate and the House of Representatives. The Constitution expresses this fact thus: 'the National Assembly shall have power to make laws for the peace, order and good government of the federation or any part thereof' in respect to any matter within the exclusive jurisdiction[42] of the federal government and including those matters over which the federal authority shares concurrent jurisdiction with the state governments. In the latter case, however, where there is an inconsistency between legislation by the National Assembly and that by the state Assembly, the state law, to the extent of the inconsistency involved, shall be null and void (s4(5)).

Though the legislative powers of the federation are vested exclusively in the National Assembly, those powers are not necessarily unfettered. All laws of the Assembly are subject to the jurisdiction of the Courts and no law of the Assembly, if it is to be binding, can exclude such jurisdiction (s.4(8)).[43] Similarly, a law of the Assembly with retrospective effect in respect of any criminal offence is to be deemed as being without any force. Subject to these limitations, only by an express act of the National Assembly can monies be appropriated from the Consolidated Revenue Fund of the federation. Admittedly, a President can authorise the expenditure of funds in the services of the federation for up to six months, given that the total sum involved does not exceed the sum appropriated for an equivalent period in the preceding financial year, without the approval of the Assembly. But thereafter, a President who is bent on challenging the legislature will find, short of being indicted for abuse of office, that he will have to come to terms with the legislature if he is to carry through his programme (s.74(2)(3) & (4)). For it is the National Assembly alone which is empowered to cause to be removed from office a President (or Vice-President) accused of gross misconduct or of undermining the Constitution.

To initiate the process for the removal of a President (or Vice-President) from office, it is necessary and sufficient for one-third of the members of the National Assembly to have a notice signed to that effect delivered to the President of the Senate.[44] Within seven days of such a notice — which is expected to contain the full particulars of the allegations made against the President (or Vice-President) — the President of the Senate is required to serve the notice to the incumbent of the office concerned (who may if he so chooses reply to the charges made) and to all the members of the National Assembly, who not later than seven days thereafter must resolve, without any debate, whether the charges are to be investigated or not. On the basis of a positive outcome — that is, a resolution supported by not less than two-thirds of *all the members* of each House of the Assembly — the President of the Senate, within seven days of the resolution being passed, is required to set up a committee of seven persons 'of high integrity, not being members of any Public Service, legislative House or political party' (s.132(5)) to investigate the charges.[45] The President (or Vice-President as the case may be) may if he so desires attend before the Committee to answer the charges against him and also be represented by a counsel of his own choice. The Committee is expected to submit its findings within three months of the members being appointed to the two Houses of the National Assembly.

A negative finding against the incumbent, that is, a finding that the charges are not proven, results in a termination of all proceedings against the incumbent concerned. On the other hand, should the findings be positive and the charges adjudged proven, then within 14 days of each House receiving the report of the Committee, the members must meet to consider the report and if on a resolution of either House, supported by not less than two-thirds of *all* the members of the House, the members decide to accept the report, the holder of the office concerned stands removed from the date of the adoption of the report.[46]

Besides removal on the grounds of gross misconduct, a President (or Vice-President) can also be removed from office on the grounds of incapacity, either of the mind or of the body. During the 'constitutional crisis' of January 1965 — when Dr Azikiwe as President of the federation refused to invite the incumbent Prime Minister, Alhaji Tafawa Balewa, to form a government after his party's success at the federal elections held in the preceding month — it was the threat of a possible removal from office on the grounds of incapacity which, it was reported, eventually made the President capitulate. Given the complicated process involved in having a President (or Vice-President) removed from office on the grounds of gross misconduct, a threat of removal for incapacity would therefore seem to be the most potent threat. Unlike proceedings to have a President removed for gross misconduct which have to start from the legislature, a move to have the President declared incapable of carrying out the functions of his office has to be initiated by members of the executive council of the federation. On the receipt of a resolution signed by not less than two-thirds of the members of the Council by the President of the Senate *and* the Speaker of the House of Representatives, the former is required to arrange for a team of five doctors — one of whom must be the President's own personal physician, the other four being persons of a 'high degree of eminence in the field of medicine' relating to the nature of the incapacity alleged — to examine the President (s.133(4)). If the panel of doctors should find the 'incapacity' to be proven, the President of the Senate, to whom the report of the panel is to be sent, would then cause a notice of the panel's report, signed by himself and the Speaker of the House of Representatives, to be published in the *Official Gazette* of the Federation and the President (or Vice-President) would be adjudged removed from office on the grounds of incapacity from the date of the publication of the *Gazette*. (s.133(3)). It might be argued that because of the way the Council of Ministers is composed — the President has to appoint at least one member (who must be an indigene) from each state — and the right of the President to dismiss, at his sole discretion, any Minister of the Federation, the likelihood of having a President (or Vice-President) removed for incapacity is very small and hence a President need fear no real threat from that source. On the other hand, since it only requires the collaboration of perhaps not more than two dozen persons to cause the President to be removed for incapacity[47] there could in fact be a realistic weapon in the hands of the opponents of an overbearing President.

Much of the ordinary business of the Assembly is conducted in committees and already there are some 26 of these in the House of Representatives.[48] Decisions of the Assembly, however, have to be reached — on the basis of a simple majority (unless otherwise prescribed) of all those present and voting — by each House sitting as a body. Committees have therefore to report to a House for the purposes of legislative decision-making and to facilitate this, each House has a Business Committee whose function is to schedule the reporting of Committee business before a meeting of the House. A House is properly constituted to take a decision if at the time a decision is to be taken there is a quorum in the House, the quorum being one-third of the total members of the House. The presiding officer in a meeting of the Senate is the President of the Senate and that for the House of Representatives is the Speaker of the House of Representatives, but in the event of a *joint meeting* of both Houses, it is the President of the Senate who presides, and only in his absence, the Speaker of the House of Representatives (s.49(2)). To enhance its legislative capability, the National Assembly and its committees have the power to conduct an investigation, or order an investigation, into any matter whatsoever. A proper appreciation of what this entails is probably best conveyed by quoting the Constitution:

s.82(1) . . . each House of the National Assembly shall have power by resolution published in its journal or in the *Official Gazette* of the Government of the Federation to direct or cause to be directed an investigation into —

    (a) any matter or thing with respect to which it has power to make laws;

    (b) the conduct of affairs of any person, authority, ministry or government department charged, or intended to be charged, with the duty of or responsibility for —

(i) executing or administering laws enacted by the National Assembly, and,

(ii) disbursing or administering moneys appropriated or to be appropriated by the National Assembly.

(2) The powers conferred on the National Assembly under the provisions of this section are exercisable only for the purpose of enabling it —

(a) to make laws with respect of any matter within its legislative competence and to correct any defects in existing laws; and,

(b) to expose corruption, inefficiency or waste in the execution or administration of laws within its legislative competence and in the disbursement or administration of funds appropriated by it.

s.83(1) For the purposes of any investigation under section 82 . . . the Senate or the House of Representatives or a committee . . . shall have power —

(a) to procure all such evidence, written or oral, direct or circumstantial, as it may think necessary or desirable, and to examine all persons as witnesses whose evidence may be material or relevant to the subject matter;

(b) to require such evidence to be given on oath;

(c) to summon any person in Nigeria to give evidence at any place or to produce any document[49] or other thing in his possession or under his control, and to examine him as a witness and require him to produce any document or other thing in his possession or under his control, subject to all just exceptions; and,

(d) to issue a warrant to compel the attendance of any person who, after having been summoned to attend, fails, refuses or neglects to do so and does not excuse such failure, refusal or neglect to the satisfaction of the House or the committee in question, and to order him to pay all costs which may have been occasioned in compelling his attendance or by reason of his failure, refusal or neglect to obey the summons, and also to impose such fine as may be prescribed for any such failure, refusal or neglect; and any fine so imposed shall be recoverable in the same manner as the fine imposed by a court of law.

(3) A summons or warrant issued under this section may be served or executed by any member of the Nigeria Police Force or by any person authorized in that behalf by the President of the Senate or the Speaker of the House of Representatives, as the case may require.[50]

These are fairly extensive powers which could be subject to abuse, particularly since their exercise is not subject to jurisdiction by the courts. In that respect, they open up possibilities of conflict between the privileges of members of the legislature acting in their investigatory capacity and the claims of the individual in so far as the protection of his rights, guaranteed by the Constitution, are concerned. For instance there is the right to freedom of expression and freedom of the press which provides that 'every person shall be entitled to freedom of expression, including freedom to hold opinions and to receive and impart ideas and information without interference' (s.36(1)). The freedom to 'hold' opinions must surely also entail the freedom to 'withhold' information and an individual summoned to appear before a House of the Assembly or any of its committees may find himself in the intolerable position in which there is a conflict between his freedom to withhold information and his obligation to provide whatever information may be demanded of him by the House or its committee.[51] Obviously these are delicate areas over which members of the legislature and those of the judiciary will have to tread warily if a head-on collision between the various arms of government is to be avoided.

Though the details of much legislative business are dealt with by the various specialised committees of the Assembly, there are certain matters which can only be taken in each House of Assembly sitting as a collective body, these being, proceedings (i) to remove the President for gross misconduct, discussed above, (ii) for the creation of states and (iii) for the purposes of amending the Constitution. Before any new state (the areas covered by the existing 19 and their respective capitals are all specified in the Constitution) can be created, a request to that effect supported by not less than two-thirds of the members representing the area concerned in the Senate, the House of Representatives, the state Assembly, and the local councils in the area in question must first be submitted to the National Assembly. If that request has the support of at least two-thirds of the people in the area concerned voting in a referendum, and the result of the referendum is approved by a simple majority of members of the House of Assembly and a simple majority of all the states in the federation, then and only then will a bill authorising the creation of the state concerned be presented to the National Assembly, which if supported by a two-thirds majority of the members of such House, becomes law and the state thereafter is created.[52]

When discussing proceedings for the purposes of altering the Constitution, a distinction should be made between provisions of the Constitution which are entrenched and those which are not. Only three sections of the Constitution are entrenched: (a) s.8 which specifies the procedure for the creation of states; (b) s.9 which outlines the process to be followed before any Act to amend the Constitution is passed; and (c) Chapter four of the Constitution which contains the provisions guaranteeing fundamental human rights. A bill of the National Assembly purporting to amend these provisions cannot be passed unless it is approved by not less than 80 per cent of *all* the members of each House of the Assembly and by a majority vote of the members of the state Assemblies in no less than two-thirds of the states (s.9(3)). A bill to amend any other provision of the Constitution is required only to be supported by not less than two-thirds of *all* the members of each House of the Assembly and a majority vote of two-thirds of the state Assemblies (s.9(2)).

To become a member of the National Assembly, a person has to be a Nigerian citizen, though not necessarily a citizen by birth; to enter the Senate a candidate must be at least 30 years old, while to enter the House of Representatives, he or she must be 21;[53] one must suffer no disabilities such as being an undischarged bankrupt, or a lunatic. The National Assembly is elected for four years after which all members vacate their seats (unless re-elected), but a member may be forced to lose his seat if he is absent from meetings of the Assembly for a total period which is not less than a third of the minimum required sitting period of 181 days in any one year.[54] The official languages of the Assembly are English and three other Nigerian languages, Hausa, Ibo and Yoruba, but the latter come into use 'when adequate arrangements have been made'.[55]

THE JUDICIARY

In any system based on the notion of 'checks and balances', such as is to characterise the second republic, it is the judiciary, ultimately, which holds the balance between the executive and the legislature on the one hand, and on the other, between those two arms of government and the ordinary citizen. Or as the Constitution puts it:

> The judicial powers . . . shall extend . . . to all inherent powers and sanctions of a court of law, [and] to all matters between persons, or between government or authority and any person in Nigeria, and to all actions and proceedings relating thereto, for the determination of any question as to the civil rights and obligations of that person (s.6(6) (a)(b)).

The institutions created to operationalise the 'judicial powers' can be described schematically as shown in Figure 5.1. There are significant differences between this structure and what obtained under the first republic. First, the Federal Court of Appeal, the Federal High Court and the State Customary Court of Appeal are all new institutions. Secondly, whereas in the first republic, appeals with respect to customary law lay from the customary courts to the Magistrates' Courts (which were graded in terms of their jurisdictional competence) and from thence to the Regional (now State) High Court,

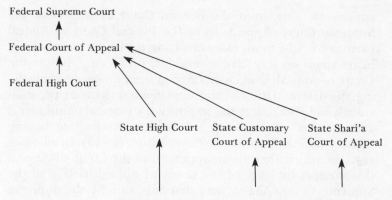

FIGURE 5.1   *Structure of the judiciary*[56]

appeals from the customary courts now lie, in the first instance, to the Customary Court of Appeal and from thence
to the Federal Court of Appeal. In the same manner, in the
first republic appeals from the Shari'a courts (which applied
Islamic personal law) went to the Shari'a Court of Appeal
and should decisions of the latter court conflict with principles of the civil law of the land, as interpreted by the Regional
High Court, such conflicts were taken and resolved by a Court
of Resolution, but in the second republic appeals from the
Shari'a Court of Appeal are to lie to the Federal Court of
Appeal.

In jurisdictional terms, the highest court of law in the
federation is the Federal Supreme Court[57] which, to the
exclusion of any other court, has original jurisdiction in all
disputes between the federation and a state or states and
between states in so far as such disputes involve the existence
or extent of a legal right; and since the exercise of legislative
power by the National Assembly and the state Assemblies is
made subject to the jurisdiction of the courts, this confers on
the Supreme Court the right of 'constitutional review', the
power, that is, to declare Acts of the National Assembly or
laws of the state Assemblies either null and void, without any
effect, or *ultra vires*, beyond the powers of the legislature
concerned. But besides the original jurisdiction of the courts,
the Supreme Court has appellate jurisdiction as well and

appeals lie only from the Federal Court of Appeal to the Supreme Court. Appeals from the Federal Court of Appeal exist as of right in all cases involving questions of law alone; in decisions on any civil or criminal proceedings before the Court of Appeal; in decisions arising from proceedings involving the determination of the fundamental rights of the individual; in appeals over the imposition of capital punishment; and in decisions involving the validity of elections to any office established under the Constitution (s.213). In all other cases in which there is an appeal from the Court of Appeal this is either by leave of the Court of Appeal itself or of the Supreme Court. Against any determination by the Supreme Court, there can be no further appeal. The court is thus not only the highest but also the last and final court.

The Federal Court of Appeal[58] was instituted to release the pressure of appellate cases on the Supreme Court and accordingly, appeals to the Court of Appeal lie from the High Courts (Federal and State), the Shari'a Court of Appeal, the Customary Court of Appeal and the Code of Conduct Tribunal. In the cases of the Shari'a and Customary Courts of Appeal, appeals to the Federal Court of Appeal are with the leave of the Court of Appeal and/or, the Shari'a and Customary Court of Appeal and are at the instance of any of the parties appearing before either of the latter courts. Appeals to the Federal Court of Appeal from the High Court (Federal or State) lie as of right over the same class of cases in which there is a right of appeal from the Court of Appeal to the Supreme Court, and in addition, questions involving the custody of minors and matrimonial cases. In appeals from the Shari'a and Customary Courts of Appeal, it is for the National Assembly, by law, to determine which class of cases are to be allowed to go before the Federal Court of Appeal.

The Federal High Court[59] replaces what used to be known as the Federal Revenue Courts which were established by the military to hear revenue cases, cases which had grown in numbers and prominence during the military regime. The jurisdiction of the court, besides covering revenue cases, has been made to include the normal powers of a state High Court and also to serve as an Electoral Tribunal to hear cases involving the validity of elections to the offices of President and

Vice-President respectively. The High Court of a State has 'unlimited jurisdiction to hear and determine any civil proceedings in which the existence or extent of a legal right . . . is in issue or to hear and determine any criminal proceedings involving or relating to any penalty, forfeiture, punishment or other liability in respect of an offence committed by any person'. It should be noted that though reference is made to a Federal High Court and the High Court of a State, this should not be read as implying a parallel system of courts. As in the first republic, the judicial system is a unified system and the Federal High Court or the High Court of State can entertain any case irrespective of whether this derives from an Act of the National Assembly or a law of a state Assembly. This is brought out quite clearly in s.251 of the Constitution, which provides that:

(1) The decisions of the Supreme Court shall be enforced in any part of the Federation by all authorities and persons, and by courts with subordinate jurisdiction to that of the Supreme Court.
(2) The decisions of the Federal Court of Appeal shall be enforced in any part of the Federation by all authorities and persons, and by courts with subordinate jurisdiction to that of the Federal Court of Appeal.
(3) The decisions of a High Court and of all other courts established by this Constitution shall be enforced in any part of the Federation by all authorities and persons, and by other courts of law with subordinate jurisdiction to that of the High Court and those other courts, respectively.

In this respect the Nigerian judicial system differs from the system that operates in the United States, which is largely a parallel system.

The question of what recognition should be accorded Islamic law in the *Constitution of the Federation* – which describes *federal* instrumentalities[60] – aroused considerable controversy (which is discussed below) during the debates of the Constitution Drafting Committee and the Constitutional Assembly. The provision of a State Shari'a Court of Appeal,[61] appeal from which is to lie to the Federal Court of Appeal, is thus something of a compromise. Essentially, the function of the court is to hear appeals from other Shari'a Courts where Islamic personal law — as this relates to questions of marriage, guardianship of infants, succession and inheritance and the maintenance of Moslems who are physically or mentally infirm, is applied. Unlike Shari'a, which is a definite and well-known system of law, and in contrast to Ghana, for example, where some attempt has been made to codify customary law with the view of deriving a body of Ghanaian 'common law', customary law in Nigeria has remained largely unsystematised and varies from one community to the other. The provision of a Customary Court of Appeal was in fact made to 'counter' the insistence of those who demanded that recognition be given to Shari'a in the Constitution. But in the absence of anything which could be called a body of customary law, all that could be done was simply to state that the 'Customary Court of Appeal[62] of a State shall exercise appellate and supervisory jurisdiction in civil proceedings involving questions of customary law' (s.247(1)).

Under the civil regime of the first republic and during the military interregnum, few cases went on appeal to the Shari'a Court of Appeal, in some years the number barely exceeded five. The experience with a Customary Court of Appeal is hardly likely to be much different. Both courts must therefore be seen as 'constitutional cosmetics', perhaps not unlike the preamble to the Constitution: 'We the People of the Federal Republic of Nigeria . . . Do Hereby MAKE, ENACT, AND GIVE TO OURSELVES the following Constitution'.

THE CONSENSUAL BASIS OF THE SECOND REPUBLIC

The basic framework of the institutional structure of the second republic was provided by the Constitution Drafting Committee (CDC) in their 'Draft'. The 'Draft' was debated by members of the Constituent Assembly and, with some minor modifications, was adopted. Thus one way of examining the consensual basis of the institutions of the second republic is to look at the representativeness of the CDC and the Constituent Assembly (CA). But when one talks of 'representativeness' in this context, there are at least two perspectives from which this could be viewed. The first is to examine the extent to which the composition of the two bodies, the CDC and the CA, could be said to be a cross-sectional representation of the Nigerian 'electorate'. The second is simply to see the degree to which the viewpoints of the members are a reflection of the dominant interests of the same 'electorate'.

The CDC members were not an elected group: they were hand-picked by the military authorities, and oddly enough there was not one female person amongst its members even though there are a good many female lawyers and social scientists — the class of persons who were thought by the Head of the federal military government to have more to offer in the drawing up of a draft constitution — among the Nigerian population. Be that as it may, of the 50 people who made up the CDC, some 19 were either university teachers or university administrators (including a Vice-Chancellor of a Nigerian University). In fact the total of these members of the CDC who had at one time or the other been either university teachers or administrators, is something like 26. In the same manner, while there were not fewer than six people who, at the time the CDC was meeting, held political office as civilian commissioners in the military administration, were one to add to this the total of those who had previously held political office — commissioners, former regional and federal ministers — then the number would go up to something of the order of 19. There were 12 lawyers among the members, including two teachers of law (one a Professor of Law), the Attorney-General of a State, and a State Chief Justice, a medical practitioner who was also a large-scale farmer and businessman, an army chaplain, a journalist cum managing director of a newspaper, a local government administrator, and some 12 businessmen (business consultants, company directors and one owner of perhaps the largest ranch in Nigeria). Another way of looking at the composition of the CDC is to say that some 80 per cent of the members belong to the broad 'class' of the intelligentsia — teachers, lawyers, doctors and administrators. In religious terms, less than 40 per cent were Moslems, though the proportion of the total population who are Moslems is larger than 40 per cent.

Unlike the CDC, members of the CA were in the main 'elected' but in the particular context of the CA that is hardly any yardstick of representativeness to go by. The electoral units were the newly elected local government councils, and few, if any of these could be said to be representative of their respective areas. First, only in seven of the 19 states were the local government elections direct, and for the country as a whole the average number of councillors per state was approximately 250, the range varying between 135 and 450. Even in areas where there were direct elections, close to 50 per cent of the councillors were returned unopposed, the range varying from a low of 12.5 per cent for Bendel to a high of 70 per cent for Anambra state. Kaduna state, where the elections were indirect, returned some 57 per cent of its councillors unopposed. Secondly, irrespective of whether the elections were direct or indirect, voter registration fell far below what was expected, even although registration periods were extended in most states. But worse still, voter turnout was reportedly, for all states, disappointing. In Kaduna state, using the number of ballot papers released by the electoral commission as a crude index of expected voter turnout, of the 3.89 million ballot papers issued, only 647,000 were utilised, giving a turnout percentage of just about 16 per cent of the expected. The outcome was to make the councils heavily unrepresentative and with the numbers involved, in effect this meant that it took the votes of an average of some 60 unrepresentative councillors to elect one member of the CA. Inescapably, this led to electoral malpractices — some very well-known personalities of the first republic had to be disqualified from membership of the CA on the grounds of electoral malpractice — which became the distinguishing characteristic of the CA elections. The fact that there was a high incidence of electoral abuse was perhaps only to be expected. Not a few of those who contested the elections to the CA saw it as a stepping-stone, an almost necessary stepping-stone, to a career in politics, and even possibly to political office. Of the nine members — that is excluding the President of the Republic and the nine Vice-Chairmen — who make up the national officers of the National Party of Nigeria, no fewer than seven were members of the CA and of the seven, four became federal ministers; one, the Political Adviser to the President; and the other two, members of the National Assembly, though it must be emphasised that it is not being suggested that any of these men came to political office by any other than fair means.

Not surprisingly, therefore, the majority of the members of the CA were businessmen and contractors, former politicians, commissioners and (usually retired) top military and police personnel and members of the professions, such as lawyers and doctors. The only woman elected to the CA, for example, was a well-known contractor. On the whole, this class of people formed close to three-quarters of the total membership of the CA. There were of course some academics but these tended, more often than not, to be 'sons of the soil' who had distinguished themselves academically and had been 'invited' by the local community to 'represent' them at the CA. If the CDC and the CA could be said to be representative of any group at all, that group would be the elite of Nigerian society: largely the intelligentsia in the case of the CDC, and the business—commercial elite in the case of the CA. In the first sense of 'representativeness' distinguished above, it could therefore be said that underlying the institutional structure of the second republic is an elite consensus of the intelligentsia and the business—commercial 'class'. The contrast, once again, is with the first republic whose consensual basis was that of the political class, using the term political class in the sense given to that term by the Italian political sociologist, Gaetano Mosca.[63]

But to say that the consensual foundation of the second republic was that of the elite is not to suggest that there was unanimity amongst that elite. Nor is it to suggest that there is anything necessarily pejorative about the term elite consensus, although it has been used pejoratively by some, critics of the CDC. In few, if any, societies has the consensual basis of the society's constitution been other than that of the elite. The masses, put simply, just do not make 'constitutions', though in some constitutions it is proclaimed that there is one and only one interest — that of the masses, the proletariat — which would of course make any talk of a consensus either otiose or meaningless.

Nowhere is the elite consensus underlying the second republic better demonstrated than in the use of the expression 'the *federal* character of the Federation' in references to the exercise of Presidential power with respect to appointments to different positions — federal ministers, Nigeria's permanent representatives overseas, chairmanship and membership of the boards of para-statals and public bodies set up under the Constitution, judicial offices, commissioned and non-commissioned personnel of the armed forces, federal permanent secretaries and Presidential advisers — in the public services of the federation. It was the competition for these offices — and hence for the resources controlled by incumbents of these offices — by the members of the elite in the different ethnic groups[64] which played such a large part in the eventual collapse of the first republic. In fact, while there was some concern over the powers of the President in the CDC's discussion of the recommendations of the report of the sub-committee on the executive (expressed in the main by those who had held political office and those with business/commercial interests), greater interest was shown over ways and means of ensuring that each state had an equal chance of providing an incumbent for the office. The sub-committee had proposed a 'zoning formula' for rotating the office between the different zones.[65] That formula would have been accepted, but for it being shown that for some states it could take no less than 144 years before that opportunity occurred and not many were confident that the second republic would last that long. When it was further realised that even then, some ethnic groups within the state might stand no chance of their members ever becoming the President, interest swung to the more realistic position of ensuring that whoever became the President had the widest possible acceptability amongst the electorate. The outcome was the 'double plurality' condition which a prospective candidate must satisfy before becoming the duly elected President.

Inter-elite accommodation was again shown over the question of the place of Shari'a courts — and hence of religion — within the institutional structure of the second republic, and here the basic divergence of views was amongst the group delineated above as the 'intelligentsia'. What was at issue was, in essence, the competitive capability of the 'Northern' intelligentsia, particularly, the 'far Northern intelligentsia', the place of Shari'a courts being used in that context to serve instrumentalist purposes. In the first republic, the competitive power position of the North had been maintained through the network of relations provided by the Native Administration, the regional bureaucracy and the party, the Northern Peoples' Congress (NPC). This network conferred on the NPC a hegemonic control over federal politics. With the breakup of the Northern region into ten states, not only had the bureaucratic and the native authority networks disappeared, but their disappearance meant that the authority bulwark which sustained the NPC had also disappeared. But if the privileges which hegemony conferred were to be retained, then some factor had to be found to counter the tendency towards separatism which 'statism'[66] would seem to be fostering. With more than two-thirds of the population of the ten 'Northern' states Moslem, Islam provided a ready-made answer, the more so as it encompassed not just the religious, but also the economic, political, social and cultural.

In the debate on the judiciary, some members of the 'Northern' intelligentsia had in fact contended that for a Moslem to live in a secular state was an 'abomination'. The least that could and should be expected would therefore be for the state to make provision to have those matters which pertain to the personal life of the Moslem adjudicated under Islamic personal law. But, it was contended, the only way to do that was to accord Shari'a federal status, the argument being that the 'received law' which the secular courts administered was in large part derived from Judeo-Christian origins. Giving Shari'a federal status meant, for the protagonists: (a) appointing persons competent in Islamic personal law, who must also be Moslems, to the Supreme Court; and (b) stipulating that only such judges should preside over the cases involving Shari'a law. Federal recognition on these terms would have the effect of ensuring that Moslems would not see themselves as 'second-class' citizens which, by implication, would be likely if the administration of Shari'a was left as a matter for the states. When the issue was presented in these terms, Shari'a became not just a subject which would cut across state lines, but a rallying call for the unity of all Moslems. But to have conceded such a claim would have amounted to recognising Islam as a 'state religion', which would have contradicted the no less accepted desire that Nigeria should remain a 'secular state'. The controversy came close to causing a split in the CDC which would have meant an end to all talk of a return to civil rule. As such an outcome was not in the collective interest of the elite — they all would have lost with no one gaining — a compromise solution had to be found, which would represent a minimal consensus, and the formula was found in the provision of a Federal Shari'a Court of Appeal.

But even that minimal solution was not acceptable to the 'Southern' intelligentsia of the CA. For that solution was just another concession to the North, or so they interpreted it, the thin end of the wedge, and this was very much the case as there was no real functional justification for a Federal Shari'a Court of Appeal. The controversy became so bitter that the CA had to adjourn sitting for a period to allow the principals to take stock of their respective positions. As in the CDC, since no one stood to gain by allowing the CA to collapse, a solution was found in the provision of a State Shari'a Court of Appeal, but a court which would have to be *established under the Constitution*.

Finally, there was the controversy over the nature and role of the state, the controversy which came the closest to having clear-cut ideological undertones. Central to the controversy was the question of who should control the 'social surplus'. For some members of the intelligentsia (at the CDC) to allow the social surplus — the surplus which accrues from the economic activity of the totality that is the society — to be appropriated by individuals would be not only conceptually wrong since part of that surplus could only have arisen as a result of the activity of the state as a collective entity — and hence could not have been contributed by the actions of individuals *qua* individuals — it would also be morally wrong as it would only serve to perpetuate the existing inequalities, gross as these were,[67] in the society. If it is conceded that a 'fundamental objective' of the state should be to 'control the national economy in such a manner as to secure the maximum

welfare, freedom and happiness of every citizen on the basis
of social justice and equality of status and opportunity'
(s.16(1)(a)), then it follows almost necessarily, or so it was
argued, that the social surplus should accrue to the state,
which would require that the state control the totality of the
means of production and distribution. One cannot restructure
social relations — which manifest themselves in the form of
class and status inequalities — without having effective control
of the means of production and distribution since social relations are none other than the manifestation of the relations
between the means of production and distribution. In effect,
what this argument amounted to was that Nigeria should be
proclaimed a 'socialist state'.

Against that stand was the position taken by the business—
managerial—professional elite that, on pragmatic grounds and
from the historical evidence available, there is not much likelihood of there being a 'surplus' unless individuals are free to
reap the rewards of their own efforts and hence share, as of
right, in the social surplus. A socialist framework was not
only antithetical to individual initiative: to adopt such a
framework would amount to no less than an imposition, a
derogation from the right which the Nigerian people, through
their elected representatives, should have, the right to determine under which form of economic system they would want
to live and work. The conflict was one between two contrast-
ing moralities, the 'socialist' and the 'liberal' morality,[68] the
resolution of which was found to lie in the formula which
enables the state 'without prejudice to its right to operate or
participate in areas of the economy other than the major
sectors of the economy', the phrase 'the major sectors of the
economy' being construed to mean:

> such economic activities as may from time to time be
> declared by a resolution of each House of the National
> Assembly to be managed and operated exclusively by the
> Government of the Federation; and until a resolution to
> the contrary is made by the National Assembly, economic
> activities being operated exclusively by the Government of
> the Federation on the date immediately preceding the day
> when this section comes into force, whether directly or

through the agencies of a statutory or other corporation or company, shall be deemed to be the major sectors of the economy (s.16(4)(a)).

As a consensual compromise, though it had the approval of the majority of the members of the CDC, it was sufficient nevertheless to force at least two members of the intelligentsia to record their dissent in the form of a separate constitutional 'draft' which, since it was presented to members of the CDC on the final day of the Committee's proceedings, could only be 'taken notice of' by the Committee. There were other minor divergences of opinion amongst and between the elite members of the CDC and the CA, but in the second sense of 'representativeness' distinguished above, the controversy over the role and nature of the state could be said to be about the only major controversy in which expressed opinions did reflect societal perspectives. In the main, then, the institutional structure of the second republic could be taken to rest on, and derive from, an elite consensus, and the Constitution which embodied that structure could be said to be a Constitution drawn up by the elite for the elite.

THE SECOND REPUBLIC AND THE NATURE OF NIGERIAN FEDERALISM

Enough has been said already about the institutional framework of the second republic to provide some indication of the way Nigeria's new federal system is structured. From that description it is fairly obvious that the balance of political power has been deliberately tilted by the 'founding fathers' in favour of the Federal authority. Even an item like local government, which in most federal systems is left the exclusive preserve of the 'component' governments (state, region, provincial — the terms used vary from one federal system to the other), has in the Nigerian system been made subject to federal control and regulation.[69] The fairly large reserves of funds controlled by the federal government make the states heavily dependent on federal allocations for their revenue needs, while the Constitution confers on the federal government the exclusive prerogative of prescribing 'minimum standards of education at all levels',[70] and with respect to trade and commerce requires that the National Assembly should not only be able to designate any class of goods and commodities as 'essential goods or commodities' but also gives the Assembly the power to 'control and regulate the prices' of the goods and commodities so designated.[71] That the balance has been thus tilted is perhaps hardly surprising. In a multi-ethnic and highly fractionalised society such as Nigeria's, the need for a central authority capable of containing the centrifugal forces inherent in such a society requires little argument.

But while a formal comparison of constitutional provisions is useful from a juridical point of view, ultimately the determination of the 'federal balance' can be said to derive not so much from constitutional provisions as from such variables as personality factors, the nature of the party system, the propensity or otherwise towards rule observance by political actors and a number of other imponderables. The significance of party, for example, is already shown in the pursuit of different policies by different states in the sphere of education, policies which could very well lead to conflicts between some states and the federal government. The result of the July 1979 elections resulted in the following configuration: of the 19 states in the federation, eight states came under the control of parties in opposition to the coalition in power at the federal level. Lagos, Ogun, Ondo and Bendel are under the United Party of Nigeria (UPN); Borno and Gongola are under the Great Nigeria Peoples' Party (GNPP); and Kano is under the Peoples' Redemption Party (PRP). One state, Kaduna, has a legislature controlled by a party different in complexion from that which controls the executive; three states are being administered by a party which is the junior partner in the federal coalition (Anambra, Imo and Plateau under the Nigerian Peoples' Party – NPP); while seven have their affairs being run by the party, the National Party of Nigeria (NPN) which is the major partner in the federal coalition.

The UPN states, consonant with their election manifesto, have all introduced a programme of 'free education' (at primary and secondary school levels) but in doing so these states have had to impose some restrictions such as that only children who are indigenous to states can qualify or, alternatively, where the children are not 'indigenes' then the parents must have been resident in the state for a specified number of years. While primary and secondary education are within the exclusive jurisdiction of the states, nevertheless, the Constitution also stipulates that:

> A citizen of Nigeria of a particular community, ethnic group, place of origin, sex, religion or political opinion shall not, by reason only that he is such a person —
> (a) be subjected either expressly by, or in the practical application of any law in force in Nigeria or any executive or administrative action of the government to disabilities or restrictions to which citizens of Nigeria of other communities, ethnic groups, places of origin, sex, religions or political opinion are not made subject; or,
> (b) be accorded either expressly, by or in the practical application of, any law in force in Nigeria or any executive or administrative action, any privilege or advantage that is not accorded to citizens of Nigeria of other communities, ethnic groups, places of origin, sex, religion or political opinions (s.39(1)).

But though the Constitution enjoins on the federal government the obligation to ensure that all governments conform to the Constitution, it has yet to make any move to correct what is patently discriminatory action by the UPN states. On the other hand, Kaduna state, where the executive is controlled by the PRP, is yet to be able to have Commissioners appointed because the state Assembly, which is dominated by the NPN, has consistently refused to ratify the list of nominees presented by the executive. Thus, short of being accused of discriminatory action, there is not much the NPN-controlled federal executive can do to make the UPN states observe the provisions of the Constitution unless at the same time it obliges the NPN members of the Kaduna state Assembly to co-operate with the PRP Governor of the State.

Central to the federal nature of the second republic is the fact that the system itself depends on the provision of executive leadership by the federal authority. For effective federal leadership to be forthcoming, the authority itself must be legitimate. But it is precisely that legitimacy which the circumstances surrounding the election of the President has brought into question — and by extension, the citizen's confidence in federal institutions. The facts of the elections are straightforward enough. In a declaration by the Chief Returning Officer, Presidential Elections, Mr F. L. O. Menkiti (supported by the Deputy Officer, Malam M. Abubakar and the Assistant Returning Officer, Mr F. J. Okono) on 16 August 1979, following the Presidential elections held on 11 August 1979, it was stated that:

CandidateAlhaji Shehu Shagari	(NPN):	Votes received 5,688,857;
Candidate Chief Obafemi Awolowo	(UPN):	Votes received 4,916,651;
Candidate Dr Nnamdi Azikiwe	(NPP):	Votes received 2,822,523;
Candidate Alhaji Amini Kano	(PRP):	Votes received 1,732,113;
Candidate Alhaji Ibrahim Waziri	(GNPP):	Votes received 1,686,489.

The declaration then went on:

Alhaji Shehu Shagari has satisfied the provision of section 34A, sub section (1)(c)(i) of Electoral Decree No. 73 of 1977, that is to say, he has the highest number of votes cast at the election. From the details of the state by state results ... this candidate has also satisfied the provision of sub section (1)(c)(ii) of the same section as he has not less than one-quarter of the votes cast at the election in each of at least two-thirds of all the states in the Federation. The Federal Electoral Commission considers that in the absence of any legal explanation or guidance in the Electoral Decree, it has no alternative than to give the phrase 'at least two-thirds of all the states in the Federation' in section 34A sub section 1(c)(ii) of the Electoral Decree the ordinary meaning which applies to it. In the circumstances, the candidate who scores at least one-quarter of the votes in 12 states and one-quarter of two-thirds, that is, at least one-sixth of the votes cast in the 13th state satisfied the requirement of the sub section. Accordingly, Alhaji Shehu Shagari is hereby declared elected President of the Federal Republic of Nigeria'.[72]

The actual wording of s.34(a)(1)(c)(i) and (ii) is as follows:

> A candidate for an election to the office of President shall
> be deemed to have been duly elected to such an office
> where —
> (c) there being more than two candidates —
>   (i) he has the highest number of votes cast at the
>   election; and,
>   (ii) he has not less than one quarter of the votes cast
>   at the election in each of at least two-thirds of
>   all the States in the Federation.

It was perhaps a bit misleading of the Chief Returning Officer
to have used the expression 'in the absence of any legal
explanation or guidance in the Electoral Decree', for though
the Decree did not provide any guidance, it is not quite accur-
ate to suggest that FEDECO did not seek legal guidance. Even
before the election results were declared, the NPN had considered the possibility of the party's candidate not securing
25 per cent of the votes in a 13th state and the party's
National Administrative Secretary and Secretary to the Campaign Committee, Alhaji Umaru Diko, had suggested that an
interpretation of the phrase 'in each of at least two-thirds of
all the states . . . ' could be taken to mean 'a quarter of the
votes in 12 states of the federation and not less than a quarter
of two-thirds of the votes in the 13th state'. The party had
then sought the advice of the Chairman of FEDECO, Chief
Michael Ani, about the acceptability of the party's interpretation of the electoral requirement. The Chairman, in turn, had
consulted the Attorney-General of the Federation and officials
of the Federal Ministry of Justice on their view of that interpretation, and had received the 'advice' that it was a plausible
and, in so far as the Ministry of Justice was concerned, an
admissible interpretation. As if to make 'assurance doubly
sure', the party and the Chairman went on to solicit the view
of members of the Supreme Military Council, who supposedly
confirmed the admissibility of the interpretation offered by
Alhaji Umaru Diko.[73] Therefore, in offering his interpretation
of the electoral requirement, the Chief Returning Office did
so in the knowledge that that interpretation would not be

objected to either by the Ministry of Justice or the Supreme
Military Council.

Be that as it may, the Chief Returning Officer's interpretation was unacceptable to the UPN candidate, Chief Obafemi
Awolowo, who then filed a petition before the Electoral
Tribunal challenging the validity of the election of the NPN
candidate, Alhaji Shehu Shagari, a petition to which he joined
as second and third respondents respectively, the Secretary to
FEDECO and the Chief Returning Officer, Presidential Election. Chief Awolowo's petition rested on the contention that '
(a) Alhaji Shehu Shagari was 'at the time of the election, not
duly elected by a majority of the lawful votes at the election
as he has not satisfied section 34A sub-section (1)(c)(ii) of the
Electoral Decree 1977'; (b) Alhaji Shagari 'had less than one
quarter of the votes cast at the election in each of at least
two-thirds of all the states in the Federation'; and (c) the
election of Alhaji Shagari was 'invalid by non-compliance
with the provisions of . . . the Electoral Decree 1977 . . . '. He
therefore requested the Tribunal to (i) declare that 'Alhaji
Shehu Shagari was not duly elected or returned and that his
election or return was void'; and (ii) order the Secretary to
FEDECO and the Chief Returning Officer 'to arrange for an
election to be held in accordance with the provisions of section 34A(3) of the Electoral (Amendment) Decree 1978'.[74]
It should be noted that before the commencement of the
trial, the Tribunal had upheld a certificate issued by the
Attorney-General of the federation claiming privilege for
certain documents subpoenaed by Counsel for Chief Awolowo
to be tendered by the Chairman of FEDECO. Another attempt
by the same counsel to have tendered two other documents:
(a) the certified copy of the Press Release made by the Chairman of FEDECO on 22 December 1978; and (b) a certified
copy of a Press Release by the Executive Secretary of FEDECO
issued on 13 November 1978 — both releases purporting to
show that FEDECO itself had interpreted the phrase 'in each
of at least two-thirds of the states . . . ' to mean *thirteen states*
— was ruled inadmissible by the Tribunal. Similarly, the Tribunal also ruled as inadmissible the request by the Petitioner
to amend his claim so as to specify that two-thirds of all the
states of the federation should mean and should only mean
thirteen states on the grounds that the request was not initially

'pleaded' which the Petitioner, being himself a lawyer, should have done if the request was considered by him central to his petition.

Shed of all the rhetoric, the arguments by counsels for the petitioner and the first respondent (Alhaji Shehu Shagari) amounted to the following. In the submission of the counsel for the petitioner, the phrase 'in each of at least two-thirds' appearing before the word 'states' could only qualify and refer to 'states' and to nothing else, which counsel for the respondent countered by claiming (a) that the referrent of the phrase could only be the terms preceding the phrase, that is, the words 'votes cast in', and (b) that had the framers of the Constitution — and the drafters of the Decree — intended the phrase 'in each of at least' to qualify states, they would have stated that expressly, but in the absence of such an express statement,[75] only a literal interpretation was admissible and the only literal interpretation of 'in each of at least two-thirds' must be 'twelve and two-thirds states'.

Before pronouncing on the substantive issue of the petition, the 'voidness' or otherwise of the election or return of Alhaji Shehu Shagari as the duly elected candidate for the Presidency, the Panel dealt with the second plea in the petitioner's claim, that FEDECO be ordered to hold an election for the office of the President on the basis of s.34A(3) since no candidate had satisfied the requirement of securing not less than a quarter of the votes in each of at least two-thirds of all the states. The Tribunal upheld the submission by counsels for the respondents that irrespective of the ruling on the substantive issue, not only would the Chief Returning Officer and the Executive Secretary of FEDECO be incompetent to order such an election, but the time required for that election to be held would have expired and thus the election sought could not be held. The plea for an election as sought by Chief Awolowo was therefore dismissed by the Tribunal. By any canon of logic, the Tribunal's ruling on this score cannot but be regarded as extremely odd, for either it must be the case that the election was valid, and hence the question of the election sought by Chief Awolowo did not and could not arise; or, the election was void, in which case the time prescribed for an election to be held by an 'electoral college' was not a *judicial* issue but an administrative—political question for decision. In reaching its decision, it seems obvious that the Tribunal had conflated two separate and distinct questions and in so doing overstepped the bounds of its own competence.

The Tribunal's ruling on the substantive issue, the interpretation of the phrase 'in each of at least two-thirds of the states . . . ' (after reviewing the submissions of the counsels for the two sides), is worthy of being quoted as it is central to the appeal which Chief Awolowo was to make to the Supreme Court. The Tribunal stated as follows:

> we intend to apply to the expression 'two thirds of all the States of the Federation' which is the gravamen of this petition, the literal construction of the expression which has been and still is the accepted canon of the statutory interpretation in the highest Court in England, and which is also approved by the Supreme Court of Nigeria. On the basis of that application, we find that the words used in the subsection are plain enough; and we cannot find any ambiguity therein. It even seems to us absurd to read anything more into the plain words of the sub-section. In our view it does not require the opinion of an expert in Mathematics or a computerist[76] to work out what two-thirds of nineteen means. It is enough to say that any student in a Primary school, tutored in the subject of "FRACTION"[77] in simple Arithmetic will have no difficulty in getting twelve two-thirds if asked to find two-thirds of nineteen. The lawmakers of that subsection must therefore be taken to have intended nothing more than that; and we so hold. Moreover, we are of the view that if the legislature intended anything to the contrary, they would have provided a 'PROVISO' to take care of any possible contingencies.[78]

But it is one thing to arrive at a conclusion from mere 'tutoring in fractions' and knowledge of arithmetic, and another to apply the conclusion so derived to a given empirical situation. In their application, the Tribunal argued that: 'as the dominant requirement in the election is the number of votes cast in each of the states, "two-thirds state" would be synonymous with two-thirds of the total votes cast in that state and not the physical or territorial area of such state'.

One could concede that the 'dominant requirement in the election is the number of votes cast in each of the states' but it is far from clear by what rule of *synonymity*[79] the Tribunal arrived at the conclusion that 'two-thirds of a state' would be synonymous with 'two-thirds of the total votes cast in that state'! Logically, if the synonymity rule adopted by the Tribunal (whatever that rule may be) were to be accepted, then the statement 'not less than a quarter of the votes cast in each of at least two-thirds of all the states' would be *synonymous* with, or logically equivalent to, the statement 'not less than a quarter of two-thirds of the total votes in all the states' and that would obviously be absurd.[80] Applying the 'canon of interpretation' used by the Tribunal, if the lawmakers had intended 'in each of at least two thirds of all the states' to mean 'two-thirds of the total votes in all the states' then they would have used the latter expression and not the more cumbrous phraseology of 'in each of at least two-thirds of all the states'.

But it was on that totally implausible, indeed, idiosyncratic notion of synonymity, that the Tribunal then went on to argue that were one to take the 'thirteenth state' to be Kano, where Alhaji Shehu Shagari polled not less than the required one-quarter of the total votes cast);

> the question therefore is: What then is the total votes cast in two-thirds of Kano State. The obvious answer is 813,842 (total votes cast in Kano was 1,220,763). A quarter or 25% of those votes will then be 203,460.5 votes . . . the total votes scored by the 1st respondent (i.e. Alhaji Shagari) is 243,423 which is obviously more than one quarter of the votes cast in two-thirds of Kano state. In the circumstances we are satisfied that the 1st respondent has satisfied the provision of section 34A(1)(c)(i) and (ii) of the Decree; and we therefore hold that he (i.e. Alhaji Shagari) was duly returned . . . as duly elected President of the Federal Republic of Nigeria.[81]

Not satisfied by the ruling of the Tribunal, Chief Awolowo

appealed to the Supreme Court, the grounds of appeal being substantially the same grounds as those raised before the Tribunal, but with the modification that even if it were accepted that the phrase 'in each of at least two-thirds of all the states' meant 'twelve and two-thirds state' as the Tribunal held, nevertheless, the Chief Returning Officer would still be wrong in declaring Alhaji Shagari the successful candidate because:

> in order to find $\frac{1}{4}$ of two-thirds of all the votes in Kano state in relation to the votes cast for any of the candidates, only $\frac{2}{3}$ of the votes received by that candidate can be used. As this was not done . . . with respect to the votes of [Alhaji Shagari] his [the Chief Returning Officer's] calculation was wrong.

The Supreme Court, reviewing the evidence and submissions by counsels for the contestant by a majority decision (five members – including the Chief Justice – out of seven) upheld the ruling of the Tribunal but added that:

> even if we had found that there had been non compliance with the said provisions, we would have invoked the provisions of section III of subsection (1) of the Decree and held that the election, which in the present context means the election to the office of President, was conducted *substantially* in accordance with the provisions of section 34A(1)(c)(ii) which is within Part 11 of the Decree.[82]

A sixth member of the Court, Mr Justice A. O. Obaseki, though agreeing with the majority view that Alhaji Shagari was validly elected, disagreed with the reasoning of the majority. In Mr Justice Obaseki's view, the central question was not whether the phrase 'in each of at least two-thirds of all the states' referred to 'states' or to 'votes' (though he agreed the phrase must refer and can only refer to 'states' in the physical, territorial sense), the central question was the grounds on which invalidation of the election was being sought by the petitioner, Chief Awolowo, and these, as stated in the petition were: "(a) . . . that Alhaji Shagari had less than one quarter of the votes cast at the election in each of at least two-thirds of all the states in the federation"; and "(b) . . . that the election . . . of Alhaji Shehu Shagari was invalid by reason of non-compliance with the provisions of Part II of the Electoral Decree 1977 to wit section 34A(1)(c)(ii) . . . ". As the Decree also provided in Part III that 'an election shall not be invalidated by reason of non-compliance with Part II of this Decree if it appears to the Tribunal having cognisance of the question that the election was conducted substantially in accordance with the provisions of the said Part II and that the non-compliance did not affect the result of the election', in the judge's view 'once a petitioner alleges a particular non-compliance and averred in his prayer that it was substantial it is his duty so to satisfy the Court or Tribunal having cognisance of the question'[83] and that neither Chief Awolowo nor his counsel had done, for as Justice Obaseki put it: 'I think that when the Decree speaks of "affecting the result" it means tilting the result in favour of the petitioner'.[84] No gross irregularities in the actual conduct of the election which would have been sufficient to vitiate the election *qua* election had been alleged, nor had it been shown that Chief Awolowo would have won the election but for the non-compliance with the sufficient requirement. On the other hand, it had been shown that Alhaji Shagari had substantially satisfied the sufficient requirement, he not only had a majority of all the votes cast, he had more than 25 per cent of the votes cast in 12 states. Since Alhaji Shagari had substantially complied with the sufficient requirement and non-compliance with that requirement could not 'tilt' the election in favour of his opponent, Chief Awolowo, it followed, in the judge's view, that Alhaji Shagari's election could not be invalidated. The plea that the election be invalidated must therefore fail.

The oddity in this line of reasoning was pointed out by the only dissenting member of the Supreme Court, Mr Justice Kayode Eso, for it amounts to saying that '*X* cannot be invalidated' entails '*X* is valid' but no such entailment can follow. Thus, from the statement 'that *p* cannot be disproved' it does not follow that *p* is thereby proved. From the statement 'that *p* cannot be proved' all that follows and can only follow is the statement 'that *p* cannot be proved'. From 'it cannot be disproved that God exists' one cannot derive the statement 'God therefore exists', the one does not entail the other and any attempt to show that such an entailment follows must necessarily fail. As Mr Justice Eso then argued, the question of substantiality with respect to compliance or non-compliance with the sufficient requirement rule (i.e. the rule that to be successful a candidate must poll not less than 25 per cent of the votes in each of at least two-thirds of all the states) is neither here nor there. The material conditions which have to be satisfied for an election to be properly so called are one thing. Necessary and sufficient conditions (rules) which have to be satisfied before any candidate can be declared a successful candidate are another. If the material conditions are not satisfied, then the question of success or failure does not arise since the election will then be a non-election and that will be all there is to it. But once an election is declared to be properly so called, then the conditions for success or failure become material and either it is the case that the conditions are satisfied or they are not; the question of 'substantial compliance' with those conditions becomes not only irrelevant, it simply does not arise at all. In Justice Eso's opinion, the phrase 'in each of at least two-thirds' can only refer to states — as spatial entities — and not to votes. But while for some purposes, the spatial entity can be sub-divided into various units, in the sense required by the 'phrase', there can be no way in which a state can be divided into three equal parts for one to talk in any meaningful way of 'two-thirds' of a state. It follows therefore that 'states' must be taken as indivisible units and 'two-thirds' of all the states, where all means 19, cannot but be 13 and not 12 and two-thirds state, the term 'two-thirds state' being meaningless.[85] Alhaji Shagari, it was shown, did not satisfy the sufficient requirement. He polled not less than 25 per cent of the votes in 12 states but in the 13th state polled only 19.4 per cent of the votes and not 25 per cent. He could therefore not be regarded as having been duly elected or returned as the successful candidate for the office of President.

The Electoral Tribunal by a unanimous decision, and the Supreme Court by a majority decision, held Alhaji Shagari to have been successfully elected and he has been duly sworn in as President. Nevertheless, for those states controlled by the UPN, Chief Awolowo's party, and states controlled by parties sympathetic to the UPN, for example, GNPP-controlled states — which together come to seven states of the 19 states of the federation — the validity of Alhaji Shagari's election remains in question and though it may not be possible at this stage to state in which way or ways the unacceptability of the legitimacy of the President may affect the behaviour of these states, that there will be some effect which will influence the nature of Nigeria's federal system cannot be denied.[86]

6

Parties and the 1979 Elections

Editor's note: The Federal Election Commission (FEDECO) report, *The General Election of 1979* (Lagos, 1981) was published after Professor Dudley's death, but unless stated otherwise, election data in this chapter are drawn from this report, not the earlier figures available to the author.

Military regimes are, by their nature, anti-party. This is not just to say that states with military regimes are no-party, or party-less states: it is to say, in addition, that military regimes are opposed to the existence of parties. Once the military takes over power, one of the first moves it makes is thus to ban all parties and quasi-political organisations and associations, the regime then depending on civil servants and the co-optation of civilians to enable it to govern. The military could proscribe parties because it does not have to rely, for the purpose of governing, on any expression of the popular will, the place of the popular will having been taken by the military's monopoly of coercive force. A vacuum is thus necessarily created with the military's decision to disengage, and parties, as 'basic institutions for the translation of mass preferences into public policy', as V. O. Key put it,[1] provide one possible instrumentality to fill such a vacuum.

But there is still the question of what form of party system there should be. During the period of decolonisation, parties had simply grown, developed, as the franchise was introduced and expanded. The element of 'choice' barely arose. With disengagement the question of choice becomes salient. In his opening address to the CDC, as was pointed out in the preceding chapter, Brigadier Muhammed alluded to the question of choice when he suggested that the CDC, considering 'the harmful effects of a proliferation of national parties', might not only want to consider ways of limiting the number of parties, but if in fact it were possible to 'discover some means by which government can be formed without the involvement of parties', then the CDC should so recommend. Out of some 350 memoranda submitted to the CDC, of the 28 that made specific references to parties and party systems, five proposed a 'no-party' state for Nigeria, one memorandum advocated a single-party state while 23 were in favour of Nigeria having a multi-party system, with two or more parties. It is difficult to visualise Nigeria as a no-party state, for if, as Sartori has suggested, a distinction is made between political development of the polity and political development of the society, the latter involving the political awakening and activation of the population at large, then a politically conscious society, a politicised public, is that which not only demands, but also requires, the electorate to take an active part in the more effective management of the public affairs of the society. As Sartori himself put it, ' "the masses" not only cannot be kept out indefinitely, but it is useful to involve them. If their enmity is dangerous, their indifference is wasteful. Parties may be repressed, but the problems raised by politicization remain. And a party-less polity cannot cope, in the long run, with a politicized society'.[2] For a society such as Nigeria's, which has undergone the process of politicisation for a period covering more than four decades, the notion of a party-less state becomes virtually inconceivable. Which leaves the choice between either the single- or the multi-party state.

Historically, the single party has been a product of either revolutionary change, the total restructuring of society through the overthrow of existing power-holders and the seizure of the means of coercion and social control by a class or a vanguard, or through the process of political channelisation, the process, that is, of controlling and ordering demands of a politicised mass public through organised and concerted action. Where the former involves, necessarily, the use of violence, the latter only presupposes the existence of organised groups or associations whose activities have to be channelised by legal or extra-legal means (but not necessarily through the use of violence) towards specified goals or ends. In most African states, with the exception of those states with a revolutionary experience — Guinea-Bissau, Algeria, Mozambique and Angola — the single-party regime has been established largely through the process of political channelisation. Here, a distinction should be made between the *de jure* and the *de facto* one-party regimes on the one hand, and on the other, the one-party dominant or hegemonic party state. In the *de jure* one-party regime — Ghana between 1958 and 1966, Tanganyika,[3] Zambia and Sierra-Leone are examples — a political party, having gained control of the machinery of state, uses the legal instrumentalities of the state to proscribe other competing parties and thereby becomes the only legally recognised political party in the society-state. In the *de facto* single-party regime — examples are Tunisia, Liberia (before the military coup of April 1980) and Guinea — competing parties are eliminated through the electoral process and the one party emerges as the only effective instrument of political expression and representation of the politicised electorate. But once having emerged as the only effective party, the single party, on gaining control of the state, invariably then uses the machinery of the state to establish itself as the *de jure* party, thereby blurring the distinction between the *de jure* and the *de facto* single-party regime. Nevertheless, the distinction is still of some significance if only for historical purposes, since it rests on the *ex ante factum* and the *ex post factum* capture of state power by the single party.[4] In contradistinction to the *de jure* and the *de facto* one-party state, the one-party dominant regime arises when a party assumes such a pre-eminence within the political system that it is in a powerful enough position to determine the performance of other parties within the system. In other words, other parties within the system have to co-operate with the 'dominant' party to survive, and function only to the extent that they are allowed specific spheres of action by the dominant party. Examples of one-party dominant states are to be found in Kenya and the Ivory Coast. But whichever is the case, the single party arises not from choice but from the activity of politics itself, from the fact that the politicised society cannot be left unchannelled. It follows from this that the single party must continuously have to justify itself, either in terms of what it achieves — the pragmatic or modernising single-party state — or in terms of prefix values and goals, in which case we have the ideological single-party state. In the context of a disengaging military regime, it seems all too obvious that the single party is not a plausible option.

The choice then was not one between the party-less state or single party on the one hand, and on the other the multi-party state; it was essentially one of what form of the multi-party system was to be allowed. In a highly politicised, multi-ethnic or segmented pluralistic society such as Nigeria, allowing parties to form on a free associational basis could very easily result in an atomised pluralistic party system,[5] and hence in an unstable political system. While it might be possible to moderate the degree of atomisation by a suitably devised electoral system,[6] it is hardly likely that this could provide an adequate mechanism to counter the fractionalisation arising from segmentation. The obvious way out therefore seemed to lie in some form of limitation, but a limitation which, though it would make for 'restricted boundedness',[7] would nevertheless preserve the principle of free associations. Basically, this amounted to stipulating specific criteria which an association would have to meet to be formally and legally recognised as a political party. The function of recognition was left to the Federal Electoral Commission. The criteria which the CDC proposed were in the main incorporated into the Electoral Decree No. 73 of 1977 and restated in the Federal Constitution.

By the provisions of the Electoral Decree (and the Constitution) 'no association by whatever name shall function as a political party unless it is registered as a political party to the Electoral Commission' (FEDECO) (s.78(i)). To qualify for registration, an association (that is, a party) is required to (a) register the names and addresses of its national officers with the Commission; (b) make its membership open to every Nigerian irrespective of his place of origin, religion, ethnic group or sex (the former Northern Peoples' Congress had in its Constitution 'the membership of the Congress is open to all people of *Northern Nigerian descent* irrespective of creed, rank or tribe'); (c) register a copy of the association's 'constitution' with the principal office of FEDECO 'in such form as may be prescribed by the Electoral Commission'; (d) register all alterations to the constitution of the party with the princi-

pal office of the Commission within 30 days of such an alteration being made; (e) ensure that the name, emblem or motto[8]
has no ethnic or religious connotation and does not give the
appearance that the activities of the association are confined
to a party only of the federation; and (f) have the headquarters
of the association located in the federal capital (which, for
the present, means Lagos). But that is not all. It is also required
that the rules and constitution of a party provide for the
periodic election 'on a democratic basis'[9] of the principal
officers or members of the executive committee or other
governing body of the party; and the officers or members of
the executive committee should reflect the 'federal character'
of the society. 'Periodic election' was interpreted to mean
not less often than once in every four years, thereby making
elections to party offices coterminous with the term of office
of the President, and the 'federal character' was taken to imply
that the members of the governing body of a party must be
recruited from the different states of the federation covering
not less than two-thirds of all the states of the federation.
Failure to fulfil these conditions could then lead to the registration of a party being cancelled or withdrawn, and as it was
also provided that only registered parties could present candidates for elections to the National Assembly, state Assembly
and the offices of President of the Federation and Governor
of a state (plus those of the Vice-President and Deputy
Governor), the withdrawal or cancellation of the certificate
of registration of any party meant it could not present
candidates for election to these offices, or, put differently,
contest any election to be held in the federation. Furthermore,
to ensure that parties, even where they ostensibly observe the
stipulations stated above, do not in their behaviour depart
from the broad objectives of the state, it is also provided that
'the programme and objects [*sic*] of a political party shall
conform with the relevant provisions of [the Fundamental
Objectives and Directive Principles of State Policy of] the
Constitution' (s.80(i)). Supposedly then, FEDECO could cancel the certificate of registration of a party if in the judgement
of the officials of FEDECO, the 'programmes and objects' of
the party are not in conformity with the Fundamental Objectives of the Constitution and since there is no appeal against

the decisions of FEDECO, this in principle leaves with the Commission a weapon which could be used to counteract destabilising tendencies inherent in, or arising from, the functioning of the party system.

There are, however, other restrictions on parties, the administration of which could prove to be extremely difficult if not almost impossible. For example, there is the provision that no person who is under the age of 18 years may become a member of a political party and parties enrolling such persons as members, or maintaining 'youth wings' of persons under that age are liable, on the facts being proven, to a fine of ₦5000 for the first offence and ₦10,000 for subsequent offences. Since parties are not obliged to submit their membership lists to FEDECO, and as births are not registered over large areas of the federation (there being in many areas no registries for that purpose or even a legal requirement to have births registered), it is difficult to see how the restrictions on membership can be enforced. Nevertheless, the existence of such a provision could provide winning parties, either at the state or federal level, with the means of harassing opposing parties. A party bent on harassing its rivals, or possibly even of eliminating its rivals, could encourage persons known to be 'under age' to enrol as members of opposing or rival parties and then seek to have such parties prosecuted by FEDECO. In such circumstances, cautious or hesitant FEDECO officials who might suspect such an intentional harassment could be placed in an extremely difficult or hazardous position: they could be reported to the Public Complaints Bureau for hesitating or failing to act, and ultimately be brought before the Code of Conduct Tribunal where they could face the possibility, should the charges against them be proved — and proof in this instance would not be all that difficult — of, at the least, losing their jobs. The possibilities open to a determined party are immense and the likelihood of the judicial system being brought to a halt is not inconceivable. The same outcome can be envisaged under the provision (s.81(3)) which stipulates that:

No political party shall hold or possess any funds or

assets outside Nigeria, nor shall it be entitled to retain any funds or assets remitted to it from abroad. Any funds or assets remitted or sent to a political party from outside Nigeria shall be paid over or transferred to the Electoral Commission for the Federation within 21 days of its receipt with such information as the Commission may require.[10]

That there could be legitimate grounds for concern, if party financing were left totally unregulated — external interests seeking to influence electoral outcomes by contributing funds to specific parties for example — cannot be denied. At the same time, however, by imposing such blanket regulations, there can be no denying the fact that in wanting to throw out the bathwater, the law makers may have ended up throwing out the baby also.

The Electoral Decree was published in January 1978 and some eight months later, at the end of September 1978, the ban prohibiting the formation of political parties — the emergency decree passed in May 1967 — was lifted. The lifting of the ban became the signal for the formation of a plethora of parties and by the end of the year some 150 parties were supposed to have been formed. The founders of a number of these certainly held little expectation that their parties would be registered by the Electoral Commission, but they could at least bargain for what they could get with leaders who stood a better chance of their organisations being registered. The party 'field' was thus seen by some as a market in which what was being offered for sale was not votes but bloc support and, not surprisingly, 'parties' emerged with names like the 'I chop, you chop' party. However, by the end of the year, the Electoral Commission announced that five parties had qualified for registration, these being the National Party of Nigeria (NPN), the Unity Party of Nigeria (UPN), the Nigerian Peoples' Party (NPP), the Great Nigeria Peoples' Party (GNPP) and the Peoples' Redemption Party (PRP). These were the parties that finally contested the elections held in July/August 1979.

THE PARTY SYSTEM UNDER THE SECOND REPUBLIC

Chief Awolowo, veteran politician of the first republic (leader of the subsequently banned Action Group (AG), first Premier of the Government of Western Nigeria, and leader of the Opposition in the Federal House of Representatives from 1960 to 1962 after which he was jailed for felonious treason until his release by General Gowon in August 1966) and now leader of the UPN, was the first to announce the formation of his party. The UPN had been in the making long before it emerged in October 1978. In fact, most of the leadership of the UPN were the same set of people as had led the AG and for much of the period during which parties were supposed to have been banned, that leadership was clandestinely engaged in keeping alive the support for the AG in readiness against such time when the ban on parties would be lifted. When before the Ad Hoc Constitutional Conference of September 1966, Chief Awolowo was made chairman of the 'Leaders of Thought'[11] – and subsequently became 'Leader of the Yorubas' – many then thought the Chief was using the 'Leaders of Thought' meetings as caucus meetings of the AG 'faithfuls' and in 1969 when Chief Awolowo offered to mediate between the then military government of the West and the rebelling farmers of the West (the Agbe k'oya revolt) relations between the Chief and the Governor of the West, Brigadier (later Major-General) Adebayo soon became strained as the latter came to believe the Chief was in fact using his mediational role not to appease the rebelling farmers but to rally support for his AG. In the same manner, a number of people suspected that Mr Bola Ige (one of the AG leaders and currently UPN Governor of Oyo state) employed much of his stewardship as Commissioner of Agriculture in Adebayo's military administration, canvassing support for the AG when he was supposedly trying to get the farmers of the West to back the government's agricultural programme. And in a manner, seemingly by proxy, of testing his acceptability by the electorate, and hence what level of support to expect, Chief Awolowo had had his son contest the local government elections in Lagos state in 1977 and his son had won with a handsome margin.

Thus when the emergency decree was abrogated and the ban on parties lifted, Chief Awolowo and his supporters of the former AG already had a party formed, awaiting just the

mere formality of an 'official' launching to set it going. The
local government elections had shown that there was strong
electoral support for Chief Awolowo — as demonstrated
by the number of former AG members who got elected — in
Lagos, Ogun, Oyo and Ondo states. In the various elections
of the first republic, the AG had elicited a strong following
in the Midwest (which after 1976 became known as Bendel)
where the party had tended to share voter support just about
equally with the National Council of Nigerian Citizens (before
1961, known as the National Council of Nigeria and the
Cameroons) just as the AG shared the vote (up until 1960)
with the NPC in what had become Kwara state. In alliance
with what used to be known as the United Middle Belt Congress, the AG had also had a good following in Benue and in
Borno (in the latter in alliance with the Bornu Youth Movement). In the calculation of Chief Awolowo and his supporters,
with the launching of the UPN all that was required to secure
a dominant position for the new party was to seek to secure
support in those states which used to form the Eastern region
and in those parts of the North that had now become the
states of Sokoto, Kano, Kaduna, Bauchi, Plateau, and Gongola.
And here the UPN thought it had a good chance — encouraged
by the creation of states — in such states as Kaduna, Plateau,
Bauchi, and Gongola where the population is more ethnically
mixed than in Kano, Sokoto, or Niger.

The UPN's expectation of electoral support in the ethnically heterogeneous states of the former Eastern and Northern
regions was based in part on the party's organisational skills
and resources, and in part on the UPN's electoral programme.
Financial support from business groups, which the Chief had
cultivated while serving as Commissioner for Finance in
Gowon's administration — and from the educated elite of
the former West — meant that the party had been able to
recruit, quite early in the game, a number of young people,
school teachers, and new university graduates, to serve as
canvassers for the party in the various states and among the
different strata of the society. And as early as 1969, in his
book, *The Strategy and Tactics of the Peoples' Republic*,
Chief Awolowo had outlined what he thought should be the
operational goals of a putative socialist government of repub-

lican Nigeria, goals which included free education at all levels (which it was thought should appeal to people in the states mentioned, particularly as they are less educationally endowed in comparison to the electorate of the former Western region and the Ibo-speaking areas of the former Eastern region), free medical health care, full social security coverage for all citizens, and guaranteed full employment (to be realised within the space of some ten years), and of course, an agricultural revolution which would make Nigeria self-sufficient in terms of her food needs within the space of five years. These ideas, worked out and suitably elaborated, became the 'ideological platform' of the UPN. Thus, while the other parties were still preoccupied with organisational questions, or in some cases contesting leadership positions, Chief Awolowo and the UPN were well on the way with a well-thought-out electoral programme and the image of the only party with an effective and efficient organisation.

But though the ideological stance of the UPN was geared to appeal to the broadest possible spectrum of the population — the intelligentsia, the working class and urban masses and the peasantry — the interests of specific groups and communities were not ignored. For the business—commercial groups for example, there was the promise not only that attempts would be made to check foreign control and domination of the economy, but also that Nigeria's oil wealth would be put to more effective use in opening up new investment opportunities — petro-chemical and agro-chemical industries — in which the state and local entrepreneurial expertise would be profitably and usefully combined in the greater interests of the total society. For the farmers there was the promise of capital aid to enable the small farmers to be more efficient and more productive, while to specific local communities, such as the peoples of the Cross River and Kaduna states — areas in which there have been strong and persistent demands to have more states created (after the creation of 19 states) — the promise was given that a UPN-controlled government would make it a matter of priority to ensure that more states were created. In the same manner, the people of Borno state were told that the Borno railway extension would be electrified should the UPN be elected to power. In overall terms, the

UPN's claim to be 'democratic socialist' in orientation has to be seen as one in which, for tactical purposes, the 'democratic' and the 'socialist' components of the party's ideology are packaged in different 'mixes' with each 'mix' being sold to different segments of the population in the hope of maximising total electoral support. For the 1979 elections, then, the UPN's tactical approach could be described as one exhibiting a strong ideological commitment which was nevertheless watered down as pragmatic considerations dictated.

In its election manifesto the NPN claimed that it was the 'only party formed out of nationwide consultation and consensus by Nigerians'. There is a sense in which that claim could be said to be correct, for whereas parties such as the UPN or the GNPP emerged with a 'ready-made' leadership — unquestioned candidates for the highest political office in the federation, the Presidency — the NPN had to wait till its first convention, held in Lagos in November 1978, to resolve the issue of the party's national political leadership. Before that date the NPN was perhaps nothing more than a collection of individuals who, in a loose sense, shared certain common interests, such as a commitment to the maintenance of a free market economy, and who, by and large, were relatively well-to-do. There had been a meeting between this class of people and those who were to become members of the PRP, in Kano in early October, the aim being the formation of a national party, but the interests of the two sets had been so divergent as to be irreconcilable and the PRP members-to-be had broken away, determined to form a separate party.

The nucleus of the NPN could be said to have been formed when various dignitaries assembled in Sokoto to celebrate the fortieth anniversary of Sir Abubakar as Sultan of Sokoto and Sarkin Mussulmi. The core of that nucleus, not surprisingly, was made up of former members of the NPC and other party sympathisers; but while there was some general recognition that a possible leader would have to come from that group, there was no agreement on who that leader was to be.[12] Since the death of the former Prime Minister of the Federation, Sir Abubakar Tafawa Balewa, and the former Premier of the North, Sir Ahmadu Bello, the Sardauna of Sokoto, there had been a leadership vacuum in the 'far' North and underlying that vacuum was the fact that there no longer seemed to be a willingness to accept the grounds on which political leadership in the past had been based. In the 1940s and early 1950s — and before that — birth and social status had been taken as unquestionable qualifications for political leadership but with the sociopolitical changes which have occurred in the North since 1966,[13] those qualities have come to be challenged. In a Nigeria-wide survey conducted in 1973/74, for example, to the question 'what qualities should suit one for political leadership?' the response set from the Northern states was as shown in Table 6.1. The claim of education, it would seem, was tending to replace the old claims of birth, status and tradition, and those vying for the leadership of the NPN embodied these conflicting claims — the intelligentsia on the one hand, and on the other the old political class of native authority councillors and wealthy contractors and mercantile interests (political power, birth and wealth correlated very closely). At the November convention of the NPN, interestingly enough, it was the business–managerial group which emerged the victors; not only did they have the resources to buy political support but the other contesting groups, it would appear, cancelled each other out. At the convention, then, Alhaji Shehu Shagari, a former commissioner under General Gowon, and a wealthy farmer, won the contest for the Presidential candidate, with Dr Alex Ekwueme, a very wealthy architect, as his Vice-Presidential running mate, and Chief A. M. A. Akinloye, a lawyer and former minister in the West, emerged as the Chairman of the party. The former regions of the North, East and West had been pulled together in a new consensus that was being forged by the NPN.

If the UPN can, with some justification, be described as a reincarnation of the AG, then the NPN can in like manner be taken as the lineal successor of the NPC. On a Left–Right ideological positioning, the NPN like the NPC could be located Right of Centre, the NPN's 'virtue', if one could use that term, lying precisely in the desire to conserve, to maintain the existing structure of the society. The distinctive feature of the NPN's electoral manifesto was the party's promise of 'more of the same': more funds to small-

TABLE 6.1   *Qualities for political leadership (percentages)*

Criteria	Kwara	Benue	Borno	Bauchi	Kano	Kaduna	Niger	Plateau	Totals
Distinguished family	0.0	0.0	36.7	4.8	14.4	10.9	0.1	0.4	317
									7.6
Devotion to tradition	2.9	26.1	11.8	3.8	6.2	0.2	1.1	1.3	235
									5.7
Popularity with masses	6.0	7.7	16.4	49.8	16.4	23.2	20.4	50.6	1131
									27.3
High education	90.4	66.1	31.4	40.0	61.7	61.6	78.1	46.1	2389
									57.7
Don't know: no opinion	0.7	0.1	3.7	1.7	1.3	4.2	0.3	1.6	72
									1.7
TOTALS	252	395	225	909	811	657	466	427	4142
	6.1	9.5	5.4	22.0	19.6	15.9	11.2	10.3	100

Note: Column totals are weighted for population using the 1963 census data.

scale farmers; more large-scale mechanised farms; more meat, dairy and livestock farming; more tree-crop farming; more housing for the urban areas and improved quality of rural housing; more educational institutions – but with private schools being allowed to co-exist side by side with state schools; more health facilities; more to be spent on defence and on law and order; protection for the disabled, the aged and the destitute; more to be spent on sports, recreation and enlightenment; more support for OPEC (Organisation of Petroleum Exporting Countries) and more of many other things. However, the business orientation of the party is brought out quite clearly – which perhaps uniquely differentiates the NPN from the other parties – in the following statement:

> as Nigerians are energetic people they should be encouraged by themselves, or where suitable, in co-operation with foreign expertise and finance, to take a leading role in the manufacturing sector of the economy. To further this objective, *it will be the fundamental policy of the party if voted into power to encourage, protect, and induce foreign capital into Nigeria so that it may contribute to the sound development of the national economy, the improvement of the balance of payments*, and the introduction of advanced technology into the economy. (Italics mine.)

For a party with predominantly business interest representation – and one which had to rely on the London public relations firm of Michael Rice and Company to handle its publicity – perhaps that was not a surprising ideological and electoral position to take.

The beginnings of the original NPP can quite possibly be traced to 'Club 400', an association initiated by Alhaji Waziri Ibrahim, ostensibly intended to serve as a platform for channelling the efforts of the moderately well-to-do neo-nationalists towards philanthropic ends: its real purpose was to provide a focus for rallying the politically ambitious with resources to gamble in the stakes for successor to the military regime. Waziri had once served as an NPC federal minister, but on the collapse of the civilian regime he had left politics for the more rewarding field of business where, within a short period, he accumulated an immense fortune as an international arms buyer for the federal government during the civil war. However, with the promise of a return to civil rule and with more than enough resources to invest in fighting to gain supreme political power, anyone with the obvious talents of Waziri would have been attracted by the lure of politics. While Waziri was looking for converts to his 'Club 400', there were others, largely young, educated men (who had got themselves to the Constituent Assembly) who had formed themselves into what was known as 'Club 19', an association aimed at bringing together the minority elements from the various states as an insulation against the domination of Nigerian politics by the major ethnic groups, the Yoruba, Hausa and the Ibo. With few resources at their disposal, 'Club 19' soon found, in Waziri, a Kanuri and a 'minority' person, a financial champion; thus was formed the 'original' NPP with Waziri as leader.

Perhaps suspecting that he stood very little chance of winning adherents to his party in the 'Western' states — Lagos, Ogun, Oyo, and Ondo — and in the former NPC strongholds — Sokoto, Bauchi, Niger, and Kaduna — (nor in the predominantly Hausa-speaking states like Kano), Waziri concentrated his efforts very early in certain sections of the country: Anambra and Imo states (the former East-Central State); the minority or ethnically heterogeneous areas, Bendel, Cross River, Rivers, Kwara, Gongola, and Plateau states, and of course, his 'home' state of Borno. Though on the face of it, a good strategic approach, it soon led the NPP into difficulties. By spreading the support base of the NPP in the way Waziri did, he left the Anambra/Imo state caucus as the largest single bloc in the party and soon there were accusations that too much power was being concentrated in the hands of Waziri (who was accused of encouraging a 'personality cult'): he was not only Presidential candidate, he was also Party Chairman, in contrast to the 'diffused' leadership structure of the NPN.

But in reality, the demand for the 'democratisation' of the leadership was more Machiavellian than appeared on the surface. It was in fact based on the realisation that, however well

the NPP performed at the elections, it was unlikely to emerge
as a 'winning coalition', in the sense of winning the presidential vote. The odds against winning would actually be considerably worsened should a caucus, like the Anambra/Imo
caucus, succeed in carving for itself a separate 'identity'. In
those circumstances, at best, all that (the remnant of) the
NPP could expect would be to become a member of a coalition
federal government. But in those same circumstances a
(breakaway) faction of the NPP could stand to gain more
bargaining on its own, more so if it were pivotal and in a
position to turn a 'blocking coalition' into a minimum winning
coalition.[14]

The challenge centred, not unexpectedly, around that
veteran Nigerian nationalist and politician, Dr Nnamdi
Azikiwe, who was also being wooed by the NPN.[15] The
leadership question was finally resolved at the Ibadan convention of the NPP. Waziri declined to give up his dual status of
Party Chairman and Presidential candidate and in the face of
that refusal, the NPP split into two factions: one centred
around Dr Azikiwe, and the other around Alhaji Waziri. The
former claimed the name of the original party, the NPP, with
the bulk of the following being made up largely of former
members of the NCNC (for example men like Mr Ogunsanya,
who became the Party Chairman, and Mr Olu Akinfosile,
former NCNC member of the House of Representatives),
while the latter became the Great Nigeria Peoples' Party
(GNPP). Ideologically, there was not much to distinguish
either party other than that whereas the GNPP sought to
make the need for consensualism ('politics without bitterness')
the focal point of its appeal to the electorate, the NPP based its
claims to support on the espousal of a liberal ethic. On an 'indi-
vidualist'/'collectivist' or a 'competitive market'/'socialistic
economy' dimension, an approximate placing of the different
parties could possibly be represented as follows:

PARTY IDEOLOGICAL POSITIONING

PRP	UPN	NPP	GNPP	NPN
LEFT		CENTRE		RIGHT

It should be emphasised that the foregoing ideological

positioning notwithstanding, ideological disputes have never been a prominent feature of Nigerian politics and while there are no doubt to be found protagonists of some form of Marxism or the other, the rhetoric of the class struggle and class conflict is not something which has won wide recognition. Generally, political beliefs are characterised more by their fluidity than by any consistency with which they are adhered to, and certainly for the political leadership, political beliefs are more a matter of convenience than one of commitment. For the vast majority of the people, the primary concerns have been, and still are, questions of food, jobs and education, which is another way of saying that, essentially, opinion distribution is single-peaked. The result of course is that, in any election, one tends to find competing parties espousing more or less identical platforms, and making more or less the same promises to the electorate with only differences in emphasis and/or campaign style to distinguish the programmatic appeal of one party from the other.

Little need be said about the fifth party, the PRP, led by the well-known radical politician, Alhaji Aminu Kano. A nationalist when it was unfashionable to be such in the early days of party politics in the old Northern region, Aminu was unable to reconcile himself to the gradualist conservatism of the NPC. Though he served as a commissioner in the military administration of General Gowon, he did so more from a commitment to federalist ideals than as a supporter of military rule, and openly opposed Gowon's decision to postpone indefinitely the return to civil rule in 1976 which Gowon had promised in 1970. With the overthrow of Gowon and the prospect of a return to civil rule, Aminu increasingly found himself isolated from the mainstream of 'northern' political opinion which he saw as conservative and too committed to a capitalist ethic. Though Aminu would like to be taken for a socialist, his 'socialism' could possibly be better described as a form of populist communalism (sovereignty belongs to the people; elected representatives are no more than 'trustees' of the people; land belongs to the people who should decide to what use it should be put; etc.) but it is a communalism which has found expression in various ambiguous statements by Aminu rather than in any coherent formulation. Aminu's ambiguity has, however, had one advantage: it has provided him with a suitable cover for drawing together, under his leadership, a wide spectrum of diverse radical opinion-holders who would have been alienated from him had he ever succeeded in giving coherent form to his ideological position. To that extent, one could describe the PRP as a 'residual party', a party of those who have been unable to reconcile themselves to the platforms of the other parties. In another sense, however, as the electoral data shows, the PRP is a 'Kano' party, an expression of Kano's claim to political primacy in the North,[16] much in the same manner as one could talk of Sokoto's claim to religious (Islamic) primacy.

From this description of Nigerian parties it can be seen that the system can be characterised, following Sartori, as one of limited pluralism,[17] which is a system composed of between three and five political parties, and distinguished from extreme pluralism where not only are there more parties, but the parties themselves tend to fractionalise, and therefore to multiply. However, besides numbers there are other characteristic features of limited pluralism which set it apart from the extreme pluralistic system. The first feature is the small ideological distance which tends to exist among the parties; that is, ideological differences, though present, are not strong, or not strong enough to result in a polarisation — the pulling towards extremes — of the parties. The second feature follows from this fact of a small ideological distance: party competition tends to be centripetal rather than centrifugal; or put differently, party competition tends to be system-reinforcing and system-legitimating, the referent of system in this context being the macro, or overall, political system. The third feature is that the formula of governing tends to be one not of *alternative* governments but of alternating *coalitions* since it is rarely the case in such a system that there is any one party with an overall majority large enough to enable it to form a government by itself. The feature of alternating coalitions is in fact closely related to the small ideological distance which separates the parties. Put briefly, coalitions alternate where, in a system in which there are five parties, A, B, C, D, and E, at a given time coalition (A,B) may form the government, and at another, it could be (A,C), (A,D) or (B,C), (B,E) and so on, in contradistinction to a system of alternative *governments* where coalition (A,B) forming the government at a given time may be succeeded at another period by coalition (C,D), (D,E) or (C,D,E) or any combinations of C, D, and E. This fact of alternating coalitions thus tends to result, as a fourth feature, in a 'bipolar coalitional configuration', that is, the appearance is given of a two-party system as the different parties group into two broad coalitions.

These features of the limited pluralistic party system should be seen as features indicating tendencies which a given system may approximate to in varying degrees, the closeness of approximation being a matter for empirical observation and not one determinable *a priori*. In the Nigerian case, the trend towards bipolarity can be seen, certainly at the state level, in the tendency for the GNPP, PRP, and UPN states to work together in close collaboration: there are regular meetings of the governors of the nine states involved.[18] At the extra-legislative national level, the same trend can be seen in the growing call for bipolarisation, based on the suggestion made by Dr Chuba Okadigbo, the Presidential political adviser (NPN) and taken up by the Senate majority leader, Dr Joseph Wayas (NPN), that the existing five parties should form into two broad coalitions — one, the Peoples' National Party of Nigeria (PNPN) to be made up of the NPN, NPP, and PRP, and the other, the Peoples' Unity Party to be composed of the UPN and the GNPP. Already within the PRP, it is possible to discern some three factions emerging, the first centred around the PRP's Vice-Presidential candidate during the elections, Mr S. G. Ikoku (who is also the party's Deputy Chairman), who, it would seem, would prefer to have the PRP enter into a formal alliance with the NPN. The second faction is centred on the party's two state Governors — Mallam Ibrahim Rimi, Governor of Kano state, and Alhaji Musa Balarabe, Governor of Kaduna State — both of whom would rather have a revamped PRP (possibly by overthrowing the national leader, Mallam Aminu Kano) work in close collaboration with the UPN; the third faction is centred on Aminu Kano himself, who would want to have the PRP retain its existing 'identity' but to work with whichever party it might be thought desirable to co-operate with given the prevailing circumstances of the time.[19]

While one will have to wait for subsequent elections to see if alternating coalitions will prevail, the trend towards centripetality can be seen in the formation at the National Assembly level of Parliamentary Study Groups — which cut across the official committee system and which embrace all the parties. However, it remains to be seen whether the existing limited pluralistic system will persist or whether, over time, there will be a move towards a definite bipolarity.

THE 1979 NATIONAL ELECTIONS

The formation and registration of the five parties heralded the way for elections which were held on 7 July (to the Senate of the National Assembly), 14 July (to the House of Representatives), 21 July (to the state Assemblies), 28 July (for the Gubernatorial offices) and 11 August (for the Presidential office). The arrangments for the elections were handled by the Federal Electoral Commission (FEDECO) and these can be very briefly described. Essentially, the arrangements involved the preparation of a voters' list of all those registered to vote; the division of the federation into single member constituencies, of which there were 449,[20] and the further division of each constituency into a number of polling stations. For each polling station there was a polling clerk to supervise the voting procedure; and for each constituency, a Returning Officer, the returning officer therefore supervising the activities of all the polling clerks in his constituency; and for each state, there was at least one Electoral Officer. To deal with the problem of disputed elections, special electoral tribunals were set up, of which there were at least one for each state. For the election to the office of the President, the Federal High Court served as the electoral tribunal. There was a right of appeal from the decision of an electoral tribunal to the Federal Supreme Court. There were separate ballot papers for each of the elections and a ballot paper showed not only the name of the candidate contesting a particular constituency, but also the symbol of the party sponsoring the candidate. A voter marked in secret the ballot paper issued to him by the polling clerk, after which the voter folded the paper before placing it in the ballot box in full view of all those legally permitted to be present at the polling station. (In the main these were the polling clerk and the polling agents; the latter, of whom there could be not more than two for each candidate, represented the interests of the contesting candidates but were formally appointed by the Electoral Commission.) After voting, the thumb of each voter was imprinted with indelible ink to prevent a voter voting more than once.

For the Federal House of Representatives, the division of the country into 449 constituencies gave the distribution of seats to the different states which is shown in Table 6.2. There

TABLE 6.2   *House of Representatives: allocation of seats by states*

State	Population total	No. of seats allocated	Population represented per MHR[21]	Index[22] of representation
Anambra	3,596,618	29	124,000	1.0
Bauchi	2,431,296	20	122,000	0.983
Bendel	2,460,962	20	123,000	0.992
Benue	2,427,017	19	128,000	1.032
Borno	2,997,498	24	125,000	1.008
Cross River	3,478,131	28	124,000	1.0
Gongola	2,605,263	21	124,000	1.0
Imo	3,672,654	30	122,000	0.983
Kaduna	4,098,306	33	124,000	1.0
Kano	5,774,840	46	126,000	1.016
Kwara	1,714,485	14	122,000	0.983
Lagos	1,443,568	12	120,000	0.968
Niger	1,194,508	10	119,000	0.960
Ogun	1,550,996	12	129,000	1.040
Ondo	2,729,690	22	124,000	1.0
Oyo	5,208,884	42	124,000	1.0
Plateau	2,026,657	16	127,000	1.024
Rivers	1,719,925	14	123,000	0.992
Sokoto	4,538,787	37	123,000	0.992

Note: The State population figures were those agreed to at the meeting of Secretaries to State Military Governments on 17 May 1977, *West Africa*, 4/7/1977. The figures differ from those given in the White Paper on the Report of the Panel on Creation of States (Ministry of Information, 1976). The former figures were used because they were more recent than those shown on the White Paper.

is a whole host of factors which make strict proportionality (index of representation = 1.0) extremely difficult, if not impossible, to achieve, and for the allocation arrived at by FEDECO, deviation from strict proportionality is far too small to be significant. (One way of putting this is to say that out of the total of 449 seats distributed, Benue and Ogun states *combined* lost one seat which was gained by Lagos and Niger states *taken together*.)

If FEDECO's allocation of seats between the states — the very close approximation to 'strict proportionality' — is to be commended, the picture with respect to the registration of voters would seem to be very different. At the end of the registration exercise, it was claimed by FEDECO that over 47 million (some 47.7 million) voters had qualified for registration and had been duly registered. However in the election with the highest total vote — the Presidential election — only 16.8 million voters cast their votes, giving a voter turnout of just about a third which is just about the lowest turnout in the whole of Nigeria's electoral history. And given the widespread allegations of vote-rigging — the same voter voting more than once, for example — and there is some evidence to support these allegations,[23] then the true vote must have been lower than the recorded vote of 16.8 million. How does one explain this low-level vote?

One explanation could be that the 1979 elections were the first ever elections in which the voting age was lowered to 18. Thus, those within the age range 18—33 years (who would have been between 5 and 20 years old when the last elections were held in 1964) would have been voting for the first time in their lives. And if, as some have suggested, voting is a matter of 'habit', then not having acquired the 'habit of voting', first-time voters will be more likely to abstain from voting than others. Secondly, voting, as Blondel and others have argued, is a mark of affirmation, of belief in the efficacy of the political system. But it is within the 15—29-year-old age group that one finds the most acute cases of the unemployment which is so characteristic of developing countries and one would therefore expect that class of the population to constitute the most alienated and hence the most likely to abstain. One might also expect abstainers among the rural population. For one thing, it is usually easier to mobilise the urban masses than the rural – the concentration of the mass media and better communication and transport facilities in the urban areas make such mobilisation more readily manageable. Besides, given the lag between the lifting of the ban on the formation of parties and the time the elections were held, a space of some nine months, it was as much as the parties could do to reach the urban electorate; to reach the rural electorate in any effective way would have required far longer. If one conceded this hypothesis of non-voting, then since demographically more than half the total population fall within the range 15–49 years old, and given the unquestionably large rural population, the non-voting hypothesis would seem a reasonable explanation of the figures.

But though voter abstention may have occurred on a considerable scale, a second hypothesis that could explain the low voter turnout could be over registration. Close to 60 per cent of the population would fall within the age range of those qualified to vote. If we assume that everyone qualified to vote was registered – a totally implausible assumption since there were numerous reported cases of non-registration – then to have registered an electorate of over 47 million would indicate a total population of some 100 million people and there cannot be many – not even FEDECO itself – who would be prepared to say that Nigeria had a population in 1978 of 100 million people. With the rejection of the 1973 census figures[24] and so much dependent on numbers – the allocation of revenue, the distribution of federal grants, aid and patronage and much else besides – the temptation to inflate voter registration must have been quite considerable and it seems almost certain the figures were inflated. For instance, for the Presidential election the number of ballot papers delivered to the state was fixed at 80 per cent of the registered vote. In Ondo state – which had one of the highest voter turnout figures for the Presidential election in the whole federation – the percentage of votes cast rose between the Senatorial and the Presidential election by (the unbelievable figure of) 143.12% – some 1,369,849 votes were cast at the Presidential election with 752,412 ballot papers returned unused. On the basis of these figures, then the registered electorate would have been (in round figures) 2.6 million. With a total population of some 2.7 million, assuming that everyone aged 18 and over was registered (which is highly improbable), then it would follow that only 0.1 million, or just about 4 per cent of the total population, was under 18 years, which would mean either that the known demographic structure is grossly misleading, or the figure of 4 per cent is totally absurd, and the latter would be the truer representation.[25] Whatever then, may be the correct position with regard to voter abstention, there can be no escaping the fact that most of the states — if not all — inflated their numbers of the registered electorate. FEDECO therefore made a bad job of the preparation of the register of voters and to that extent contributed in no small way to the allegations of large scale electoral abuse.

The elections which, it was generally agreed, were conducted in an orderly manner, and were in the main, free and fair, were held at weekly intervals, the first being, as stated above, for the second chamber of the National Assembly, the Senate. The count for the Senatorial contest gave the result shown in Table 6.3.

The outcome of the Senatorial vote could be seen as a near-accurate predictor for the rest of the elections as the distribution of seats and the percentage of votes won by the various parties in the elections to the House of Representatives and state Assemblies followed fairly closely the pattern established in the Senatorial contest. The results of the contests for the House of Representatives and the state Assemblies are shown in Tables 6.4 and 6.5.

From the three elections — to the Senate, the House of Representatives and the state Assemblies — the pattern, as it emerged, showed that certain states could quite clearly be associated with particular parties, as shown in Table 6.6. Though the GNPP had retained control of Gongola, it was nevertheless clear that the party's hold on the state was tenuous and that Gongola was very much a 'marginal' state. The positions of Bendel and Kwara had been reversed in the three elections, for whereas in Bendel the NPN got a majority of the Senate votes but lost the state to the UPN in the House of Representatives and state Assembly elections, the

Source: The General Elections of 1979: Report by the Federal Electoral Commission

TABLE 6.3 *Election to the senate*

State	GNPP	UPN	NPN	PRP	NPP	Total
Anambra	13,782	10,932	210,101	19,574	699,157	953,546
%	1.45	1.15	22.03	2.05	73.32	
Bauchi	187,805	28,959	323,327	127,279	42,148	709,518
%	26.47	4.08	45.57	17.94	5.94	
Bendel	42,528	330,537	264,369	2,055	70,214	709,703
%	5.99	46.57	37.25	0.29	9.89	
Benue	46,452	14,925	332,967	2,491	73,524	470,359
%	9.88	3.17	70.79	0.53	15.63	
Borno	278,342	22,145	184,633	31,508	3,256	519,884
%	53.54	4.26	35.51	6.06	0.63	
Cross River	163,753	78,479	310,061	—	68,203	620,496
%	26.39	12.64	49.97	—	10.99	
Gongola	223,121	124,747	203,225	67,744	17,836	636,673
%	35.04	19.59	31.92	10.64	2.80	
Imo	100,688	9,404	141,856	8,609	758,186	1,018,743
%	9.88	0.92	13.92	0.85	74.42	
Kaduna	232,924	84,994	400,888	278,669	43,399	1,040,874
%	22.38	8.17	38.51	26.77	4.17	
Kano	35,430	13,831	233,985	683,367	—	966,613
%	3.66	1.43	24.21	70.70	—	
Kwara	32,383	126,065	154,302	639	1,493	314,882
%	10.28	40.04	49.00	0.20	0.47	
Lagos	14,480	428,578	34,587	2,556	53,901	534,102
%	2.71	80.24	6.48	0.48	10.09	
Niger	71,498	13,363	175,475	8,984	867	270,187
%	26.46	4.95	64.95	3.32	0.32	
Ogun	3,078	405,047	53,099	—	730	461,954
%	0.67	87.68	11.49	—	0.16	
Ondo	4,861	501,492	49,612	245	7,239	563,449
%	0.86	89.00	8.81	0.04	1.28	
Oyo	11,272	757,696	200,382	—	8,897	978,247
%	1.15	77.45	20.48	—	0.91	
Plateau	40,487	19,624	154,792	19,017	220,278	454,198
%	8.91	4.32	34.08	4.19	48.50	
Rivers	47,185	20,154	153,463	2,271	87,396	310,469
%	15.20	6.49	49.43	0.73	28.15	
Sokoto	380,806	34,145	571,562	38,255	—	1,024,768
%	37.16	3.33	55.77	3.73	—	
TOTAL	1,930,875	3,025,117	4,152,686	1,293,263	2,156,724	12,558,665
%	15.37	24.09	33.07	10.30	17.17	
Seats won	8	28	36	7	16	95
% seats	8.4	29.50	37.90	7.30	16.90	
Seats − PR	15	23	31	10	16	
Differential	+7	−5	−5	+3	—	

Source: The General Elections of 1979: Report by the Federal Electoral Commission
PR = proportional representation

TABLE 6.4   *Distribution of seats: House of Representatives*

State	Total seats	GNPP	UPN	NPN	PRP	NPP
Anambra	29	–	–	3	–	26
Bauchi	20	1	–	18	–	1
Bendel	20	–	12	6	–	2
Benue	19	–	–	18	–	1
Borno	24	22	–	2	–	–
Cross River	28	4	2	22	–	–
Gongola	21	8	7	5	–	1
Imo	30	–	–	2	–	28
Kaduna	33	1	1	19	10	2
Kano	46	–	–	7	39	–
Kwara	14	1	5	8	–	–
Lagos	12	–	12	–	–	–
Niger	10	–	–	10	–	–
Ogun	12	–	12	–	–	–
Ondo	22	–	22	–	–	–
Oyo	42	–	38	4	–	–
Plateau	16	–	–	3	–	13
Rivers	14	–	–	10	–	4
Sokoto	37	6	–	31	–	–
TOTAL	449	43	111	168	49	78
% seats	100	9.6	24.7	37.4	10.9	17.4

reverse was the case in Kwara where the UPN had won a majority of the Senate vote but lost the state to the NPN in the House of Representatives and state Assembly elections. The fourth election in the series, that for the Gubernatorial office, held on 28 July, followed much the same pattern but with the one surprising difference, that the NPN lost Kaduna state to the PRP (discussed below) (see Table 6.7).

Of the five candidates who contested the Presidential elections – Alhaji Ibrahim Waziri for the GNPP, Chief Obafemi Awolowo for the UPN, Alhaji Shehu Shagari for the NPN, Dr Nnamdi Azikiwe for the NPP, and Mallam Aminu Kano for the PRP – two, Azikiwe and Aminu Kano, had initially had their candidacy questioned by FEDECO on the grounds

TABLE 6.5 *Distribution of seats: state Assemblies*

State	Total seats	GNPP	UPN	NPN	PRP	NPP
Anambra	87	1	—	13	—	73
Bauchi	60	9	—	45	2	4
Bendel	60	—	34	22	—	4
Benue	57	6	—	48	—	3
Borno	72	59	—	11	2	—
Cross River	84	16	7	58	—	3
Gongola	63	25	18	15	1	4
Imo	90	2	—	9	—	79
Kaduna	99	10	3	64	16	6
Kano	138	3	1	11	123	—
Kwara	42	2	15	25	—	—
Lagos	36	—	36	—	—	—
Niger	30	2	—	28	—	—
Ogun	36	—	36	—	—	—
Ondo	66	—	65	1	—	—
Oyo	126	—	117	9	—	—
Plateau	48	3	—	10	—	35
Rivers	42	1	—	26	—	15
Sokoto	111	19	—	92	—	—
TOTAL	1347	157	333	487	144	226
% seats	100	11.7	24.7	36.2	10.7	16.8

TABLE 6.6 *Party control of states*

GNPP	UPN	NPN	PRP	NPP
Borno	Bendel	Bauchi	Kano	Anambra
Gongola	Lagos	Benue		Imo
	Ogun	Kaduna		Plateau
	Ondo	Kwara		
	Oyo	Cross River		
		Niger		
		Rivers		
		Sokoto		

TABLE 6.7 *Gubernatorial office (including Deputy Governors): by states*

GNPP	UPN	NPN	PRP	NPP
Borno	Bendel	Bauchi	Kano	Anambra
Gongola	Lagos	Benue	Kaduna	Imo
	Ogun	Cross River		Plateau
	Ondo	Kwara		
	Oyo	Niger		
		Rivers		
		Sokoto		

of alleged irregularities with their tax payments, or, in the case of Aminu Kano, non-payment of tax. Azikiwe had challenged the decision of FEDECO not to have him registered before the Anambra state High Court and had won his case, the court ruling that he had duly and properly paid the taxes for which he was assessed. Though Aminu Kano had earlier claimed that since he earned no income in the three years preceding the elections, the mandatory period for which tax receipts had to be produced for a candidate to be eligible for registration, and hence could not be liable for tax, he subsequently did pay tax and with the approval of the military authorities, was duly registered as a candidate. The outcome of the Presidential election is given in Table 6.8a–d.

Given the controversy which surrounded the election of the President (discussed in the last chapter), it might be helpful to look at the 'minority' vote (Table 6.9). It is not of course being suggested that the 'minority' vote could resolve the legal and conceptual issues involved in the controversy. But it does provide a way of looking at the electoral appeal of the different candidates among groups with which they are, in the main, not ethnically identified. Essentially, the notion of 'minority' used here can properly be conceived of in politico-ethnic terms. Historically,[26] certain areas of the federation have been known as 'minority areas'. These were areas which had ethnically heterogeneous populations which were ethnically different from the main ethnic group in the regions in which these areas were geographically located. Thus, before the Midwest (now Bendel) was carved from the former Western region, it counted as a 'minority area' because the total population of the area is ethnically different from the main ethnic group in the Western region, the Yorubas. Also, the population of the area is ethnically mixed, being made up of Binis, Urhobos, Ika-Ibos, Ijaws, Itsekiris, and many others. The same thing could be said of such areas as Calabar, Ogoja and Rivers provinces which now made up the Cross River and Rivers states respectively, and also the territories which presently form Kwara, Benue, Plateau, Bauchi and Gongola states. In using the term 'minority state' in the present context, one sense then of that term is this historical usage. But it has been found necessary to qualify that historical usage by

TABLE 6.8(a)   *Presidential election*

State	GNPP	UPN	NPN	PRP	NPP	Total votes cast
Anambra	20,228	9,063	163,164	14,500	1,002,083	1,209,038
Bauchi	154,218	29,960	623,989	143,202	47,314	998,683
Bendel	8,242	356,381	242,320	4,939	57,629	669,511
Benue	42,993	13,864	411,648	7,277	63,097	538,879
Borno	384,278	23,885	246,778	46,385	9,625	710,951
Cross River	100,105	77,775	425,815	6,737	50,671	661,103
Gongola	217,914	138,561	227,057	27,750	27,856	639,138
Imo	34,616	7,335	101,516	10,252	999,636	1,153,355
Kaduna	190,935	92,382	596,302	437,772	65,321	1,382,712
Kano	18,482	14,973	222,998	932,803	11,082	1,200,338
Kwara	20,251	140,006	190,142	2,376	1,830	354,605
Lagos	3,943	681,762	59,515	3,874	79,320	828,414
Niger	63,273	14,155	295,366	14,555	4,292	391,641
Ogun	3,974	689,655	46,358	2,338	2,343	744,668
Ondo	3,561	1,294,666	57,388	2,479	11,752	1,369,846
Oyo	8,029	1,197,983	177,999	4,804	7,732	1,396,547
Plateau	37,400	29,029	179,458	21,852	269,666	537,405
Rivers	15,025	71,114	499,846	3,212	98,754	687,951
Sokoto	369,021	46,103	886,094	45,077	12,503	1,358,798
TOTAL	1,696,488	4,928,652	5,653,753	1,732,184	2,822,506	16,833,584

TABLE 6.8(b)   *Percentage vote (Presidential election)*

State	GNPP	UPN	NPN	PRP	NPP	Total votes cast
Anambra	1.68	0.75	13.49	1.20	82.88	1,209,038
Bauchi	15.44	3.00	62.48	14.34	4.74	998,683
Bendel	1.23	53.23	36.19	0.74	8.61	669,511
Benue	7.98	2.57	76.39	1.35	11.71	538,879
Borno	54.05	3.36	34.71	6.52	1.35	710,951
Cross River	15.14	11.76	64.41	1.02	7.66	661,103
Gongola	34.09	21.68	35.53	4.34	4.36	639,138
Imo	3.00	0.64	8.80	0.89	86.67	1,153,355
Kaduna	13.81	6.68	43.13	31.66	4.72	1,382,712
Kano	1.54	1.25	18.58	77.71	0.92	1,200,338
Kwara	5.71	39.49	53.62	0.67	0.52	354,605
Lagos	0.48	82.30	7.18	0.47	9.57	828,414
Niger	16.16	3.61	75.42	3.72	1.09	391,641
Ogun	0.53	92.61	6.23	0.31	0.32	744,668
Ondo	0.26	94.51	4.19	0.18	0.86	1,369,846
Oyo	0.57	85.78	12.75	0.34	0.55	1,396,547
Plateau	6.96	5.40	33.39	4.07	50.18	537,405
Rivers	2.18	10.34	72.66	0.47	14.35	687,951
Sokoto	27.16	3.39	65.21	3.32	0.92	1,358,798
Percentage vote recorded	10.08	29.28	33.58	10.29	16.77	16,833,583

a 'political' criterion, a criterion derived from the first election, that to the Senate. In other words, in addition to that historical usage, or in qualification of that usage, a state is furthermore regarded as a 'minority state' if at the first election, no one party polled 70 per cent or more of the total votes cast in that state.[27] In other words, states in which a particular party

TABLE 6.8(c)   *Senatorial and Presidential elections: total votes by parties*

Party	Senate total (1)	% (2)	Presidential total (3)	% (4)	Differential % (4) − (2)
GNPP	1,930,875	15.37	1,696,489	10.08	−5.29
UPN	3,025,117	24.09	4,928,652	29.28	+5.19
NPN	4,152,686	33.07	5,653,753	33.58	+0.51
PRP	1,293,263	10.30	1,732,184	10.29	−0.01
NPP	2,156,724	17.17	2,822,506	16.77	−0.4

TABLE 6.8(d)   *Percentage vote difference: Senatorial/ Presidential elections*

State	GNPP	UPN	NPN	PRP	NPP
Anambra	0.23	−0.4	−8.54	−0.85	9.56
Bauchi	−11.03	−1.08	16.91	−3.6	−1.2
Bendel	−4.76	6.66	−1.06	0.45	−1.28
Benue	−1.9	−0.60	5.6	0.82	−3.92
Borno	0.51	−0.9	−0.8	0.46	0.72
Cross River	−11.25	−0.88	14.44	1.02	−3.33
Gongola	−0.96	2.09	3.61	−6.3	1.56
Imo	−6.88	−0.28	−5.12	0.04	12.25
Kaduna	−8.57	−1.49	4.62	4.89	0.55
Kano	−2.12	−0.18	−5.63	7.01	0.92
Kwara	−4.57	−0.55	4.62	0.47	0.05
Lagos	−2.23	2.06	0.7	−0.01	−0.52
Niger	−10.3	−1.34	10.47	0.4	0.77
Ogun	−0.14	4.93	−5.26	0.31	0.16
Ondo	−0.6	5.51	−4.62	0.14	−0.42
Oyo	−0.58	8.33	−7.73	0.34	−0.36
Plateau	−1.95	1.08	−0.69	−0.12	1.68
Rivers	−13.02	3.85	23.23	−0.26	−13.8
Sokoto	−10.00	0.06	9.44	−0.41	0.92

TABLE 6.9   *'Minority' vote: Presidential election*

State	GNPP	UPN	NPN	PRP	NPP	
Bauchi	154,218	29,960	623,989	143,202	47,314	
Bendel	8,242	356,381	242,320	4,939	57,629	
Benue	42,993	13,864	411,648	7,277	63,097	
Borno	384,278	23,885	246,778	46,385	9,625	
Cross River	100,105	77,775	425,815	6,737	50,671	
Gongola	217,914	138,561	227,057	27,750	27,856	
Kaduna	190,936	92,382	596,302	437,772	65,321	
Kwara	20,251	140,006	190,142	2,376	1,830	
Niger	63,273	14,155	295,366	14,555	4,292	
Plateau	37,400	29,029	179,458	21,853	269,666	
Rivers	15,025	71,114	499,846	3,212	98,754	
TOTAL	1,234,635	987,112	3,938,721	716,058	696,055	7,572,581
Percentage of total	16.30	13.04	52.01	9.46	9.19	
Comparable percentage Senate election	22.56	14.26	43.87	8.93	10.38	6,057,243
Differential (+) or (−)	−6.26	−1.22	+8.14	+0.53	−1.19	

Total 'minority' vote as % of total vote: Presidential election (A)	44.98
Total 'minority' vote as % of total vote: Senatorial election (B)	48.23
Change (A) − (B)	−3.14

Total 'minority' vote: Presidential election	7,572,581
Total 'minority' vote: Senatorial election	6,057,243
Percentage differential 'minority' vote	25.01
Percentage differential overall vote Presidential/Senatorial elections	34.04

Note: Benue included as a 'minority' here although excluded by Dudley on the basis of his functional definition of minority. See pp 206–11.

is electorally dominant — a 'party-dominant state' — are excluded irrespective of the fact that such a state might otherwise have counted as a 'minority area'. The application of the politico-ethnic criterion thus immediately eliminates nine states from being regarded as 'minority states': Lagos, Ogun, Oyo and Ondo where the UPN polled 70 per cent of the votes are in the main, Yoruba-speaking states, the ethnic group with which Chief Awolowo is identified; Imo and Anambra states where the NPP polled over 70 per cent of the votes are Ibo-speaking states and identified ethnically with Dr Azikiwe; Sokoto is Hausa-Fulani and identified with Alhaji Shehu Shagari, a Fulani; and Kano, another Hausa-Fulani state, is identified with Mallam Aminu Kano, also a Fulani. There are, however, two 'oddities' involved in the application of this criterion; Borno state, an essentially Kanuri state linked with Alhaji Waziri Ibrahim, a Kanuri, is classed as 'minority' whereas Benue, normally and conventionally taken to be a 'minority' state, is eliminated, even though none of the Presidential or Vice-Presidential candidates is ethnically linked with any of the groups within the state. However, since the NPN polled over 70 per cent of the votes in Benue, that state can be regarded as a 'party-dominant state' in contrast to Borno, where the GNPP succeeded in polling only 53.8 per cent of the votes and the NPN 35.7 per cent. Borno could with justification be classed as 'competitive'. Be that as it may, apart from Benue, no state which would normally be taken as a 'minority state' is excluded by the application of the criterion, and in fact, the exclusions cancel each other out and in no way affect the distribution shown in Table 6.10.

With this presentation of the electoral data, the 'voting decision' can now be examined, doing so on a party-by-party basis.

THE VOTING DECISION

The first striking feature of the voter support for the UPN is the remarkable consistency of that support, a consistency which would suggest the existence of a predisposition among

TABLE 6.10(a)   *Party electoral appeal: proportion votes polled in states*

Party		Less than 5%	5–9%	10–19%	20–29%	30–49%	50–59%	More than 60%
GNPP	(1)	6	2	4	4	2	1	—
	(2)	9	3	4	1	1	1	—
UPN	(1)	9	2	1	1	2	—	4
	(2)	8	2	2	1	1	1	4
NPN	(1)	—	2	2	3	8	2	2
	(2)	1	3	3	—	5	1	6
PRP	(1)	14	1	2	1	—	—	1
	(2)	15	1	1	1	1	—	1
NPP	(1)	10	1	4	1	1	—	2
	(2)	11	2	3	—	0	1	2

Note (1) Senatorial election; (2) Presidential election.

TABLE 6.10(b)   *Party electoral appeal: collapsed*

Party		Not larger than 20%	21—59%	60% and over
GNPP	(1)	12	7	—
	(2)	16	3	—
UPN	(1)	13	2	4
	(2)	12	3	4
NPN	(1)	4	13	2
	(2)	7	6	6
PRP	(1)	17	1	1
	(2)	17	1	1
NPP	(1)	15	2	2
	(2)	16	1	2

Note: (1) Senatorial election; (2) Presidential election

a set of the electorate to vote for the party. Voter predisposition does of course derive from a number of different variables: categoric variables such as age, sex, or ethnic identity; or social characteristics such as education, class, occupation or religious affiliation.[28] In the case of the UPN, the high degree of localisation of its support would indicate that, of the set of predisposing factors, the most salient is that of ethnic identity. All four states in which the UPN had overwhelming support (over 80 per cent of the votes) are Yoruba-speaking states — Lagos, Ogun, Ondo, and Oyo. It is obvious, however, that the ethnic variable cannot possibly explain the fairly considerable support which the UPN had in such states as Bendel and Gongola, though it would account for the party's one-third share of the vote in Kwara where a significant proportion of the electorate is Yoruba-speaking.

In Bendel, the UPN's share of the vote rose from 46.57 per cent in the Senatorial election to 53 per cent in the Presidential election. It won all but one of the seats in the state to the federal House of Representatives and secured 57 per cent of the seats in the state Assembly besides winning the gubernatorial contest in the state. In Gongola, the UPN polled about a fifth of the votes in the Senatorial and Presidential elections and won roughly the same proportion of the seats in the state Assembly and in the House of Representatives. What is now known as Bendel had been part of the former Western region, an area in which, traditionally, the AG had significant support, even after Bendel became a separate state, and much of that support must have been transferred to the UPN during the elections. The basis of that support itself lies in intercommunal conflicts and rivalries, for example, Itsekiri–Urhobo rivalries; and intra-communal struggles, such as those amongst the Edos (Binis), between members of the Ogboni fraternity and those opposed to the fraternity, a conflict which in itself is a reflection of the struggle for power within the 'Bini state' system. For the 1979 elections, such inter-communal conflicts were compounded by intra-community leadership disputes which had the effect of amplifying support for the UPN.[29] Much the same thing occurred in Gongola where the NPN surprisingly chose to recruit the local party chairman and secretary from the non-Fulani ethnic groups, thereby antagonising the Fulani who then gave their support to the GNPP and the UPN.

But there are other areas which in the past supported the AG and in which one would have expected the UPN to have won a sizeable following — areas such as Benue, Cross River and the Rivers states. The UPN vote in these states ranged between 2.57 per cent and 13 per cent in the Senatorial and Presidential elections. But then AG support in these areas in the past was mainly 'negative' support, more a case of opposition to the dominant parties in the regions of which these states formed a part — in Benue, opposition to the NPC and in the Rivers and Cross River areas, opposition to the NCNC — than of positive support for the AG.[30] There is also not much doubt that, as in Bendel and Gongola states, intra-community struggle for leadership — particularly in the Cross River state — influenced the pattern of voting, though adversely against the UPN.

The second striking feature of the UPN vote is the size of the support the party received in those states with which the party is ethnically linked. In no other state or states did any party win a comparable level of support. An explanation becomes all the more necessary when it is realised (a) that in no time in the past (other than in 1959) did the AG poll up to 50 per cent of the votes in the same areas; (b) that in 1961, for example, the votes in these areas, though not the seats, had been split almost equally between the AG and the NCNC; and (c) that in a state like Lagos whose population is more ethnically mixed than in the other three Yoruba-speaking states (the Yoruba-speaking elements in Lagos constituting just about two-thirds of the total population) and where political support had tended to vary between the NCNC and the AG in the past, it seems highly improbable that the UPN could have won more than 80 per cent of the votes with no other party polling as much as 10 per cent.

Conceivably, the UPN's slogan, *'Ti wa n'ti wa'* (lit: what is ours is ours, an appeal, in other words for the ethnic fold to close ranks) must have played a part in rallying support, particularly in those areas — Ilesha, Akure, Ibadan, Owo, and Abeokuta — where the AG had in the past had a marginal following. But this can hardly be an adequate explanation as that slogan does not seem to have had a similar impact in the Ogbomosho division of Oyo state. There are, however, three other possible explanations: (i) that the welfarist electioneering cues of the UPN were sufficiently compelling to sway large numbers of voters; (ii) that the leadership qualities of Chief Awolowo, who it should be remembered had earned himself the title of 'Leader of the Yorubas' in 1966 (during the crisis that preceded the civil war), were paramount in determining voter preferences; and (iii) that there was large-scale manipulation, 'rigging', of the vote. The first two factors, though salient, can nevertheless be discounted. Were the cue theory to be sustainable, then one would have expected it to have attracted greater voter support in the less advantaged areas — Bauchi, Plateau, Rivers, and Cross River states for example — than in the more advantaged former Western region. Besides, there was nothing particularly new in the campaign platform of the NPN. The AG had campaigned on a more or less identical platform in 1959 and had lost the elections. Equally, though Chief Awolowo's qualities as a leader need not be disputed, this is not to say that they are in any way unique,[31] and quite a number of others have questioned his entitlement to be styled 'Leader of the Yorubas'.[32]

The most plausible explanation of the UPN's overwhelming support in the Yoruba-speaking 'West' would therefore seem to lie in a fairly large-scale rigging of the vote. First, though the overall vote difference showed a rise of 34.2 per cent between the Senatorial and the Presidential elections, the recorded increases in Ogun (Chief Awolowo's home state) and Ondo were 70.26 per cent and 158.16 per cent respectively. In few states, such as Rivers (225.71 per cent)[33] was the latter percentage increase exceeded. The Ogun figure, for example, was one and a quarter times the increase in Sokoto (Shagari's home state), one and a half times the rise in Anambra (Azikiwe's home state), twice the increase in Borno (Waziri's home state) and twice Kano's (Aminu Kano's state). The figures for Oyo (58.11 per cent) and Lagos (59.08 per cent) were surpassed only by Bauchi (92.99 per cent) and Niger (68.32 per cent). Since it seems hardly credible to argue that the senatorial vote must have been unbelievably low in the first case, then a more than doubling of the vote in the presidential election can only be attributed to a fairly large-scale rigging.[34] This seems all the more likely when it is realised that the mass of polling clerks and polling agents responsible for the administration of the elections were all locally recruited, and from the class of people, schoolteachers and lower-cadre civil servants, who had in the past provided strong support for the AG and to whom the slogan of *'ti wa n'ti wa'* would have a highly charged emotional appeal.

Significantly, the voters of Ogun, Ondo, and Oyo states rejected the NPP (senate elections 0.16, 1.28 and 0.91 per cent; presidential elections 0.32, 0.86 and 0.55 per cent, respectively) much in the same way that the voters of Anambra and Imo states rejected the UPN (Senatorial elections 1.15 and 0.92 per cent; Presidential elections 0.75 and 0.64 per cent respectively). Obviously, the Ibos identified the UPN with the Yorubas, and the Yorubas identified the Ibos with the NPP. The 1979 elections therefore saw the reincarnation of the old conflicts between the NCNC and the AG, and both ethnic groups voted accordingly, the Yorubas for the UPN and the Ibos for the NPP. The Ibos, though, are more closely knit than the Yorubas and interview findings would seem to suggest that there was significant pressure at the grass-roots level — of the 'compound' and the clan — to have voters vote for the NPP.[35] In overall terms, however, the NPP's performance was the worst of all the parties. Other than in Plateau where in the Presidential election the NPP polled just over 50 per cent of the votes, in no state did the party receive as much as 15 per cent of the vote. Its share of the 'minority' vote in the Presidential election was only marginally more than that of the PRP and whereas the PRP (with considerably fewer resources) improved its share of the 'minority' vote between the Senatorial and the Presidential elections (+0.53 per cent; percentage computed with Benue included in minority states), the vote for the NPP actually fell (−1.19 per cent), and that despite the fact that the 'minority' vote between the two elections rose by 25.02 per cent.[36] It would seem that in initiating, or rather engineering, a split within the original NPP, Azikiwe not only succeeded in making the electorate at large equate the NPP with the Ibos, but in that very success, alienated large segments of the electorate who would have interpreted the move as just another attempt by Azikiwe to ensure that the Ibos were not left out in the leadership stakes, a game Azikiwe had played with consummate skill in 1959. In Plateau, the NPP vote was not only an anti-Hausa-Fulani vote, an assertion of the determination of the local indigenes — the Biroms, the Angas and many others — to claim a major share in the economy of the state (which has been dominated by the Hausa migrants), it was also a mark of the success of the indigenous intelligentsia in their struggle for political dominance against the traditional rule by community 'elders' and chieftains. The anti-Hausa sentiment is very clearly brought out in an opinion survey (referred to above) carried out in 1973. (Though the survey was conducted when Nigeria had 12 states, the data have been disaggregated to reflect the 19-state structure which emerged after 1976. Thus to the question, 'Would you be unhappy to see a Hausa man as President of Nigeria', the response set was as shown in Table 6.11. It might therefore be more helpful to see the NPP as a

TABLE 6.11 *Unhappy if Hausa is president of the federation*

	Kwara	Plateau	Benue	Borno	Bauchi	Kano	Kaduna	Niger	Row total (%)
Yes	4.5	89.4	36.0	6.1	23.2	20.5	19.5	1.5	25.6 (1062)
No	94.2	10.2	59.6	82.7	76.6	78.1	68.8	98.2	70.3 (2913)
Don't know	1.3	0.4	5.0	11.2	0.2	1.4	15.7	0.3	4.0 (167)
% of sample	6.1	10.3	9.5	5.4	22.0	19.6	15.9	11.2	100.0
N	252	427	395	225	909	811	657	466	(4142)

coalition of two factional groups, an Anambra/Imo faction on the one hand, and a Plateau faction on the other, both factions coalescing in what could prove to be a temporary 'marriage of convenience'. Should that be the case, then it is not unlikely that the NPP could end up becoming a highly localised party like the PRP. But then, the more localised some of the existing parties become, the greater is the likelihood that there could be a move towards bipolarity.

The Jihad had assured Sokoto a claim to the religious leadership of the emirates of the north; Kano on the other hand, had always had pretensions to a like political leadership.[37] When parties were in the process of being formed and Aminu discovered that because of his 'radicalism' — amongst other reasons — he was thought not quite acceptable as a leader of the 'party of the North', it seemed only natural that he would want to found a party of his own, assured at least, that such a party would receive the support of the people of Kano. But the PRP not only received sweeping political support in Kano, it also managed to secure a limited following in part of the rest of the country. A party with the fewest resources of all the five parties,[38] the PRP not only won the gubernatorial election in Kaduna state — largely as a result of UPN and GNPP voters being asked by the leaders of both parties to vote the PRP ticket in order to defeat the NPN candidate[39] — but its share of the vote between the Senatorial and the Presidential elections fell in only six states in contrast to the UPN's ten and NPN's and GNPP's twelve. Nevertheless, it must be admitted that other than in Bauchi, Borno, and Gongola (where PRP support ranged between 6 and 17 per cent,[40] PRP support in the rest of the country was marginal, a marginality which holds little promise for the future. In the 'minority' areas of the south, the party's share of the vote rarely exceeded 3 per cent vote support, which can be attributed to the PRP's ideological orientation — and in the UPN- and NPP-dominant states of the 'West' and 'East', the PRP polled less than 1 per cent of the votes. One must therefore conclude that though ideological considerations are not without some interest to a very small segment of the electorate, such considerations are as yet not a significant factor in Nigerian politics, and are unlikely to be in the near future if the perceptions of inequalities that appear to be significant continue to be not those arising from interpersonal comparisons, or comparisons between functional groups (workers versus elites of different categories for example), but those deriving from inter-ethnic group comparisons.

If the voter support for the UPN and the NPP leads one to see these parties as ethnically based parties, the same thing can hardly be said of the GNPP and the NPN. From its 'idealistic' origins, one would expect the GNPP vote to be a 'protest vote' — those opposed to the domination of the political arena by the main ethnic groups — and not surprisingly its main support (apart from Borno) came from Bauchi, Cross River, Gongola, and Niger states[41] where the party polled between a sixth and just over a third of the votes. Though its share of the 'minority' vote fell by 6.26 per cent (Benue included) between the Senatorial and Presidential elections the party nevertheless polled, on the average, about a fifth of the 'minority' vote in both elections. In the two elections, and between them, in those to the House of Representatives and the state Assemblies, the principal competition came not from the UPN or the NPP, but from the NPN. Relative to the 'minority' vote, one could therefore say that the GNPP and the NPN were competing for the same party-defined space. To explain what is here meant by a party-defined space, one should compare that notion with another, the notion of a 'policy space'. A 'policy space' can be defined by dimensions representing issues or underlying policy divisions (ideological orientations) which, for example, can be represented by some sort of a continuum, eg. a 'Left—Right continuum' and within which parties are free to move. Thus, a 'policy space' cannot be defined in terms of predispositions of voters, which restrict free movement of parties. In contrast to a 'policy space', a 'party-defined space' is a space whose end-points or limiting positions are made up of some 'ideal' party position, and within which individuals can be arrayed in terms of their degree of identification with, or propensity towards voting for, such a party. A party-defined space is thus a space derived from a rational calculus of voting propensities.[42] If the assessment that the GNPP and the NPN, relative to the 'minority' vote, are competing for the same party-defined space is accepted, it would seem to follow that either the GNPP will have to create for itself a different party image and hence carve out a distinct party space, or it will sooner, rather than later, face extinction. To see the logic of that conclusion it is necessary to examine the 'minority' vote.

Several theories have been put forward to explain why people vote the way they do: for example, the 'social group theory' which holds that individuals are predisposed to vote in a particular way because of the social groups they belong to. Thus the 'working man' would vote, for example, for a 'Labour' party because of the characteristics of his own social position, characteristics which he identifies with the 'Labour' party; or the Yoruba person would most likely vote for the UPN because he sees the UPN as a party of, and for, the Yorubas. Alternatively, there is the 'cue theory' that party programmes and electioneering platforms, party ideological positions, are really cues which serve to 'prompt', or cue the voter to vote in a particular way, in much the same way that an actor behaves according to the cues he receives. Party programmes, etc., are thus 'signalling devices' indicating ways a voter could follow. Of the different cues that there might be in a given election, the voter simply selects that bundle which he most prefers, and votes accordingly; depending on which bundle he selects, he may vote for different parties at different elections. Then there is the 'rational choice' theory which sees the voter simply as a consumer with resources to expend, the resource in this case being his vote. Like any consumer, the voter has an 'objective function' which he seeks to maximise, and he expends his resources voting for that party which he believes would best maximise his objective function. The objective could be power, status position or some special interest or the other.[43]

In the Nigerian context there can be little dispute that the key objective of minority groups, who in the past had had their interests subordinated to those of the dominant ethnic groups, would be the maximisation of their political power position, a necessary condition for ensuring that their interests are catered for in any share-out of the 'national cake'. The 'calculus of rationality' for the minority groups would thus run something like the following. Whichever party wins the Presidential elections will control the ultimate political power in the federation. Given the population distribution between the different states, the party most likely to win the Presidential election will be the party which wins the greatest support in the 'northern' states, and if past experience is any guide, it is unlikely that either the UPN or the NPP – with their ethnic basis – stands a chance of winning such support. Of the other parties, the PRP's ideological commitment is more likely to restrict its electoral appeal than win it widespread support. The GNPP, on the other hand, has the needed financial resources to fight the elections but the unpreparedness of Waziri to 'democratise' the leadership of the GNPP cannot but be inhibiting. Besides, being a Kanuri – and a 'renegade' so to speak from the 'northern ranks' (the old NPC) – it is highly unlikely that his party will receive much support from the more orthodox Hausa-Fulani states. The best bet would therefore seem to be the NPN. In fact, in the elections, though the NPN's share of the overall vote rose from 33.07 per cent in the Senatorial elections to 33.58 per cent in the Presidential, an increase of 0.51 per cent, its share of the 'minority' vote for the same elections rose from 43.87 per cent to 52.0 per cent, an increase of 8.14 per cent. Relative to the 'minority' vote, there was actually a shift between the two elections, from the GNPP (−2.56 per cent), the UPN (−0.79 per cent) and the NPP (−1.1 per cent) towards the NPN. The NPN's vote share in the 'southern' minority states – Bendel (36.19 per cent), Cross River (64.40 per cent), Rivers (72.65 per cent) – is of particular significance in this respect.

The NPN won the Presidential stakes and it did so, essentially, on the 'minority' vote. But that itself was made possible because of the creation of states. By dismantling the old structure of regional government, the coercive machinery through which the regional governments manipulated the vote in the minority areas, such as the bureaucracy and parastatal bodies, was also destroyed, and if the 1979 elections proved anything at all, it was that no party can win ultimate political power without the active support of the minority areas or states. The variable 'state' has become a significant factor in the geography of Nigerian elections.

THE ELECTIONS AND THE CONSTITUTION

For all the care taken in the new Nigerian Constitution — and in the Electoral Decree — to play down the element of ethnicity in Nigerian political life and prominence given to the need for national integration, the 1979 elections showed quite clearly that the actuality of electoral behaviour was still a far cry from the ideals of the framers of the Constitution. In what used to be the Western region (after the excision of the Midwest, now Bendel) and in Anambra and Imo states of the former Eastern region, the voters voted out of a sense of ethnic commitment. In the former North itself, the majority of the voters in Sokoto voted for the NPN and Alhaji Shagari, as did the voters in Kano for Aminu Kano and the PRP. An outcome of this pattern of voting has been to make the legislative assemblies of the states concerned reflect not just the dominant party but also the main ethnic group, thereby undermining the ideal the Constitution sought to achieve — to make political institutions reflect the 'federal character' of the nation. Other than in the presidential election in which the Presidential candidate and the Vice-Presidential candidate are of different ethnic groups, *in no election did any of the parties present candidates who were not indigenous to the state in which such candidates were contesting.* No matter how able a Nupe person resident in Bendel state may be, no matter for how long he may have been resident in the state, no matter what contributions he may have made to the socio-political life of the state, should current practice persist, such a person could not possibly stand any chance whatsoever of holding political office outside his state of 'origin'. In fact unless such a person maintains regular contacts with his 'home state', cultivates a constituency in his 'state of origin' — and to do so would entail his not being able to make the optimum contribution to his 'state of residence' — then he stands no chance whatsoever of holding political office anywhere in the federation. But this, in effect, means that a large reservoir of potential political skills is lost to the federation, a reservoir of skills which could cut across the restrictiveness of ethnicity.

Alvin Gouldner has tried to argue that the distinguishing

characteristic of intellectuals — and of the intelligentsia in general — is the commitment to a 'culture of critical discourse' which Gouldner abbreviates as CCD. CCD, as he puts it, 'is characterized by speech that is relatively more situation-free, more context or field "independent" '.[44] The commitment to CCD not only links the intellectual (considered as a class) to his cultural heritage, it also frees him from the past and by orientating the class to the 'totality', CCD endows the intelligentsia 'with a cosmopolitanism facilitating political diagnosis, the decoding of events in the largest context, from a national, international, and increasingly, a world-system standpoint'.[45] The introduction of 'fundamental objectives' into the Constitution could be seen as part of this facilitative 'political diagnosis'. The electoral evidence, however, would suggest that faced with the competitiveness demanded by a cosmopolitan/ nationalistic outlook or the preservation of the privileges which ethnicity encourages, the Nigerian intelligentsia chose the latter. In that respect, its members are as yet to rise to the challenges of their class. But until they do so, the idealistic underpinning of the Constitution will remain a 'dialectic' confronting the intelligentsia with possibilities rather than realities, which could be all that the 1979 elections proved.

Conventional wisdom might suggest that one way of matching the reality of actual behaviour to the ideals of the Constitution could be to alter radically the electoral system, for instance, in the direction of a system of proportional representation based, say, on a list format. The rationale for this is not far to seek. A list system could encourage parties when composing the slate of candidates to make a more 'balanced' choice, if only to escape the accusation of ethnic or local bias. In principle, it should be possible by such an approach for an Ibibio person to find himself sitting in the Oyo state Assembly and an Urhobo likewise sitting in the Sokoto state Assembly. On the other hand, the problem with this approach to 'social engineering' — unless there is a concrete desire for change — is that, far from helping to actualise the ideal, it could introduce those tendencies which the ideal seeks to eliminate and hence make political institutions little more than a caricature of the ideal.

Though there were variations in the percentage poll by

TABLE 6.12   *Distribution of seats on a PR system*

Party	Av. % poll	House of Representatives			State Assemblies		
-------	-----------	Seats won	PR	Difference	Seats won	PR	Difference
		Seats won	PR	Difference	Seats won	PR	Difference
GNPP	11.0	43	49	+6	157	148	−9
UPN	26.0	111	117	+6	333	350	+17
NPN	36.0	168	162	−6	487	485	−2
PRP	10.0	49	45	−4	144	135	−9
NPP	17.0	78	76	−2	226	229	+3

the various parties between the senatorial and the presidential elections, if we even out these variations by taking the average percentage poll of the two elections and assume that this represents a close approximation to the 'true' poll of the different parties, then on a basis of a system of proportional representation (PR), the distribution of seats in the House of Representatives and in the state Assemblies between the various parties would be as shown in Table 6.12. Given the present pattern of voting, obviously a PR system would not make much of a difference to the distribution of seats. And though an argument made in favour of PR is that it tends to reward smaller parties and disfavour larger ones,[46] in the Nigerian case the reverse would seem to be true: the PRP, the smallest of the five parties, loses the most seats, although it might be retorted that this is no objection to PR but a consequence of the extreme localisation of the PRP. But as can be seen by comparing the NPN's position with that of the UPN, a party with a wider spread of support (the NPN) is disadvantaged while one with an ethnically located voter support is rewarded, a consequence which could reinforce ethnic voting. On the other hand, the real challenge of a PR system based on a list format lies not in such considerations, but in the possibilities which it opens up for actualising the fundamental objectives listed in the Constitution. It is, then, either the case that Nigerians are willing to radically alter existing institutions or they might as well learn to live with the realities of their own political life.

7

The Economy

In 1960 when Nigeria became independent, the total revenue of the federal and regional governments combined amounted to no more than £143 million. Twenty years later, the expectation is that by 1981 the federal government will derive, from oil alone, a revenue put at some ₦21 billion, while federal government spending covering the last nine months of 1980 was put at some ₦7 billion. To put the difference another way, the federal government now spends in one day almost twice as much as was spent by the government in one month, 20 years ago. In the 1962—68 Six Year Plan for Development, the total planned expenditure for the then Northern region was £88.9 million. The same region, now subdivided into ten states, is expected to expend some ₦4.4 billion under the Third National Development Plan (1975—80). In 1964, at the time of the general strike, the number of those under wage employment was put at some 800,000 people; eleven years later — 1975 — that figure had risen to some 2.18 million.[1] Again, over the 20 years since independence, whereas in 1960 there were 2.9 million enrolled in primary schools in the federation, that figure had grown to 11.5 million in 1980. The comparable figures for those in teacher-training institutions and in secondary (post primary) schools are 27,400 and 254,370 (teacher-training), and 134,000 and 552,063 (secondary schools) respectively.[2] In GNP terms, excluding Egypt and South Africa, Nigeria is by far the 'wealthiest' state in Africa, with a GNP estimated in 1974 at $22.4 billion in contrast to Algeria's $11.7 billion and Libya's $11.9 billion.[3] It is hardly surprising therefore to find that

Nigeria is increasingly being referred to as 'the giant of Black Africa'. But before one uncritically accepts that description, it is perhaps well to note that of the 18 African states (out of a total of 44 excluding Egypt and South Africa) with per capita incomes (1974) of $300 and above, Nigeria ranks 15th, surpassing Senegal, Mozambique, and the Republic of the Congo. The rank order for some commonly accepted indices of social welfare are as follows: school age (put at 5—19 years) per teacher, 16th; per capita expenditure on health, 18th; population per physician, 18th; infant mortality rate (defined as deaths under 1 year per 1,000 livebirths), 15th; and life expectancy (expectation of life at birth), 15th. The data on which the rank ordering is based (with the rank orders) are shown in Table 7.1.

The foregoing contrasts have been expressed in the way they have to indicate a possible form which a discussion of the economy could take; in terms first, of the management of the economy as a whole, the problem of economic planning; second, of the relation between the states and the federal government, the problem of federal finance; and third, that of the individual and the state, the problem of distribution, social justice or equity.

ECONOMIC PLANNING AND MANAGEMENT

Though the term 'planning', whether economic, social, or political, has now become very much an 'in' word, a mark of some kind of approbation or approval, as an exercise, it is something of fairly recent origins in the Nigerian experience, an exercise which could be said to have been begun, in any meaningful sense, only within the last two decades. Before that, the only instrument of economic management was the annual appropriations bill, the budget, which was not related to any specified economic goal, other than the orthodoxy inherited from the colonial administration, that the budget somehow or the other had to be 'balanced': expenditure, whether recurrent or capital, had to be fitted within the constraints of 'expected revenue'. Even then, and all too often, that limited 'goal' was not realised: between 1957 and 1962, in overall terms, Nigeria consistently recorded balance of

TABLE 7.1 Military and social expenditures in $(US): selected African states 1974

COUNTRY	GNP ($US 10^6)	HUMAN RESOURCES				MILITARY EXPENDITURE ($US)						EDUCATION					
		GNP PER capita	Soldiers ('000)	Teachers ('000)	Doctors ('000)	Per capita	Rank (a)	Per Soldier	Rank (a)	Per Capita	Rank (a)(b)	School age (%) population in school (c)	Rank (a)(b)	School age population per teacher (c)	Rank (a)(b)	Literary % (d)	Rank (a)(b)
Algeria	11,711	771	63	75	2.2	17	66	4,127	70	50	42/ 2	50	73/ 8	67	74/ 6	26	90/ 6
Angola	4,488	711	na	20	0.4	–	–	–	–	9	98/16	24	114/15	111	108/14	12	117/15
Botswana	193	312	1	3	0.1	–	–	–	–	11	86/14	42	91/10	82	91/10	20	101/11
Congo	560	426	5	6	0.2	2	116	3,000	84	26	66/ 7	61	41/ 4	76	82/ 8	20	101/11
Gabon	1,029	2002	2	3	0.9	21	62	5,500	48	49	43/ 3	79	86/ 9	44	48/ 2	30	89/ 5
Ghana	4,013	413	18	57	0.9	5	96	2,833	88	13	80/12	43	98/11	66	72/ 5	25	12/ 7
Ivory Coast	2,906	611	6	17	0.4	9	79	7,000	40	46	45/ 4	40	109/13	99	103/13	20	101/11
Liberia	581	382	6	6	0.1	3	112	800	124	7	107/17	26	26/ 2	86	94/11	10	120/16
Libya	11,914	5089	32	30	2.0	175	17	12,781	25	185	20/ 1	66	32/ 3	28	24/ 1	22	97/10
Mauritius	565	648	–	7	0.3	–	–	–	–	25	67/ 8	63	109/13	49	55/ 3	62	66/ 1
Morocco	6,997	412	56	58	1.4	12	72	3,500	75	18	72/10	26	123/18	117	110/15	20	101/11
Mozambique	3,122	353	na	11	0.5	–	–	–	–	4	116/18	20	114/15	284	132/18	7	132/18
Nigeria	22,378	365	210	160	2.8	14	69	4,029	64	13	80/12	37	102/12	141	116/16	25	92/ 7
Zimbabwe	3,184	500	8	30	0.9	11	74	8,625	33	16	76/11	23	118/17	82	90/ 9	10	92/ 7
Senegal	1,535	359	6	9	0.3	6	90	4,168	61	10	91/15	53	65/ 5	169	125/17	36	120/16
Swaziland	188	393	–	3	0.1	–	–	–	–	19	65/ 5	51	69/ 6	61	67/ 4	32	83/ 3
Tunisia	3,522	624	24	32	1.1	8	82	2,000	99	34	56/ 5	51	69/ 6	70	78/ 7	40	87/ 4
Zambia	2,784	565	16	21	0.4	18	65	5,312	50	30	63/ 6	51	69/ 6	87	95/12		79/ 2
TOTAL AFRICA 44 STATES	140,316	402	762	1094	35.3	11		5,096		14		30		116		22	
USA	1412400	6666	2174	2387	350.6	405	5	39,359	3	379	3 –	84	2 –	25	13 –	99	1 –
UK	190630	3419	355	565	77.0	176	15	27,718	9	203	18	84	2 –	23	7	98	14
France	265990	5059	502	504	75.5	191	11	19,952	12	273	14	69	17	25	13	99	1 –
USSR	703100	2789	3525	2500	697.4	333	6	23,830	7	166	22	64	30	27	21	99	1
Brazil	8512	943	254	800	65.0	20	63	8,102	37	33	57	50	73	48	54	68	60

Notes:

(a) Rank-order position based on 138 countries.

(b) Rank-order position of 18 states – all African

(c) Age 5–19 years

(d) Percentage of population over 15 years able to read and write

(e) Deaths under 1 year per 1000 live births

(f) Expectation of life at birth

(g) Per capita supply of food, including fish, in calories per day

n.a. = not applicable.

TABLE 7.1 (continued)

| COUNTRY | HEALTH | | | | | | | | | | NUTRITION | | | |
	Per capita	Rank (a)(b)	Population per Doctor	Rank (a)(b)	Population per hospital bed	Rank (a)(b)	Infant(e) mortality rate	Rank (a)(b)	Life expectancy yrs (f)	Rank (a)(b)	Calorie (g) supply per capita	Rank (a)(b)	% of required	Rank (a)(b)
Algeria	9	61/ 6	6901	85/ 5	326	64/ 8	126	90/ 5	53	72/ 3	2138	92/12	89	104/12
Angola	5	78/13	15788	111/16	511	82/12	200	138/18	37	138/18	2021	111/16	86	115/16
Botswana	7	66/ 9	9762	96/ 9	345	66/ 9	97	67/ 2	44	105/ 9	2040	105/15	88	107/14
Congo	7	66/ 9	7964	90/ 7	225	49/ 2	175	129/16	44	105/ 9	2260	81/ 9	102	69/ 6
Gabon	31	41/ 2	4759	83/ 3	98	18/ 1	178	133/17	41	117/15	2228	85/10	95	89/10
Ghana	6	74/12	11339	103/11	781	108/17	133	96/ 7	46	97/ 7	2318	79/ 7	101	74/ 8
Ivory Coast	8	63/ 8	13597	108/14	497	79/11	160	119/14	43	114/14	2654	45/ 1	115	41/ 1
Liberia	5	78/13	11169	102/10	596	88/13	159	117/12	45	100/ 8	2170	90/11	94	91/11
Libya	103	20/ 1	1135	44/ 1	238	52/ 3	125	88/ 4	53	72/ 3	2570	53/ 4	109	51/ 2
Mauritius	15	53/ 3	3230	73/ 2	256	55/ 4	46	45/ 1	66	45/ 1	2458	62/ 5	108	52/ 3
Morocco	5	78/13	12144	105/12	702	100/14	149	107/ 8	53	72/ 3	2611	49/ 2	108	52/ 3
Mozambique	3	91/17	17027	115/15	766	106/15	150	109/10	44	105/ 9	1975	119/17	84	122/17
Nigeria	1	116/18	21884	122/18	1378	125/18	162	124/15	41	117/15	2085	100/13	88	107/14
Zimbabwe	7	66/11	7071	88/ 6	323	63/ 7	122	85/ 3	52	72/ 6	2593	51/ 3	108	52/ 3
Senegal	4	86/16	15214	112/15	746	104/15	159	117/12	41	117/15	2309	80/ 8	97	84/ 9
Swaziland	8	63/ 7	8852	93/ 8	270	57/ 5	149	107/ 8	44	105/ 9	1950	122/18	84	122/17
Tunisia'	11	59/ 5	5128	85/ 4	423	73/10	128	94/ 6	54	69/ 2	2440	63/ 6	102	69/ 6
Zambia	13	54/ 4	12267	106/13	311	61/ 6	157	116/11	44	105/ 9	2052	103/14	89	104/12
TOTAL AFRICA 44 STATES	4		9952		561		150		45		2055		87	
USA	182	10	604	17	138	30	17	18	71	18	3504	7	133	13
UK	159	14	728	25	106	22	16	12	72	9	3349	22	133	13
France	277	7	696	23	95	15	14	9	72	9	3411	15	135	8
USSR	63	29	361	1	89	10	28	33	70	27	3540	5	138	8
Brazil	2	100	1600	53	260	56	82	64	61	55	2516	58	105	59

Notes:
(a) Rank-order position based on 138 countries.
(b) Rank-order position of 18 states — all African.
(d) Age 5–19 years.
(e) Percentage of population over 15 years able to read and write.
(e) Deaths under 1 year per 1000 live births.
(f) Expectation of life at birth.
(g) Per capita supply of food, including fish, in calories per day.

n.a. = not applicable.

payments deficits one year after the other, the deficits ranging from £35 million to £72 million,[4] deficits which were only made up by a systematic whittling down of the reserves accumulated in the past by the Central Produce Marketing-Board (instituted in 1949). Since those reserves were derived from the price differential, between what was paid to the farmer and what the Board earned in export earnings, of export produce — palm products, cocoa, hides and skins, etc. — it need hardly be pointed out that for close on a decade, Nigeria existed only through the exploitation of her farmers. And until the advent, in recent years, of petroleum, that picture barely changed.

Admittedly, there had been the colonial 'Ten Year Plan of Development and Welfare' of 1946 and the 'Economic Programme' of the federal and regional governments of 1955—60, but neither of these could be said to be 'economic plans' in the commonly accepted usage of that term. The former was really nothing other than programmes of aid designed by the Colonial Office to help 'restore' the economies of the colonies which had been kept at a 'standstill' during the Second World War. The 1955—60 Economic Programme, revised in 1958 and extended to 1962 was, in essence, governmental 'shopping lists' (three regional and one federal) of items the governments wanted to see instituted. The programmes enunciated no goals or objectives, were unco-ordinated, and lacked even the virtue of consistency. It was with the 1962—68 National Development Plan, formulated with the aid of American economic consultants,[5] that planning really began in Nigeria. That plan embodied three main objectives which can be described briefly as: (a) the achievement of a growth rate of 4 per cent per annum for the economy as a whole; (b) the rapid development of opportunities in education, health, and employment; and (c) the achievement of a modernised economy compatible with the democratic aspirations of the people and the equitable distribution of welfare among the people and between the regions. Given those objectives, the strategy of implementation was aimed at the optimum mobilisation of resources with the aim of shifting the emphasis of economic activity from the production of primary commodities for export towards the domestic production of previously imported items — the strategy of import-substitution – and the transference of ownership of productive enterprises increasingly from expatriate to indigenous hands. At the regional level, though, the emphasis not only differed from the strategic approach of the federal government, it also varied from one region to the other. Where the North placed its emphasis on rapidly increasing agricultural output, the East aimed at an economy in which agriculture and manufacturing would be complementary, while the West saw in industrial development, the opportunities for structural transformation of its economy. But whatever the varying objectives and strategic approaches, the plan as a whole was vitiated from the start in that it was hoped, and accordingly built into the plan, that close on 50 per cent of the resources needed to finance the plan would be forthcoming from external sources. In the first two years of the plan, that is before the political chaos which was to lead to the collapse of the civilian regime, for which there were reasonable 'Progress Reports', the maximum amount of external finance for the plan received by the governments amounted to no more than 14 per cent of the sums expected. With the start of the civil war, all talk of the National Plan just about disappeared as the energies and resources of the state were directed to the successful prosecution of the war, and not until the end of the war in January 1970 was talk about economic planning to be resumed once again.[6]

Unlike the 1962–68 Plan, the Second National Development Plan 1970–74 was very much 'homespun' but the differences in approach and conception went much further than that. In the 1962–68 exercise there had been extensive consultations between the federal government and the regional authorities, and regional plans were largely the products of regional planning ministries, with federal planning experts having the task, besides producing a 'federal plan', of having also to co-ordinate and rationalise the various plans within the framework of an overall input–output matrix which they had developed for that purpose. With the 1970–74 Plan, however, the approach to planning was radically different, this being largely technocratic and bureaucratic. The fact that the plan was formulated – and was expected to be implemented – under a military regime no doubt contributed to this orientation. But there can be no denying that that orientation was also a reflection of the dissatisfaction of the economic technocrats with the planning strategy of the past — which they regarded as having been too much concerned with the need to be politically accommodating, with not enough attention paid to the demands and logic of economic rationality. To further the latter end, federal technocrats produced and circulated to the state governments 'Guidelines' which state planning functionaries were enjoined to adhere to strictly, as failure to do so could result in state plans being rejected and federal items substituted. The Second Plan was going to be a *national* plan and the federal technocrats would not hesitate to wield the 'big stick' to make it so. But the federal planners need not have bothered. Most of the states, the six in the 'North' for example, had only been in existence for under three years (before the Plan was launched) and had had little, if any, experience of 'planning' besides lacking the necessary personnel to undertake such a task. As for the Rivers and the East-Central states, even though they too were created in 1967, they could be said to have existed as effective administrative agencies only either just before the end of the civil war (the Rivers state) or only after the cessation of hostilities (the East Central state) and thus, it would hardly make much sense to talk of them putting together an economic plan. The Second National Plan was therefore, for all practical purposes, a *federal government* plan and could justifiably be described as an exercise in 'planning from above'.[7] For a final confirmation of the technocrats' concern with economic rationality, one could do no better than read the 'aims and objectives' of the plan which were stated as the creation of (a) a united, strong and self-reliant nation; (b) a great and dynamic economy; (c) a just and egalitarian society; (d) a land bright and full of opportunities for all the citizens; and (e) a free and democratic society. As these were written into the plan after it had been formulated, almost as some kind of a postcript, or an after-thought, reading the Second National Plan is like reading two different documents, one, a short, and ambiguous political testament, and the other, a lengthy and technically complex document, with little if any relationship between the two. In this respect, if an economic plan can be said to be an operationalisation of the political will and goals of a nation, then one could hardly describe the Second National Plan as an 'economic plan'. Perhaps the plan could be described as the technocratic description of the bureaucrats' conception of the economically rational.

For the technocrats, the objectives to be achieved during the plan period were to (i) foster the growth and diversification of manufacturing industry directed both at import substitution and the creation of an export potential; (ii) aid the rapid development of indigenous managerial and technical manpower; (iii) promote a locational policy which would ensure the more effective utilisation of local resources, maximise output and thus create greater employment opportunities; and (iv) increase the proportion of indigenous ownership of industrial investment while at the same time ensuring the greater participation of local personnel with the requisite skills in managerial capacities. With these as objectives, the next step was to find a function the maximisation of which could be regarded as a necessary condition for the satisfaction of the delineated objectives and this was found in the notion of 'value-added', which formed the basis for the rank ordering of priorities. A threefold rank order was established: the first was given to agriculture (with a view to agri-based industries), industries (particularly those which offered the best prospects for forward and backward linkages – though steel was accorded a first-order necessity), transportation and manpower development. Next came social services and public utilities, power, communications and water supplies, and finally, the third category, a residual category, into which almost everything else was put. Defence and security, as might have been expected in a military regime, was made a 'special class', to which, in fact, all the other priorities were subordinated. In the case of industry, as a matter of public policy, certain items were reserved for direct state control and ownership – iron and steel, petrochemicals, fertiliser production and the like – while it was also laid down as policy that the government would hold a 55 per cent equity share ownership in certain specified enterprises – mining, banking and insurance, for example. All other enterprises would be run as 'mixed' ventures with government and private indigenous participation being fixed at not less than 35 per cent of the equities.[8] Overall, federal government capital for the plan was put at some ₦4 billion, an astronomical sum compared to the standards of the 1962–68 Plan which covered a six-year period as against the former's four years.

If the Second National Plan was thought ambitious, the Third Plan, covering the period 1975–80, was more ambitious still, with public expenditure put at ₦33 billion which was subsequently revised upwards to ₦43 billion (though it was estimated effective expenditure would amount to no more than ₦26.5 billion). These huge sums reflected the euphoria which followed the 1973/74 oil boom when the plan was being prepared. It was then thought that oil production would rise to about 3 million barrels a day by 1980 to yield the large balance-of-payments surpluses which, it was expected, would pay for the cost of the plan. As the planners put it, 'finance is unlikely to be a major problem during the Third Plan period'. But far from these optimistic predictions being realised, oil production actually fell, first, to just about half the projected output, before rising slightly to the present average daily output of 1.9 million barrels. Not only did the output of oil fall, the price also fell (though again, this was subsequently to improve), with the effect that far from the large balance-of-payments surpluses expected, the country in fact had payments deficits of ₦259.3 million in 1976 and ₦656.5 million in 1977. And in place of money being no constraint, Nigeria has in fact had to borrow externally, some $2.0 billion, to help pay for the plan. The assumptions underlying the plan were extraordinarily unrealistic, but it will nonetheless be of interest to glance briefly at its approach to development.

The architects of the Third Plan thought that more emphasis should be given to a rapid improvement in 'the infrastructure necessary for sustained industrialisation'; that more effort should be put towards improving the poor performance of the agricultural sector; and that more should be done to promote the 'welfare of the average Nigerian' and particularly the welfare of those in the rural areas. But despite these shifts of emphasis, the goals of the Second Plan — a self-reliant country, the indigenisation of investment — and the basic objectives of industrialisation, remained unaltered. But the approach to planning this time was different. Though 'Guide-lines' were once again issued by the federal planners, the states, which by 1974 were more firmly established than many had been in 1969, played a greater role in drawing up their own plans. To illustrate what significance was attached to the federal guidelines, it might be instructive to recount the experience of this writer who was then a member of the Midwest state planning committee. Though it is not being claimed that that experience can be generalised for all the states, this writer found that it was by no means unique, for friends and colleagues who were members of similar commit-tees in other states had a not too dissimilar experience.

The first task for the Midwest planning ministry was to determine as best as it could what funds it could reasonably expect to have to finance planned projects. This meant esti-mating what the state could expect to receive from the federal government, and what it could itself save from its recurrent budget, savings which could then be transferred to the capital budget. The next step was to list all the various projects or schemes the government would want to see implemented in the state; and to this was added the 'demands' emanating from the various communities within the state. (Communities had earlier been asked to list what their most urgent needs were — water, schools, markets, electric lighting, clinics, quays and motor-propelled river transport in the riverine areas — needs which they would want to see the government satisfy.) Finally, there were what came to be known as 'commissioners' projects'. Still believing that the military would hand over power to civilians in 1976 — this was before General Gowon announced, on 1 October 1974, that the set date for a military handover was no longer 'realistic' — the civilian commissioners on the Midwest Executive Council had been asked by the Military Governor to enumerate what three projects they would want to have the government execute in their respective communities, projects which they, the commissioners, 'would be remembered by' by their communities,[9] for insertion in the plan.

The set of 'projects' was then costed and the total cost was compared to expected financial resources and a rule of selec-tion was found to be necessary as the former far exceeded the latter. The decision on priorities was simple enough: priority one went to the state's projects; the second, to 'commissioners' chosen schemes'; and lastly came the community 'needs', or, for purposes of clarity, 'communal needs' since even 'commissioners' projects' were also meant to satisfy community needs. The process of elimination obviously followed the rank ordering of priorities, the one constraint on the pruning being that each community was to be allowed at least one 'communal project'. In the end, 'planned' projects still exceeded total expected financial resources and the government simply decided to accept the consequence of deficit financing. (It was only after this 'planning' process was completed that the 'economic planning committee' – a body supposed to advise the government on planning problems – was summoned to comment on the 'draft plan', at which stage they discovered that their real function was to be no more than a legitimating body.) It only needs to be added that with the overthrow of Gowon, and faced with severely reduced funds, the successor government had little choice but to remove the various 'commissioners' projects' from the Midwest Plan. Similar pruning exercises were carried out by the other state governments, as indeed they were by the successor federal military authority but not even that could rid the plan (revised) of its original 'shopping list' character.

The above description of the approaches to planning has been made not with the purpose of pinpointing the shortcomings and weaknesses inherent in the planning process – to do that in a satisfactorily convincing manner would require an expertise which the writer does not possess, and some economists have argued that judged by the performance of the economy there are no good grounds to show that employing the sophisticated tools of modern macroeconomic analysis is to be preferred to an ad hoc 'shopping list' approach given the nature of the economy – but only to show that what passes for 'economic management' amounts to no more than management by the bureaucrats and top political decision-makers for the bureaucrats and top political decision-makers. Admittedly there are visible landmarks to indicate the successes of 'planning'. In educational terms, enrolment for the

Universal Primary Education has risen from 8.3 million when the system began[10] in 1976 to the present (1980) figure of 11.45 million while the total number of universities has more than doubled over the last decade, the numbers rising from six in 1970 to the present-day figure of 17. The output of power has increased by over 300 per cent, from 190 MW in 1969 to just about 750 MW in 1977 while there are already plans to increase the output from the Kainji Dam, the country's first hydroelectric power station, from the initially installed capacity of 400 MW to 800 MW and new contracts have been awarded for the construction of two additional hydroelectric power plants with a combined output of some 1145 MW. Nevertheless, despite the remarkable increase in power generation, it has been estimated that between 20 and 33 per cent of industrial output is lost annually as a result of continuous power failures.[11] In addition to the increased output of power, there is the ever-changing landscape as the country is traversed by an increasingly widening network of modern roads and the towns are dotted with a proliferation of high-rise office and residential blocks. In place of one oil refinery which in the 1960s could only produce enough refined oil to meet 40 per cent of Nigeria's needs for petroleum products, the country now has three refineries with the capacity not only to meet domestic demand but also to produce a surplus for an export market. New institutions have also been created – the Nigerian Investment and Development Bank, the Nigerian Bank for Commerce and Industry, the Nigerian Agricultural Bank, and the Nigerian National Insurance Company; these, together with a considerable expansion of the previously existing commercial banking institutions, now exist to facilitate the granting of credit to entrepreneurs and to 'oil the wheels of industry and commerce'. To these must be added a burgeoning stock market which has been made possible through the institution of the Capital Issues Committee (which fixes the prices of shares to be opened up for sale on the stock market) and the Nigerian Acceptances Limited (through whose agencies new stocks and shares are marketed).

Structurally, there have also been some significant changes in the nature of the economy. Thus, for instance, whereas private consumers' expenditure accounted for 87.4 per cent of the Gross Domestic Product in 1958/59, this had fallen to 46.4 per cent by 1975/76. On the other hand, and for the same periods of time, the proportion of capital formation to GDP rose from 11.1 to 28.9 per cent. But perhaps the most startling change was the ratio of government consumption expenditure to GDP which rose from 5.2 per cent in 1958/59 to 22.8 per cent in 1975/76. The details of the composition of final expenditure are presented in Table 7.2. The changes in the export structure are no less interesting. Cocoa, which accounted for 19.9 per cent of total exports (by value) in 1962 and 15.1 per cent in 1970 had fallen to a mere 3.6 per cent in 1975. As against that, crude oil, which provided just 9.9 per cent of total exports (again by value) in 1962, rose to 57.6 per cent in 1970 and 92.7 per cent in 1975. When we turn to the industrial composition of the GDP, we see that whereas agriculture accounted for 65.9 per cent of GDP in 1958/59, and 41.8 per cent in 1971/72, by 1975/76, this had declined to 24.5 per cent or just over half the percentage value of four years earlier. In contrast, the proportion from industrial production (which includes for this purpose, mining and quarrying, manufacturing and craft, electricity and water supply, and building and construction) rose from 9.2 per cent in 1958/59 to 32.4 per cent in 1971/72 and by seventeen percentage points to 49.1 per cent in 1975/76, but perhaps it should be noted that of the figure of 49.1 per cent, actual manufacturing (including crafts) amounted to only 7.4 per cent. The details of the export structure and the industrial composition of the GDP are provided in Tables 7.3—7.5. The favourable picture presented by 'industry' in the composition of GDP by 1975 can be accounted for in large measure by 'building and construction' which in fact grew by 40.8 per cent from the plan forecast of 14.4 per cent to 55.2 per cent (from the 1974/75 level).

But though one could talk of structural changes in the Nigerian economy, in many respects, the changes are not as impressive as the 'planners' make them out to be. For one thing, much of what passes for 'manufacturing' amounts to little more than the reprocessing and repackaging of imported

TABLE 7.2 *Composition of final expenditure (as a percentage of GDP at market prices) for selected years*

	1958/59	1964/65	1971/72	1975/76
Private consumers expenditure	87.4	85.3	72.9	46.4
Government consumption expenditure	5.2	6.1	7.7	22.8
Gross fixed (domestic) capital formation	11.1	12.8	14.7	28.9
Exports	15.8	15.1	25.0	34.8
Less imports	19.5	19.3	20.4	33.1
TOTAL	100	100	100	100

Source: Figures for 1958/59—1971/72 from O. Teriba and M. O. Kayode, chapter 2 of Teriba and Kayode (eds.) *Industrial Development in Nigeria* (Ibadan: Ibadan University Press 1977), p. 19. Those for 1975/76 computed from *First Progress Report on Third National Plan* (Lagos: Central Planning Office, n.d. Table 2.8, p. 17.

TABLE 7.3   *Nigeria's exports, selected years (% of
total by value)*

Item	1962	1967	1971	1975
Crude oil	9.9	29.8	73.4	92.7
Cocoa	19.8	22.6	11.0	3.6
Palm oil	5.3	0.5	0.3	0.0
Palm kernels	10.0	3.2	2.0	0.27
Groundnuts	19.2	14.6	1.9	0.0
Groundnut oil	3.6	3.0	1.0	0.0
Groundnut cake	1.4	1.7	0.5	0.06
Raw cotton	3.5	2.7	0.8	0.0
Rubber	6.7	2.6	1.0	0.30
Tin and metal ore	4.1	5.4	1.8	0.50
Other commodities	16.5	13.7	6.3	1.04
TOTAL	100	100	100	98.47(a)

Source: Teriba and Kayode, *op. cit.,* p. 21 and *First Report on
Third National Plan,* Table 2.12, p. 19. (a) does not add up to 100%
because figures for Hides and skins, and Timber and timber products; are not shown — these figures were omitted in order to show
comparability with the 1962—71 data.

TABLE 7.4   *Industrial composition of GDP: selected years*

	1958/59	1966/67	1970/71	1975/76
Agriculture	65.9	53.8	41.8	24.5
Industry	9.2	19.8	32.4	49.1
Transport and communication	4.1	4.0	3.7	3.2
Distribution	12.5	12.4	11.5	10.5
Government	3.1	3.2	5.3	7.9
Social services	3.0	4.2	3.2	3.7
Others	2.1	2.6	2.1	1.6
TOTAL	100	100	100	100

Source: Teriba and Kayode, *op. cit.,* p. 18; *First Report on Third National Plan,* Table
2.6, p. 16.

TABLE 7.5   *Import content of intermediate inputs of Nigerian industry: 1959/60 and 1972/73*

	1959/60		1972/73
Agriculture	67.4%	Dairy products	40.85%
Livestock, fishing and Forestry	79.4	Grain mill products	99.75
Textiles	18.3	Miscellaneous food products	60.35
Agricultural processing	4.8	Animal feeds	30.70
Clothing	29.3	Beer brewing	46.0
Drink and tobacco	75.7	Soft drinks	45.55
Food	22.4	Made-up textile goods (except wearing apparel)	79.65
Metal mining	39.0	Carpets and rugs	100.0
Non-metal mining	80.3	Paper containers, boxes and boards	44.95
Chemicals	39.4	Basic industrial chemicals	87.30
Transport	49.0	Fertilisers and pesticides	43.50
Utilities	32.4	Drugs and medicines	45.45
Trade	13.8	Other chemical products	61.05
Construction	39.5	Tyres and tubes	44.75
Transport equipment	68.1	Pottery products	92.10
Non-metallic mineral	43.0	Glass products	65.35
Metal manufacturing	71.9	Concrete products (other than cement, bricks and tiles)	44.55
Wood, leather, etc.	32.0		
Miscellaneous manufacturing	65.6		

Source: Teriba and Kayode, *op. cit*, p. 26; *Federation of Nigeria, Third National Development Plan,* 1975–80, p. 148.

components, with not much evidence of the 'backward linkages' much sought after by the planners. This is readily seen by looking at the import content of selected items for 1959/60 and 1972/73 (two lists are shown as the elements in each set are not identical).

An iron and steel plant which has been on the drawing boards of the planners since 1959 is yet to materialise, though the first products from the mill (at Ajaokuta) are expected in 1983[12] while a liquefied natural gas plant – which with petroleum refining was to provide the basis for Nigeria's petrochemical and fertiliser industry – is yet to be constructed as no firm contracts have been negotiated for the sale of the plant's product. At present, much of the natural gas from associated and non-associated oil fields – revenue from which is expected to outstrip that from oil in the 1980s – is flared, while Nigeria imports phosphates from Poland to feed its existing fertiliser plants.[13] Thus for all the planners' talk about the need for industrialisation, the following comment by the Nigerian Manufacturers' Association perhaps provides a not unfair summary of the planners' efforts: 'Nigerian manufacturers are beset with a host of problems, such as frequent power cuts, inadequate water supply, shortage of trained manpower and non-availability of facilities for additional working capital, which not only result in reduced production, but also discourage expansion of existing plants'.[14] One effect of that 'discouragement' is shown by the fact that the index of industrial production, which stood at 137.1 in 1976 (1972 = 100), only rose to 142.5 in 1977, and even that figure is regarded by some observers as an exaggeration.

If industrial activity presents a not too bright picture, that offered by agriculture, in which in 1965, 80 per cent of the active population was employed, comes very close to being a disaster. According to the Third National Plan, 64.0 per cent of the total labour force of 29.2 million was estimated to be working in agriculture, a percentage which was expected to drop to 61.2 per cent – out of a labour force estimated at 32.74 million – by 1980. (The corresponding figures for the wage labour force and those in wage employment are: 62.5 per cent (2.18 million) of a wage labour force of 3.49 million in wage employment, giving the percentage of 'unemployed' of 37.5. The 1980 estimated figures are put at 73.8 per cent (2.76 million) of a wage labour force of 3.7 million in wage employment, and 'unemployment' at 26.2 per cent.) But although, according to the Central Bank of Nigeria, the index of food crop production between 1960 and 1975 had been rising by 1.8 per cent per annum – on the average – that for demand had risen steadily by 7.4 per cent per annum. The result of this stagnation – if not decline – in foodcrop production has been an astronomical increase in the annual food import bill. Thus, for instance, whereas the food import bill rose by 24 per cent between 1976 and 1977, by 1978 that figure had jumped to 79 per cent.

Translating the increases in the food import bill into specific figures is quite illuminating. In 1976, for example, Nigeria, which previously produced enough rice for its domestic needs, imported some 60 million kilos of rice. By 1977, that figure had risen to 246 million kilos (a rise of 310 per cent) and was to rise again in 1978 to 1939.4 million kilos (an increase of 688 per cent). In the months of March and April 1980 alone, the federal government imported 200,000 tonnes of rice and by the end of September 1980, the President of the Republic was asking the National Assembly for legislation to lift the restriction on the importation of some 13 food items, which included rice.[15] The situation with vegetable oils (including palm oil of which before 1962, Nigeria was the world's largest exporter) is hardly different. In 1976 some 1002 tonnes of vegetable oils were imported, but by 1977 that figure had risen to about 178,488 tonnes (133,866 tonnes imported within the first nine months of the year), representing an increase of 17,813.2 per cent. Groundnuts, the output of which stood at 1.12 million tonnes in 1972 (again, Nigeria used to be the world's largest exporter of groundnuts), had by 1976 fallen to 2000 tonnes with the result that in that year, Nigeria had to import some 14,000 tonnes of nuts and oil for domestic use. In the same manner, the import of fish – in which Nigeria was previously self-sufficient – rose, between 1977 and 1978, by 120 per cent. The table (Table 7.3) showing the structure of Nigeria's exports tells the story of some of the other agricultural commodities – such as cocoa, cotton and cotton seed, and rubber – which formed part of the country's traditional exports. With output stagnant, demand rising, and an economy fuelled by petroleum revenues, it is therefore hardly surprising to find that the consumer price index (1960 = 100) for food, which in 1974 was 258.9 had risen a year later to 367.8. Given that incomes in the urban sector have tended to rise faster than in the rural — aided by the 'Udoji' awards of 1975 and recent legislation which fixed the minimum urban wage at ₦100 per month (from the previous figure of ₦60) — the urban/rural terms of trade have in fact moved against the farmers and their incomes may not only have declined relatively but may have fallen in absolute terms.

In more recent years, particularly since July 1975, there have been some attempts to stem, and possibly reverse, the adverse trend in agricultural production. These attempts include high cost but ineffective 'publicity' conscious campaigns, such as 'Operation Feed the Nation' (OFN) which was launched in 1976,[16] the creation of specialised and centralised commodity Marketing Boards (which replace the former State Marketing Boards) to buy and market Nigeria's export crops (and by paying more to the farmers, offer price incentives towards increased production), the creation of integrated farming schemes through the institution of some eleven River Basin Authorities (for irrigation, etc.), and the provision of new inputs at subsidised rates (fertilisers and seeds, tractors, threshers and irrigation pumps), the provision of credit — ensured by a ruling by the federal government that at least 6 per cent of all commercial bank loans should go to the agricultural sector and the central banking undertaking to underwrite 75 per cent of bank loans up to ₦50,000 to individuals engaged in agriculture (₦1.0 million in the case of co-operatives) — and the setting up of specialised agencies — the Root Crops Production Company and the Cereals and Grains Board — to produce and market particular crops. At the same time agricultural production has been removed from Schedule III to Schedule II of the Nigerian Enterprises and Promotions Decree (the so-called Indigenisation Decree) thereby permitting up to 60 per cent of foreign ownership in Nigerian agriculture. It would be one of the most interesting twists of history if a government of the independent state of

Nigeria brought about, through its policies, the introduction of an expatriate 'farmer–settler' community in the country, something which the colonial administration, beginning with the term of office of Sir Hugh Clifford as Governor, did all it could to prevent.

For plan after plan, one perennial comment has been that plan implementation has been hampered by the shortage of critical manpower — skilled workmen, professional and technical assistants, senior administrative and managerial staff and high-level professional and technical personnel. Yet, one of the objectives of planning, it has always been stated, has been to eliminate this bottleneck. Either the problems involved in securing the requisite high-level cadre of staff have been underestimated, or the planners could not have given sufficient consideration to the constraint posed by the shortage of critical manpower. Whatever is the case, it therefore seems hardly credible that a plan such as the Third National Plan could have been designed which would require a workforce of about 450,000 including 12,000 senior professionals, 22,000 intermediate staff and 250,000 skilled and semi-skilled staff simply to complete the building and construction projects of the public sector, unless, of course, which would be still less credible, the Third Plan was meant to be no more than a 'cosmetics' exercise to cover some other design the planners and the governments may have. By the end of the first year of the plan, the unrealistic manpower requirements had become all too apparent. The First Progress Report, for example, noted 'that the vacancy rate in respect of senior administrative staff including accountants was 55% as at April 1976; and for senior professional staff e.g., engineers, quantity surveyors etc., the vacancy rate was as high as 64%'. The Report goes on to say: 'the situation in the public corporations is not in any way better than in the civil service . . . vacancy rates in respect of senior administrative/managerial staff were about 45% as at April 1976, and as high as 60% for senior professional/technical staff'.[17] Even with the revision of the plan and a 60 per cent increase in the number of expatriates recruited under the 'expatriate quota scheme' — in itself a measure of the difficulties with the manpower situation — it is hardly likely that the manpower requirements of the plan will be met. Nor is the situation improved by the civil service losing part of its already short supply of administrative/managerial/technical/professional staff to the private sector where salaries are higher and the perquisites of office much more rewarding. But this already points to some of the issues to be taken up in a later section of this chapter.

So far attention has been focused on the macro-issues of 'planning', with hardly anything said on the subject of the day-to-day management and monitoring of the economy. Essentially, of course, that function is one which is undertaken by the 'executive' ministries of finance, works, transport, communications and the like. Until fairly recent times, conventional administrative behaviour tended to remain that of ensuring that monies voted by the authorities were expanded and where possible, accounted for. And one only has to read the annual reports of the various Auditors-General of the different governments to realise that even the accounting function was all too often not properly observed as numerous audit queries went unanswered. Even the annual ritual of the preparation of the budget involved little more than building an 'inflationary' factor on the preceding year's budget, adjustments then being made to equate the new 'estimates' with expected revenue. That budgeting had to be related to specific objectives or even to past performance was little talked about.[18] For example, for the 1962—68 Plan period, plan fulfilment or underfulfilment was measured essentially in terms of the proportions of the voted sums expended. Thus, plan targets were said to have been 'underfulfilled' (or overfulfilled) where there were cases of underspending (or overspending) and fulfilled just in those cases where expenditure equalled allocations of funds. The experience with the Second National Plan 1970—74 was not much different.

One consequence of this form of behaviour has been that decision-making — and, in general, policy-making — has tended to be *ex post factum*, designed to deal with past exigencies (and not infrequently the conditions have themselves changed) rather than anticipatory and therefore designed to bring about desired or preferred 'social states'. The Public Service Review Commission (the 'Udoji Commission') which was set up in 1972 but which issued its report some two years later[19] noted, for instance, that while the nature of the economy had been changing, becoming more 'development-oriented', the civil service had barely changed and had remained basically 'maintenance-oriented'. Hence in their report, the commission was able to say 'our main message in this report is the need for introducing a new style public service',[20] 'new style' being defined in terms of a service which is results-oriented and employs all the techniques of modern management science — 'management by objectives', 'project management', 'programme and performance budgeting systems', 'programme evaluation and review techniques', and other similar tools; in which recruitment would be based on the possession of specialised skills with opportunities for continuous training and upgrading of the holders of those skills; and in which there would be built-in motivational incentives to ensure adequate performance, for instance, by making upward mobility dependent on such performance. To bring about such a 'new style' civil service would require, the commission argued, a complete restructuring of the civil services of the federation. But apart from bringing all those employed in the 'public sector' under a uniform salary structure and paying out a nine-months 'arrears' of salary (contrary to the commission's recommendations)[21] — the 'Udoji awards' — hardly any attempt has been made to carry out the restructuring suggested by the commission. Rather, the government preferred to effect a 'purge' of the public services and, it would appear, lost the chance to bring about a more radical institutional change, at least for the immediate foreseeable future. Even if it were true that 'the science of muddling through' approximates more closely to the observed behaviour of public servants than the 'rational decision-making' models of the rational choice theorists, it does not thereby follow that a 'virtue' has to be made out of 'muddling through' but that would seem to be the situation that the civil services in Nigeria are left with.[22]

FEDERAL–STATES RELATIONS: THE PROBLEM OF FEDERAL FINANCE

It is generally accepted that there are two basic sets of forces which operate within any federal system. There is, first, a set of forces tending to pull the federation apart — centrifugal forces — which stem from real or imagined differences in culture and history, perceptions, whether real or imagined, of relative deprivation, the feeling that a given unit or component of the federation is not doing as well as it believes it should and would therefore be better off on its own or in association with some other, different grouping — or insecurity, such as the fear Ibo-speaking peoples experienced after the killings of May, July and September/October 1967, fears which finally led to the former Eastern region seceding and proclaiming itself 'Biafra'. Then, there is a second set of forces which tend to hold or pull together the component units — centripetal forces — which gain strength from considerations such as the greater security of a large collective, and the various supposed benefits which derive from the economies of size — larger domestic market, better prospects for investment and hence for growth, greater diversification of resources and the like. Supposedly, where the centrifugal forces exert a greater pull than the centripetal, then there is a very strong likelihood that the federation will break up, and, of course, the reverse would hold, that the federation would persist where the latter forces, the centripetal, exert the greater pull. And if the two forces are evenly balanced, the federation, it appears, will persist. Usually, in the 'life' of any federal system, these two kinds of forces exert contrary pulls with the result that federal systems are always subject to various stresses and strains in the relationship between the component units, and between the component units and the federal authority, and one such stress is that which arises from the allocation of resources, and, specifically, the allocation of revenue.

It is part of what is meant, in saying of a system that it is a federal system, that there is a constitutional division of jurisdiction between the component units and the federal authority, a division which entails that each component part, and the 'overall authority', should have some 'independent' source of revenue to execute those functions constitutionally allocated to it. In an 'ideal' world in which the component units were comparable one to the other in basic essentials — geographical area, population (including the composition — for example of age and sex — and the distribution of certain attributes, such as educational, professional and technical skills), income levels, service and welfare levels, and resource levels (agricultural and mineral resources for example) — the problem of revenue allocation would be relatively easy to solve. Provided the component units could agree with the federal authority as to what proportion of the total revenue of the country should go to the federal, and what proportion to the component units, then one would simply divide that proportion available to the component units equally among the units. Unhappily, there are hardly any 'ideal' worlds to be found anywhere, and in the 'real' world nothing is as neatly ordered as one would expect of the 'ideal'. For historical and other reasons there are various differentials between the component units, differentials which often lead to the more favourably endowed wanting more, not only to maintain the level and standard of what there is, but also to improve on the existing levels. On the other hand, the less well endowed demand more both simply because they are less 'well off' and because they want to 'catch up' with the better-off units. With limited resources, it is unlikely that there could be any one distribution of revenue which would leave all the component units believing they were all equally well off, or put differently, that there could be any one distribution which would not leave at least one unit believing it was worse off than what it was before the new distribution.

It follows from the foregoing, that for a country which is relatively poor, or which is striving to 'develop' at the most rapid rate possible, such as Nigeria is, the problem of 'fiscal federalism' will remain for quite some time, a continuous and pressing problem. To appreciate how significant the problem is, it will help to look at some of the differentials which exist between the different states. (In Tables 7.6 and 7.7 the '12-state structure' has been used, since it is that for which there are available comparable data even though that data are not all too reliable.) Whatever the reliability we want to attach to the figures, it can at least be agreed that Lagos is a much 'richer' state than either the North-Eastern or North-Western states even if we do not accept that Lagos is more than thrice as 'rich' as either of those two states.

TABLE 7.6 *Per capita GDP 1960/61–1975/76 (at constant 1962/63 prices) (in Naira units)*

State	1960/61	1965/66	Percentage change	1970/71	Percentage change	1975/76	Percentage change
Benue Plateau	40	44	10	50	13.6	80	33.3
Kano	35	40	14.2	50	25.0	80	60.0
Kwara	41	42	2.4	50	19.0	85	70.0
North Central	40	42	5.0	50	19.0	90	80.0
North-Eastern	33	35	5.7	45	28.6	75	66.6
North-Western	33	35	5.7	40	14.3	75	87.5
East-Central	45	55	22.2	58	5.5	100	72.4
Rivers	70	80	14.3	80	0.0	140	75.0
South-Eastern	48	55	14.6	58	5.5	95	31.8
Lagos	120	130	8.3	170	30.8	220	29.4
Midwest	50	60	20.0	70	16.6	120	87.5
Western	55	70	27.3	75	7.1	110	46.6

Source: Report of the Panel Appointed by the Federal Military Government to Investigate the Issue of the Creation of More States and Boundary Adjustments in Nigeria (Dec. 1975 unpublished) Table 4. GDP figures for the states were said to have been derived by averaging assumed populaton and income figures. The percentage changes were computed by the author. It need hardly be emphasized that the figures should be read as strictly indicative'.

TABLE 7.7   *Per capita state government revenues by sources: 1971–1975 (₦)*

	1971/72			1973/74			1975/76		
	Total	Federal source	Internal	Total	Federal source	Internal	Total	Federal source	Internal
Benue Plateau	4.6	3.8	0.8	5.0	3.8	1.2	14.1	12.0	2.1
Kano	4.2	3.2	1.0	5.5	4.5	1.0	19.9	6.3	3.6
Kwara	5.9	4.8	1.1	6.6	5.3	1.3	17.4	15.0	2.4
North-Central	5.9	4.5	1.4	6.0	4.0	2.0	15.0	12.0	3.0
North-Eastern	3.5	3.0	0.5	3.9	3.3	0.6	11.0	9.5	1.5
North-Western	3.6	2.8	0.8	4.2	3.4	0.8	11.0	8.3	2.7
East Central	4.8	3.0	1.8	7.4	4.0	3.4	18.5	13.0	5.5
Rivers	14.5	12.5	2.0	17.0	14.6	2.4	57.6	51.6	6.0
South-Eastern	7.4	6.0	1.4	8.2	5.2	3.0	22.4	17.0	5.4
Lagos	17.1	6.1	11.0	19.8	8.0	11.8	33.2	16.4	16.8
Midwest	17.7	12.8	4.9	30.8	27.2	3.6	48.0	41.5	6.5
Western	5.5	4.4	1.1	4.4	3.0	1.4	21.0	14.2	6.8

Source: Report of the Commission on the Creation of States, Table 6.

But then it might be argued that figures like GDP are too 'gross' to be really useful — for one thing, their computation does raise conceptual difficulties, some of which are not easily resolved, even if one ignores the problems of measurement. From the point of view of the component authorities, what may perhaps be more important is what the state actually gets as revenue, what it can actually expect to spend. Though the figures cover only the period 1971—76, looking at the amounts of revenue raised from internal sources it is easily seen that it bears little relation to per capita levels of GDP. However one interprets the proportion of state revenues derived internally, the figures do point to the fact that some states (East-Central, Lagos, West and Midwest) have tended to generate more revenues internally (Lagos, percentage of internal to total revenue 64.3 per cent in 1971, 50.6 per cent in 1975; East Central, 37.5 per cent and 29.7 per cent; and West, 20.0 per cent and 32.3 per cent) than others (for example, Benue-Plateau with comparable percentages of 16.7 per cent and 14.8 per cent; North-Eastern, 14.3 per cent and 13.6 per cent; and Rivers 13.8 per cent and 10.4 per cent). This could be due to a number of factors: (a) a greater 'extractive capacity' where 'extractive' relates essentially to bureaucratic capacity; (b) greater exercise of political will, the determination of the state to tax by imposing its will on the 'citizens'; and (c) a broader economic base available to be tapped for revenue. That administrative capacity could be very salient is suggested by the fact that in terms of secondary school enrolment, the three states (Lagos, East-Central and West) provided 63.6 per cent of the total number of students enrolled in secondary schools in 1973 and 60.07 per cent of the total estimated enrolment for 1975, while in terms of university education, the same three states similarly accounted for 60.65 per cent of total enrolment in 1970 and 47.34 per cent in 1975, figures which also point to another form of inequality between the states. Were the percentage of Midwest students enrolled in universities to be added to the figures for the three states, the resulting percentages would be 73.7 per cent in 1970 and 59.2 per cent in 1975. If one were to take employment in the public sector under federal jurisdiction, where competition is, in principle, free and open (all the states maintain restrictive practices of one form or the other in state employment), then the chances of a graduate from the Western state would appear to be sixteen times that of his counterpart from Rivers, North-East, North-West and Kano; ten times that of the person from Lagos, and Benue Plateau; and five times that of the individual from the South-East and Kwara. And since much of political competition in Nigeria (as in most other countries) is concerned with, in the words of Harold Lasswell, 'who gets what, when and how?' (and supposedly one should add 'and why'), it becomes easier to appreciate why revenue allocation should continue to remain a highly controversial issue in the country.

Several separate though related issues or questions are involved when we talk of 'fiscal federalism'. For example, there is the question of who should be the taxing authority and who should be the collecting authority; or whether the taxing should also be the collecting authority. Then there is the question of whether what is collected should be retained in whole or in part by either the federal or the component authorities, or whether some taxes should be allocated to the federal authority and others to the component units. Finally, should certain taxes be reserved to the component units, on what basis should this be decided, or, put differently, what principles should govern the allocation of revenue between the states? Over the years, particularly during the period between 1953 and 1964, it has been the latter question, that of the principles of allocation, which has provided the focal point of controversy, controversy which in certain cases became so divisive as to lead to threats of secession by one region or the other — for example, the Western region in 1953/54 and the Eastern region a decade later.

Generally, issues of revenue allocation tended — at least up until 1966 — to be conjoined with those of constitutional reform. The first exercise in revenue allocation was that conducted by Sir Sydney Phillipson and Mr Simeon Adebo in 1946, and it was made necessary by the introduction of the 'Richards Constitution', the constitution which put Nigeria on the way to federalism. The review of that constitution in 1948/49 — which led to the introduction of the 'MacPherson constitution' in 1951 — saw the institution of another revenue allocation commission, this time under Professor Hicks and Sir Sydney Phillipson.[23] It was the Hicks—Phillipson Commission which first attempted to spell out the different principles or criteria which might be applied in the allocation of revenue, such as those of derivation, need, population size, 'even development' (of the regions), and common national interest. But although the commission noted that in putting forward their formula of allocation they had taken these principles into consideration, it was never shown what weighting was given to which principle, a shortcoming which, with the approach to Whearean federalism in 1954, was to lead to the appointment of yet another commission, the Chick Commission.[24]

The influence of the Chick Report was just as short-lived as it was to be superseded, with the approach of independence, by that produced by Sir Jeremy Raisman in 1958.[25] By 1964, with oil just beginning to make an impact on the economy, yet another commission was appointed to examine the basis of revenue allocation[26] but the report of that commission was more or less overtaken by the crisis which accompanied the federal elections held in December of that year. At the start of the civil war in 1967, then, the general revenue allocation situation could be summarised briefly as follows:

SYSTEM OF REVENUE ALLOCATION AS AT MAY 1967[27]

A. Revenues raised, collected and retained by the Federal Government:

> Company tax (100 per cent); import and excise duties on beer, wines and liquor, import duties (except on motor spirit, diesel oil and tobacco), 66 per cent; and mining rents and royalties, 15 per cent.

B. Revenues raised and collected by the federal government and transferred to state governments on the principle of derivation:

> Export duties on primary produce (100 per cent), import and excise duties on motor spirit, diesel oil and tobacco (100 per cent); and mining rents and royalties (15 per cent).

C. Revenues raised and collected by the federal government, credited to the Distributable Pool Account and shared among the states on a specified percentage basis:

> Import duties (except on beer, wines, liquor, motor spirit, diesel oil and tobacco), 35 per cent, and mining rents and royalties, 35 per cent.

D. Revenues raised, collected and retained by state governments:

> Personal income and poll tax, sales tax on produce (except on tobacco, motor fuel, diesel oil, hides and skins), licence and government service fees, fines, rents on government property, revenue from lotteries, etc.

The Distributable Pool Account (DPA) served in the main as a 'correction factor' to even out the disparities which the use of a derivation criterion, on which the allocation system was in effect based, might introduce. Allocation from the DPA gave the North a share of 42 per cent, the East 30 per cent and the West 28 per cent though it was never clear how exactly those percentages were derived. With the creation of the Midwest in 1963, the West's share of 28 per cent was reduced to 20 per cent and the difference of 8 per cent allocated to the newly created region, presumably on the basis of the population size of the Midwest. That presumption gains in plausibility in that when states were created by Decree in 1967, the breakdown of the East's share closely reflected the relative populations of the three states into which that region was divided (East-Central 17.5 per cent, South-East 7.5 per cent and Rivers 5 per cent) as also did the distribution of the Western region's share of 20 per cent between the Western state (18 per cent) and the Lagos state (2 per cent). In the North, on the other hand, the region's share was split equally (7 per cent to the North-East, North-West, North-Central, Kano, Kwara and Benue Plateau respectively) between the six states into which the North was broken. But this may reflect not so much a departure from 'principle' as the fact that in the 'uncertain' conditions then prevailing in the North,[28] a move away from equality could have raised more difficulties than it solved.

The outcome of the allocation system with respect to regional revenues (before the creation of the Mid-West) is shown in Table 7.8. Significantly, the two regions, the West (in 1953) and the East (in 1958) which placed the greatest emphasis on derivation as a principle of allocation, showed the highest rates of increase. In 1953, the West had insisted on derivation while the North wanted allocation based on population, and the East on 'need'; but by 1958, with the first trickle of revenues from oil, the East had changed its tune, the region then playing the 1953 tune of the West while the West itself had come to find some 'wisdom' in the notion of uniform economic development. Budgetary demands, and not the larger issues of 'principle', invariably dictated how each region chose to play the 'allocation game'.[29]

TABLE 7.8   *Current revenue federal and regional governments: 1953–60 (£'000)*

	Federal government	Regional governments total	North	East	West
1953	50,906	18,938	8,540	4,730	5,668
1954	59,256	18,993	6,338	5,348	7,307
1955	62,481	36,238	13,123	9,397	13,718
1956	59,950	38,150	13,748	9,008	14,381
1957	70,567	43,276	14,549	12,184	15,522
1958	70,945	44,475	14,319	13,380	15,709
1959	77,316	53,323	15,059	14,216	16,649
1960	88,824	53,323	16,608	14,875	19,681
1953–60	74.4	181.5	94.4	214.4	247.2

The military coup of 1966, the crisis that followed, and the outbreak of civil war in July 1967 temporarily relegated all considerations about revenue allocation to the background. But with the approach to an end of the civil war, talk of a second national plan of 'reconstruction and rehabilitation', and, more particularly, the likelihood of rising revenues from oil to look forward to, it seemed reasonable to re-open the question of revenue allocation. Besides, the ad hoc arrangements which had had to be made when states were created in 1967 hardly seemed adequate for the demands of the 1970s. In 1968 the military government appointed the 'Dina Commission' 'to look into and suggest any change in the existing system of revenue allocation as a whole . . . including the Distribution Pool'. The commission was requested to submit its report within four months. Though the commission was highly critical of previous allocation exercises, their main ground for rejecting the past was conceptual: previous attempts were made too closely dependent on constitutional changes. As the commission put it, '. . . revenue allocation should be properly conceived not as a constitutional exercise but as a means of financing development programmes'.[30] In other words, it was just another tool of overall economic management, and it was from that perspective that they presented their proposals for reform which, if one ignores those particulars which related to changes in the proportions in which revenue from specific taxable items was split between the federal and the state governments,[31] were that: (a) the complex division of taxing authorities should be rationalised, with the federal government taking on the role of the principal tax-imposing authority; (b) the federal government should take over some of the functions which then fell to the states, functions which the states were not adequately equipped to execute, such as higher education; (c) portions of certain revenues should be put into a special fund under the control of the federal government and from which 'special grants' could be made to the states for well-stated purposes: (d) the criteria for distribution from the DPA — which the commission wanted renamed 'States Joint Account' — should be more properly defined and the commission suggested as such criteria, 'basic need or nominal budget gap, minimum national standards and balanced development' (with weights for each shown, including the rationale for the weights given); (e) in so far as revenue from petroleum was concerned, a distinction should be made between revenues derived from 'off-shore wells' and that from 'on-shore wells' with the total revenue from the former accruing to the federal government.

Shed of its rhetoric and the aura of technical expertise, the effect of the Dina Commission's recommendations on state revenues, taking the DPA alone, would have been to seriously reduce the revenues going to the 'oil-producing states', the Midwest, Rivers and South-Eastern states, including the war ravaged East-Central state, while increasing the shares of states like the Western, Lagos, Kwara and North-Eastern. The share of the East-Central state, which had a population roughly comparable to that of the Western, would have declined by 6.5 per cent while that of the Western state would have increased by 1.3 per cent. In the same manner, the North-East, with a population roughly comparable to the West's though the former has a geographical area which is more than five times the size of the latter, would have been entitled to a share percentage of 7.7 per cent while the West would have had 19.3 per cent, two and a half times as large as the North-East's. When the committee submitted their report in January 1969 and the federal government announced it was not accepting the findings of the committee, the rejection came as no surprise.

In the absence of the controversy normally associated with party politics, it did not prove difficult for the military to reject the Dina recommendations, but having done so, it had itself to find a new formula for allocation, as one was needed if the Second National Plan was to get under way. The simplest approach would of course have been to accept that solution which not only came closest to the then existing practice — to which the military governors were accustomed — but which if it departed from the accepted practice, would not deviate too radically from the developmental aspirations and expectations of the governors, and this was found in a division of half the total sum in the DPA among the states on the basis of equality, and the other half on the basis of the relative size of population. The military government came out with its solution in the Decree (Distributable Pool Account) No. 13 of 1970 which was given retroactive effect from April 1969. The new distribution, compared with the Dina recommendations and the then constitutionally prescribed distribution (by the Decree (Financial Provisions) No. 15 of 1967), is shown in Table 7.9.[32] Some other changes were made in the fiscal system later on. Following the 'boom' in oil revenues after the price increases of 1973, the federal government

TABLE 7.9 *Distributable pool account: share of states, April 1969 – comparative figures (%).*

	From April 1969 (1)	May 1967 provisions (2)	Difference col. (1) and (2) (3)	Dina committee suggestions (4)	Difference cols. (1) and (4) (5)
Benue Plateau	7.8	7.0	0.8	7.7	+0.1
Kwara	6.3	7.0	−0.7	8.3	−2.0
Kano	9.3	7.0	2.3	6.0	+3.3
North-Central	7.8	7.0	0.8	7.7	+0.1
North-Eastern	11.3	7.0	4.3	9.9	+1.4
North-Western	9.3	7.0	2.3	8.8	+0.5
East-Central	10.6	17.5	−6.9	11.0	−0.4
South-Eastern	7.4	7.5	−0.1	6.9	+0.5
Rivers	5.6	5.0	0.6	1.6	+5.0
West	12.7	18.0	−5.3	19.3	−6.6
Lagos	5.5	2.0	3.5	5.9	−0.4
Midwest	6.4	8.0	−1.6	6.9	−0.5

decided to take over the responsibility for fixing income taxes throughout the federation in 1974. Though revenue from income tax remained a state revenue, it was now left to the federal government to fix the rates, thereby eliminating the considerable variation in the 'take-home pay' that existed between the states among peoples with the same incomes and comparable commitments. It also meant that the federal authority had to compensate some of the states for loss of revenue (the differential between the state and federal rates) from income tax. In the main, the principal beneficiaries from the uniform income tax were those from the Western and East-Central states, which before the change had the highest rates of income tax in the federation.

The uniform tax 'reform' was succeeded in the following year by another change in the DPA, this time in its composition rather than in the distribution, which remained unaltered. By the change, customs and excise duties which were formerly paid to the states were transferred to the DPA while the federal government surrendered (to the DPA) its share of the royalties from both on-shore and off-shore drilling. Basically, the changes had the effect of eliminating the derivation element in the states revenue make-up, leaving only the 20 per cent from mining rents and royalties which still accrued to the states on the basis of derivation.

The cumulative effect of these changes has been to swell the total amount which now accrues to the states, but this really should be attributed to the considerable rise in federal revenues brought about by oil. But if state revenues have risen, the rate of increase has nevertheless not kept pace with the rate of increase in federal revenues — the latter has risen much faster than the former. More important, however, is the fact that there does seem to be an inverse relation between the increases in state revenues and the incentive on the part of the states to generate more of their revenue from 'internal' sources.[33] A possible consequence of this would be to make the states less responsive and accountable to the state electorate. Admittedly notions of 'responsibility' and 'accountability' are problematical in the context of a military regime, but in a civil regime they become quite important for, as has been shown in various studies,[34] the citizen's sense of identification with the political system and its ruling authorities, his sense of his subjective competence — that is, his estimation of his ability to influence the decisional outcomes of the system — and his general cognitive level, his knowledge of the system, are all directly related to the degree of responsiveness and accountability of the state to its citizens. Already (1980) the governors of the nine states controlled by the UPN, GNPP and PRP have demanded an increase in the proportion of revenue allocated to the states in order, as they put it, 'to enable the governors of all the 19 states to fulfil the promises made by Senators, Representatives, State Assemblymen and the governors to the electorate during the electioneering campaigns.' 'These promises', the governors added, 'cannot be fulfilled unless a reasonable share of the national revenue goes to the states and the local governments'.[35] In other words, electioneering promises cannot be met unless the federal government makes funds available, but the corollary to that is simply that citizens cannot hold the states accountable for non-fulfilment for then the fault would not lie with the states but with the federal authority. In any case, there would not be much point in the citizens demanding accountability since not having 'paid' for that for which the demand is made, there would be nothing to 'account' for.

The division of the country into 19 states in 1976 more or less rendered outdated the system of allocation which existed before the states were created. To meet that exigency ad hoc arrangements, rather in the spirit of May 1967 when the 12 states were decreed, had to be made. The military had in fact taken their attempts at 'reform' as interim measures and in his address to the CDC the late General Murtala had suggested one of the things the CDC might want to look into was the system of revenue allocation. The CDC, however, thought the issue was best left to an expert committee, a position which the Constituent Assembly also accepted. With the handover of government to a popularly elected civilian government, the new government took the appointment of a revenue allocation commission as a matter of priority and as a result set up the 'Okigbo Commission' to undertake the task of reviewing the system of allocation with the request that in carrying out its task the commission should give due regard to the principles of allocation, particularly those of derivation, population, equality of states, even development, equitable distribution and national interest.

The commission's report, which was submitted to the President at the end of June 1980,[36] has already aroused some controversy even though it is yet to be published. However, from comments made by those opposed to the commission's recommendations, the main proposals have become known. These would seem to be that of federally collected revenue, 53 per cent should be retained by the federal government, 30 per cent should be allocated to the states, 10 per cent should go to local governments, and 7 per cent should be put in a 'special fund', from which approved sums would be made available to the oil-producing states as compensation for ecological damage arising from oil exploration and production. And of the 30 per cent which the commission recommended should be allocated to the states, it was suggested that 40 per cent should be shared between the states on the basis of population, 40 per cent on the basis of 'minimum responsibility', and 15 per cent on primary school enrolment (the federal government presently pays to the states ₦40 per pupil enrolled under the universal primary education scheme), while the balance of 5 per cent should be distributed in proportion to the amount of revenue internally collected.[37]

For its own part, the federal Ministry of Finance, presumably advocating the 'federal viewpoint', had wanted (in the Ministry's submission to the commission) the federal government to retain 70 per cent of federally collected revenues, with 20 per cent going to the states and 10 per cent to the local authorities. Furthermore, the Ministry had argued that 3 per cent of the value of minerals derived from a given state should be statutorily allocated to it in the form of compensatory grants while 1.0 per cent of federal income was to go into a 'national relief fund'. With the submission of the commission's report, the federal government has intimated it would be prepared to accept a 55 per cent share of federally collected revenues with 30 per cent accruing to the states, 12 per cent to local governments and 3 per cent to a 'special fund'.

As might be expected, the commission's recommendations

have not met with complete approval. The governors of nine of the 19 states have issued a public statement saying they would want to see the states have a 40 per cent share of federally collected revenues with 10 per cent accruing to the states. In addition to that the governors of the main oil-producing states, Rivers, Cross River and Bendel (the Governor of Bendel state also subscribed to the views of the 'nine') have said the 'Okigbo recommendations' were unacceptable to them, arguing that the recommendations were not only 'politically tainted, prejudiced, insensitive and biased', but also that they involved a 'deliberate and dangerous mix up of the principle of derivation with the Special Fund meant to clear up the mess of the debris left by the process of exploitation and exploration of minerals'.[38] Given the distinction made between 'on-shore' and 'off-shore' oil, it seems inescapable that oil will play a crucial part in the controversy over the 'Okigbo report'. (The Governor of Imo state, an oil-producing state, has already disputed the claim by his Cross River counterpart that the Cross River state is the third largest producer of oil.)[39]

Until more is known of the rationale on which the commission based its recommendations, little in the way of useful comment can be made. But that there will be vigorous opposition from the states seems already certain. The tying of 5 per cent of the share-out between the states to 'internally' derived revenues would no doubt work in favour of those states — for example, Oyo, Ondo, Ogun, Bendel, Imo and Anambra — with high urban concentrations, and to the disadvantage of those with large rural populations, such as Borno, Sokoto, Niger and Gongola, and one would expect the latter to oppose such a recommendation, desirable as it may be on other grounds. The pattern of opposition already cuts across party lines so that a resolution on the basis of party alignments is hardly to be expected. A parliamentary coalition of National Assemblymen from states opposed to the commission's recommendations could prove extremely embarrassing to the executive branch of the government, and unless care is taken, could easily degenerate into a head-on collision between the two 'arms' of the government with unforeseeable consequences. Oil may have greased the wheels of government and thus made its working easier and smoother, but it may yet clog the whole machine.

THE STATE AND THE CITIZEN: THE QUESTION OF SOCIAL WELFARE

Large sums are expended by the various governments annually (Federal government; 1970/71 ₦302 million, 1973/74 ₦331.5 million, 1975/6 ₦1,053.6 million, 1979/80 ₦8,805.2 million; and States governments: 1970/71 ₦393.0 million, 1973/74 ₦528.8 million, 1975/76 ₦1,317 million, 1979/80 ₦2,263.13 million – the last figure does not include the sum of ₦300 million local government expenditure for 1979/80), and one may well be anxious to find out what impact these sums have had on the 'life chances' or 'life styles' of the average Nigerian. Put in terms of the 'goals' of the Second National Plan, how 'just and egalitarian' has the society become?

As a first approximation, some of the areas in which governmental activity can be seen to make a direct contribution to the life styles of the citizens are those of health and education. But when one looks at the expenditure pattern of the federal government for 1979/80 for example (and that was a year in which expenditure on health and education was more or less double the previous year's annual expenditure), per capita expenditure on health by the federal government amounted to no more than ₦1.1 while the expenditure on education was ₦4.19 (on a population figure of 88 million). On the other hand, per capita expenditure on defence was ₦5.92 (₦8.17 if one thinks in terms of 'security', that is the armed forces and the police) but expenditure per soldier came to ₦3476.[40] Per capita expenditure on defence, health and education by the federal government is shown in Table 7.10. But these figures give no indication of the degree of variation that exists between the states, some idea of which can be gained from looking at state capital expenditures on health and education under the Third National Plan, taking just the first year of the Plan (Table 7.11).[41] Health and Education formed 17.74 per cent of total expenditure (capital) in Benue Plateau state, 19.01 per cent in the East-Central, 19.41 per cent in Kano, 18.72 per cent in Kwara, 10.66 per cent in

TABLE 7.10 *Federal Government: military and social expenditures –*
1971/72–1978/79[42]

	Defence		Education		Health	
	₦ million	Per capita (₦)	₦ million	Per capita (₦)	₦ million	Per capita (₦)
1971/72	285.89	3.24	5.16	0.06	15.43	0.17
1973/74	420.16	4.71	12.21	0.14	19.97	0.23
1975/76	1166.69	13.26	295.23	3.35	69.77	0.79
1978/79	597.85	6.79	779.36	8.85	81.0	0.92

Source: Recurrent and Capital Estimates of the Government of the Federal Republic of Nigeria.

Lagos, 13.49 per cent in the Midwest, 20.76 per cent in the North-Central, 25.83 per cent in the North-East, 12.59 per cent in the North-West, 22.73 per cent in the Rivers, 18.91 per cent in the South-East and 17.96 per cent in the West. In the main, then, other than in Lagos (which has the lowest population), the Midwest and the North-West, expenditure on health and education was roughly comparable for most of the states, the average expenditure being about 18 per cent. However, in per capita terms, while the ratio of the minimum expenditure on health to the maximum is 1:23, that on education is 1:33 (North-Central and Lagos in the former case, North-East and Rivers in the latter). Other things being equal then, one might want to say that individuals in the 'West' are by far and away better off in health terms (services received) than their counterparts in the North-Central, and that the same thing holds between individuals, in educational terms, in the Rivers and the North-Eastern states (and like comparisons could be made pairwise for all the states). But before one jumps to such a conclusion, while it cannot be denied that states like Lagos, the West and the East Central are better served in health and educational terms than most of the other states, care should be taken in comparing the latter set of states, for the figures may reflect no more than the low base from which some states started and hence the considerable emphasis placed on either health or education, in the attempt simply to raise that which is barely existent.

TABLE 7.11   *Capital expenditure on health and education: Third National Plan, year 1975–76*

	Health				Education			
	Total 1975–80 (₦ million)	Per capita (₦)	1975–76 (₦ million)	Per capita (₦)	Total 1975–80 (₦ million)	Per capita (₦)	1975–76 (₦ million)	Per capita (₦)
Benue Plateau	30.7	6.06	2.2	0.43	69.35	13.8	7.3	1.43
East-Central	62.6	8.69	3.1	0.43	70.66	9.8	15.98	2.22
Kano	32.4	5.68	0.9	0.16	68.82	11.9	14.27	2.46
Kwara	28.5	12.39	9.7	4.2	46.12	20.1	5.87	2.54
Lagos	53.9	37.43	0.7	0.5	30.64	21.2	5.78	4.01
Midwest	39.7	16.54	1.6	0.6	49.10	20.45	4.32	1.8
North-Central	23.8	5.80	0.4	0.09	75.10	18.3	3.27	0.79
North-Eastern	49.1	6.0	2.1	0.25	90.50	11.06	1.92	0.20
North-Western	30.6	5.27	1.8	0.31	44.89	7.73	2.76	0.47
Rivers	34.8	19.33	3.3	1.83	74.3	41.27	12.16	6.75
South-East	22.9	6.36	2.7	0.75	65.9	18.3	8.47	2.35
West	43.0	4.57	21.0	2.23	81.33	8.65	20.0	2.14

More interesting, however, is a comparison of the minimum and maximum per capita expenditure on health and education respectively between the states, and here the minimum ratios are 1:2 and 1:3, figures which indicate the greater emphasis placed on education generally and which are a testimony to the belief that education remains the principal avenue for upward mobility in the society as a whole. It also points to the fact that the less educationally advantaged states (that is most of the states other than Lagos, Bendel, Oyo, Ogun, Ondo, Anambra, and Imo states) are prepared to invest in education not only to improve their own manpower supply but also to ensure that indigenes from their states stand a reasonable chance in the struggle for the control of the instrumentalities of state power, the bureaucracy, the para-statals, the defence and security services. Be that as it may, it is also the case that the educationally more advantaged states spend, in per capita terms – and on average – three times as much (owing to the larger proportion of persons of school age being in schools and hence having a larger 'absorptive capacity' for education) – as the less favoured states. In effect, therefore, in the absence of any specially designed schemes to further aid these states – for example, federally sponsored and financed 'crash programmes' (which could raise charges of 'favouritism' and therefore have political consequences) – it does not seem likely that the existing disadvantage can be eliminated. But should the existing educational inequalities persist, they could become increasingly potent 'flashpoints' of instability in the society as a whole.[43]

There are other aspects to the same problem, the urban–rural dimension. Even although the urban–rural dichotomy is often not very clear-cut (for instance in states like Oyo, Ogun, Anambra, Imo, and to a lesser extent Bendel) and there are hardly any published figures of the distribution of schools (nor of educational facilities in general) between the urban and rural areas of the various states, it is observationally true that the urban areas are better served with schools than the rural, with the result that with rising expenditure on education, which can be easily seen from federal recurrent spending (which rose by 2317.77 per cent between 1973/74 and 1975/76, and 163.98 per cent between 1975/76 and 1978/79)[44] the main beneficiaries have been the urban residents and not the already deprived rural inhabitants. The Universal Primary Education (UPE) scheme, which was launched in 1975/76 has in fact worsened the comparative disadvantage of the rural areas, for with urban wages rising faster than the rural, migration from the rural to the urban areas has increased, thereby denuding the rural areas of their able adult working force and leaving the children of schoolgoing age to fill the gap in farm labour created by migration. Noticeably, the UPE scheme, though free, is not compulsory and with the worsening urban—rural terms of trade, the rural population requires the labour of children of schoolgoing age if rural incomes are not to fall still further.

When we turn to the urban population itself, we find that the children of the urban working 'class' (the lower income groups) are at a disadvantage compared with those of the middle and upper income brackets. To make generalisation easier, we can use salary scales — questionable as some may regard this method — to demarcate the 'lower' from the 'middle' and 'upper' income groups and say that those on Grade Levels (GL) 1 to 7 (the minimum wage for those on GL 1 is now ₦100 a month) fall into the 'lower' category (about two-thirds of all those within that category would be between GL 1 and GL 4) while those within GL 8 and 12 are in the 'middle' income group, and the 'upper' income group is constituted by those within GL 13 and 17 (starting salary for GL 17 is ₦1083 a month which gives a ratio of approximately 1:11 between the minimum of GL 1 and GL 17). Most of the lower income group pay, on average, about 30 per cent of their monthly wage on house rents: the equivalent for the upper income group, whose rents are subsidised with a fixed upper limit of ₦300 per annum, is 2.4 per cent, and in most urban centres the density of occupancy ranges from 5:1 to as high as 7:1.[45] Given the environmental handicaps that children from lower income families have to contend with as a result of this situation, and with about eight children competing for every single place in the secondary schools, it is hardly surprising that most find it more difficult than their counterparts from the upper income groups to get a place in the secondary schools. When one adds to this the unevenness in the quality of secondary schools, and the fact that to get into a good secondary school may mean having to board far away from home (the school population of each of the federally sponsored, so-called unity schools, of which there are 39 scattered throughout the federation, is 591 compared to 1500 in the state schools), given the high correlation between entry to a university and attendance at a good secondary school, then the declining proportion of students from lower income families attending universities — a result confirmed by O'Connell and Beckett[46] in their survey of the social origins of university students enrolled at the universities of Ahmadu Bello, Ibadan, Lagos and the University of Nigeria — becomes readily understandable. Admittedly, the federal government has ruled that boarding fees should be reduced from ₦120 per term to ₦60, but even that reduced figure still represents 15 per cent of the gross annual income of the lower income group, a proportion few can pay given that the lower income group is usually worse-hit by inflation, which before 1980 was rising by more than 14 per cent (at the official figures) per annum, than their upper income counterparts. Should this tendency — for the offspring of the urban working class and the rural population to lose out in the competition for higher education places — continue, then the likely outcome would be for the elite (the upper income groups) to become a self-recruiting elite and to the extent that it is the elite who control and manipulate the instrumentalities of the state and also wield political power, the elite also become a self-perpetuating oligarchy. Paradoxically, though by lowering boarding fees the government had aimed at easing the financial burden of education on the lower income groups, the outcome has been in reality for that group to subsidise the education of the children of those in the upper income groups and help entrench the elite in their position of power. As the Hausa statement has it, though the context is somewhat extended, '*Zuriyan Sarki ba talakawa ne ba*' which translated means 'the descendants of a Chief never become commoners'.

But it is not only the educational system which has tended to benefit more than proportionately the elite and hence to reinforce the existing patterns of inequality: several aspects of the planning process have contributed to the same outcome. For example, programmes aimed at agricultural regeneration have done exactly this. Apart from various schemes to help 'small farmers' — by the supply of subsidised fertilisers, improved seeds and seedlings, minor mechanical aids and credit facilities — the emphasis has been on large mechanised schemes directly managed by the state or by private individuals operating on their own or in collaboration with external financial interests. The projects range from the integrated farming schemes centred around the various River Basin authorities such as the Chad Basin Development authority scheme covering some 66,000 hectares; the Hadeija Jemaare Basin project for 22,000 hectares for the first phase and another 35,000 hectares in the second and third phases; and the National Grains Company project involving some 4000 hectares, to the scheme to clear not less than 3000 hectares in each of the 19 states, which area would then be subdivided among individual farmers. In most of these schemes the land has been acquired through the dispossession of the small farmers who are expected to be compensated for their loss, or where possible resettled. But more often than not they have neither been resettled nor compensated, and even where some compensation has been paid, this has in numerous cases been quickly spent, leaving the small rural farmer landless and without the means of earning a steady income or a living of any kind. Whatever then may be the economic rationales for these schemes, they have inevitably led to the creation of a steadily rising number of landless 'peasants'.

Not only have these schemes succeeded in converting the small farmer into a landless, unemployed individual; part of the land he has been told to vacate has been taken over by members of the elite — the upper ranks of the armed forces and the bureaucracy, the contracting—commercial class and the professional/managerial groups — who with ready access to bank loans and other agricultural credit[47] have been better placed to take up the challenges of large-scale mechanised farming. It is also this class who, with aid from government-financed housing corporations and bank loans, have gone into the acquisition of urban real estate (in a number of cases the land acquired has been developed at public expense by the governments), about one of the most profitable forms of private investment in contemporary Nigeria. An indication of how profitable this can be is shown by the following quotation from the report of the Constitution Drafting Committee:

> The value conferred upon state land by the expenditure of public funds is inflated and exploited when plots of it have been allocated to private persons. A plot of state land in Victoria Island now sells in the markets for well over ₦30,000; at Enugu it has recently risen to between ₦20,000 and ₦25,000. For the individual allottee this is so much unearned and therefore undeserved income. If he gets more than his due share of state land, he would have unjustly enriched himself at the expense of the rest of the population. This inequality and inequity are aggravated when the allottee builds houses on the plots with a loan from financial institutions. The rent is fixed at a level far beyond the means of the wage earner to afford. The position has resulted that only a few private individuals can afford to pay the rent charged at Victoria Island. The land there being concentrated in the hands of a few direct allottees from the state, the rest are denied the opportunity of ever owning plots in the Island or renting accommodation there. This is a position that should not be tolerated in a country of equal opportunities that we all envision.[48]

What the CDC wrote of Victoria Island could just as well have been written about most of the major urban centres in Nigeria. It is perhaps not without some interest that though the CDC debated at length on the desirability of imposing a constitutional limitation of the number of state lands which individuals can own, the committee was unable to reach any agreement and had to leave the issue open.

The same phenomenon can be observed when one looks at public housing. To ease the shortage of housing in the urban centres, the federal government, in the Third National Plan, had proposed building 60,000 house units which were to be sold at cost to the public (there being state housing schemes to complement the federal programme). Under the civilian government, that number has been upgraded to 200,000 units

annually and loans are to be made available through the
Federal Mortgage Bank to enable buyers to purchase houses
on an 'owner—occupier' basis. The loans fall into three categories: social, economic, and commercial. The first category,
social loans, have a ceiling of ₦65,000, are for 'owner—occupier' purchases and are repayable over a 15—20-year period.
The economic category, which covers loans in excess of
₦65,000, is meant to serve the needs of those interested in
urban housing as a commercial venture and are repayable
over a period not exceeding 10 years, while the commercial
class of loans is for those wanting to invest in the construction
of specialised buildings such as commercial stores, industrial
premises, and warehouses. Commercial loans are repayable
within 7 years. Taking the social class of loans alone, with
interest rates at about 8 per cent, it needs hardly any insight
to realise that the first-year repayments on a loan of, say,
₦45,000 (about the average cost of houses meant for the low
income groups) far exceed the total annual wage of an employee on Grade Level 8 who is at the top of the scale for his
grade level. Whoever then the beneficiaries of the government-
sponsored housing scheme may be, it seems most unlikely
that they will be the low income groups who bear the highest
burden of rent in the whole federation.

So far top administrators and the professional cadres of
the public sector have found sufficient reward in real estate
investment, and though some may have acquired significant
financial interests in manufacturing and commerce through
the promulgation of the Nigerian Enterprises and Promotions
Decree in 1972 by buying equity shares in enterprises previously wholly owned by foreign business groups, with the
passing of the Nigerian Enterprises Decree (No. 3) of 1977, the
scope for such acquisition has been somewhat reduced. The
latter decree was passed, in part, as a result of criticisms that
the original decree left too much room for a few individuals to
accumulate a more than proportionate share of the wealth of
the country. However, the 1977 Decree, by expanding the
range of indigenous participation in the economy — through
bringing a number of enterprises which previously required
only a 40 per cent equity shareholding to be in Nigerian hands
into Schedule 11 which made a 60 per cent equity sharehold-

ing by Nigerians mandatory — has also had the effect of bringing state bureaucrats and technocrats into closer contact with foreign business and financial interests. This has come about through the state having to nominate bureaucrats and technocrats to the membership of the boards of those enterprises in which the governments of the federation have themselves taken up an equity shareholding. The closer working collaboration which membership of boards has engendered has been twofold: first, it has widened the opportunities of access to credit, loans and other forms of economic inducement; and second, it has led some of the very able among the administrators, from the contacts already made, to leave the public for the private sector where rewards are not only higher but where job security, particularly after the 'purges' of 1975, is better guaranteed. Overall, and put summarily, the outcome has been to bring the 'state' and the 'economy', or put in Parson's terms,[49] the 'goal setting' subsystem and the 'integrative' subsystem into greater congruence than ever before.

In principle, it could be argued that such an outcome could lead to a better management of the economy, if only because, again in principle, it would have the effect of making information about the private sector more readily accessible to state planners and other managers of the economy.[50] But such an expectation must, however, remain questionable not least because, though indigenisation may have broadened the pattern of ownership in the major industrial and financial enterprises,[51] it has also left the shareholding by foreign interests concentrated and, in consequence, left the control of these enterprises unaltered. Effective control still lies with expatriate managers, leaving the indigenous managerial or directorate complement as simply 'compradorial' elements. One need not therefore dispute the statement of one of the goals of the Second National Plan which was to create 'a land of bright and full opportunities for all citizens', except to make the qualification that in place of the phrase 'for all citizens' one should read 'for the few'[52] which is perhaps a more palatable way of denying one other goal of the Second National Plan, the creation of a 'just and egalitarian society'.

8

External Relations

The capacity to enter into relations with other states is now regarded as one of the attributes of statehood, like maintaining a standing army, having a national emblem or a national anthem, and Nigeria, on becoming a sovereign state on 1 October 1960, thus became responsible for the conduct of its inter-state relations. But relations to what purpose? The traditional and conventional answer would be to say: to further the 'national interest'. Except that that leaves open the questions: what is meant by the 'national interest'? and who determines that interest?

Several answers have been proposed to the former question, one such being by Brian Barry. Barry's answer would be to say that the 'national interest' is the interest of a 'non-assignable group',[1] a residual interest which is left once the various interests of the different groups in the society have been taken into consideration and each has cancelled the other out. But this seems to be like Rousseau's 'General Will', the 'will' that is left when the pluses and the minuses have been added, subtracted and cancelled out. The difficulty of course being that it is far from clear what is left when the cancelling-out processes have been completed.

The difficulty is compounded when the question is asked whether, conceptually, it is possible to talk of an interest which is not, in some form or another, the interest of a group. The boundaries of that group may be difficult to define with any precision, but to say that, is not to say that the group is 'non-assignable' if by 'non-assignable' is meant non-definable. The issue of assignability or non-assignability is related to the question of who defines the 'national interest'. One way of pursuing this is to do so negatively, by excluding for a start those of whom it can reasonably be said that they are not involved in, or responsible for, the definition of the 'national interest'. Put in this way it seems obvious that the defining group is neither the electorate nor the legislature. The broad outlines of a foreign policy posture or commitment may feature in the electoral programme of a party but it would be absurd to identify the 'national interest' with the broad outlines of a policy, outlines which more often than not do no more than indicate the general international orientation which a party proposes to take should it find itself forming the government of the day. In other words, while such 'outlines' may help to indicate the possible trend of policy, they in no way determine policy, which must have to await events in the international political arena. The same argument applies to the legislature which, though it may have to give legal effect to policy outcomes of inter-state relations, does so only *ex post*, after the event. Nor could the defining group be claimed to be the executive considered as a collective body. For one thing, inter-state relations often demand a certain delicacy of approach, sometimes entailing secrecy or such extreme urgency that there is hardly time for the consultation and deliberation which executive decision-making requires. These arguments apply with all the more force to the legislature.[2]

By a process of elimination, one is then left with the 'professionals' — the body of top civil servants and/or political appointees who are actively engaged in the day-to-day management and administration of the state's relations with other states, agencies of other states, formal and non-formal quasi-autonomous governmental and non-governmental organisations, international institutions and organisations and various other international actors. For the external relations of a state cover not only the formal relations with other states, relations which often give rise to treaties, agreements and understandings, but also commercial, scientific and cultural undertakings in which the participants are not necessarily states *qua* states, but actors covering a wide range of description. The activities embraced in a state's external relations are so variegated that the demands for professionalism, for expert knowledge and negotiating skills are often of a different order from what is usually demanded in the management of the domestic affairs of the state. In these circumstances, the executive political head responsible for overseeing the external relations of the state may therefore do no more than stipulate the parameters which govern or determine policy outcomes and to that extent there is a fundamental difference between foreign relations and domestic decision-making. Ultimately, then the 'national interest' may be defined as whatever the professionals who manage the state's external relations say it is.

But to say this is not to suggest that the professionals should therefore be cast in the garb of some kind of platonic 'philosopher king'. It might thus be useful, in this context, to make a distinction with reference to decision-making in the external political arena, between 'determinants' and 'constraints'. A mathematical analogue might be helpful. Consider for example, a function $f(x)$ where $f(x)$ is taken, for illustrative purposes, to represent a linear equation of the form $f(x) = a_0 + a_1 x_1 + a_2 x_2 + \ldots + a_{n-1} x_{n-1} + a_n x_n$, where $(a_0, a_1, \ldots, a_n)$ are, as usual, parameters, and the x's, $(x_1, x_2, \ldots, x_n)$ are variables of the function. Given whatever values the variables can take, once the parameters are known, then the value of the function $f(x)$ is determined. We could call, for the present purposes, the set of parameters, the 'constraints' and the set of variables, the 'determinants'. In the determination of the value of the function, the respective roles of the executive/political head and the professionals could be said to consist in the former determining the values of the parameters, and the latter, the professionals, the range of values which the variables can take. In determining the value of $f(x)$, there is a dynamic relationship between the parameters and the variables. The contrast between domestic and external decision-making suggested above, then, lies precisely in the reversal of roles in the determination of the values of the parameters and the variables.

If the foregoing is seen as a simplified form of a paradigmatic model of foreign relations decision-making, one can then proceed to examine how that model has been, or could be, applied in the determination of Nigeria's external relations. In a lecture by the Nigerian High Commissioner to Trinidad and Tobago – given at the Institute of International Relations, University of the West Indies, St Augustine campus – the High Commissioner, Mr Emmanuel Kolade, suggested that Nigeria's foreign relations could be seen to have passed through three distinctive phases: the first, covering the period 1960–65 (the first republic) was, he said, marked by caution and relative inactivity; the second, from 1966 to 1969, the civil war period, was devoted mainly to maintaining the integrity of the nation; while the third, beginning from 1970, was said to have been notable for a new Nigerian initiative on the diplomacy of the West African sub-region. It was a period 'characterised by personal diplomacy, bold diplomatic initiatives and concrete cooperative agreements'.[3]

That periodisation was put forward before the overthrow of General Gowon in July 1975. Two months after the overthrow, in a television interview given on 24 October 1975, the new Federal Commissioner for External Affairs was to modify that picture by drawing a contrast between the period 1970 to July 1975 and the post-July 1975 era. According to the new Commissioner, Col. (later Major-General) Joseph Garba, Nigeria's foreign policy 'was in the main sound, but I think it was in the application that left a lot to be desired'. Col. Garba went on to add that

> the former regime overplayed the game. Now this tended to make us react to developments, thus negating the need for a firm stand on most major issues . . . either out of fear of committing blunders or maybe some other considerations [the regime] couldn't come out with a firm stand on major issues and so in fact because of that we did not have a policy at all.

Unlike the posture of the 1970–75 period, then, the post-July 1975 administration 'is probably going to be more aggressive . . . this government will come out more firmly and state its stand on any issue that involves Nigeria or the international community at large'.[4] One may not accept the characterisation of the different periods as presented either by

Mr Kolade or by Col. Garba, but the periodization that both men offer — 1960—65; 1966—69; 1970—75; and post-1975 (at least till October 1979 when the second republic came into being on 1 October) — does offer a useful starting point within which Nigeria's external relations may be examined.

THE FIRST PHASE: 1960—65

Though Nigeria maintained some form of external representation before she became independent, such representation was kept more on a tutelary basis — with Britain as the overseeing authority — than as a mark of sovereignty. In fact when the first conference of independent African states met in Accra (Ghana) in 1958, Nigeria was not invited, something which Nigeria was to construe as a 'slight' and which was to influence the relations between Ghana and Nigeria throughout the whole period. In the main this was the period when the institutional requisites for conducting foreign relations were in the process of being built up and symptomatic of the 'teething' problems which the federation had to face was the dispute between the Ministry of Information — which insisted that anything that had to do with information and publicity, both domestic and external, had to be within the purview of the Ministry — and the Ministry of External Affairs, which rightly claimed that anything not 'domestic' must necessarily fall within the jurisdiction of 'external affairs', a dispute which was only resolved by the intervention of the Prime Minister who ruled in favour of the latter ministry.

Basically, there were two main policy fields which were of primary concern to Nigeria within this period. The first was Nigeria's relations with her erstwhile colonial master, Britain, and by extension, Nigeria's relations with the other Commonwealth countries, a Commonwealth of which Britain was the 'head'; the second concerned the relations between Nigeria and the other African states. Nigeria signalled her tutelage relationship to Britain in her first act as an independent state by entering into a defence pact — the Anglo-Nigerian Defence Pact — with Britain, a pact which gave Britain military facilities, including the training of her military personnel, in Nigeria. But within a year after independence, when the pact came up for renewal, it was to be abrogated by Nigeria, due largely to opposition from university students who proclaimed the pact a neocolonial arrangement. But that fact notwithstanding, Nigeria maintained a special relationship with Britain throughout the period under consideration. It was largely under British direction that, for some two years after independence, Nigeria denied the USSR the facility to open an embassy in Lagos, even though the USSR had expressed a desire to open diplomatic relations with Nigeria. Though the ostensible reason given was that Nigeria did not have the resources at that stage to reciprocate with an embassy of her own in the Soviet Union, the more plausible explanation would seem to be that Nigeria's leaders had not quite got over the image of the Soviet Union created by the colonial administration. For much of the forties, Soviet literature had been banned from circulation in Nigeria and Nigerians educated in the Soviet Union were denied employment in the administration. When eventually the government permitted the Soviet Union to establish an embassy in Nigeria, it was on the understanding that the number of embassy staff would be restricted; it was claimed that that was the advice of the British government, the understanding being that since Nigeria did not have the personnel to keep Soviet representatives under effective surveillance, the numbers to be allowed had to be such that the British High Commission could keep a check on them.

The caution and the restrictiveness applied not only to the USSR but to the other East bloc countries as well. As against that, however, most of the West European states were permitted to open embassies unchecked, as was the United States, a policy which was to cast serious doubt on Nigeria's proclaimed stance of 'neutralism'. For soon after independence the Prime Minister had proclaimed, as a general guideline of the country's foreign policy, that while old associations would be maintained and strengthened, Nigeria would seek to remain neutral between the two contending world powers, the USSR and the United States.[5] It was never exactly clear what the policy of neutralism entailed. Even as late as 1975, in the television interview given by Col. Garba referred to above, the ambiguity still persisted. The Commissioner stated that:

We want the nation to be positively neutral in the sense that we want to take an independent stand on major issues

and we don't want to sit on the fence. What was happening
was that when we sent delegations out on national service
to international conferences we usually failed to brief
them about our stand. Hence when they had to take a
stand, they sat back rather than commit themselves on any
issue. What I think we want to do is to be neutral. When
you are neutral you tend to be in a better position to assess
an issue objectively when it comes to your own turn to
intervene. You will not be committing yourself to anyone.
I think this is what we want.[6]

Perhaps what is being called 'neutralism' would be better
described as 'non-alignment', the deliberate refusal of a nation
to be seen to be aligned or committed on major international
issues to either bloc in a bipolar-power world, but the seman-
tics of 'neutralism' and 'non-alignment' have become too
complex — and often confusing — to be gone into here. What
seems reasonably certain is that for the period 1960—65,
judging from its voting record at the United Nations, Nigeria
was neither 'neutral' nor 'non-aligned'.[7] On most issues of
any significance — for example, on disarmament — Nigeria
tended to vote with the Western powers.

But the foregoing should not be construed to mean that
Nigeria followed Britain uncritically, in the formulation and
determination of her foreign policy. Thus, for example, when
South Africa became a republic in 1962, Nigeria was among
the commonwealth states which insisted that South Africa
be excluded from the Commonwealth, even though at the
same time Nigeria still maintained some trading relations with
South Africa. And when France exploded its first nuclear
device in the Sahara in 1963, in spite of all the assurances
given by France and reinforced by Britain that there would
be no ill effects to Nigeria, Nigeria as a result of this went
ahead and broke diplomatic relations — at least for a time —
with France. On the other hand, when Rhodesia unilaterally
proclaimed itself an independent state in 1965, Nigeria, unlike
some other Commonwealth African states — for example,
Tanzania — thought the incident not sufficiently important
to warrant breaking diplomatic relations with Britain. Instead,
Nigeria accepted the British view that 'limited economic

sanctions' and not force of arms would be adequate to bring Southern Rhodesia 'to heel' and hence were the more appropriate reaction to UDI (Unilateral Declaration of Independence).

In a sense, it could be argued that during the first half of the period Nigeria was prepared to follow in the footsteps of Britain largely because, as a newly independent state, it had yet to acquire the expertise required to formulate an independent foreign policy, besides being predisposed in that direction both from its past association with Britain and from the balance of power within the federation itself, a balance which placed the Northern Peoples' Congress in a dominant position in the federal parliament. From 1964, however, there was evidence that Nigeria was beginning to acquire a self-confidence sufficient to strike an independent stance of her own. Some idea of the strength of a relationship between countries can be gained from a look at the volume, value and direction of trade; and certainly by 1964 there was enough evidence to show some swing in Nigeria's external trade away from Britain towards the European Economic Community (EEC) countries. By 1965, the desire to diversify the pattern of trade was sufficiently pronounced for Nigeria to appoint an Ambassador Plenipotentiary to the EEC to negotiate an associate status for Nigeria with the EEC countries. The coup of 1966, however, was to interrupt that trend and lead not only to a recall of the ambassador but also a termination of the negotiations. The negotiations were not resumed until close to a decade later, by which time Britain herself had negotiated entry into the community as a fully fledged member.

If Nigeria caused hardly a ripple on the international scene, in Africa the picture was somewhat different. In 1958, when the first conference of independent African states was held, there were only 10 independent states in the continent — which number included the ancient kingdom of Ethiopia; Liberia, which was settled with freed American slaves as an independent state; and South Africa (although South Africa is normally excluded when the count of 'African' states is taken). The conference — to which were invited a few yet-to-be-independent states — resolved among other things to work towards (a) the total liberation of Africa from foreign domination; and (b) 'continental African unity now'. The latter was construed to mean a pan-African political organisation under which the separate states would subsume their sovereignty and which would serve as the common forum through which Africa would express itself in the international political arena. Two years later, the number of independent states had grown to 26 and by 1963 when the Organisation of African Unity (OAU) was finally established, to 34. But by 1960, when half the total number of African states had become independent, an ideological divide had developed between the states, a divide which grouped the various states into three classes: the 'Casablanca group', the 'Brazzaville group' and the 'Monrovia group'. Underlying this tripartite division was a more fundamental division, that between the 'radicals' — states like Ghana, Guinea, Mali, Algeria and Congo (Brazzaville) — and the 'moderates', countries such as Sierra-Leone, Senegal, the Ivory Coast, Liberia and Nigeria. While the former wanted a political union of all the African states, the demand for 'continental unity', the latter talked in terms of a 'functional association', arguing that in the circumstances of the times, talk of 'continental unity' was not just premature, it was unrealistic. Though not opposed in principle to the notion of 'continental unity', the 'moderates' thought such unity was something that needed to be nurtured, to develop over time from a 'functional association' of separate sovereign states.

Amongst the moderates, Nigeria provided leadership, and smarting from not having been invited to the 1958 conference, sought to isolate the more radical in the 'radical' camp while selling to the moderates of the radical group the logic of functional association. When therefore the African states assembled in Addis Ababa in 1963 to resolve the differences between the contending groups, Nigeria was reasonably confident that the position she had championed — with Liberia and Sierra-Leone — would win the day. In the 1962 'treason' trials involving Chief Awolowo and some 21 other members of his party, evidence had been adduced that Ghana had not only encouraged the alleged subversive activities of those charged, but had actually provided military training for a number of the accused persons. It was hardly surprising then, to find Article III of the Charter of what became the Organisation of African Unity stating that: 'member states adhere to the principles of sovereign equality, non-interference in the internal affairs of member states [and] respect for territorial integrity ...', a proposal which had been advocated by Nigeria. But having played an active role in fostering the establishment of the OAU, Nigeria surprisingly withdrew into a relatively isolationist posture. Where the Francophone states were struggling with the problems of 'regional security', (in the formation, for example, of the Organisation Commune Africaine et Malgache (OCAM)) or the East African states, with the dilemmas of economic cooperation (in the translation of the East African Common Services Organisation into the East African Community), Nigeria's leaders sought only to immerse themselves in their own domestic problems, preferring to talk more of the Commonwealth than of the OAU. About the last act the regime of the first republic was to undertake was to host a meeting of the Commonwealth Heads of governments in Lagos, and that at a time when the Western region was close to being in a state of anarchy. A day after the meeting ended the 1966 coup took place, which was to cost the Prime Minister and two of the regional Premiers (among others) their lives. Nkrumah, who was himself to be overthrown in a military coup a month later, said of the Balewa regime that the tragedy of the regime was that the Prime Minister never quite understood the forces which brought about the downfall of his regime. It was perhaps a harsh judgement but many would probably agree that it contained a large element of truth and, in some respects, it is a not unfitting epitaph for a regime which, though sovereign, behaved as if it were still a colonial state.

THE CRISIS ERA: 1966—69

For much of this period Nigeria was fighting to contain the threat of secession and possible disintegration, and policy was dominated by the one primary consideration of maintaining the unity of the state. The first indication that Nigeria might have to revaluate her existing foreign policy came when she attempted to blockade the shores of the former

Eastern region after the territory had been proclaimed the new state of 'Biafra' by the then Military Governor, Col. Ojukwu, at the end of May 1967. The blockade had been necessitated by the need to prevent (a) arms and ammunition being smuggled in to the territory, and (b) the shipment from the area of petroleum, which would have provided export income that could be used for the purchase of arms and war materials; the area at that time produced two-thirds of the total crude oil output of the country. Though the naval boats involved in the blockade were operating within Nigerian territorial waters, Britain, which then operated the largest concession of oil wells in 'Biafra', proclaimed the blockade to be against international law. Obviously, for Britain, getting the rewards for her investment was more important than whether Nigeria survived or not as a single political unit. This was followed, a year later, after hostilities had begun, by Britain's embargo — though this was subsequently lifted — on the sale of arms to the Federal government. Other countries — France, the Netherlands, Czechoslovakia and the United States (which was to claim that she recognised Nigeria as being within the sphere of influence of Britain and would model her policy in respect of the civil war accordingly) — were to follow the British example. Admittedly the British embargo had been placed on 'humanitarian' grounds, but then Britain had always been the traditional arms supplier to Nigeria.

The revaluation of policy led to one fundamental conclusion: for developing countries like Nigeria, there could be no clear division of areas in the international political arena, no clear 'whites' or clear 'blacks'. All areas were 'grey' areas and the essence of international morality lay in getting what you wanted at the time you wanted it: how you got what you wanted must of necessity be secondary to the getting of that which was desired. In addition, there had to be a preparedness to balance short-term interests against long-term ones and the way in which this was done had to be dictated by the circumstances of the time. In relation to the first, that of morals, if Britain wanted to hold Nigeria to ransom over arms supplies, then Nigeria would have to get the arms she needed from any source possible and, in this instance, it meant the Soviet

Union. From being a country to be dealt with cautiously, the Soviet Union became an ally, seemingly overnight. From supplying Nigeria with arms at the time Nigeria needed the arms, it was a short step to securing a billion naira contract to build Nigeria's first steel plant, and still more contracts to lay oil pipelines for the distribution of Nigeria's oil products. In the now familiar pattern of inter-state relations of the developing countries, trade and other exchanges followed the supply of arms.

Conceivably it was the need to ensure a supply of arms that made Nigeria sign the Nuclear Non-Proliferation Treaty in January 1968, a treaty which obliged Nigeria not to seek to develop a nuclear capability either then or in the future. It is arguable if it could be said that signing such a treaty was in the 'national interest' of Nigeria (however that term is interpreted) even if it could be shown that Nigeria could hardly expect to acquire the skills or the resources needed to develop such a capability. Few states, by any rational consideration, would want to bind its future actions, or the possibility of action, in the way Nigeria did by signing the treaty. Admittedly, Nigeria had been elected a member of the United Nations committee on nuclear proliferation, but it would be absurd to suggest that that committed Nigeria to becoming a signatory to the treaty. In 1968, of course, Nigeria had no clear policy on nuclear energy, though since that time some moves have been made towards developing a policy and in the absence of a policy, a non-committal approach would have been safe and have fitted Col. Garba's picture of the policy output process, of delegations 'sitting back rather than commit themselves'. Obviously that picture could at best only have reflected a partial view of the policy-making process. In signing the non-proliferation treaty, Nigeria simply discounted the future heavily in favour of the present. Given the exigencies of the civil war and pressure from the great powers who would obviously be opposed to third-world countries developing nuclear pretensions, Nigeria could perhaps have had little choice but to sign the treaty.

The exigencies of war also made Nigeria rethink her policy towards her African neighbours. When 'Biafra', acting through favourably disposed states like the Ivory Coast, Tanzania and

Uganda, demanded that the civil war be discussed by the OAU, Nigeria could easily have claimed that the war was an internal affair and under the provisions of the charter objected to the OAU discussing the war on the grounds that to do otherwise would amount to interference in the internal affairs of Nigeria — a move which Nigeria in fact did make in the early stages of the war. But to have persisted in that move would only have antagonised the other African states, and this it was not prepared to do. France had not quite forgotten the federal government's opposition to her nuclear tests in the Sahara, and there were allegations that 'Biafra' had offered substantial oil concessions to France to secure a regular supply of arms. Smaller states are, of course, easier to control and manipulate than larger ones, and given France's orientation towards a clientilist relationship with her former colonies, a break-up of the federation would make it possible for France to maintain 'Biafra' as another client state. And there were grounds to believe that France was putting pressure on the Francophone African states to accord 'Biafra' recognition as an independent state. Obviously, the larger the number of African states to recognise 'Biafra' as a separate state, the easier it would be for the metropolitan powers to give a similar recognition, as they could then claim to be only following the lead already given by the African states and thereby escape the charge of interfering in African affairs with an aim at a re-Balkanisation of Africa. And once the metropolitan powers made a move towards the recognition of Biafra, the more 'internationalised' the conflict would become and the less tractable a resolution of the conflict would become. To minimise the risk of 'internationalisation', it was therefore imperative that the federal government ensured that the minimum of African states gave recognition to Biafra.

This meant winning over as many of Nigeria's neighbours — and other states, such as Ethiopia for example — as possible. Admittedly, there was an element of 'self-interest' involved in African states not giving recognition to 'Biafra'. Most of these states are ethnically heterogeneous and not a few were faced with secessionist or potential secessionist claims — Chad, the Sudan, Ethiopia, Kenya, and Uganda are well-known examples. A successful secessionist bid by 'Biafra' would not only strengthen minority groups already fighting for a separate existence, it could also encourage latent groups to stake their own claims. But in 1968/69 Nigeria's problem was to ensure that she had sufficient support among the African states to win OAU validation of her position *vis-à-vis* the claims of 'Biafra'. Thus the support of states like Niger, the Cameroun, Togo, Dahomey (which later became the Republic of Benin), Ethiopia, Algeria, Kenya, Zaire, and Guinea was carefully cultivated — in some cases, by proposals of joint collaborative ventures — while attempts were made in other cases to ensure, if not their support, then their neutrality — as for example, with Senegal. In some respects one can see a similarity with what was later to emerge as the Economic Organisation of West African States (ECOWAS) in this early excursion into the art of winning friends and influencing people.

The pay-off to Nigeria from reorientating her policy towards the other African states can be easily judged from an examination of the role of the OAU in seeking to bring about a 'peaceful solution' to the Nigerian civil war. The question of the civil war had been raised for the first time at the meeting of the OAU in Kinshasa in September 1967. On that occasion, besides setting up a Consultative Committee of five, charged with the responsibility of finding ways of bringing the war to an end, the OAU had enjoined on the contestants the need for a peaceful settlement. Though the federal government had objected to having the civil war, which it took to be a domestic issue, included on the agenda of the OAU, it had no objection to the war being discussed informally. For the 'Biafrans', the fact that the civil war was discussed at all was taken to be a moral victory, a recognition of the legitimacy of their claims and Col. Ojukwu, the 'Biafran' leader, announced that in 'the OAU we recognise . . . an essential instrument for the achievement of meaningful unity . . . the Republic of Biafra must work more positively for the realisation of the objectives of the Organisation [of African Unity] which has thus far eluded it'.[8]

A second attempt by the OAU to mediate — the Kampala conference of May 1968 — proved fruitless. After a week of talks the 'Biafran' delegates walked out of the conference with nothing achieved. However, in April and May 1968, four

African states, Tanzania, Gabon, the Ivory Coast and Zambia, formally recognised 'Biafra' as an 'independent' state, a recognition which led to a renewal of federal effort to win support from the other states for its cause. How successful the renewed efforts proved to be became apparent from the subsequent attempts at mediation by the OAU. Thus, at the Niamey (July 1969), Addis Ababa (August 1969) and Algiers (September 1969) talks, far from winning any sympathy, the 'Biafran' delegation in each case were simply told to look for ways to 'co-operate' with the federal government.[9] When the OAU made its final attempt at mediation — before the end of the civil war — by summoning the contestants to a conference in Monrovia, the 'Biafrans' hardly bothered to attend. With the collapse of 'Biafra' in January 1970, the civil war came to an end and from the war experience came a salutary lesson: in any foreign policy calculus, Africa must remain an area of primary interest for Nigeria. But it was still to take another five years before that realisation was to be formulated into a coherent doctrine.

THE THIRD PHASE: 1970—75

During the crisis period, foreign policy was left much to the 'professionals'. In the period 1960—65 Nigeria's missions abroad had been headed by political appointees. With the military takeover, however, most of such appointments were rescinded and career diplomats replaced those chosen on party political grounds to work in the country's missions abroad. Even when politicians were brought into the Executive in May 1967 and a civilian commissioner was appointed to head the Ministry of External Affairs, the exigencies of civil war conditions kept the Executive preoccupied with domestic issues so that external relations were left more or less exclusively to career diplomats. Much of this was to change with the end of the war when the Head of State, General Gowon, for all practical purposes took over the external affairs of the federation. As Brigadier Garba was later to put it after the overthrow of General Gowon, 'our external image was based on two things — the former Head of State himself, because he toured extensively — and oil'. Foreign policy became, after the war, a matter of 'personal diplomacy' as Gowon sought to create for himself an *'international persona'*, presumably to complement the domestic persona which his successful prosecution of the civil war had gained for him.

There is of course nothing necessarily undesirable in the pursuit of foreign policy objectives through a style of 'personal diplomacy' provided it can be shown that there is some coherence about the objectives being pursued. The difficulty, however, was that in a number of instances the objectives tended to be too obscure to be readily appreciated. A good example of this was Gowon's agreement to pay the salaries of Grenadian civil servants following his visit to the island after attending the Commonwealth Heads of Governments Meeting at Kingston in early 1975. Admittedly, the offer could be construed as a form of aid to a 'friendly' government then on the verge of bankruptcy. But this is hardly plausible as Grenada had hardly featured in any meaningful way in Nigeria's list of friendly states. In any case, it is questionable if an offer to pay the salaries of civil servants of a foreign state for a couple of months is the most desirable way to offer aid. This would be to mistake personal generosity for aid, though why a Head of State should choose to display his personal form of generosity with public funds is something which few could pretend to understand, other than of course within the context of a 'personal diplomacy'. Much the same thing could be said of Nigeria's decision to commit ₦19.5 million towards the expansion of the Commonwealth Fund for Technical Co-operation, particularly when Nigeria was already involved in bilateral agreements over technical co-operation with countries such as Britain, Canada and India, through which agreements Nigeria was more likely to obtain the technical expertise she needed. It was also the pursuit of 'personal diplomacy' which took Gowon to China in 1974, but apart from an acrobatic troupe and a team of 'experts on small-scale industries' (experts on woodwork and leatherwork) visiting Nigeria, it is not easy to see what Nigeria gained from Gowon's journey to China. There is certainly no evidence to suggest that the relations between Nigeria and China have in any way been improved thereby.

There were other aspects to the 'personal diplomacy' of General Gowon apart from the direct initiatives taken by him. Thus, after the Egypt—Israeli war of 1973, Nigeria suddenly broke off diplomatic relations with Israel, a posture which might have made some sense following the 'Six-day war' of 1967 when there was reason to believe that Israel's sympathies were with 'Biafra' but no such step was taken then. One can only explain the 1973 action in terms of some attempt by Gowon to 'appease' the Islamic susceptibilities of the peoples of the Northern region of Nigeria, though why this should have been thought necessary remains obscure, more so as Nigeria stood to gain more from technical cooperation with Israel than from any of the Arab states. If religious factors may have played a part in explaining the breach with Israel in 1973, it is difficult to see how the same factors could be said to have influenced Gowon's expression of Nigeria's support,

> for the joint efforts by Morocco and Mauretania [to solve] the question of the Spanish Sahara, when the solution being proposed — when the foreign Ministers of the two states called on Gowon to discuss the question of Spanish Sahara — was the division of the territory between Morocco and Mauretania contrary to the OAU's declaration that colonial territories were entitled to independence on the basis of the boundaries inherited from the metropolitan powers. In fact that expression of support was contrary to Gowon's own declared policy, made at the UN in 1973, that African states should seek to liberate at least one colonised territory every three years.[10]

If the position taken over the Spanish Sahara seems somewhat arbitrary, no less arbitrary was that taken by Gowon over the foreign oil companies operating in Nigeria. Soon after the end of the war, Nigeria had expressed a desire to take over a controlling share in the operations of the various petroleum-producing companies. This would ensure that Nigeria got a fair return from a wasting natural resource, and it conformed to the practice in most petroleum-producing countries. Thus in 1973/74 the government proceeded to purchase a 55 per cent shareholding in these companies, but Shell—BP was left out of the process, presumably because negotiations with Shell—BP were yet to be completed. But after a state visit to Britain by Gowon in 1974 and talks with the Heath government, it transpired that rather than a 55 per cent share, Nigeria had agreed to take over only 35 per cent of the shares in Shell—BP. The successor military administration to Gowon's was to bring Shell—BP's status on the same level with the other companies[11] and it was difficult for observers to understand why Gowon should have made a special concession to Shell—BP other than to say that that was yet another example of Gowon's form of personal diplomacy. (There cannot have been many African Heads of State to have been awarded an honorary degree by Cambridge University as Gowon was during his state visit to Britain.)

It should not be thought, however, that Gowon's style of diplomacy was altogether inopportune. Having won praise from the international press for his conciliatory approach to the defeated 'Biafrans' and with money not an immediate constraint following the rise in petroleum prices, it would not have been unreasonable for someone like Gowon to think that the image of an outward-looking Nigeria would be in the best interests of the country, particularly after the charges of genocide which had been made against the federal government during the civil war. Though Britain had been hesitant at a certain stage about the supply of arms to Nigeria — and there had been considerable pressure on the British government to halt all shipment of arms to the federal government — nevertheless the supply of arms to Nigeria did continue throughout the civil war. The concession to Shell—BP could therefore be seen as some mark of appreciation for the support which Nigeria had received from Britain during the civil war. Besides, with the war ended and priority given to the problems of post-war reconstruction and rehabilitation, Nigeria could do with all the help she could get, and much of this could be expected to come from Britain and the European community countries, which would mean gaining the support also of countries such as France and Western Germany. In the Spanish Sahara dispute, France is known to be sympathetic to the claims of Morocco, which could well explain Nigeria's expression of support made to the Foreign Ministers of Morocco and Mauretania — an attempt to gain the approval of France.

The desire to gain the support of France and Germany could also explain the decision of the federal government to award to both countries the contracts to establish car assembly plants — for Peugeot and Volkswagen cars in Nigeria — even though both countries had been critical of the federal government during the civil war.[12] But the exercise of winning back former 'friends' and establishing new spheres of influence was not restricted to Europe alone. Relations with Tanzania and Zambia, two countries which had recognised 'Biafra', were re-established, while in West Africa, negotiations for the federal government to embark on joint enterprises with states such as Guinea (for the exploitation of iron ore in Guinea) and the Republic of Benin and Togo (for cement processing) were initiated and as in the case of Tanzania and Zambia, relations were re-established with the Ivory Coast and Gabon. By 1974 Nigeria had even agreed to supply the Ivory Coast refinery with crude petroleum, even though the Ivory Coast continued to provide refuge for the one time-leader of 'Biafra', Col. Ojukwu.

The joint-venture approach to economic co-operation which had been begun with the Republic of Benin and Togo, states on the western border of Nigeria, was followed up with the establishment of the Chad Basin Authority which embraced Nigeria, Niger and the Chad Republic. Towards the east, the latent hostility which had existed between Nigeria and the Cameroun — a latent hostility which stemmed from the excision and eventual amalgamation with Nigeria of the northern section of the former British Cameroons following the plebiscite held in the area in 1961 — was finally resolved after a series of meetings — first at the level of officials of both states, and finally, at a meeting between the two Heads of State. But the real achievement of the period could be said to be the establishment of the Economic Community of West African States (ECOWAS), the instrument establishing which was finally to be agreed to by all the states involved in 1975.

ECOWAS can rightly be claimed to be the product of Gowon's style of personal diplomacy. The basic conception was to create the West African sub-region into a free trade area, the eventual aim being that the free trade area would develop into an integrated economic region, more or less on the model of the EEC. It has often been argued that contributing to the underdevelopment of most of the African states are such factors as smallness of population, interpreted to mean, in this instance, effective market size (the population of Nigeria, for example, is more than twice the total population of all the other West African states put together). Other such factors are lack of skills; complementarity of economies which restricts inter-state trade; the low level of inter-state trade compared to the total volume of export and import trade; and of course the more usual constraints such as lack of capital and the reliance on the export of one or two agricultural items for the bulk of foreign exchange earnings. The list is indicative and is not meant to be exhaustive of the several factors impeding growth and development. A number of these factors could be eliminated, or their impact meliorated, if larger regional groupings could be formed from the existing states. ECOWAS is meant to be one such grouping.

There have been examples of such regional formations but few have proved successful. The Central African Federation was one such example which lasted for a couple of years before it collapsed, but it could be argued that that is not a good example to cite. For one thing, the federation was externally imposed — on what was then Northern Rhodesia, Southern Rhodesia and Nyasaland — by Britain and not an autonomous growth based on the consensus of the federating units. For another, it involved racial policies which were unacceptable to the majority of the peoples in the federating states. Another example of a regional grouping is OCAM, the organisation embracing most of the Francophone African states, but this owes its continued existence more to the dependence on France of the constituent states, than to anything the organisation could be said to have achieved. It is in fact an organisation for mutual defence and not strictly an economic association. The most successful example of regional co-operation among African states was the East African Community (of Uganda, Kenya and Tanzania) but even that has, for all practical purposes, collapsed owing to dissatisfaction by some of the component states over benefits expected from the community. Given the experience of such examples, the hopes for ECOWAS cannot be all that sanguine. Even though the constituent states have all agreed, in principle, to the charter setting up the organisation, the charter itself is yet to be ratified by all of the states involved. Nevertheless to have secured the agreement of the states concerned must be counted a diplomatic achievement by the two states which have largely championed the formation of the organisation, Nigeria and Togo.

In some respects, ECOWAS can be regarded as a significant departure from the traditional practice of foreign relations by Nigeria, a practice which has in the main been marked more by its isolationism than by its adventurousness, and characterised by conservatism rather than radicalism. The departure becomes all the more significant since, in the short run at least, the other member states have more to gain from ECOWAS than has Nigeria. There cannot be much doubt that the absence of party political considerations and wealth from petroleum contributed in facilitating the change. It is open to question if Nigeria could have proceeded with the same confidence that she showed over the formation of ECOWAS if she had had to operate within the same financial constraints as the civilian regime had had to. Wealth from oil certainly made it easier for Nigeria to become a member of the 'Group of 77', the group of African Caribbean and Pacific (ACP) states which negotiated a special status for the group's member states with the EEC. The Convention governing the relationship between the EEC and the ACP states (the Convention was signed at Lome and is usually refered to as 'Lome I') covers trade co-operation, stabilisation of export earnings, industrial and technical co-operation, services, payments and capital movement, institutions, and general provisions.

Basically, the convention provided that all products originating from ACP states should be free of customs duties and charges having equivalent effect when imported by EEC countries, and also that imports from the ACP should not be subject to quantitative restrictions. Though relations between the ACP and the EEC states were to be based on the principle of non-reciprocity, the ACP countries undertook not to discriminate among member states of the Community and to grant to the Community treatment no less favourable than the most-favoured-nation treatment. In the determination of the origin of products, the EEC would regard the whole of the ACP states as one territory. With respect to the stabilisation of export earnings, the ACP states would be entitled to ask for a transfer from the stabilisation fund (which is a fixed sum set up by the EEC) if earnings from a product covered by the scheme — such as groundnuts, cocoa, coffee, coconut and palm products, raw hides, skins and leather, bananas, tea, raw sisal, iron ore and wood products — represented at least 7.5 per cent of total earnings from all products (2.5 per cent in the case of the least-developed or landlocked or island territories) in the year preceding the year of application for aid from the fund. States benefiting from the stabilisation fund were expected to contribute towards the 'reconstruction' of the fund (waived in the case of the least-developed or landlocked or island states) should there be a significant improvement in total earnings above the base year (that is the year of receipt of transfers from the fund). Though the fund covered much of Nigeria's traditional exports, since crude oil represented such a large proportion of total earnings from all exports, it meant Nigeria could not benefit from the stabilisation fund.

Nigeria can expect to benefit from membership of the ACP only indirectly through the fund for Financial and Industrial Co-operation. The Lome Convention provided for 10 per cent of the total aid money available from the EEC (3390 million units of account; that is, the value of the dollar before it was devalued in 1971) to be set aside for regional development. Organisations like the Chad Basin Authority can apply for development aid from that fund and only to the extent that funds are made available to such organisations can Nigeria, provided she is a member of such an organisation — as she is in the case of the Chad Basin Authority — expect to benefit from her inclusion in the ACP group of states. ACP member states can conclude bilateral agreements with the EEC or individual EEC countries on industrial co-operation for the development of agro-allied industries, mineral and other energy products, but since such agreements can be concluded outside the framework of the ACP, there is not much to benefit Nigeria on that score. At best, then, if Nigeria loses nothing by being included in the ACP, she also gains little if anything from her membership. Inclusion in the ACP can therefore be seen as part of a determination by Nigeria to closely identify herself with the third world, particularly in terms of the overall debate over the creation of a new international economic order, of which the so-called 'North–South dialogue' is but just an aspect.

Though the initiative towards the formation of ECOWAS and Nigeria's membership of the ACP group of states have been discussed in terms of Gowon's style of 'personal diplomacy', in the main they represent the influence of the civil servants and career diplomats on the foreign policy-making process. In the discussions leading to the formulation of the Four Year Plan for Reconstruction and Development (1970– 74) – and extrapolations from that – there had been a growing awareness among the technocrats that there could be no meaningful talk of Nigeria's economic future outside the economic prospects of the West African sub-region. If Nigeria was to become an industrial nation, as the planners hoped, then a long-run strategy of industrial development for Nigeria could not afford to ignore the West African sub-region as a potential economic market. Thus, moves towards the creation of such a market must count as a priority in Nigeria's foreign-policy objectives. But if such moves were not to give rise to fears of hegemonic designs on the part of Nigeria, then they would have to be seen in the context of a more radical approach to the as-yet-unresolved problems of Africa; problems such as those of neocolonialism and colonialism, particularly in those areas still under 'white domination' – Mozambique, Angola, Rhodesia, Namibia and South Africa.

This in effect meant taking a more aggressive attitude towards apartheid, for example, and Nigeria's fortunate chairmanship of the UN Special Committee Against Apartheid afforded adequate opportunities for this. Criticism was, however, not restricted to the UN. At the domestic level, holders of South African passports – even those with South African visa entries in their passports – were denied entry into Nigeria. When in 1975 the federal government gave permission for the International Press Institute to hold a conference in

Lagos, and it became clear South African journalists would be present at the conference, the government, while not rescinding its permission, made it clear South African journalists would be disallowed entry into Nigeria. The venue for the conference was eventually moved from Nigeria. But though Nigeria maintained a relatively hard line on apartheid and on the white-dominated territories, in general terms Nigerian foreign policy with respect to broader international issues conformed to the framework outlined in the previous periods — a guarded acceptance of the Eastern bloc, at least in so far as trade and commerce were concerned, and a general support for the West. But some of this was to change with the overthrow of General Gowon's administration.

THE FOURTH PHASE: 1975–79

Immediately after the overthrow of General Gowon, the new administration set up a committee, made up of persons drawn from the armed forces, the universities and the career diplomats from the Ministry of External Affairs, to review the whole basis of Nigerian foreign policy and to formulate new guidelines. Though the committee was requested to make its report with the utmost urgency, events in other parts of Africa were to bring about a radical change in policy even before the committee could complete its task. The basic impetus to the change was the South African invasion of Cunene province of southern Angola, an invasion ostensibly geared to the protection of the Cunene dam, but in fact made in support of UNITA (Union for the Total Independence of Angola), one of the three factions involved in the struggle for Angolan independence, the other two being the FNLA (National Front for the Liberation of Angola) and the MPLA (Popular Movement for the Liberation of Angola). All three had external backers: UNITA was backed by South Africa; FNLA by the Western powers, particularly Britain and the United States; and the MPLA by the Soviet Union and Cuba. However, MPLA had the widest support of the three in Angola. Initially, the federal government's attitude had been to support moves towards the unification of the three factions, but once it was clear UNITA was prepared to rely on South

African military aid there was hardly any option left to the Nigerian government but to support the MPLA: Henry Kissinger, the then US Secretary of State (a man who had not cared to mask his contempt for Africa) had in fact asked the Nigerian government to use its influence to act as a counterweight against Soviet and Cuban support for the MPLA, obviously not out of concern for the peoples of Angola but in furtherance of his conception of great-power politics and their respective 'spheres of influence'. In taking the decision to back the MPLA diplomatically and financially — the federal government later gave ₦13.5 million aid to the MPLA — the Nigerian government acted in total opposition to the West, thereby signifying a commitment no longer to tolerate a situation in which Africans would be used for the advancement of racist policies in Africa.

The new orientation to a policy of total commitment to the liberation of Africa was further clarified in August 1977 when Nigeria was host to the World Conference for Action against Apartheid. On that occasion, Nigeria's new Head of State, Lt.-General Obasanjo, attacked multinational corporations for 'contributing in no small measure to the evil machinations of apartheid', adding that Nigeria was 'mounting surveillance on all those enterprises who depend on our raw materials and markets but continue to help our enemies'. 'Such enterprises', he said, 'must decide now to choose between us and our enemies' and he promised that Nigeria would be setting up an economic intelligence unit to monitor the activities of these enterprises. Contractors and enterprises known to have links or connections with South Africa had been barred from operating in Nigeria and the economic intelligence unit would be used to further that policy.[13] Two years later, when it was revealed that British oil companies had broken the oil embargo on Rhodesia, the Federal government proceeded to nationalise Shell—BP (Nig.) Ltd. That action was in fact taken while the Commonwealth Conference was being held in Zambia. Prior to the conference the British Prime Minister had announced that Britain would recognise whichever regime emerged successfully after the elections then scheduled to be held in Zimbabwe, even though most of the African member states of the Commonwealth were

opposed to the elections being held on the grounds that such
an election could only favour the administration then headed
by Bishop Abel Muzorewa whose African National Congress
was in alliance with Ian Smith's Rhodesian Front (the white
supremacist party which unilaterally proclaimed Rhodesia an
independent state in 1965). Since the Patriotic Front (PF)
parties headed by the two nationalist leaders, Joshua Nkomo
and Robert Mugabe, were then proscribed, lifting the ban just
before the elections could hardly give the PF time enough to
organise and campaign. More importantly, the ground rules
for the elections and the constitutional framework to follow
were yet to be agreed to by all the parties concerned. The
decision of the British government to proceed with the elections could therefore only be interpreted as an attempt to
impose a puppet regime on the majority of the African population. In deciding to nationalise Shell—BP (Nig.) Ltd, the
Nigerian government, it was suggested, was seeking to persuade the UK government of the likely consequences that
could follow any precipitate action which did not conform
to the will of the majority of the peoples of Zimbabwe.
However one interprets the Nigerian move — whether as a
retaliation against British oil companies breaking the oil
embargo or an attempt at persuasion — the fact remained
that she was prepared to use what resources she had to back
her foreign policy objectives in Africa.

It should not, however, be thought that because of her
support for the MPLA and opposition to Britain over Zimbabwe, Nigeria is thereby anti-West in some sense or the
other. In his address to the OAU summit meeting at Khartoum
in July 1978, Obasanjo made it quite clear that Nigeria's
objective was and is the independence of Africa and its
freedom from external control or intervention from whatever
source. That address was significant not only for its being the
clearest statement of Nigeria's foreign policy position but
also for it having been made against the background of the
second invasion (in May 1978) of the Shaba province of Zaire
by Zairean dissidents from Angola (backed by Cuban troops).
The invasion had led to French and Belgian paratroopers
intervening to airlift Europeans living in the province, and to
proposals emanating from France and some Francophone

African states for a Pan-African force bolstered by European aid to maintain order and security in Zaire, both of which General Obasanjo was to condemn as 'a most naked and unashamed attempt to determine (by external force) what Africa's true collective interests should be'.

Nigeria's position, as defined by Obasanjo, was that Africa should be left alone to determine its destiny, and hence East and West alike should cease, or be prevented from, intervening in the affairs of the continent. However well-meaning such intervention may appear to be, the end effect, more often than not, is to leave Africa worse off. As he put it: 'to the Soviets and their friends, I should like to say that having been invited to Africa to assist in the liberation struggle and the consolidation of national independence, they should not overstay their welcome. Africa is not about to throw off one colonial yoke for another'. What Africa needed was economic and technological assistance to enable Africans solve their own problems and not 'sterile ideological slogans which have no relevance to [our] African society'. Soviet aid to the MPLA was no doubt helpful in ensuring Angolan independence from Portugal, but similar aid to Ethiopia had led to disaster in the Horn of Africa with the result that the Soviets, through such aid, ran the risk 'of being dubbed a new imperial power, as indeed they are already being called even by those with whom they have had long association' — an obvious reference to states like Guinea, which had had to sever relations with the Soviet Union on the grounds that the USSR was seeking to impose a hegemonic relationship over Guinea.

The castigation of the great powers was also extended to the West, for Obasanjo continued thus:

to the Western powers, I say that they should act in such a way that we are not led to believe they have different concepts of independence and sovereignty for Africa and for Europe. A new Berlin-type conference is not the appropriate response to the kind of issues thrown up by the recent Kolwezi episode [the reference here being to Belgian and French intervention in Zaire to rescue European residents]. Paratroop drops in the twentieth century are no more acceptable to us than the gunboats of the last century were to our ancestors.[14]

Though the 'Kolwezi incident' may have prompted the reference to 'paratroop drops', the concern should also be seen to extend to the stationing of foreign troops in Africa. The presence of French troops in the Chad Republic has never been acceptable to Nigeria, and with the deepening of the civil war in Chad, Nigeria has not only spearheaded the move for an African peacekeeping force in Chad, but has also insisted on the withdrawal of the French military presence from Chad.

To say that Africans should be left free to determine their own 'destiny' does not imply that one African state is thereby entitled to intervene in the affairs of another, and not surprisingly therefore, just as Obasanjo had criticised the East and the West, so he was later to condemn the intervention of Tanzania in the overthrow of Idi Amin of Uganda. Consistency may demand that the principle of 'hands off Africa' should be generalised, but as the criticism of Tanzania over Uganda showed, this can pose a dilemma. Few, if any, regimes have been changed through constitutional means and, confronted by an arbitrary and tyrannical government, there may not be much of an option left to oppositionist forces seeking a regime change but to appeal to external interests. As General Obasanjo also noted in the same address, African states cannot blame all their difficulties on foreigners and a start has to be made in departing 'from the diplomatic practice of closing our eyes to what should be deprecated simply because it is happening in an African country . . . the idea of divine leadership in Africa is as past as the idea of divine leadership in Europe . . . we can no longer hide behind real or imagined foreign machinations for our own failings'.

Simply to 'deprecate' the failings of some African states may be inadequate in bringing about desired change or putting an end to arbitrary rule. 'Emperor' Bokassa's regime of terror in the 'Central African Empire' was brought to an end only with the aid of French troops and it required the armed force of Tanzania to enable Uganda to overthrow Idi Amin. If objection is taken, on principle, to the former, pragmatic considerations could be adduced to justify the latter and not to distinguish the one (Central African Empire) from the other (Uganda) could be to condemn millions of people to acquiescing in that which most people would regard as insufferable. But to accept such a distinction would involve making radical changes to the Charter of the OAU. It could even mean an end of that organisation, and for a country such as Nigeria, with the largest armed force in Black Africa, it could raise fears of 'imperial' designs from her smaller neighbours. It could well be such considerations which led the Obasanjo regime not to differentiate between forms of intervention. It may well be that the proposal — being championed by some African states, including Nigeria — to formulate an African Charter of Human Rights is what the logic of 'good housekeeping', encapsulated in Obasanjo's statement, demands. But it is difficult to see how such a Charter can be enforced without some alterations being made to the organisational form of the OAU. That could well be a challenge which the new civilian regime in Nigeria may want to accept in what seems to be the evolving pattern of Nigeria's foreign policy.

One marked effect which the new emphasis given to African liberation by the Muhammed/Obasanjo administration has had on Nigerian foreign policy is that greater coherence now exists in foreign policy-making. In place of the ad hoc approach to policy making characteristic of the past administrations, relations with other states are to be evaluated — and appropriate responses formulated — in so far as the behaviour of such states is perceived as conducive or not to the goal of total liberation. Thus, for instance, with respect to the Western powers, relations with the United States showed a marked improvement — measured in this case in terms of bilateral economic relations and the setting-up of joint working groups of senior officials examining questions of investment, transfer of technology, agriculture and rural development, and educational expansion — once it was seen that the Carter administration was prepared to be more receptive to African opinion over such matters as Namibia and Southern Africa. Brigadier Garba, Nigeria's Commissioner for External Affairs, in a speech made in June 1978 at Cleveland, Ohio, commented on this when he said:

relations between the US and Nigeria have taken a new
turn since the advent of the Carter administration. This
remarkable warmth . . . has been based on the changing
attitude of the US Government to Africa and African
problems. It seems to us that the aspirations of the African
peoples for freedom and genuine independence are now
shared by the American Government and people.[15]

Though these relations were somewhat shaken following the
second Shaba invasion, when it seemed that the US was prepared not only to throw her weight behind the French-inspired
proposal for a Pan-African Defence Force to intervene in
Zaire but also to return to the rhetoric of great-power politics,
subsequent clarification of US policy has restored the confidence which Nigeria placed in the US. One might, of course,
want to argue that the new relationship between Nigeria and
the US is to be attributed more to the fact that Nigeria is one
of the US's key suppliers of petroleum and less to do with
whatever might be the US's attitude to the problems of
Namibia and South Africa. Already, the balance of payments
between the two countries, estimated at $4000 million in
1980, has moved in favour of Nigeria, and that figure is
expected to double by 1982/83. There are therefore good
economic reasons why the US would not want to appear to
be antagonistic towards Nigeria.

The 'economic argument' can be reinforced by drawing a
parallel with the relationship between Nigeria and Britain.
When Britain had to rely on Nigeria for part of her oil supplies,
relations between the two countries were extremely cordial.
But since the advent of North Sea oil and Britain's relative
self-sufficiency in crude petroleum, the need for pretence no
longer exists and Britain could afford to ignore Nigerian
opinion if it suited her and was in her interest to do so. But
while there can be no denying that economic considerations
do play a significant part in the determination of inter-state
relations, it would certainly be a mistake to attribute everything to the economic. For one thing, the economic cannot,
for example, altogether account for the variations in the relations between the US and Nigeria; and though Britain no
longer has to depend on Nigeria for any of her petroleum

needs, Nigeria remains, next to Europe and the United States, Britain's largest export market, with exports in 1977 totalling more than £1000 million. Admittedly that figure fell to less than half that value in 1978/79 when owing to severe balance-of-payments difficulties Nigeria had to cut down drastically on her overall imports. However, with the expected improvement in Nigeria's foreign exchange position, trade with Britain is expected to improve and there is therefore a limit to which Britain can afford to ignore the susceptibilities of Nigeria over matters relating to race relations in Africa. The readiness with which the British Prime Minister changed her declared position over 'Rhodesia' during the Commonwealth Conference at Lusaka in 1979 in itself is indicative.

The change in Nigeria's foreign policy stance since 1975 can be attributed in a large measure to the influence of the radical intelligentsia on the policy-making process. Admittedly, most of those who came to power after the coup that overthrew Gowon were people who had had direct experience of war at the front during the civil conflict, had seen at first hand the effects of foreign intervention, and were therefore better placed to appreciate situations such as that which Angola presented. Nevertheless, it was the pressure from the intelligentsia for the recognition of the MPLA which finally persuaded the government into taking that step. The South African incursion into Cunene merely served as a catalyst. The role of the intelligentsia in this respect points to a difference in the policy-making process during the Gowon administration and that of his successor. Whereas in the former period, foreign policy-making and foreign policy management was undertaken by Gowon himself and the professional, career diplomats, in the latter period, the inputs from academics and various advisory bodies took on greater prominence, a characteristic which marked not only the foreign policy scene but the system of administration as a whole. This is not to say that the career diplomats thereby lost whatever influence they may have had. Given the caution with which the post-Gowon administration treated the bureaucratic elite, civil servants simply resorted to closer co-operation with those academics and other members of the intelligentsia who had access to the administration in order to exercise the same degree of influence as they had previously had.

THE POST-1979 PERIOD: THE SECOND REPUBLIC

However one evaluates the foreign policy posture of the Muhammed/Obasanjo administration, few would deny that under that administration there was a more concerted move towards greater independence in foreign policy-making. The word 'independence' is here chosen in preference to terms like 'neutralism' or 'non-alignment'. Not only has the descriptive content of these terms varied over time, but they are in fact very closely tied to specific images of the international political scene, images which all too often are subjectively tainted. Looked at from the perspective of time, perhaps what emerges most clearly is the trend towards a more independent assessment of events, the formulation of objectives on the basis of such an assessment and the determination of action in the light of the objectives. During the first republic, it was the 'British connection' more than any other factor which helped to shape the basic framework of Nigerian foreign policy. Not only had the key political actors worked with — many had in fact worked under — British colonial officials, but even the career diplomats had served their apprenticeship in, and had their induction into the international diplomatic scene from, British High Commission offices, consulates and embassies. A large proportion of members of both sets — political actors and career diplomats — had also been educated in Britain and to some extent had been imbued with the ideals and values transmitted by British higher education institutions. It was thus only to be expected that these men would look to Britain for 'guidance' particularly in a field which to most of them was new — the diplomatic field.

The Gowon administration effected little change within the framework it inherited. Within the context of the civil war there was little change the administration could in fact effect as much of the effort of the society was directed towards a prosecution of the war. The post-civil war period did witness the start towards some change. The career diplomats had had some time to learn on the job; besides, with the war over, there was more opportunity for a reassessment of policy and to profit from the reassessment. The start made after the civil war was intensified on the change in administration following the overthrow of Gowon. Africa became the focus of primary concern, with special consideration being given to Nigeria's immediate neighbours in the desire to consolidate the internal security of the state. Relations with other states were then to be determined, first in terms of the interests of the nation, and second, in terms of the orientation of such states to the problems of national liberation in those areas still under white rule (now primarily Namibia — or South West Africa — and South Africa) and the perpetuation of apartheid in South Africa.

The acceptance of the foregoing as the basic goals of foreign policy has resulted in some revaluation of policy with reference to the United States, the Soviet bloc countries, the West European states and the countries of the Middle East. The extent to which the framework so far established will be maintained by the new civilian government is yet to be seen. If the recent agreements reached with the United States in such fields of interest as investment in industry and agriculture — including nuclear technology — are anything to go by,[16] these being a continuation of the improved relations between Nigeria and the US begun by the last military administration, then the indications could be that there is not much likelihood of a major reversal of policy. But such a conclusion must be seen to rest on the premise that the existing federal coalition, the NPN/NPP coalition, remains in power. Should a different coalition emerge to control federal power — for instance, a coalition of which the UPN is the major partner — then it is not unlikely that there could be some changes in the direction of Nigeria's foreign policy, but here one moves into the realm of speculation and not of fact.

Notes and References

CHAPTER 2: THE CONCEPTUAL FRAMEWORK — VALUES AND POLITICS

1. One can hardly talk of a political tradition in the African political scene because of the relative 'newness' of political institutions and more particularly because of the rapidity with which they change. Consequently political socialisation has proved extremely difficult thereby resulting in the absence of behavioural norms or rules. Huntington has sought to describe this absence by saying that what characterises African polities, and others like them, is not political development but political decay. S. P. Huntington, *Political Order in Changing Societies* (New Haven: Yale University Press, 1968). The basic argument of that text can be found in Huntington's 'Political development and political decay', *World Politics*, 17 (1965).

2. A. P. d'Entreves. *The Notion of the State* (Oxford: Clarendon, 1967).

3. E. Kedourie, *Nationalism* (London: Hutchinson, 1960).

4. The items selected are not intended to be exhaustive or even representative, merely indicative of a fairly large body of literature.

5. Sociologists in fact borrowed their ideas of functionalism from social anthropologists, particularly from the writing of Malinowski and that of his student Radcliffe Brown. For variants of functional theory, see W. Michell, *Sociological Analysis and Politics* (New York: Prentice Hall, 1967).

6. L. W. Pye. 'The non-western political process', *Journal of Politics* (1958), 20. One should perhaps note that the Almond and Coleman volume appeared two years after the Pye article.

7. C. B. MacPherson, *The Political Theory of Possessive Individualism* (Oxford: Clarendon Press, 1962).

8. D. Apter, *The Politics of Modernisation* (Chicago: Chicago University Press, 1965).

9. This formulation follows Galtung's presentation in general outline; see J. Galtung, 'A structural theory of imperialism', *African Review*, 1 (1972); for other formulations see B. J. Berman, 'Clientelism and neo-colonialism: centre—periphery relations in African states', *Studies in Comparative International Development* (1974); R. Vengroff, 'Neo-colonialism and policy outputs in Africa', *Comparative Political Studies*, 8 (1975); S. Amin, *Unequal Development: An Essay on Social Formations in Peripheral States* (New York: Monthly Review Press, 1976); T. M. Shaw and K. A. Heard (eds), *The Politics of Africa: Dependence and Development* (London, Longmans, 1979).

10. J. Plamenatz, *Man and Society*, vol. 2 (London: Longmans, 1963), chapter on Marx.

11. In a fairly recent survey of the use and utility of this concept, Dennis Kavanagh writes that 'for our purposes we may regard the political culture as a shorthand expression to denote the emotional and attitudinal *environment* within which the political system operates', D. Kavanagh, *Political Culture* (London: Macmillan, 1972), p. 10. This will suggest that the political culture is not part of the political system. But for Dahl, Pye, Beer and numerous other users of the notion, political culture is very much part and parcel of the political system; S. H. Beer and A. Alam, *Patterns of Government* (New York: Random House, 1962).

12. A generalised analysis of the various political writings of Max Weber is given by D. Beetham, *Max Weber and the Theory of Modern Politics* (London: Allen & Unwin, 1974); also A. Giddens, *Politics and Sociology in the Thought of Max Weber* (London: Macmillan, 1972).

13. M. MacDonald, 'The language of political theory', *Proceedings of the Aristotelian Society* (1940/41), reprinted in A. Flew (ed.), *Logic and Language*, first series (Oxford: Blackwell, 1951) and (same editor) in the Anchor Books edition which contains the first and second series of *Logic and Language* (Doubleday, 1965).

14. T. Gurr, *Why Men Rebel* (New York: Princeton University Press, 1970); and H. Echstein and T. Gurr, *Patterns of Authority* (New York: John Wiley, 1975).

15. D. Apter and C. F. Andrain (eds), *Contemporary Analytical Theory* (New York: Prentice Hall, 1972) Introduction, esp. pp. 18—19.

16. R. Dahl, 'The concept of power', *Behavioural Science*, 2 (1957); and generally, R. Bell, D. V. Edwards and R. H. Wagner (eds), *Political Power: A Reader in Theory and Research* (New York: Free Press, 1969).

17. See D. S. Shwayder, *The Stratification of Behaviour* (London, Routledge & Kegan Paul, 1965) pp. 247—9.
18. The survey was carried out under the 12-states system and disaggregated to reflect the 19-states structure. However, difficulties encountered during the interview period were such that data for Sokoto and Gongola areas were regarded as being somewhat erratic and hence not shown. I am grateful to Dr D. G. Morrison, who at the time of the survey was Acting Director of the Computer Centre, University of Ibadan, for the analysis of the data, including statistical checks for reliability and significance.
19. See Abner Cohen, *Custom and Politics in Urban Africa* (Berkeley: University of California Press, 1969).
20. Cf. B. Bosanquet, *The Philosophical Theory of the State* (London: Macmillan, 1899).
21. K. Wiredu, *Philosophy and an African Culture* (Cambridge: Cambridge University Press, 1980), p. 4.
22. See the discussion in B. J. Dudley, 'Bogged down with speed money', *CERES (FAO)*, Sept./Oct. 1973.
23. A. Peace, 'Prestige, power and legitimacy in a modern Nigerian town', *Canadian Journal of African Studies*, **13** (1—2; 1979) 50.
24. E. A. Ayandele, *African Historical Essays* (London: Frank Cass, 1979) pp. 287—8.

CHAPTER 3: POLITICAL INSTITUTIONS OF THE FIRST REPUBLIC

1. Joan Wheare, *The Nigerian Legislative Council 1923—47* (London: Faber & Faber, 1949).
2. The Nigerian members were nominated from the various native administrations, though provision was made for directly elected members to represent Lagos (three members) and Calabar (one member).
3. See B. J. Dudley, *Parties and Politics in Northern Nigeria* (London: Frank Cass, 1968) *passim*.
4. Thomas Hodgkin, *African Political Parties* (Harmondsworth: Penguin, 1961).
5. Between 1957 and 1959 Nigeria had a 'national government' composed of the NPC, the NCNC and the AG. This was supposed to facilitate the formation of a consensus to enable Nigeria win independence.
6. By 1969 when Chief Awolowo wrote *The Peoples' Republic* (Ibadan: Oxford University Press, 1969) this had become the 'linguistic principle', but it was a principle which would have grouped together some 13 million Yoruba-speaking peoples which

would have made the political unit formed by the application of such a principle the next largest unit in the federation. Chief Awolowo, of course, thought the Yorubas were culturally 'superior' to all other groups in Nigeria.

7. *Report of the Coker Commission of Enquiry* — 4 volumes (Ibadan: Government Printer, 1962). In fact some £11 million of government funds were funnelled through the NIPC, of which £6.5 million ended up in the AG's coffers.

8. The NIPC was not the only source of funds for the AG. NPC leaders claimed to have evidence that the Israeli company, the Nigerian Water Resources Company, also provided funds for the AG's campaign.

9. For example, Chief Shonibare, who became one of the key figures of the NIPC, was one of the earlier sponsors of the AG.

10. That is, after the death of Chief Adegoke Adelabu who was NCNC leader of Ibadan and also leader of Mobalaje Grand Alliance, the association of the key ward leaders of Ibadan.

11. See Ajayi, J., and Smith, R. S., *Yoruba Warfare in the 19th Century* (Cambridge: Cambridge University Press, 1964); also R. S. Sklar, *Nigerian Political Parties* (Princeton: Princeton University Press, 1963).

12. These constraints were highlighted by the crisis in the East Regional Assembly where, though the legislature had passed a vote of no confidence in the executive and had refused to pass the regional appropriations bill, the Lt. Governor, acting in his executive capacity as head of government, over-rode the decision of the legislature. It should also be noted that under the MacPherson constitution, a regional legislature could not be dissolved unless the federal legislature was also dissolved. The collapse of the MacPherson constitution finally came when the NPC members of the federal legislature could not agree with their NCNC and AG colleagues over the date of independence and the legislature had to be adjourned *sine die*.

13. The West introduced a free primary education system in 1954 and was followed by the East in 1955, but difficulties with finance led to the reintroduction of school fees in the East, which in turn led to riots and protests. The East finally introduced a free primary education system in 1957. On these and related issues, see D. Abernethy, *The Political Dilemma of Popular Education* (Stanford: Stanford University Press, 1969).

14. Regionalisation not only covered direct governmental institutions but also included such para-statal instrumentalities as the Central Produce Marketing Board and but for the restraining influence of the colonial administration could have been extended to cover the railways and post and telecommunications.

15. The North, even before regionalisation, had its local authority 'police force', the Yan Doka. Only the West seized upon regionalisation to create a local police force, which was to become a problem when that force had to be integrated with the Nigeria police force in 1958. The West's 'regional police force' was for all practical purposes nothing other than a para-political extension of the Action Group.

16. The conference was held in 1958 and also considered the Report of the Commission Appointed to Enquire into the Fears of Minorities and the Means of Allaying them (the Wellinck Commission), Cmnd 505, 1958.

17. The pact was agreed to at the 1958 constitutional conference and Chief Awolowo was a signatory to the pact. In opposing the ratification of 'heads of items' of the pact, the issue before the legislature, Chief Awolowo was plainly being Machiavellian.

18. This was one instance when pressure groups proved effective in influencing public policy. A key point raised by newspaper editors was that it was absurd to hold, as the Act required, newspaper editors liable for the accuracy of every report sent in by their reporters. The Act also would have required editors to personally deliver to the Ministry of Information a signed copy of every edition of a newspaper printed.

19. V. O. Key Jnr: 'A theory of critical elections', *Journal of Politics*, 17 (1955).

20. The legal tussle between Chiefs Akintola and Adegbenro is highly interesting for the light it throws on the relationship between the political and the legal. Sixty-five members of the regional assembly signed an affidavit to the effect that they no longer had any confidence in the Premier, Chief Akintola. The Governor was then requested to appoint Chief Adegbenro instead as Premier, an action which the Governor complied with; whereupon Akintola sought an injunction in the regional High Court, to restrain the Governor from appointing Adegbenro as his successor, an action which he lost. Akintola then appealed to the Supreme Court, which gave a decision in his favour (Justice Lionel Brett dissenting). Adegbenro followed by challenging the decision of the Supreme Court in the Privy Council, with the Privy Council giving a decision in his favour. The federal government then reacted by ignoring the ruling of the Privy Council, and by abolishing the right of appeal to the Privy Council; in effect it thus upheld the decision of the Supreme Court. Thus, contrary to the ruling of the regional High Court and the Privy Council, Akintola ended up becoming Premier of the West.

21. Dr Michael Okpara's NCNC-controlled East regional government sought an injunction from the Supreme Court in an attempt to

restrain the federal government from using the census figures as the basis for policy-making. The Supreme Court, however, ruled that since the census came under executive action, it could not entertain any motion for an injunction.

22. The code, among other things, enjoined on party leaders the obligation to desist from using language likely to incite or provoke the electorate to violence. It also sought to restrain governmental leaders from restricting free movement of goods and persons between the regions.

23. Constitutionally, Sir Abubakar still retained his office as Prime Minister, that is, for as long as the President did not appoint another person to replace him. Given the election results, the President could not possibly have appointed anyone other than Sir Abubakar, but that the President refused to do. There was thus the absurd situation that Sir Abubakar had *de facto* to continue in office yet *de jure* was denied office by the President.

24. Welby-Everard also sought separate legal advice from Professor Gower, who was then Dean of the Lagos University Faculty of Law. Gower's advice, given in a three-page memorandum, was to the effect that the Prime Minister, as head of government, was the effective minister responsible for the armed forces and thus the military's obligation lay with the Prime Minister. On this and related issues, see J. P. McIntosh, *Nigerian Government and Politics* (London: Allen & Unwin, 1966).

25. The President gave way when he realised there was a move to declare him medically incapable of continuing in office. Under the constitution, a certificate signed by two medically qualified persons is necessary and sufficient to declare a President unfit to continue in office. There was an attempt to use just such a move to remove the President. Faced with that prospect, the President succumbed.

26. See note 25 above. Had the Prime Minister gone to the Supreme Court there was a good chance that the Court would have ruled in his favour since constitutionally the President was under an obligation to act on the advice of the Prime Minister who also happened to be the man with the largest following in the legislature. On the other hand, since most members of the Court were thought to be UPGA sympathisers, there was just the possibility that the Court could have ruled in favour of the President, which would have created an unresolvable legal and constitutional crisis.'

27. The West's finances had been in a critical state, in fact, as far back as 1962. Even before the split in the AG, Chief Akintola, concerned over government spending on education, had wanted to increase secondary school fees but he had been overruled by his party leader, Chief Awolowo. (One can actually trace the origins of the crisis in

the party to Chief Awolowo's attempt to run the government of the West from Lagos.) By 1964 the government was having to rely heavily on federal aid even to pay the salaries of its employees. In the rural areas there were allegations that primary school teachers were not having their salaries paid, and these teachers formed the main support, together with junior civil servants, of the UPGA. The blatant rigging of the election results so alienated this segment of the population that they in fact became the 'unofficial' opposition to the government.

CHAPTER 4: THE MILITARY AND POLITICS

1. D. S. Shwayder, *The Stratification of Behaviour* (London: Routledge & Kegan Paul, 1965).
2. For a formulation of this view see S. E. Finer, *The Man on Horseback* (London: Pall Mall, 1962). In the main, we could divide most theories of military coups into two broad categories: (a) those who see the cause in sociopolitical factors — Finer and many others belong to this group; and (b) those who take the cause to be inherent in certain characteristics of the military — Janowitz and others belong to this latter group.
3. There were two key actors in the January coup — Major Nzeogwu who led the troops in the North in a successful action, and Major Ifeajuna who had control in the South where the coup failed, owing largely to the intervention of Major-General Ironsi. Nzeogwu at one stage threatened to march on the South, a threat which Ironsi exploited in having the federal executive (the Prime Minister and the Minister of Finance were both killed in the coup) hand over power to him.
4. The exception was Lt. Col. Unegbu, the Quarter-Master General, who was reportedly killed by 'accident'. On the whole, some 27 people were known to have been killed in the coup.
5. There was an agreement among the top military hierarchy, after the coup, that there should be a moratorium on promotions in the army, but in April Ironsi unilaterally promoted some 18 majors to the rank of Lt. Col. and over 80 per cent of these were Ibo-speaking. When Ironsi announced his ill-fated plan to appoint military prefects, many in the North saw it as an attempt by Ironsi to pack the North with his new appointees, a step towards complete control of the North — so it was thought — by the Ibos.
6. Mr Aper Aku, the man who swore the affidavit, was elected governor of Benue State in the July 1979 elections. Perhaps more significant than the pronouncement of the innocence of the governor by Gowon was the statement made by the Attorney-General and Com-

missioner for Justice, Dr Taslim Elias, that the judiciary should no longer entertain such affidavits. Dr Elias justified his position on the grounds that he was making that rule with the approval of the Judicial Advisory Committee, but most people saw the announcement as a move by Gowon to protect his governors from judicial enquiry. It was known that some five other people had prepared affidavits they were to swear against other military governors.

7. The Public Service was defined as including all those who were paid from public funds. The procedure adopted was for the head of each section to put forward a list of all those who for any of the reasons stated could be said to qualify for removal. For example, at the University of Ibadan where the author was working at the material time, Heads of Departments were to prepare lists of those to be removed within their departments; the Deans were to provide lists of Heads of Departments to be removed and the Vice-Chancellor was supposed to provide a similar list of Deans. (In the case of the University of Ibadan, the Vice-Chancellor refused to have anything to do with the exercise.) The Registrar was required to perform the same exercise for the administration.

8. The issue is taken up in more detail in the text further on.

9. Proposals for demobilisation had been prepared as early as 1968 but Gowon stalled over each proposal submitted to him. It must be admitted that there were powerful elements in the Army who did not quite support the idea of demobilisation and who thought that the size of the army should in fact be increased. Muhammed himself, in 1972, was in favour of increasing the size of the armed forces.

10. Apart from Muhammed, the only people killed in the attempted coup were Muhammed's aide de camp and the Governor of Kwara State, Col. Ibrahim Taiwo. On Obasanjo's becoming Head of State, his place as Chief of Staff, Supreme Military Headquarters was taken by Col. Shehu Yar'adua, who was at that time the Commissioner for Transport and the man reputed to have masterminded the overthrow of Gowon.

11. The figures from 1973 to 1977 are as follows: 1973, 51.2 per cent; 1974, 45.4 per cent; 1975, 45.9 per cent; 1976, 29.8 per cent; 1977, 42.0 per cent. See the paper (mimeo) by J. F. E. Ohiorhenuan: 'The Military and Capitalist Development in Nigeria', University of Ibadan, Dept of Economics, 1980.

12. Cf. Lt.-Gen. Danjuma, Army Chief of Staff talking to a representative of the *New Nigerian*, 2/1/76 on 'Tackling the manpower problems of the army'. There Danjuma stated that 'more than 90% of our defence budget [is spent] on paying salaries alone'. In another

statement (*Daily Times*, 18/1/76), Danjuma had said it would take 60 per cent of Nigeria's national income to arm and equip the army. For other statements about the problem of demobilisation, *Daily Times*, 20/8/75, 18/10/75, 13/1/76; *New Nigerian*, 27/10/75, 10/12/75, 12/12/75, 22/12/75, 13/1/76, 14/11/76.

13. Gowon has, not without some justification, been criticised for his inability — or perhaps, one should say, unwillingness — to take decisions. But from his experience, particularly during the period 1 August 1966 to 31 May 1967, when the federation came close to being torn asunder, he, more than any of his colleagues, knew what tenuous bonds held the federation together. As someone who kept in close touch with the NCOs, he also had a good insight into how the 'rank and file' viewed the issue of demobilisation.

14. This was the administration's own evaluation made in a statement by the Chief of Staff, Supreme Military Headquarters, Brigadier (later Lt. Gen.) Shehu Yar'adua, in a televised programme on 1 October 1977.

15. There were a few other members, including the Inspector General of Police and the Chief of Staff, Army (then Lt. Col. Gowon).

16. Ironsi did not spell out what he meant by 'group of provinces', for instance whether the North would become two or more 'groups of provinces'. However, after his speech it became fashionable to refer to the regions as 'the Northern (Eastern, Western, etc.) group of provinces'.

17. This was in sharp contrast to the Kano massacres of September 1966 (when troops of the 4th Battalion mutinied) when Hassan personally led the attempt to restore order.

18. Some of the key bureaucrats concerned were H. Ejueyitse, who was the head of the service, A. A. Ayida, P. Asiodu, E. Ebong and Y. Gobir. The breakup of the North followed more or less the lines put forward by the Middle-Belt representatives in the Northern delegation to the Ad Hoc Constitutional Conference in August 1966.

19. Information provided by a regional military governor.

20. Information supplied by the head of one of the state civil services who accompanied his State Governor to some of the SMC meetings.

21. Related to the author in discussion with a member of the FEC. Mr Ayida in his Presidential Address to the Nigerian Economic Society, 1973, put it quite delicately in the following manner: 'If civil commissioners appear to exercise less power than the former Minister's, it is not because their functions have been usurped by Permanent Secretaries and other senior civil servants. . . . Commissioners were not appointed to run the government as political masters but as

servants of the military, the new political masters'. (All quotations
from the Ayida address are from the mimeographed version. Quotation cited from p. 23.) Again, on p. 22 Mr Ayida commented: '. . .
properly conceived such civilians are to assist the military to govern
by interpreting the wishes of the people to the military and vice
versa. Unfortunately, there is abundant evidence that the basis of
civilian participation in the military administration is not abundantly
clear even to some civil commissioners'.

22. In most of the attempts to have affidavits charging corruption
sworn against military governors — Midwest, East Central, South-
East, and Kano — the necessary information was claimed to have
been supplied by civil servants.

23. For a slightly different formulation of the same set of options, see
Ian Campbell, 'Army reorganisation and military withdrawal', in
S. K. Panter-Brick (ed.) *Soldiers and Oil* (London: Frank Cass,
1978) p. 64.

24. By mid-1971 a number of federal commissioners who had embarked
on overt attempts at forming political parties in the expectation of
a return to civil rule had abandoned these attempts while odd
remarks made by people like Mr Asika, the Administrator of the
East Central State, and Brigadier S. O. Ogbemudia, military governor of the Midwest state, left little room for doubt that the
military were no longer keen on returning to the barracks.

25. Examples are Mr Tayo Akpata, Commissioner for Education in the
Midwest, and Mr Femi Okunnu, Federal Commissioner for Works
who were strong advocates of the idea of a 'national movement'. It
should be pointed out that there was some support for this among
some academics in the Universities. Mr Asika was alleged to have
been billed for the role of 'party ideologist'.

26. Mr Eme Ebong headed a team that went to Egypt to study the
Egyptian Arab Socialist Movement.

27. The Zaria conferences were usually attended by academics, top
army and civil service personnel, and 'natural rulers'. Often these
conferences provided a forum for the military — through the army
men and civil servants who attended these conferences — to float
current thinking within the government.

28. Mr Asiodu was careful in his remarks (made while chairing one of
the panels at the conference) not to be openly identified with the
proposal for a 'national movement', but there was not much doubt
where his sentiments lay. In the discussion that followed, the author
remembers well a comment by Lt. Col. Yar'adua (as he then was)
that an officer might be very able, professionally extremely competent but would not be of much use as a commander of troops if

he could not win the loyalty of his men. Professional expertise cannot be a substitute for sound political judgment.

29. At the Ad Hoc Constitutional Conference most of the delegates, former politicians like Chief Awolowo, Tony Enahoro, Joseph Tarka, Aminu Kano, Sir Ibrahim Kashim and many more — had come out with proposals which would have amounted to a breakup of the federation. See Memoranda Submitted by the Delegations to the Ad Hoc Conference on Constitutional Proposals for Nigeria (Lagos: Ministry of Information, 1967); also my *Instability and Political Order* (Ibadan: Ibadan University Press, 1973) pp. 151—64.

30. A. A. Ayida, *op. cit.* (note 21), quotations on pp. 3, 22, 37—9.

31. This could be easily seen in the reaction, as evidenced in several letters, comments and articles in the press, to Dr Azikiwe's proposal for his form of 'dyarchy', the sharing of power between the military and elected civilians but with the military holding a veto power.

32. This group included men such as Dr Mahmud Turkur, Mallam Ibrahim Tahir, Dr Suleiman Kumo, and many more. Some of these men belonged to that influential circle which came to be known as the 'Kaduna Mafia', a group which also included non-academics.

33. The 'influence' as seen by this group was not just 'southern' it was also Christian and 'missionary'. There was thus a religious dimension to the opposition.

34. The incident was reported to the author by a member of the North's intelligentsia on the periphery of the 'Mafia' and was repeated by one of the state commissioners. But whereas the latter saw the incident as representing something of conceit on the part of the academics — Gowon was alleged to have said he left the group overwhelmed — the former saw it as an indication of the 'arrogance' of Gowon.

35. There are a number of school photographs which testify to the links between the military and the intelligentsia. One example of such linkages is provided by Generals Muhammed and Shuwa who were classmates of Dr Jibril Aminu and Mr Justice Uwais. General Muhammed, as is well known, was a nephew of Alhaji Inuwa. He was also related to one of Kano's leading families, the Wali family.

36. Three illustrative cases will suffice.

Case (1) Joseph Gomwalk, Governor of Benue Plateau State. On taking office in May 1967, Gomwalk (who was to be executed in 1976 for being implicated in the attempted coup that led to the dealth of Murtala Muhammed) was supposed to have a sum of ₦200 in his savings account and ₦430 in his current account. But while he was governor, he acquired the following: (a) a house in Naraguta Avenue, Jos, valued at ₦70,000; (b) a block of four flats in Pankshin, valued at ₦60,000 for which he had collected rent of ₦40,000 from the Federal Military Government through the Benue Plateau state government; (c) a house in Langtang Street, Jos, which was rented by Voteniski (a firm of contractors in which the governor had an interest) for a sum of ₦24,000 a year; (d) another house, 12 St Patrick Avenue, Jos, rented by Voteniski for ₦20,000; (e) a house in the Government Reservation Area, Pankshin, said to have been bought from another contracting firm, Bepco, for ₦26,000 but which was valued at ₦140,000; (f) 1500 (50K) shares in UAC, 1300 (₦1.00) shares in J. Holt, 910 (₦20) Incar Motors shares; (g) two blocks (each of six flats) of flats at Victoria Island, Lagos, built for the governor by Julius Berger (a West German contracting firm) for having been awarded the contract to build the Liberty Dam (Jos) and the Jos Waterworks; (h) a house, 14 Nguru Rd, Kaduna, and another at Makera village; and (i) several other properties for which he had collected rent totalling ₦73,400.

Case (2) − Governor O. Ogbemudia of the Midwest who became Acting Governor of the Midwest (later made substantive) after the fall of Benin to federal troops on 20 September 1967 and eight years later had acquired: (a) a farming estate at Nsukwa; (b) The Palm Royal Motel valued at ₦149,759 and from which he was earning a monthly income of ₦10,000, (c) a house at 27b Eguadese St, Benin City; (d) another at 17/H Ogbeide Ward, Government Reservation Area, Benin; (e) another property in Benin, 26 Iheya St; (f) still another Benin property in Urubi Quarters, (g) a piece of land in Victoria Island, Lagos, (Plot 855), (h) several undeveloped landed properties; (i) Investments in shares worth N28,940, and (j) farms in the following villages − Ignovbiobo, Ekae, Isiohor, Okhoro, Igwosa, Uwelu, Irua and Iniye.

Case (3) − Mr Ukpabi Asika, who became Administrator of Enugu (later East-Central state) in November 1967, and who, eight years later had acquired: (a) Bladi Court, Warri, valued at ₦120,000; (b) Plot R, in the GRA, Onitsha, valued at ₦76,000; (c) an apartment, 1229 La Torre, in Spain; (d) another property in Spain, 9 Torremeloes, Spain; (e) a house, 6 Mayohaung Road, GRA Kano; (f) undeveloped land in Burutu, Lagos, Enugu and Onitsha; (g) shares in Glaxo and Mid-Diversified Investments Ltd; (h) Plot II, Aba Industrial Estate; (i) Plot 8/15 Block 25 New Haven Layout, Enugu; (j) property at 17 Abakaliki Rd, Enugu; (k) a house at 2 Old Cemetery Rd, Onitsha.

These cases are by no means unusual. Governor Usman Faruk of

Sokoto, for example, accumulated over 21 separate properties. Gomwalk's properties were listed by the *New Nigerian*, 3/12/75, Ogbemudia and Asika's in *New Nigerian*, 9/2/76, the same issue which lists properties owned by Musa Usman (North-East), Bamigboye (Kwara), Diete-Spiff (Rivers), Abba Kyari (North-Central) and Esuene (South-East).

37. *New Nigerian*, 31/7/75.

38. Since the assassination of Muhammed there has been some controversy as to who initiated what, the suggestion being that Muhammed's No. 2, Obasanjo, was really the 'ideas man', but to pursue such a controversy would be futile and unrewarding in this context.

39. Various policy positions are treated under one or the other of the three categories but no chronological sequence should be read into the treatment.

40. Most of those involved in the coup became members of the new SMC, but the two key figures are reputed to have been Shehu Yar'adua and Col. Ibrahim Taiwo, the Governor of Kwara state, who was said to have been the 'link man' between the members. Taiwo was the only other top military officer to die in the attempted coup of 13 February 1976.

41. Obasanjo, The Chief of Staff, Supreme Military Headquarters (as he then was) was supposed to have been largely responsible for influencing the decision to have an Ogun state created. Certainly Obasanjo was strategically placed to influence such a decision.

42. Various Rental Control Decrees were passed by the military, but except where elite housing was concerned, none had much effect. The Rent Decrees are best seen as 'symbolic' acts of the military.

43. The Decree was issued on 4 December 1975, at about the same time that another Decree was passed which made it an offence punishable by a sentence of 10 years' imprisonment or a fine of ₦10,000 to attempt to bribe any member of the SMC or the FEC, the state military governors and members of the States' Executive Councils.

44. There really was nothing for the CPIB to do, just as there was no need to pass any Decrees specifying harsher punishments for attempts at corrupting members of the SMC (see note 43 above). The police have the skills and training to deal with all reported or suspected cases of corruption. If it was thought that something more needed to be done, this could have taken the form of strengthening the police and updating the resources available to them. The CPIB Decree was thus a largely 'cosmetic' Decree, but it had the implication that the administration did not have full confidence in the capabilities of the police, which could explain the lack of co-operation the Board received from the police and why the Board

was so impotent. The cynic might want to argue that that was what the administration aimed at from the beginning.

45. The 'abandoned properties' were properties owned by Ibo men previously resident in places like Port-Harcourt but which they had had to abandon during the civil war for fear of advancing federal troops. Most of these were either taken over by the non-Ibo-speaking peoples of the Rivers state or simply requisitioned by the government of the state with often no compensation paid. About a third of all properties in Port-Harcourt fell into the category of 'abandoned properties' — ignoring properties destroyed or partly destroyed in the war.

46. More accurately, the Nigerian Enterprises Promotions Decree (1972) passed with the aim of making Nigerians take over 'the commanding heights of the economy'. A schedule to the Decree listed 22 activities — retail trade (other than department stores and supermarkets), most urban services (such as hairdressing) and some small scale manufacturing — which were to be reserved to Nigerians. Non-Nigerians operating in these areas were expected to sell their businesses to Nigerians by a certain date. A second schedule which included wholesale trade, department stores and supermarkets, construction and a number of manufacturing enterprises — some 33 items — were precluded to non-Nigerians unless above a stipulated size (fixed capital of not less than ₦200,000 or a turnover of of not less than ₦500,000) and having at least 40 per cent of their equity in Nigerian ownership. In 1977 the Decree was amended to cover 40 and 57 activities respectively and the equity shareholding by Nigerians was raised to 60 per cent. On the operation of the 1972 Decree, see O. Aboyade 'Indigenizing foreign enterprises: some lessons from the Nigerian Enterprises Promotions Decree', in O. Teriba and M. O. Kayode (eds), *Industrial Development in Nigeria* (Ibadan: Ibadan University Press, 1977).

47. ICSA and ESIALA were organisations set up in 1967 and 1970 respectively to oversee investments held in common after the breakup of the Northern and Eastern regions in May 1967. The items coming under the supervision of these organisations included universities and broadcasting, institutions which could not be split and their assets shared.

48. The federal government took over the universities of Benin, Ahmadu Bello, Ife and the University of Nigeria, Nsukka. New universities (or Colleges of Science and Technology converted into universities) were established at Ilorin, Jos, Kano, Port-Harcourt, Calabar and Maiduguri. To facilitate co-ordination and planning, the Universities Commission was reconstituted and given executive powers in 1975.

49. Though a panel under Monsignor (Brigadier) Pedro Martins was subsequently created to review cases of wrongful dismissals or retirements, at the time of the purge, those affected were not given any opportunity to defend themselves. Most did not even know on what grounds they were being removed and only knew of their removal from radio announcements. The high-handed arbitrariness of the purge is perhaps best shown by the case of Professor H. O. Thomas, Vice-Chancellor, University of Ibadan, who was retired, not for anything connected with his administration of the university but for conduct said to be 'unbecoming of a Vice-Chancellor', which arose from his administration of the estate of his deceased sister and her husband. Professor Thomas was later to be fully exonerated, but by then the damage had already been done and his reputation besmirched by an administration which did not even have the decency to let it be publicly known that they had wronged someone of the standing of Professor Thomas.

50. This was subsequently to be admitted by various members of the administration in private discussions.

51. Compare the following statements from Ayida, *op. cit.* (note 21) pp. 14—15:

> . . . the most sensitive potential threat to the stability of the Nigerian federation was and remains a North—South confrontation and it was of great strategic importance, that the number of states in the 'northern' parts of the country should be seen to be equal to the number of 'southern' states (this was an important consideration which could not be made explicit in the days of the gathering storm early 1967) and . . . there had to be a 'Lagos state without splitting Yoruba heartland', as part of the strategy of containing the former conditional secessionists in the then Western region, who were convinced that if the Nigerian federation disintegrated through the breakaway of the Eastern region, Lagos would automatically become part of the new Republic of Oduduwa.

52. See note 18 (above) for the North. With respect to the Eastern region, though there had been demands for the creation of a COR (Calabar-Ogoja-Rivers) state in the East, to have created such a state would have left the peoples of the Rivers as a permanent 'minority' in the COR state. The Rivers state had therefore to be carved out of the COR state. Besides, in late 1965, a rebellion had broken out in the Rivers — the 'Boro Rebellion' — in support of a Rivers state (Isaac Boro, who led the rebellion, had been a student

at the University of Nigeria before taking to arms). The Boro rebellion was quelled only after the January 1966 coup and Isaac Boro himself was imprisoned. He was released during the civil war to join the 3rd Division of the Nigerian army that liberated the Rivers. Boro was killed in the operations which led to the taking of Port-Harcourt by federal troops.

53. See my *Parties and Politics in Northern Nigeria* (London: Frank Cass, 1968) ch. 8, especially, pp. 268–82.

54. See A. D. Yahaya, 'The creation of states' in S. K. Panter-Brick (ed.), *op. cit.* (see note 23), p. 216. Dr Yahaya was a member of the Irikefe Commission.

55. See *Federal Military Government Views on the Report of the Panel on Creation of States* (Lagos: Federal Ministry of Information, 1976).

56. Report on the Panel Appointed by the Federal Military Government to Investigate the Issue of the Creation of More States and Boundary Adjustments in Nigeria (unpublished, mimeo, Dec. 1975) p. 81.

57. *Ibid.,* p. 66.

58. For instance in terms of foreign private investment – which in 1963 represented 68.1 per cent of all investment in industry – the share of the two regions was 40.3 per cent of the total (in terms of number of establishments) and 50.4 per cent (in terms of value) respectively. See A. N. Hakam, 'The locational patterns of foreign private industrial investments in Nigeria', in O. Teriba and M. O. Kayode (eds), *op. cit.* (see note 46), pp. 149–62. In revenue terms, breaking the Western state into three states meant the federal allocations to that area rose from 1/12th to 3/19th, and in the East-Central, the amount rose from 1/12th to 2/19th. On the implications of this, S. E. Oyovbaire, 'The politics of revenue allocations' in Panter-Brick (ed) *op. cit.* (see note 23).

59. There were some councils known as 'Emir-and-Council' and 'Federated Councils' but these were of little importance. See my *Parties and Politics in Northern Nigeria*, pp. 241–4.

60. For more detailed discussion, C. E. F. Beer, *The Politics of Peasant Groups in Western Nigeria* (Ibadan: Ibadan University Press, 1976).

61. For perspectives on the reform 'as seen from Ibadan' and 'from Kaduna', see the contributions by O. Oyediran and Alex Gboyega, and Y. A. Aliyu respectively in S. K. Panter-Brick (ed.) *op. cit.* (see note 23).

62. Federation of Nigeria, *National Development Plan 1962–68* (Lagos: Government Printer, 1962) p. 21.

63. P. C. Packard, 'A note on concentration and profit rates within the manufacturing sector, 1963 and 1965', in O. Teriba and M. O. Kayode (eds), *op. cit.* (see note 23) , p. 126.

64. See G. K. Helleiner, *Peasant Agriculture, Government and Economic Growth in Nigeria* (New Haven: Yale University Press, 1966).

65. See *Sunday Sketch*, 4/5/80.

66. Central Bank of Nigeria, *Annual Reports; Economic and Financial Review*, various issues.

67. *Government Views on Second Report of the Federal Assets Investigation Panel* (Lagos: Federal Ministry of Information, 1978) p. 15.

68. See note 46 above.

69. See note 36 above.

70. As one example of the sums involved, the rent bill for rent-subsidised housing for the staff of the University of Ibadan rose from just about ₦1,000,000 to over ₦2,000,000 after the Decree. One of the houses rented by the University belonged to the Head of State, the rent of which rose from ₦6000 to ₦8000. Between 1976 and 1979 the Head of State was Visitor to the University of Ibadan.

71. I use this term in contrast to the more 'Marxian' notion of 'industrial capitalism'. The Nigerian businessman was more of a merchant who specialised in buying and selling and who relied very heavily on the state for the success of his activities. He therefore took few risks and certainly was not much involved in 'production'.

72. The literature is quite extensive and varies. The following can be said to have held one form or the other of the 'modernisation thesis': H. Bienen, *The Military and Modernisation* (New York: Aldine-Atherton, 1971); M. Janowitz: *The Military in the Political Development of New Nations* (New Haven: Yale University Press, 1964); E. Feit, 'Pen, sword and people: military regimes in the formation of political institutions', *World Politics*, 25, 2 (1973); J. J. Johnson (ed.), *The Role of the Military in Underdeveloped Countries* (New Jersey: Princeton University Press, 1962); M. Lissak, 'Modernisation and role expansion of the military in the developing countries', *Comparative Studies in Society and History*, 9, I (1966); C. E. Welch, Jr.; *Soldier and State in Africa – A Comparative Analysis of Military Intervention and Political Change* (Evanston: North-western University Press, 1970); S. Decalo, *Coups and Army Rule in Africa* (New Haven: Yale University Press, 1975).

73. On the components of 'modernity' and a profile of the 'modern' individual, see A. Inkeles and D. H. Smith, *Becoming Modern: Individual Change in Six Developing Countries* (Cambridge: Harvard University Press, 1974).

74. Ali Mazrui, 'Lumpenmilitariat and the Lumpenproletariat', in *Political Studies*, 21, 1 (March 1973).

75. FESTAC was estimated to have cost Nigeria some ₦800 million, but that included the cost of the National Theatre (put at ₦80 mil-

lion) and the so-called 'FESTAC village', the blocks of flats and chalets built to accommodate the participating artists.

CHAPTER 5: POLITICAL INSTITUTIONS OF THE SECOND REPUBLIC

1. It was the attempt by the defeated candidate, Dr Albert Margai, to prevent Dr Siaka Stevens, after his party's success in the 1967 elections, from forming a government, which led to the coup that brought the military in in the first place.
2. See D. Austin and R. Luckham (eds), *Politicians and Soldiers in Ghana, 1966—72* (London: Frank Cass, 1975).
3. s.274(5) provides that 'nothing in this Constitution shall invalidate the following enactments, that is to say —
   (a) The National Youth Service Corps Decree 1973;
   (b) The Public Complaints Decree 1975;
   (c) The Nigerian Security Organisation Decree 1976;
   (d) The Land Use Decree 1978; and the provisions of those enactments . . . shall not be altered or repealed except in accordance with the provisions of s.9(2) of this Constitution.'
   On the patterns of military withdrawal, V. P. Bennett, 'Patterns of demilitarisation in Africa', *Quarterly Journal of Administration*, 9, 1 (1974) 5—15.
4. When the composition was first announced, there were 51 members (which included the Chairman) but one of the nominees, Chief Awolowo, declined to serve on the Committee, bringing the numbers to 50.
5. From the Address of Brigadier (later General) Murtala Muhammed, 'Address by the Head of State of the Federal Military Government, Commander-in-Chief of the Nigerian Armed Forces at the Opening Session of the Constitution Drafting Committee on Saturday 18th October 1975' (hereafter referred to as 'Address') and reprinted as prefix pp. xli—xliii to the *Report of the Constitution Drafting Committee*, vol. 1 (Lagos: Ministry of Information, 1976). The CDC Report is in 2 volumes: vol. 1 which contains the Report, Address, and the Draft Constitution, and vol. 2 which contains the Reports of the six Sub-Committees of the CDC set up to prepare proposals on various aspects of the Draft Constitution.
6. All quotations from the 'Address', pp. xlii and xliii.
7. Report, in vol. 1 of the CDC Draft Constitution, p. v, para 3.2—2. Hereafter, references will be given in terms of numbered paragraphs.
8. *Ibid.*, para 2.2—1.
9. With respect to the North, see B. J. Dudley, *Parties and Politics in Northern Nigeria* (London: Frank Cass, 1968) *passim*.

10. The Electoral Decree No. 73 of 1977 provides – s.77(1) that 'no association other than a political party shall canvass for votes for any candidate at an election . . . '. In effect, therefore, the situation provided for in s.73(b) of the Constitution – the situation of the 'independent candidate', cannot logically arise. But one could argue that since s.73(b) does imply that there could be independent candidates, then s.77(1) of the Decree cannot possibly apply. Obviously there are, here, all the ingredients for a legal tussle between the individual candidate and the Federal Electoral Commission (FEDECO) – a rich field for the constitutional lawyer. It should be noted that nothing in s.73(b) prevents two parties forming an alliance, provided that when such an alliance is so formed, members of the parties forming the alliance identify themselves by the name of the alliance and not of their previous parties. Since however, such an alliance would have to be 'recognised' by FEDECO before it could have a legal existence, it follows that such alliances can only come into existence as legal entities in between elections.

11. These are listed in the Fourth Schedule to the Constitution. Section 2 of the Schedule – which was added by the Constituent Assembly to the CDC Draft – provides for local councils' participation in such councils of the state government as would be responsible for the provision and maintenance of other natural resources other than mines.

12. s.149(1) states: 'the Federation shall maintain a special account to be called "the Federation Account" (this was previously known as the Distributable Pool Account) into which shall be paid all revenues collected by the Government of the Federation . . . '.

13. 'Having an interest' here means the voter believes he has certain legal claims which have been denied by the state.

14. There is nothing in the Constitution to stop a state governor, exercising the executive powers vested in him, from dissolving, for one reason or the other, the elected councils within his area of jurisdiction. In fact, since the elections of July 1979, and the assumption of office on 1 October by elected state governors, many have dissolved councils elected in 1977 and there is no evidence that such states have had their 'local government allocations' withheld.

15. Report, para. 7.5.

16. Pt. 11 of the Fifth Schedule to the Constitution gives a list of offices classed as 'public offices' for the purposes of the Code of Conduct – a list which covers the holders of all elective offices, members of the armed forces, civil services and universities, and offices the emoluments of which are a fixed charge on the Consolidated Fund of the Republic but excludes 'chairmanship or membership of ad hoc tribunals, commissions or committees'.

17. Fifth Schedule, Pt 1, s.7.

18. *Ibid.*, s.3. This provision was inserted by the Constituent Assembly. The CDC debated this issue but agreed not to make any provisions governing foreign accounts on the grounds (a) that those who should be deterred are unlikely to be found out (because of the secrecy of Swiss bank accounts), and (b) that innocuous persons such as scholars who studied abroad and have had to maintain — of necessity — accounts abroad (usually small accounts used for paying membership fees of learned societies, subscriptions to journals, etc.) are likely to be unnecessarily penalised.

19. It is worth observing that *8 months* after taking office, no public officer has yet declared his assets, etc. as required by the 'Code'. The President explained this lapse by saying the Senate has yet to ratify the appointment of the members of the Code of Conduct Tribunal. See *Daily Times*, 5 May 1980.

20. The public services cover a population of some 700,000 people. On the conservative estimate of each of these having one spouse and one child under the age of 16 and a declaration of assets at the start of a 4-year period and another at the end, this works out at just over four million 'declarations'.

21. The Bureau is to be composed of not less than nine members; they will be responsible to the National Assembly and are to be appointed by the President subject to the approval of the Senate. Fifth Schedule, Pt 1. s.15(2).

22. Made up of three members, the Chairman (included among the three members) being a person 'who has held or is qualified to hold office as a Judge of a superior Court of Record'. *Ibid.*, s.17(2). He is to be appointed by the President on the recommendation of the Federal Judicial Service Commission; *ibid.* s.17(3).

23. The CDC recommended 15 years.

24. Fifth Schedule, Pt 1, s.20(2).

25. Since state structures are largely replicas of the federal, it will not be necessary to give a separate description of state institutions. Attention will therefore be focused on federal instrumentalities.

26. These are summarised in the 'Report', para. 7.1–7.

27. s.75(1). The CDC's Draft expressed this as 'before the commencement of the financial year' — Draft, s.94(1).

28. s.76, cf. the CDC's recommendation of a period of one year — Draft, s.95.

29. s.80(1). The CDC's recommendation was that the President should make his appointment from three names submitted by the Public Service Commission. CDC Draft, s.91(1).

30. s.80(2). The recommendation of the CDC was for such an appointment to be made by the President of the Senate or the Speaker of

the House of Representatives. CDC Draft, s.91(3). The President would have to receive senatorial approval if the period of *acting* by the Auditor-General were to exceed 6 months (s.80(3)). The Auditor-General can only be removed from office on a prayer of the National Assembly supported by a two-thirds majority of each House (s.81(1)), cf. the recommendation of the CDC that removal be effected by the President of the Senate but with the same majority approval of the National Assembly (s.92(1)(a)) of Draft.

31. The presumption would therefore be that in the appointment of Permanent Secretaries or other chief executives, there is no restriction that these be from the civil service whether of the Federation or of the states.

32. s.195(3). The CDC's proposal with respect to the appointment of the Inspector-General is the reverse of that approved by the Constituent Assembly. The CDC — Draft s.163(2) — recommended that the appointment be made by the Police Service Commission *after consultation* with the President.

33. s.141(1)(2) and (3). The composition of these bodies, their functions and the tenure of office of the members are outlined in the Third Schedule, Pt 1 to the Constitution. There are some divergences between what the Constitution provides and what the CDC proposed in their Draft, viz:

    (a) The Council of States — with respect to the membership of all former Chief Justices, the Constitution adds the qualification 'who are citizens of Nigeria', a qualification absent in the Draft. The qualification was no doubt inserted to exclude people like Sir Alexander Darnley, a non-Nigerian, who would otherwise have been qualified to sit as an *ex officio* member of the Council of States

    (b) The Federal Public Service Commission — the Constitution provides for a membership of not more than nine members (excluding the Chairman). The CDC proposed a membership of not less than eight and not more than 12 — Draft, s. 137.

    (c) The Federal Judicial Service Commission — (i) where the CDC makes the Chairman someone who 'shall not hold any judicial office', the Constitution provides that the Chairman shall be the Chief Justice; (ii) of the four non-*ex-officio* members, where the CDC proposed that two should be persons who had been qualified to practise as advocates in Nigeria for a period of not less than 15 years and the other two should be drawn from those teaching law at a university or other institution of learning (one of whom was to be versed in Islamic law) for a period of not less than 10 years, the Constitution requires the

first two persons to be appointed from a list of four recommended by the Nigerian Bar Association, and the other two to
be persons 'not being legal practitioners', who are, in the
opinion of the President, persons of 'unquestionable integrity'.

(d) The National Population Council — the CDC proposed a Chairman and other members being not less than seven and not
more than nine. The Constitution fixed on a Chairman and
one person from each state of the Federation.

34. Though the Constitution requires the National Assembly to enact
provisions which would require Nigerian citizens to undergo compulsory military training, the President is also required, before such
an enactment is passed, to maintain 'adequate facilities in any
secondary or post-secondary education institution' for giving such
military training, a requirement the President has yet to comply
with.

35. s.5(3).

36. There are only three circumstances when the constitutional stipula-
tion expressly requires a two-thirds majority of *all* the members of
either House: (a) when there is a move to remove the President;
(b) when a state of emergency is to be declared; and (c) when there
is a move to amend the provisions of Ch. IV of the Constitution
and s.8 — which describes the process for the creation of states.
The word '*all*' is defined to refer to the 450 members of the Assembly — irrespective of any vacancies that there might be in the
House. (At present there are 449 members since one member is
expected to represent the Federal Capital Territory, i.e. the new
capital, but as that capital is yet to be built, it does follow that no
action can be undertaken with respect to the three circumstances
mentioned above.) It would therefore follow that in all other cases
when a two-thirds majority is stipulated, this must mean two-
thirds of those present and voting.

37. s.123. The CDC proposed a minimum age of 40 years, Draft, s.110.

38. The qualifier, 'in which the territory of Nigeria is physically
involved', was added by the Constituent Assembly to the CDC
Draft s.112(3).

39. The Presidential candidate is required to have a 'running mate' —
who is the Vice-President and both contest on a single ticket. The
Vice-President is considered to have been elected when the Presidential candidate is elected. The Constitution does not have too
much to say about the Vice-President. Generally, the President is
required to meet with the Vice-President and the Ministers of the
Government in the process of exercising his powers. The President
can delegate any functions of his office as he deems fit to the
Vice-President. But the Vice-President is a member of the Council

of States, and of the National Security Council (of which he is the Deputy Chairman) and he is the Chairman of the National Economic Council.

40. A situation which could arise if a competitor withdraws before the close of the nomination and no other nomination is made; or he dies after the close of nomination or disappears, or is otherwise incapacitated. In any of these circumstances, FEDECO is empowered to extend the time of nomination (s.124(3)). An election to the office of President is to be held 'on a date not earlier than 60 days and not later than 30 days before the expiration of the term of office of the last holder of that office', s.124(2). The CDC Draft only stipulated that the date of the election should be announced at a time not less than 7 days before the last holder vacated office. Draft s.111(2).

41. The phrase 'in each of at least two-thirds' was amended by the military government to read 'in at least two-thirds' before the military handed over power.

42. Over treaties between the federation and other states, the National Assembly can legislate irrespective of whether a matter is in the Exclusive Federal List or not, s.12(2). Legislation passed with respect to giving effect to treaties does not require to be assented to by the President, s.12(3).

43. This provision was inserted into the CDC Draft by the Constituent Assembly.

44. s.132(2). The CDC proposed the petition be signed by 25 per cent of the National Assembly members and submitted to either the President of the Senate or the Speaker of the House of Representatives — CDC Draft s.117(2).

45. The CDC, in place of the two-thirds majority of *all* the members proposed two-thirds of those present and voting, Draft, s.117(4)(a); and in place of an independent committee of seven, the CDC recommended a committee of 12 from each House of the Assembly, s.117(6). Members of the committee were to be nominated by the President of the Senate and subject to approval by the Senate, appointed by the President of the Senate.

46. A President once removed from office for gross misconduct cannot seek redress or question any part of the process of the grounds, for example unfairness, before any Court of Law. This is the only instance when action by the legislature is constitutionally disbarred from judicial enquiry, s.132(10).

47. The Constitution is silent on whether the report of the panel of doctors has to be unanimous or not. Presumably this need not be the case. If so, since four members of the panel are appointed by the President of the Senate at his discretion, there is nothing to stop a determined President of the Senate appointing a team cal-

culated to produce an outcome that he might favour. The 'whip hand' could thus lie with the Senate President.

48. Though the Constitution provides for the setting-up of committees by the National Assembly, only one committee is constitutionally prescribed, the Joint Committee on Finance, composed of equal members from each House, s.58(3).

49. The requirement 'to produce any document' was amended by the military to allow for executive privilege.

50. The whole of ss.82 and 83 was introduced by the Constituent Assembly. Neither section is to be found in the CDC Draft.

51. An example, though in a somewhat different key, is provided by the case of Miss Vera Ifudu, a Nigerian Television Authority (NTA) reporter attached to the Senate. Miss Ifudu had recorded an interview with a Senator who alleged that a sum of ₦2.8 billion belonging to the Nigerian National Oil Corporation might have been misappropriated. The taped interview was released over the television network. However, when the House of Representatives' committee set up to investigate the Senator's allegation demanded to see a copy of the tape, it was told that the tape had already been cleaned. But Miss Ifudu had made a copy of the interview on her personal tape. When the NTA demanded the release of her tape for submission to the House of Representatives Committee, Miss Ifudu refused, claiming quite properly that the tape was her personal property. Miss Ifudu was then suspended and subsequently dismissed. See the report by Stanley Macebuh — *West Africa*, 19 May 1980, pp. 876–7.

52. Boundary adjustments between any two (or more) states require a request supported by two-thirds of all legislators from the area concerned (including members of local councils), approval by a simple majority of members of the state Assembly in respect of the area concerned; and a simple majority of each House of the National Assembly.

53. For the Senate, the CDC recommended 35 years rather than 30, Draft s.63(a).

54. The CDC recommended loss of seat only if absence exceeded 100 days, Draft, s.66(f).

55. The proposal of the CDC was 'or such other Nigerian language as the National Assembly prescribes', Draft, s.53(1). There are provisions governing 'unqualified' persons attending meetings of the National Assembly — they are liable to imprisonment for a period not exceeding 6 months or a fine not in excess of ₦1000 and imprisonment for longer periods and fines in excess of ₦1000 for each other day of illegal attendance, s.53.

56. The structure proposed by the CDC differs from that adopted by the Constituent Assembly and embodied in the Constitution. The

CDC proposed there should be a Federal Shari'a Court of Appeal and made no provisions for a Federal High Court. There also were no provisions in the CDC Draft for a State Customary Court of Appeal, Draft Ch. VII; also pp. xxxiv–xxxxv.

57. The Court is made up of not more than 15 members (CDC Draft s.180-(1)(b) proposed a composition of not less than 15). For ordinary purposes, a panel of the Court would be made up of five judges, but when the Court exercises its original jurisdiction the panel has to be not less than seven members. Membership requires not less than 15 years post-qualification experience.

58. Composition: President and not fewer than 15 other judges of whom at least three should be specialists in Shari'a law and at least three should be specialists in Customary law. Membership requires not less than 12 years post-qualification experience.

59. Composition – Chief Judge and such other judges as may be prescribed by the National Assembly. Qualification for membership – not less than 10 years post qualification experience.

60. Cf. A. W. Livingston, *Federalism and Constitutional Change* (London: Oxford University Press, 1957).

61. Composed of a Grand Kadi and such number of Kadis as the state Assembly may prescribe. To hold office as a Kadi, a person must have attended and obtained 'a recognised qualification in Islamic personal law from an institution approved by the State Judicial Service Commission and held the qualification for a period not less than 10 years' or have 'considerable experience in the practice of Islamic personal law' or be 'a distinguished scholar of Islamic personal law', s.241(3).

62. No qualifications for office are shown in the Constitution, and the composition of the Court is simply said to be 'such number of judges as may be prescribed by law for a sitting of the Court', s.248.

63. Mosca's definition of the 'political class' was that group 'who perform all political functions, monopolizes power and enjoys the advantages that power brings'. G. Mosca *The Ruling Class* (trans. by Hannah D. Kahn, with an Intro. by A. W. Livingston, New York: McGraw-Hill, 1939) p. 50.

64. See, for example, White Paper on the New Political Alignment in Western Nigeria (Western Nigeria Official Document, No. 1, 1964); and *A rejoinder to Dr Ikejiani's statement on recent accusations of tribalism in the University of Ibadan* (Ibadan: NNDP Bureau of Information, 1964).

65. Report of the CDC – vol. 2.

66. 'Statism' could be interpreted as the equivalent of 'regionalism' as that term was used in Chapter 3.

67. There is not much data. let alone reliable data. on the level of

inequality in Nigerian society, but few would dispute that there are gross inequalities. Prof S. A. Aluko, in a paper on 'Wages and Prices' presented to the Conference on National Reconstruction and Development held at the University of Ibadan, 27 March 1969, did attempt to give some rough measures of inequality by suggesting that, taking earned incomes alone, while the ratio of the lowest to the highest income in Nigeria was something of the order of 1:30, the comparable figures for the US and the USSR were 1:7.5 and 1:4.5 respectively. In other words, 'unequal' as American society is supposed to be, in terms of earned incomes, the level of inequality in Nigeria is four times that of the US, and seven times that in the USSR.

68. See W. B. Gallie, 'Socialist morality and liberal morality', in P. Laslett (ed) *Philosophy, Politics and Society*, 1st series (London: Blackwell, 1956).

69. Second Schedule, Pt 11, item 11. 'The National Assembly may make laws for the Federation with respect to the registration of voters and the procedure regulating elections to a local government council'. Though this item comes under the 'Concurrent List', item 12 in the same list states that though a state Assembly is not precluded from making laws with respect to local government elections, such laws must not be 'inconsistent with any law made by the National Assembly'.

70. Second Schedule, Pt 1, item 57(e).

71. *Ibid.*, item 59(e).

72. Quoted from *How Shagari Became President: Decisions of the Courts* (published by the NPN, 8 Jibowu Street, Yaba, Lagos; and printed by the New Nigerian Newspapers Ltd, n.d). This reproduces the judgment by the Electoral Tribunal and the Supreme Court. It is cited with page references hereafter as *How Shagari Became President*.

73. Interview results. Subsequently, the NPN's legal adviser (later appointed Attorney General after being defeated as NPN Gubernatorial candidate for Oyo state), Chief Richard Akinjide, was to restate Umaru Diko's interpretation in a TV debate in Ibadan. As a result the 'formula' has been attributed to Chief Akinjide, though it was first suggested by Umaru Diko.

74. s.34(a) subsection 3 provided that in the case of there being no clear winner — with more than two candidates contesting — the two candidates satisfying a required condition should be presented to an electoral college of all members of the legislatures in the federation. The Electoral (Amendment) Decree 1978 did not alter the requirements expected of a candidate to be declared successful.

75. Counsel for Alhaji Shagari, Mr Richard Akinjide, had cited in support the Companies Decree 1968 where reference to 'one-third' of the Board of Directors had been explicated by the qualifier 'if their number is not three or a multiple of three, then the number nearest to one-third'.

76. The reference is to the evidence by Prof. A. Awojobi, Professor of Mechanical Engineering at the University of Lagos, who had argued, in support of Chief Awolowo, that, taking the local government divisions of Kano state into consideration, there were 38,760 possible ways of deriving two-thirds of a state.

77. Capitals in the original.

78. *How Shagari Became President*, p. 16. The Tribunal was made up of Justice B. O. Kazeem (Chairman) and Justice A. I. Aseme and A. B. Wali (members). Principal counsel for Chief Awolowo was Chief A. A. Adesanya; for Alhaji Shagari, Mr R. Akinjide; and for the Chief Returning Officer and the Executive Secretary to FEDECO, Mr S. S. A. Ojomo and Mrs R. A. Osijo, both from the Federal Ministry of Justice.

79. For somewhat differing views on synonymity, cf. Quine, W. V. O., 'Two dogmas of Empiricism', in Quine, W. V. O., *From a Logical Point of View* (Cambridge, Mass.: Harvard University Press, 1953) and *Word and Object* (Cambridge Mass.: M.I.T. Press, 1960), also *Philosophy of Logic* (Englewood Cliffs: Prentice Hall, 1970) and *contra* H. Putnam, *Philosophy of Logic* (Harper Torchbooks: New York, 1971). For a very summary view on the notoriety of dealing with the problem of synonymity, S. Haack, *Philosophy of Logics* (Cambridge, Mass.: Cambridge University Press, 1978) 173–5.

80. If that view were correct, then a candidate would need to poll no more than 17 per cent of the total votes cast to poll the equivalent of 25 per cent of two-thirds of the votes cast. In other words, 25 per cent of two-thirds of the total votes cast would be about equal to 17 per cent of the total votes cast.

81. *How Shagari Became President*, p. 17.

82. *Ibid.*, p. 26. The Court did not take up Chief Awolowo's claim that the Chief Returning Officer and the Electoral Tribunal erred in calculating Alhaji Shagari's share of the votes in two-thirds of the 13th state. The majority ruling was given by the Chief Justice, Mr A. Fatayi-Williams with Justices A. G. Irikefe, M. Bello, O. Idigbe and M. L. Uwais concurring.

83. *Ibid.*, p. 38.

84. *Loc. cit.*

85. *How Shagari Became President*, pp. 46–7.

86. One incident which aroused considerable uneasiness in non-NPN

states was the deportation of the GNPP majority leader of the Borno state Assembly, Alhaji Shugaba from Nigeria on the grounds that he is a non-Nigerian citizen. It is highly improbable that the immigration authorities could have taken such a serious step without the full knowledge of the Ministries of Internal Affairs (which has charge of immigration) and of Justice. Some have seen this as an attempt by the executive branch to coerce opposition states. Supporters of Alhaji Shugaba did appeal to the courts against his deportation and as a result he has been allowed back in Nigeria pending the determination of his citizenship status by the judicial authorities. And in at least one respect, non-NPN states have refused to co-operate with the federal authorities. These states have refused to recognise the President's liaison advisers deputed to the states. Though the Constitution requires the National Assembly to determine the numbers of persons to be appointed Presidential advisers, there is no evidence to suggest that in the appointments so far made — some 29 advisers — the National Assembly had any say in the determination of the numbers. The advisers appointed so far are: 19 states liaison advisers and the following — National Assembly Liaison — Dr K. O. Mbadiwe; Political Affairs — Dr C. Okadigbo and Prof G. A. Odenigwe; Petroleum and Energy — Alhaji Yahaya Dikko; Information — Chief O. Adebanjo; Economic Affairs — Prof E. C. Edozien and Dr J. Ojama; Director of Budget (Budget Affairs) — Chief T. A. Akinyele; National Security — Dr B. Shuaibu; Statutory Boards — Dr O. Olaifa. The Vice-President has a comparable list of advisers.

CHAPTER 6: PARTIES AND THE 1979 ELECTIONS

1. V. O. Key, Jnr, *Public Opinion and American Democracy* (New York: Alfred Knopf, 1961), p. 433.

2. Giovanni Sartori, *Parties and Party Systems*, vol. I (Cambridge Mass.: Cambridge University Press, 1976) p. 41.

3. It is conventional to distinguish between Tanganyika, the former German colony which became a British mandated territory after the First World War, and Tanzania, the name given to the union of Tanganyika and Zanzibar. The reference in the text is to the former German colony.

4. See, e.g. the excellent summary by S. E. Finer, 'The one party regimes in Africa: reconsiderations', in *Government and Opposition*, 4, 2 (1967).

5. Sartori, *op. cit.* (see note 2), pp. 125–6.

6. Colin Leys, 'Models, theories and the theory of political parties', in *Political Studies*, 7 (1959).

7. The analogue here is a formalised language in which some of the variables of the language are 'restrictedly bounded', meaning by this that the variables can only take a specified range of values to yield a 'well-formed formula' of the language.

8. Cf. the following nomenclatures of parties in the first republic: The *Northern Peoples'* Congress; the *Northern* Elements Progressive Union; the *Bornu* Youth Movement; the United *Middle Belt* Congress; the *Igbirra* Progressive Union; the *Igala Tribal* Union; the *Midwest* Democratic Front, and many more.

9. Cf. the practice in the first republic where elections to party offices were the exceptions rather than the rule. For the NPC, for example, the last party elections were held in 1954, and in the NCNC none were held after 1958. Elections to party offices split the AG in 1962.

10. s.81(1) requires parties to publish and to submit to FEDECO a statement of their assets and liabilities in such a manner as FEDECO may require, while s.81(2) requires an annual statement of sources of funds, assets and statement of expenditure to be similarly submitted to FEDECO. s.81(6) imposes a penalty of ₦10,000 for failure to comply with the above requirements and an additional ₦2000 for each succeeding month of non-compliance. For failure to show funds received from abroad, the penalty is put at ₦5000 for every day (after the initial 21 days) a party unlawfully retains such funds or assets.

11. On this, see B. J. Dudley, 'Western Nigeria and the Nigerian crises', in S. K. Panter-Brick (ed.) *Nigerian Politics and Military Rule* (London: Athlone Press, 1970).

12. Essentially, there were three main contestants: Alhaji Shehu Shagari; Alhaji Adamu Ciroma, former Managing Director of New Nigerian Newspapers, and a one-time Governor of the Central Bank of Nigeria; and Professor Iya Abubakar, former Vice-Chancellor of Ahmadu Bello University.

13. For example, Emirs having to take second, if not third place, to young Army officers; something that would have been undreamed of before the coup.

14. See W. Riker, *Theory of Political Coalitions* (New Haven: Yale University Press, 1967). However, in the simple case of a 5-person committee, A, B, C, D, and E voting on an issue and a split such that (A,B) are 'for', and (C,D) are 'against', with E abstaining, should E then decide to cast his vote for (CD), the addition of E to (C,D) makes E 'pivotal' in the coalition (C,D,E). (A,B) and (C,D)

are 'blocking' coalitions. The inclusion of E to (C,D) gives (C,D) the minimum majority it requires to govern. (C,D,E) is a 'minimum' winning coalition: Gamson would refer to the same coalition as the 'cheapest' winning coalition.

15. Chief Agbaje, formerly a prominent NCNC politician from Ibadan, was, for example, deputed to see Azikiwe to win him over to the NPN. Chief Agbaje was killed in a car accident on his way back from Onitsha where he had been to see Dr Azikiwe.

16. See J. N. Paden, *Religion and Political Culture in Kano* (Berkeley: University of California Press, 1973). On the advantages of ambiguity, K. Shepsle, 'The strategy of ambiguity: uncertainty and electoral competition', *American Political Science Review*, **66** (1972) 551—72.

17. Sartori, *op. cit.* (see note 2), pp. 173—4; 178—9.

18. *Sunday Sketch*, 27/4/80. This has been followed for example by the decision of the NPN/NPP federal coalition to extend the federal practice to the states in a manner comparable to the meeting of the UPN, PRP, GNPP Governors. *Daily Times*, 26/4/80.

19. *Sunday Sketch*, 27/4/80; *Daily Times*, 25/4/80.

20. One seat is allocated to the federal territory to bring the total to 450, but the federal capital territory is yet to be established.

21. The figures are derived by dividing the figures in col. 2 (population totals) by those in col. 3 (seats per state). The computation of the index was done by my son, Jeremy Dudley.

22. The index of representation (Ir) is derived as follows:

where N = total population of the federation;
S = total seats in the House of Representatives;
p = total population of the state;
s = seats allocated to the state; then,
$Ir = p/s \times S/N$.

23. As an amusing aside, a former colleague at the University of Ibadan complained he had not minded being told how he should vote, but he was disgusted at the suggestion, and that coming from another academic colleague, that he should have voted more than once. 'Everyone did it', the colleague was reported to have said.

24. After the July coup which overthrew General Gowon, the successor military regime scrapped the census figures produced in 1973 which would have given Nigeria a total population of over 88 million. (One Professor at the University of Ife has told the story of how he aided the inflation of the 1963 census figures for his village in order to ensure the village got a grammar school, 'to compete with the adjoining village').

25. The Electoral Commission had yet to release its figures on the elec-

tions. Those given are from *How Shagari Became President*, pp. (i)—(ii).

26. Report of the Commission Appointed to Enquire into the Fears of Minorities and the Means of Allaying Them, Cmnd. 505, 1958.

27. The comparison here is with Rae's definition of a two-party system as that system in which the two main parties together poll not less than 70 per cent of the votes cast. See D. Rae, *The Political Consequences of Electoral Laws* (New Haven: Yale University Press, 1968), *passim*.

28. Ian Budge and Dennis Farlie, *Voting and Party Competition* (London: John Wiley, 1977) ch. I.

29. For example, in Bendel, the Urhobos who might have voted for the NPN were prevented from doing so because some of the NPN candidates, e.g. Mr Okumagba, a gubernatorial candidate, were unacceptable to the electorate. They voted instead for the UPN.

30. See B. J. Dudley, *Parties and Politics in Northern Nigeria* (London: Frank Cass, 1968).

31. B. J. Dudley, 'The political theory of Awolowo and Azikiwe', in O. Otite (ed.), *Themes in African Social and Political Thought* (New York: Africana Publishing Co., 1978) pp. 199—216.

32. For example, when in 1967 Chief Awolowo came out with his notion of 'conditional secession', that if the East were to secede the West would also be forced to follow suit, many questioned the right of the Chief to make such pronouncements on behalf of the Yorubas, claiming no one had formally elected him 'Leader of the Yorubas'.

33. The geographical conditions in the Rivers state could easily explain the increase. It would hardly be surprising if, in some parts of the state, people had not voted in the first elections. In fact, on seeing the low poll in the first election, some effort was made to get out the vote in subsequent elections.

34. It should not be understood that I am suggesting that there was no 'rigging' in some of the other states: only that it would not have been on the same scale as the figures for the 'wild, wild West' would suggest.

35. On the general significance of local institutions for the political behaviour of the Ibo-speaking peoples, see, e.g. A. C. Smock, 'NCNC and ethnic unions in Biafra', *Journal of Modern African Studies*, 7 (1969); also J. P. MacIntosh (ed.), *Nigerian Government and Politics* (London: Allen & Unwin, 1966), ch. 7.

36. In states like the Rivers and Cross River, opposition to the NPP would have been seen as a 'hangover' from the civil war, exacerbated, in the case of the Rivers, by the controversy over 'abandoned properties'.

37. In the first republic, for instance, the rival claims of Sokoto and Kano — the duality between religion and politics — was symbolised in the conflict between the Emir of Kano, Alhaji Sanussi (who was forced into exile — to Azare — in 1964 by the then Northern government) and the Premier of the North, Alhaji Ahmadu Bello, Sardauna of Sokoto.

38. Unlike the UPN — whose leader was able to cover the federation using a helicopter to campaign — at the end of the elections the UPN was still owing over ₦183,000 in unpaid printing bills (*New Nigerian*, 26/4/80) — or the NPN which could afford to employ a London-based public relations firm to run its campaign (contra the Electoral Decree provisions on external funds), and the NPP whose leader was said to have been paid to lead his party's campaign, the PRP could barely afford to cover the principal towns of the North, let alone the whole federation.

39. A clear case of 'insincere voting', see R. Farquharson, *Theory of Voting* (Oxford: Blackwell, 1969).

40. These were areas which in the past used to provide support for Aminu's former party, the Northern Elements Progressive Union (NEPU). It should be noted, however, that cue-wise, the PRP and the GNPP were competing for the same party-space in these states.

41. The original NPP had a not inconsiderable following in Imo and Anambra states but lost such support when Zik entered the political arena. One might want to speculate on what the outcome of the elections could have been had Zik and Awolowo not been active participants.

42. Budge and Farlie, *op. cit.* (see note 28), *passim*, but especially pp. 4 and 71.

43. *Ibid.*, *passim*, for an analysis and review of the relevant literature.

44. A. W. Gouldner, *The Future of Intellectuals and the Rise of the New Class* (London: Macmillan, 1979) p. 28.

45. *Ibid.*, p. 85.

46. D. Rae, *op. cit.* (see note 27), *passim*.

CHAPTER 7: THE ECONOMY

1. Sayre P. Schatz: *Nigerian Capitalism* (Berkeley: University of California Press, 1977) p. 34.

2. The 1960 figures are from my *Parties and Politics in Northern Nigeria* (London: Frank Cass, 1968); those for 1980 were from *West Africa*, 29 Sept., 1980, p. 1898.

3. Ruth Leger Sivard, *World Military and Social Expenditures, 1977* (Leesburg, Virginia: WMSE Publications, published under the

auspices of the Rockefeller Foundation, 1977). The rank-orders for the African states were recomputed. While there is no rank correlation between the absolute size of GNP and social expenditures, that between per capita GNP and social expenditures gave $r_s = 0.77$, $p = 0.05$. The recomputed rank and the original rank ordering based on 138 states gave $r_s = 0.96$, $p = 0.05$.

4. United Africa Company: *Statistical and Economic Review*, Issue 29 (1964) p. 15.

5. W. Stolper, *Planning Without Facts* (Cambridge: Harvard University Press, 1966).

6. Preliminary discussions on the Second National Plan started in 1968, discussions which were followed by an International Conference held at the University of Ibadan in March 1969. The basic strategic approach to the plan was outlined at the conference but the conference itself was more of a publicity exercise aimed at securing international confidence in the federal government rather than an economic 'pug-wash' as some people thought.

7. The two key architects of the plan were Professor O. Aboyade, Professor of Economics at the University of Ibadan, and Mr A. A. Ayida, then Permanent Secretary of the Federal Ministry of Economic Planning. It is an interesting fact of history that though Aboyade, in his numerous writings as critic of past planning approaches, has been a key proponent of 'planning from below', when called upon to put his 'teaching' into practice, he turned the archetypal technocrat. Some have seen in this an indication of the intellectual schizophrenia which has been said to be characteristic of the African academic inducted into a public role.

8. *Second National Development Plan 1970–74* (Lagos: Ministry of Information, 1970) *passim*.

9. The existence of 'commissioners' projects' came to light when members of the EPC, unable to accept what seemed to be gross absurdities in the Midwest Plan, insisted on an explanation. The commissioner for economic planning and the bureaucrats present, unable to offer a convincing explanation, finally admitted the items complained about were 'commissioners' projects'. But as the inclusion of these had the express approval and support of the military governor, nothing further could be said about the 'projects'.

10. The former Western region was the first to initiate a UPE scheme in 1954. The reference to 1976 is to the federally supported scheme.

11. *The Financial Times* (London) — Special Supplement on Nigeria, 30 August 1978, p. 17.

12. A steel reduction plant located at Aladja in Warri with a capacity of 100,000 tons is also expected to come into production by 1983.

13. *The Financial Times*, Supplement (see Note 11). *West Africa*, 13 October, 1980, p. 2038 reported that the federal government was about to call for a new tender for a single liquefied natural gas plant expected to cost some ₦7 billion with tenders to come from, it is hoped, Japanese, European and American groups. It stated further that the federal government has ruled that the flaring of natural gas — 'associated gas' — which comes with the production of oil, should cease by 1984, when work on the liquefied natural gas plant is expected to commence.

14. Quoted from *The Financial Times* — Supplement, p. 28 (See Note 11).

15. *West Africa*, 29 September 1980, p. 1931.

16. OFN was an extension of — and subsequently replaced — the National Accelerated Food Production Scheme.

17. *First Progress Report on the Third National Plan*, pp. 26—27.

18. Federal government spending rose, on average, by about 10 per cent per annum between 1966 and 1967. The civil war — and oil money — accelerated that increase but since 1977 the pace of federal spending has slowed down, with annual increases conforming with past experience. See Dr Mbanefo, 'The Economics of Federal Expenditure', seminar paper, Department of Economics, University of Ibadan.

19. *Report of the Public Service Review Commission* (Lagos: Federal Ministry of Information, 1974), especially the 'Main Report'.

20. *Ibid.*, Main Report, p. 7.

21. *Government's Views on the Report of the Public Service Review Commission* (Lagos: Ministry of Information, 1974).

22. D. Braybrooke and C. E. Lindblom, *A Strategy of Decision* (Glencoe: Free Press, 1963); Y. Dror, *Ventures in the Policy Sciences* (New York: Elsevier, 1971); W. J. M. MacKenzie, *Models of Collective Decision-Making in the Social Sciences: Problems and Orientations* (Hague: Mouton for UNESCO, 1968); H. A. Simon, *Administrative Behaviour* (Glencoe: Free Press, 1957).

23. *Report of the Revenue Allocation Commission — Hicks—Phillipson Report* (Lagos: Government Printer, 1951).

24. Report of the Fiscal Commissioner, Cmnd 9026 (London, 1953).

25. Report of the Fiscal Commissioner, Cmnd 481 (London, 1958).

26. *Report of the Fiscal Review Commissioner — K. J. Binns* (Lagos: Federal Ministry of Information, 1965).

27. The summary is taken from E. Oyovbaire, 'The politics of revenue allocation', in S. K. Panter-Brick (ed.), *Soldiers and Oil* (London: Frank Cass, 1978) p. 226. An excellent review and analysis of revenue allocation exercises between 1953 and 1965 is given by O. Teriba, 'Nigerian Revenue Allocation Experience 1952—65: A

Study in Inter-Governmental Fiscal and Financial Relations' — *Nigerian Journal of Economic and Social Studies,* **8** (1966).

28. Before the creation of states in May 1967, relations between the peoples from the 'minority areas' of the North — who wanted their own states — and those from the dominant Hausa-Fulani emirates had become so strained that for a time there was even fear that hostilities could break out between soldiers from these areas.

29. As shown, for example, in the table below:

Surpluses (+) or deficits (−) of governments on current account 1960–64 (£'000)

	Federal government	*North*	*West*	*East*
1960	+7075	+2057	−2471	+2014
1962	+5241	−2925	+2121	+2300
1964	+ 138	+ 417	+ 565	+1302

Source: *Federal Government Digest of Statistics* — which provided the source for the table (in the text) showing current revenues of the various governments for the period 1953–60.

30. *Nigeria — Report of the Interim Revenue Allocation Committee* (Chairman: Chief I. O. Dina, 1969), p. 27.

31. *Dina revenue allocation recommendations (summary)*

Account	*Excise duty*	*Import duty*	*Export duty*	*On-shore Rents*	*Mining (on-shore) royalties*	*Off-shore rent and royalties*
Federal government	60	50	15	—	15	60
States derivation	—	—	10	100	10	—
Joint states	30	50	70	—	70	30
Special grants	10	—	5	—	5	10
TOTAL	100	100	100	100	100	100

32. Other changes effected by the 1970 Decree include: (a) excise duty on tobacco and petroleum products previously paid to the states on a derivation basis was now to be shared between the federal government and the DPA; (b) export duties, similarly paid to the states on the basis of derivation, were now to be shared between the states (60 per cent) and the DPA (40 per cent); (c) the ratio

for distributing mining rents and royalties previously put at 50 per cent (states), 15 per cent (federal government) and 35 per cent (DPA) was now to be replaced by a 45:5:50 distribution; and (d) import duties on motor fuel formerly paid to the states on the basis of proportions sold within a state was to be shared equally between the federal government and the DPA. Comparing the Dina recommendations and the federal government's formula for distributing the DPA, the coefficient of variation of the differences of the government's formula and the Dina proposals from the formula provided for in the May 1967 Decree gave $V = 1.37$ for the former and $V = 2.8$ for the latter. If we accept the original (May 1967) distribution as fair, then we would have to accept that the April 1969 ruling was a fairer distribution than that proposed by the Dina committee.

33. Between 1967/68 and 1976/77, whereas state revenues grew by 650 per cent, those of the federal government rose by 1574 per cent. Also where in 1968/69, 40 per cent of state revenues were internally generated, by 1974/75 that figure had declined to 28 per cent. The relative disparities between federal and state revenues is shown by the fact that out of a total of ₦11 billion appropriated for 1980, only ₦2 billion (18.18 per cent) was allocated to the 19 states.

34. For example, G. Almond and S. Verba, *The Civic Culture* (Princeton: Princeton University Press, 1963); R. Bendix, *Nation-Building and Citizenship* (New York: Wiley, 1964); P. E. Converse and G. Dupeux, 'Politicization of the Electorate in France and the United States', *Public Opinion Quarterly*, **26** (1962) and J. Linz and A. De Miguel, 'Eight Spains', in R. L. Merritt and S. Rokkan (eds), *Comparing Nations* (New Haven: Yale University Press, 1966).

35. *West Africa*, 7 July 1980, p. 1223.

36. *Ibid.*, p. 1221 where it is reported that the Report

   is in four volumes. The first . . . lists names of persons, organisations, and interest groups who made submissions, together with their memoranda, the second incorporates submissions by governments and evidence received by the commission . . . the third volume comprises the commission's comments, findings and recommendations and the fourth is a minority report co-authored by Prof A. Phillips of the University of Ibadan and former finance commissioner in Ogun state, and Dr G. B. Leton, former federal commissioner, who comes from the oil-rich Rivers state.

37. *West Africa*, 1 September 1980, pp. 1641—2. Okigbo also recommended that housing, agriculture and the UPE be transferred to the

state governments. In a bill sent to the National Assembly (*West Africa*, 10 November, 1980, p. 2259), the President has proposed the following distribution: Federal government 55 per cent; States 34.5 per cent; local governments 8 per cent; and initial development of the Federal capital territory 2.5 per cent. Of the 34.5 per cent allocation to the States, 30 per cent should go to all the states; 3.5 per cent to the oil-producing states and 1.0 per cent for ecological reparation.

38. *Ibid.*, p. 1641.

39. 72.56 per cent of all crude produced in 1979 (842 million barrels) was on-shore, leaving 27.43 per cent as off-shore production. Of the off-shore output, Bendel accounted for 61.47 per cent and Cross River for 38.52 per cent. Production from Rivers, Ondo and Imo are classified as 'on-shore'. Overall distribution of total oil produced in 1979 was Bendel 53.08 per cent, Rivers 28.74 per cent, Cross River 11.75 per cent, Imo 6.17 per cent and Ondo 0.11 per cent.

40. The expenditure per soldier given by Sivard for 1974 was $4029 while the figure for 1978/79 is as shown, ₦3476, which converts to $5561.6 (at the conversion rate of ₦1 = $1.6). Thus, though expenditure between the two periods, that is expenditure on defence, fell by 13.7 per cent and the size of the armed forces also fell by 28.8 per cent, expenditure per soldier rose by 38 per cent.

41. The choice was dictated largely by (a) availability of data, and (b) the need to maintain comparability and avoid the complications associated with the creation of states (19) in 1976.

42. Preparations for, and the launching of, the UPE scheme easily account for the huge increase in education which started to show in the budget for 1975. The federal government initially accepted full financial responsibility for UPE but it was later to share this with the states when it found the burden too heavy to bear alone.

43. A case in point was the controversy which arose when figures for admission into the various universities were released by the Joint Admissions and Matriculation Board in October 1979, a controversy which led to a closure (after students 'rioted') of three universities (Maiduguri, Jos and Kano). Only the subtle defusing of the controversy by the authorities averted a crisis.

44. See note 41 above.

45. The Human Resources Research Unit of the University of Lagos surveys of house occupancy rates suggest that 73 per cent of whole families in Lagos live in single rooms. The percentage for Ibadan is only marginally lower.

46. J. O'Connell and P. A. Beckett, *Education and Power in Nigeria* (London: Hodder & Stoughton, 1977).

47. The distribution of loans given by the NAB as at July 1976 showed 52 private agricultural companies, 35 individuals, 16 state institutions, 11 co-operatives through state governments and three direct co-operatives to have benefited from the sum of ₦173 million lent by the NAB at that date. See *First Progress Report of Third National Plan*, para. 43, p. 56. Usually, small farmers would benefit through co-operatives.

48. *CDC Report*, vol. 1, para. 3.6—7, p. xii.

49. For an exposition of Parsons' 'system' theory, see W. C. Mitchell, *Sociological Analysis and Politics — The Theories of Talcott Parsons* (New Jersey: Prentice Hall, 1967).

50. A perennial complaint of planners in Nigeria, classically stated in the title of W. Stolper's book, *Planning without Facts* (Cambridge, Mass.: Harvard University Press, 1966), is the inadequacy, and sometimes total lack, of information.

51. Indigenisation not only broadened the pattern of ownership, it also dispersed, particularly after the 1977 Decree, the form of ownership. One of the arguments made in support of indigenisation — howbeit tangentially — is that it should reduce the loss of foreign exchange through the repatriation of profits. The available evidence (as shown in the First Progress Report on the Third Plan), would suggest that this effect has been marginal. For one thing, indigenisation in no way affected preference shares, the bulk of which are foreign-owned.

52. One other possible consequence of the congruence between 'state' and 'economy' is worth mentioning. Nigerian businessmen have been content to restrict their activities, in the main, to commerce and general contracting, where the returns are high and immediate and the risks minimal. With bureaucrats and technocrats moving into the private sector as active 'compradors', there is a strong likelihood that sooner or later there could be a sharp conflict of interest between the Nigerian business elite and 'comprador' bureaucrats, for as manufacturing becomes less risky or the return to 'buying and selling' less rewarding, the business groups may want to move into manufacturing (with the demand, as one would expect, that the activities of expatriates in the manufacturing sector be regulated and curtailed). But then, they may find some resistance, resistance which may not be so easy to beat by nationalistic appeals for the ending of foreign domination and exploitation — since 'champions' of the foreign interests would also be Nigerians.

CHAPTER 8: EXTERNAL RELATIONS

1. Brian Barry, *Political Argument* (London: Routledge & Kegan Paul, 1967).
2. W. Lipman, *The Public Philosophy* (New York: Mentor Books).
3. O. Oyediran (ed.), *Survey of Nigerian Affairs 1975* (Lagos: OUP for the Nigerian Institute for International Affairs, 1978), p. 311.
4. *Ibid.*, p. 188.
5. Alhaji Sir Abubakar Tafawa Balewa; *Nigeria Speaks* (London: Cambridge University Press, 1962) *passim*.
6. O. Oyediran, *op. cit.* (see note 3) p. 188.
7. See e.g. A. B. Akinyemi, *Foreign Policy and Nigerian Federalism* (Ibadan: Ibadan University Press, 1975); I. A. Gambari, 'The Domestic Politics of Major Foreign Policy Issues in Nigeria' (Ph.D dissertation, Columbia University, 1974), and Thomas Hovet Jnr, *Africa in the United Nations* (Northwestern University Press, African Studies Series, No. 10, 1963).
8. C. Odumegwu Ojukwu, *Random Thoughts*, vol. 2 of *Biafra — Selected Speeches with Journals of Events* (New York: Harper & Row), p. 182. Generally on the international politics of the civil war, see J. Stremlau, *The International Politics of the Civil War* (Princeton: Princeton University Press, 1974).
9. Stremlau, *op. cit., passim*; B. J. Dudley, *Instability and Political Order* (Ibadan: Ibadan University Press, 1973), ch. 9.
10. A. B. Akinyemi, 'Nigerian Foreign Policy in 1975: National Interest Redefined', in O. Oyediran (ed): *op. cit.* (see note 3), pp. 107–8.
11. In 1976, the Muhammed/Obasanjo regime took over 55 per cent of the shares in Shell—BP and subsequently, in 1979, nationalised the company.
12. Stremlau, *op. cit., passim* (see note 8); A. B. Akinyemi, in O. Oyediran (ed), *op. cit.* (see note 10).
13. *The Financial Times* (London) Survey — Nigeria, 30 August 1978, sec. xviii, p. 28.
14. *Loc. cit.*
15. *Ibid.*, p. 29.
16. *West Africa*, 4 August 1980, p. 1460.

Select Bibliography

CHRIS ALLEN

Professor Dudley died before he could himself compile the guide to further reading which forms part of each volume in the series. This listing, which mirrors the book's emphasis on post-independence politics, the economy and Nigerian society, has been compiled with the help of Ali Yahaya and Gavin Williams, though the final selection is mine.

I. GENERAL WORKS [see also 140]

1. Graf, W. D. (ed.), *Towards a Political Economy of Nigeria: Critical Essays* (Benin City: Koda Publishers, 1981).
2. Williams, G. and Turner, T., 'Nigeria', *West African States*, ed. J. Dunn (Cambridge: Cambridge University Press, 1979) pp. 132–72, 240–45.
3. Williams, G., *State and Society in Nigeria* (Lagos: Afrographika, 1980).
4. Williams, G. (ed.), 'Nigeria Issue', *Review of African Political Economy*, 13 (1979).

II. THE ECONOMY

History, Description, Analysis [see also 30, 79, 107, 110]
5. Hopkins, A. G., *An Economic History of West Africa* (London: Longman, 1972).
6. Smith, S., 'Colonialism in economic theory: the experience of Nigeria', *Journal of Development Studies*, 15, 3 (1979) 38–59.

7. Perham, M. (ed.), *Economics of a Tropical Dependency* (London: Faber, 1946) 2 vols.
8. Bauer, P. T., *West African Trade* (Cambridge: Cambridge University Press, 1954).
9. Freund, W., *Capital and Labour in the Nigerian Tin Mines* (London: Longman, 1981).
10. Eicher, C. K. and Leidholm, C. (eds.), *Growth and Development of the Nigerian Economy* (East Lansing: Michigan State University Press, 1970).
11. Aboyade, O., *Foundations of an African Economy* (New York: Praeger, 1966).
12. International Monetary Fund, *Surveys of African Economies*, vol. 6. (Washington: IMF., 1975) pp. 281–380.
13. Callaway, B., 'The political economy of Nigeria', *The Political Economy of Africa*, ed. R. Harris (New York: Schenkman, 1973) pp. 93–135.
14. Onoh, J. K. (ed.), *The Foundation of Nigeria's Financial Infrastructure* (London: Croom Helm, 1980).
15. Schatzl, L. H., *Petroleum in Nigeria* (Ibadan: Oxford University Press, 1969).
16. Turner, T., 'Multinational corporations and the stability of the Nigerian state', *Review of African Political Economy*, 5 (1976), 63–79.
17. Turner, T., 'Nigeria: imperialism, oil technology and the comprador state', *Oil and Class Struggle*, ed. P. Nore and T. Turner (London: Zed, 1980) pp. 199–223.
18. Forrest, T., 'Recent developments in Nigerian industrialisation', *Industry and Accumulation in Africa*, ed. M. Fransman (London: Heineman 1982).
19. Kilby, P., *Industrialisation in an Open Economy: Nigeria 1945–66* (Cambridge: Cambridge University Press, 1969).
20. Teriba, O. and Kayode, M. O. (eds), *Industrial Development in Nigeria* (Ibadan: Ibadan University Press, 1977).
21. Biersteker, T. J., *Distortion or Development: Contending Perspectives on the Multinational Corporation* (Cambridge, Mass.: MIT Press, 1978).
22. Akeredolu-Ale, E. O., *The Underdevelopment of Indigenous Entrepreneurship in Nigeria* (Ibadan: Ibadan University Press, 1975).

23. Nafziger, E. W., *African Capitalism: a Case Study in Nigerian Entrepreneurship* (Stanford: Hoover, 1977).
24. Collins, P., 'Public policy and the development of indigenous capitalism: the Nigerian experience', *Journal of Commonwealth and Comparative Politics*, 15, 2 (1977) 127–50.
25. Nigerian Economic Society, *Poverty in Nigeria* (Ibadan: the Society, 1976).
26. Bienen, H. and Diejomoah, V. P. (eds), *The Political Economy of Income Distribution in Nigeria* (New York: Africana, 1981).
27. Stolper, W., *Planning Without Facts* (Cambridge, Mass.: Harvard University Press, 1966).
28. Dean, E., *Plan Implementation in Nigeria 1962–66* (Ibadan: Oxford University Press, 1972).
29. Ayida, A. D. and Onitiri, H. M. A. (eds), *Reconstruction and Development in Nigeria* (Ibadan: Oxford University Press, 1971).

Rural Economics; Rural Development [see also 7, 8]

30. Helleiner, G. K., *Peasant Agriculture, Government and Economic Growth in Nigeria* (Homewood: R. D. Irwin, 1966).
31. Galletti, R., Balwin, K. D. S. and Dina, I. O., *Nigerian Cocoa Farmers* (London: Oxford University Press, 1956).
32. Hill, P., *Rural Hausa* (Cambridge: Cambridge University Press, 1972).
33. Hill, P., *Population, Prosperity and Poverty: Rural Kano 1900 and 1970* (Cambridge: Cambridge University Press, 1977).
34. Tiffen, M., *The Enterprising Peasant: Economic Development in Gombe Emirate* (London: HMSO, 1976).
35. Berry, S. S., *Cocoa, Custom and Socioeconomic Change in Rural Western Nigeria* (Oxford, Oxford University Press, 1975).
36. Onitiri, H. M. A. and Olatunbosun, D. (eds.), *The Marketing Board System* (Ibadan: NISER, 1974).
37. Wells, J. C., *Agricultural Policy and Economic Growth in Nigeria 1962–68* (Ibadan: Ibadan University Press, 1974).

38. Heyer, J. *et al.* (eds), *Rural Development in Tropical Africa* (London: Macmillan).
39. Oculi, O., 'Dependent food policy in Nigeria 1975–79', *Review of African Political Economy*, 15/16 (1979) 63–74.
40. Wallace, T. *Rural Development through Irrigation: Studies in a Town on the Kano River Project* (Zaria: ABU Centre for Social and Economic Research, 1979).
41. Apeldoorn, G. J., *Perspectives on Drought and Famine in Nigeria* (London: Allen & Unwin, 1981).
42. Norman, D. W. *et al.*, *Technical Change and the Small Farmer in Hausaland* (East Lansing: Michigan State University, African Rural Economy Program, 1979).

III. SOCIETY

Community, Ethnicity, Religion, Gender [see also 32, 53, 56, 63, 79, 86, 89 and 109]

43. Eades, J. S., *The Yoruba Today* (Cambridge, Cambridge University Press, 1980).
44. Cohen, A., *Custom and Politics in Urban Africa* (London: Routledge, 1969).
45. Sudarkasa, N., *Where Women Work: A Study of Yoruba Women in the Market Place and Home* (Ann Arbor: University of Michigan, 1973).
46. Smith, M., *Baba of Karo* (London: Faber, 1954).
47. Paden, J. N., *Religion and Political Culture in Kano* (Berkeley: University of California Press, 1973).
48. Peel, J. D. Y., *Aladura: a Religious Movement among the Yoruba* (London: Oxford University Press for the International African Institute, 1968).

Urban Society and Politics; Labour [see also 44, 78, 79]

49. Mabogunje, A. L., *Urbanisation in Nigeria* (London: University of London Press, 1968).
50. Aronson, D. R., *The City is our Farm: Seven Migrant Ijebu Yoruba Families* (Cambridge, Mass.: Shenkman; Boston: G. K. Hall, 1978).
51. Cole, M., *Modern and Traditional Elites in the Politics of Lagos* (Cambridge, Cambridge University Press, 1975).

52. Wolpe, H., *Urban Politics in Nigeria: a Study of Port Harcourt* (Berkeley: University of California Press, 1974).
53. Lloyd, P. C., *Power and Independence: Urban African's Perception of Social Inequality* (London: Routledge, 1974).
54. Cohen, R., *Labour and Politics in Nigeria* (London: Heinemann, 1974).
55. Peace, A. J., *Choice, Class and Conflict* (Hassocks: Harvester Press, 1979).
56. Lubeck, P., 'Class consciousness and Islamic nationalism among Nigerian workers', *Research in the Sociology of work*, vol. 1, ed. R. L. and I. H. Simpson (Greenwich, Conn.: JAI Press, 1980).
57. Fashoyin, T., *Industrial Relations in Nigeria* (London: Longman, 1981).
58. Diejomoah, V. P. 'Industrial relations in Nigeria', *Industrial Relations in Africa*, ed. U. K. Damachi *et al.*, (London: Macmillan, 1979), 169—200.

Rural Society and Politics [see also 32, 35, 43]
59. Beer, C. E. F., *The Politics of Peasant Groups in Western Nigeria* (Ibadan: Ibadan University Press, 1976).
60. Peel, J. D. Y., 'Inequality and action: the forms of Ijesha social conflict', *Canadian Journal of African Studies*, 14, 3 (1980) 473—502.
61. Clough, P., 'Farmers and traders in Hausaland', *Development and Change*, 12, 2 (1981), 273—92.

Education and Elite Formation
62. Ayandele, E. A., *The Educated Elite in the Nigerian Society* (Ibadan: Ibadan University Press, 1974).
63. Van Den Berghe, P. L., *Power and Privilege at an African University* (London: Routledge, 1973).
64. Beckett, P. and O'Connell, J., *Education and Power in Nigeria: a Study of University Students* (London: Hodder & Stoughton, 1977).
65. Nduka, O. *Western Education and the Nigerian Cultural Background* (Ibadan: Oxford University Press, 1964).

IV. POLITICS

Colonial Administration and Politics [see also 47, 51]
  66. Kirk-Greene, A. H. M. (ed.), *The Principles of Native Administration in Nigeria: Selected Documents 1900–1947* (London: Oxford University Press, 1965).
  67. Yahaya, A. D., *Native Authority System in Northern Nigeria* (Zaria: ABU Press, 1979).
  68. Nicolson, I. F., *The Administration of Nigeria 1900–60* (Oxford, Clarendon, 1969).
  69. Smith, M. G., *The Affairs of Daura* (Berkeley: University of California Press, 1978).
  70. Smith, M. G., *Government in Zazzau 1900–1950* (London: Oxford University Press, 1960).
  71. Isichei, E., *A History of the Igbo People* (London: Macmillan, 1976).
  72. Igbafe, P. A., *Benin under British Administration 1897–1938* (London, Longman, 1979).
  73. Fika, A. M., *The Kano Civil War and British Overrule 1882–1940.* (Ibadan: Oxford University Press, 1978).
  74. Crowder, M. and Ikime, O. (eds), *West African Chiefs* (Ife: University of Ife Press, 1970).
  75. Atanda, J. A., *The New Oyo Empire: Indirect Rule and Change in Western Nigeria 1894–1934* (London: Longman, 1973).

The Late Colonial Period, Decolonisation, and the First Republic [see also 47, 51, 52, 54, 59, 62, 74, 95, 96, 97, 100, 101, 102, 104, 105, 106]
  76. Hodgkin, T. L., *Nationalism in Colonial Africa* (London: Muller, 1956).
  77. Coleman, J. S., *Nigeria: Background to Nationalism* (Berkeley: University of California Press, 1960).
  78. Post, K. W. J. and Jenkins, G. D., *The Price of Liberty: Personality and Politics in Colonial Nigeria* (Cambridge, Cambridge Univeristy Press, 1973).
  79. Williams, G. (ed), *Nigeria: Economy and Society* (London: Collins, 1976).
  80. Olusanya, G. O., *The Second World War and Politics in Nigeria 1939–53* (London, Evans, 1973).

81. Post, K. W. J., *The Nigerian Federal Election of 1959* (London: Oxford University Press, 1963).

82. Awa, E. O., *Federal Government in Nigeria* (Berkeley: University of California Press, 1964).

83. Tamuno, T. N., *The Police in modern Nigeria 1861– 1965* (Ibadan: Ibadan University Press, 1970).

84. Smock, A. C., *Ibo Politics: the Role of Ethnic Unions* (Cambridge, Mass.: Harvard University Press, 1971).

85. Dudley, B., *Parties and Politics in Northern Nigeria* (London: Frank Cass, 1968).

86. Whitaker, C. S., *The Politics of Tradition: Continuity and Change in Northern Nigeria 1946–66* (Princeton: Princeton University Press, 1970).

87. Otite, O., *Autonomy and Independence: The Urhobo Kingdom of Okpe in Modern Nigeria* (London: Hurst, 1973).

88. Frank, L. P., 'Ideological competition in Nigeria: urban populism v. elite nationalism', *Journal of Modern African Studies*, 17, 3 (1979) 67–87.

89. Melson, R. and Wolpe, H. (eds), *Nigeria: Modernisation and Politics of Communalism*, (East Lansing: Michigan State University Press, 1971).

90. Anifowose, R., *Violence and Politics in Nigeria: the Tiv and Yoruba Experience 1960–66* (Lagos: Nok, 1980).

91. Mackintosh, J. P. (ed.), *Nigerian Government and Politics* (London: Allen & Unwin, 1966).

92. Sklar, R. L., *Nigerian Political Parties* (Princeton: Princeton University Press, 1963).

93. Post, K. W. J. and Vickers, M., *Structure and Conflict in Nigeria 1960–65* (London: Heinemann, 1973).

94. Osoba, S. O., 'The Nigerian power elite', *African Social Studies*, ed. P. C. W. Gutkind and P. Waterman (London: Heinemann, 1976).

Biography and Political Thought [see also 78]

95. Azikiwe, N., *My Odyssey* (London: Hurst, 1970).

96. Jones-Quartey, K. A. B., *A Life of Azikiwe* (Harmondsworth: Penguin, 1956).

97. Awolowo, O., *Awo* (Cambridge: Cambridge University Press, 1960).

98. Awolowo, O., *The People's Republic* (London: Oxford University Press, 1968).
99. Shagari, S., *My Vision of Nigeria* (London: Frank Cass, 1981).
100. Bello, Sir A., *My Life* (Cambridge: Cambridge University Press, 1962).
101. Abdulkadir, D., *The Poetry, Life and Opinions of Sa'adu Zungur* (Zaria: Northern Nigerian Publishing Corp., 1974).
102. Feinstein, A., *African Revolutionary: the Life and Times of Nigeria's Aminu Kano* (New York: Quadrangle, 1973).

The Army and Military Rule [see also 16, 18, 55]
103. Luckham, R., *The Nigerian Military* (Cambridge: Cambridge University Press, 1971).
104. First, R., *Barrel of a Gun* (London: Allen Lane, 1970).
105. Panter-Brick, S. K. (ed.), *Nigerian Politics and Military Rule: Prelude to the Civil War* (London: Athlone Press, 1970).
106. Dudley, B., *Instability and Political Order* (Ibadan: Ibadan University Press, 1973).
107. Panter-Brick, S. K. (ed.), *Soldiers and Oil: The Military and the Political Transformation of Nigeria* (London: Frank Cass, 1978).
108. Oyediran, O. (ed.), *Nigerian Government and Politics under Military Rule 1968–79* (London: Macmillan, 1979).
109. Peil, M., *Nigerian Politics: the People's View* (London: Cassell, 1976).
110. Kirk-Greene, A. and Rimmer, D., *Nigeria Since 1970* (London: Hodder & Stoughton, 1981).
111. Dent, J. M., *Nigeria: the Politics of Military Rule* (London: Frank Cass, forthcoming).

The Civil War
112. Kirk-Greene, A. H. M. (ed.), *Crisis and Conflict in Nigeria: a Documentary Source Book 1966–69* (London: Oxford Press, 1971).

113. Nzimiro, I. *The Nigerian Civil War: a Study in Class Conflict* (Enugu: Fourth Dimension, 1978).
114. Akpan, N., *The Struggle for Secession 1966–70* (London: Frank Cass, 1971).
115. De St. Jorre, J., *The Nigerian Civil War* (London: Hodder & Stoughton, 1972).
116. Stremlau, J. J., *The International Politics of the Nigerian Civil War 1967–70* (Princeton: Princeton University Press, 1977).
117. Cronje, S., *The World and Nigeria: the Diplomatic History of the Biafran War 1967–70* (London: Sidgwick & Jackson, 1972).
118. Ojukwu, C. O., *Biafra* (New York: Harper & Row, 1969), 2 vols.
119. Obasanjo, O., *My Command: an Account of the Nigerian Civil War 1967–70* (London: Heinemann, 1980).
120. Madiebo, A. A., *The Nigerian Revolution and the Biafran War* (Enugu: Fourth Dimension, 1980).

Administration and Local Government [see also 82]
121. Murray, D. J. (ed.), *Studies in Nigerian Administration* (London: Hutchinson, 1978).
122. Murray, D. J., *The Work of Administration in Nigeria: Case Studies* (London: Hutchinson, 1969).
123. Adebayo, A., *Principles and Practice of Public Administration in Nigeria* (Chichester: Wiley, 1981).
124. Collins, P. (ed.), *Administration for Development in Nigeria* (Lagos: African Education Press, 1980).
125. Ngosu, H. N. (ed.), *Problems of Nigerian Administration: a Book of Readings* (Enugu: Fourth Dimension, 1980).
126. Adamulekun, L. and Rowlands, L. (eds), *The New Local Government System in Nigeria* (Ibadan: Heinemann, 1979).
127. Oden, G. W. E. (ed.), *A New System of Local Government* (Enugu: Nwamife Press, 1977).

External relations
128. Akinyemi, A. B., *Foreign Policy and Federalism* (Ibadan: Ibadan University Press, 1974).

129. Gambari, L. A., *Party Politics and Foreign Policy: Nigeria During the First Republic* (Zaria: ABU Press, 1979).

130. Akinyemi, A. B. (ed.), *Nigeria and the World* (Ibadan: Oxford University Press, 1978).

131. Ogunbadejo, O., 'Ideology and pragmatism: the Soviet role in Nigeria', *Orbis*, 21, 4 (1978) 803–30.

132. Idang, G. J., *Nigeria: Internal Politics and Foreign Policy (1960–66)* (Ibadan: Ibadan University Press, 1973).

133. Shaw, T. M. and Fajehun, O., 'Nigeria in the world system', *Journal of Modern African Studies*, 18, 4 (1980), 551–73.

134. Aluko, O., *Essays in Nigerian Foreign Policy* (London: Allen & Unwin, 1981).

Return to Civilian Rule and the Second Republic

135. Kumu, S. and Aliyu, A. (eds), *Issues in the Nigerian Draft Constitution* (Zaria: Institute of Administration, 1977).

136. Ofonagoro, W. I. and Ojo, A. (eds), *The Great Debate: Nigerian Viewpoints on the Draft Constitution 1976/77* (Lagos: Daily Times, n.d.).

137. Graf, W. D., *Elections 1979: the Nigerian Citizens' Guide to Parties, Politics and Issues* (Lagos: Daily Times, n.d.).

138. Dent, M. and Austin, D. (eds), *Implementing Civil Rule: the First Two Years* (Manchester: Manchester University, 1981).

139. Koehn, P., 'The Nigerian Elections of 1979', *Africa Today*, 28, 1 (1981) 17–45 (and see 47–58).

140. Madunagu, E., *Problems of Socialism: the Nigerian Challenge* (London, Zed, 1981).

Index